Collective Bargaining and Changing Industrial Relations in China

Labour, Education & Society

Edited by György Széll,
Heinz Sünker, Anne Inga Hilsen
and Francesco Garibaldo

Volume 30

PL ACADEMIC RESEARCH

Siqi Luo

Collective Bargaining and Changing Industrial Relations in China

Lessons from the U.S. and Germany

PL ACADEMIC RESEARCH

Bibliographic Information published by the Deutsche Nationalbibliothek
The Deutsche Nationalbibliothek lists this publication in the Deutsche Nationalbibliografie; detailed bibliographic data is available in the internet at http://dnb.d-nb.de.

Zugl.: Frankfurt (Main), Univ., Diss., 2012

Printed with financial support of the Hans Böckler Foundation.

Library of Congress Cataloging-in-Publication Data

Luo, Siqi, 1980-
Collective bargaining and changing industrial relations in China : lessons from the U.S. and Germany / Siqi Luo.
pages cm. — (Labour, education & society, ISSN 1861-647X ; volume 30)
ISBN 978-3-631-62646-7
1. Collective bargaining—China 2. Collective bargaining—United States. 3. Collective bargaining—Germany. 4. Industrial relations—China. 5. Industrial relations—United States. 6. Industrial relations—Germany. 7. Wages—China. I. Title.
HD6837.L86 2013
331.890951—dc23
2013010037

D 30
ISSN 1861-647X
ISBN 978-3-631-62646-7

PL Academic Research is an Imprint of Peter Lang GmbH.

Peter Lang – Frankfurt am Main · Bern · Bruxelles · New York · Oxford · Warszawa · Wien

www.peterlang.de

Acknowledgments

This book would not have been possible without the support of many people. I wish to express my gratitude to my supervisor, Dr. Boy Lüthje who was abundantly helpful in offering me invaluable guidance, support, and assistance. I am also grateful to my second reviewer Dr. Wilhelm Schumm and other colleagues in the Institut für Sozialforschung in Frankfurt.

I would also like to convey thanks to Hans Böckler Stiftung for providing financial support. The staff there was always warm-hearted and quickly responded all my questions. In particular, I would like to thank Prof. Dr. György Széll for his insightful comments on this work and for his guidance on my academic career.

I would like to thank many people who saw me through this book. Many supported me during my field study including arranging interviews and offering factory access, while others helped me in proofreading and editing. I also thank the editors who agreed to publish this manuscript.

Finally, I wish to express my love and gratitude to my husband, Min and the rest of my family, who supported and encouraged me through the duration of the study.

Siqi Luo
Goyang city, South Korea
February 12, 2013

Contents

Introduction

The issue of low wages in China has become a recurring problem in the Chinese national economy. As China is now widely acknowledged as the "workshop" of the world, its low wages, no doubt, have been an attraction for manufacturing. Nevertheless, the same low wages have also become a major bottleneck for further economic growth and social development. First, the necessity of increasing domestic consumption was addressed in the 2008/9 global recession. Clearly, the over-dependency of China on foreign demand in the past is no longer able to sustain its overproduction of industrial goods in the long run. Besides, the generally low skill levels of the industrial workforce have led to a vicious "low-wage/ low-skill/ low-value-added" trap. "Made-in-China" mainly means labor-intensive, low-end and low-tech products, or in many cases, high-tech products but with core design and technologies controlled outside China and a strictly limited input from Chinese workforce. At the same time, the high turnover rates and frequent labor disputes (e.g. in the electronics industry) reflect the lack of employees' loyalty and their unwillingness to cooperate. As an innovation and upgrading strategy may necessarily reduce the demand on unskilled labor or require skill development, only a trustful labor relations can make the strategy successful primarily by soothing workers' insecurity of employment and relevant concerns. Consequently, the unstable situations in Chinese industries make any innovation or industrial upgrading extremely difficult. Further, low wages have become the top cause for several major waves of labor unrest. For instance, the recent slew of suicide cases at Foxconn and the Honda strike in 2010 were argued by Chinese media and Internet forums as a sign that the era of rock-bottom wages in China was passing (Yang 2010).

However, a question remains as to how this low-wage development path can change. The average incomes of Chinese manufacturing workers have been pushed to an extreme, for instance, they were only one fourteenth of the average wages of South Korean workers in 2003.[1] According to the sixth national survey of the All-China Federation of Trade Unions (ACFTU) on employment in 2007, 26.7% of ordinary workers had not any form of wage increases in the last five years.[2] Apparently, the wage increases have been far behind the growth of productivity. From 1998 to 2004 the productivity grew 187%, but workers' average wages increased only 134% (Zhang and Zhao 2006). In 2010, the strike

1 Chosun News, The wages of manufacturing workers in South Korea are 14 times of in China, http://chn.chosun.com/site/data/html_dir/2003/08/26/20030826000024.html

2 ACFTU Research Department, General Report on the Sixth National Survey of Employees and Workers, Theory & Practice of Trade Unions, No. 16, 2008, p3-18

wave and the Foxconn labor crisis resulted to a 30% wage increase by Foxconn and the collective agreement signed by the Honda Nanhai supplier. Nevertheless, many foreign observers suspect whether such “success” can be actually implemented or is able to last in a long term.

Specifically, collective bargaining has been the center of the public discussion, although at the policy level, it has been written into the law in China since the 1990s. In the early days of capitalist development, the importance of collective bargaining had already been recognized soon after the beginning of the industrial revolution, and later it became the dominant form of wage determination, such as during the post-war era of Fordism in the United States and in Germany. In fact, collective bargaining is not only a mechanism of determining wages and other labor standards, but also one of, if not the most important ways of adjusting industrial relations. It is usually conducted between collective labor organizations and employers or employers' associations. The basic idea is to overcome the inferior position of the relatively powerless wage workers, compared to employers in terms of property and administration rights, e.g. lowering workers' costs of demanding on wages (Offe and Wiesenthal 1980). Primarily, the liberal idea of regarding labor and capital as "equivalent", which used to be dominant in academics and practice, would be simply mistaken. According to Marx (1887), laborers possess nothing but their own labor-power and labor-power is a peculiar commodity. For the means of subsistence, the "owner" of labor-power is forced to enter into a wage contract. As labor power cannot be physically separated from its "owner", the employment of a laborer involves submitting to the authority of the capitalist for a specific period of time. On the contrary, capitalists can decide whether to employ a laborer or not, and what and how to work if employed. Capitalists can also release themselves partially from their dependence upon the workers by introducing labor-saving technologies, thereby depressing the wage rate. Given such conditions, effective collective bargaining is desired, in which two relatively balanced powers determine wages and other working conditions together.

Apparently, collective bargaining is the mechanism that could potentially improve the current wage system and channel the conflictual labor-capital relations in China. Therefore, this study aims at exploring the very existence and more likely, the future possibility, of effective collective bargaining in China. There are two major questions: what is collective bargaining in practice? what can it become in the future?

In short, collective bargaining in China has to be analyzed in the context of the changing industrial relations. As the national economy has been expanding at a nearly unprecedented speed and consequently impacting other economies through global networked production, industrial relations in China are attracting increasing attention worldwide. At the same time, the state-controlled system of industrial relations has come under criticism. At the international level, its low wages and export orientation have often been regarded as being against trade rules and labor standards (She and Fu 2001). The debate about the nature of the official trade union, especially its close linkage with the state, continues. Domestically, the large-scale dismantlement of state-owned enterprises, combined with a growing low-wage sector, has resulted to increasing inequality in the distribution of economic, social, cultural and information resources (Lu 2002). Given the ambiguous statuses of both trade unions and management in labor relations, and the inconsistent industrial policies of the government, labor-capital conflicts have frequently emerged, and from time to time burst into open labor unrest (e.g. Lee 2007). As a response to international and domestic pressures and state policies aimed to build harmonious labor relations, the system of collective bargaining and collective contract has been written into the Chinese law and officially promoted by the trade unions.

Significant labor-related changes have taken place, mostly in a top-down manner directed by the state. A capitalist market system has been introduced with the following features: the establishment of an employment contract system, a labor market, multiple types of enterprise ownership, and distribution according to production factors. The capitalist labor relations have become a matter of fact. In a few recent studies, China has been identified as "capitalism with Chinese characteristics" - a version of state-led capitalism driven by entrepreneurial rural China in the 1980s (Huang 2008: xvi), or as a "market-liberal state capitalism" (Ten brink 2010). No matter how we look at it, the economy is in accordance with many key features of capitalism, such as competition-driven accumulation, social stratification, economic-political structural interdependence and the inter- and transnational capitalist system integration. Thus, it is fruitful to look at the Chinese collective bargaining system in the much broader trajectory of the global economy and labor polity, of which, undeniably, China has already become an inseparable part.

It is recognized that collective bargaining is a key mechanism of industrial relations, but may take distinctive forms and exert different degrees of influence in a specific country. At present, the fundamental elements that compose an effective model of collective bargaining remain to be a quite confusing field in China. For instance, as revealed in the field study of this research (see chapter 3), the majority of trade unionists and managers are or pretend to be ignorant of the social norm in typical collective bargaining procedures in which wages follow the inflation increase plus the increase in labor productivity. Thus, this study attempts to clarify the elements of collective bargaining by first comparing the formation and functioning of the historical models of collective bargaining in the U.S. and Germany, during periods of the rise and fall of Fordism.

The U.S. was chosen because it was the first country that developed mass production method as well as Fordist wage regulation, which was centered on collective bargaining. In the 1930s and 1940s, collective bargaining had reached the greatest influence in the U.S. with the largest coverage ever since. Following the US, Germany was a late comer to the modern mass production of automobiles, but its well-known model of "high wage, high skill, high quality", based on industry-wide bargaining, enabled the country to rapidly become a leading player in the global market. Importantly, the two cases show a comparison of industrial relations in two distinctive political traditions and economical orders. In fact, both countries had experienced massive labor conflicts and the labor movement waves during the heyday of the development of the automobile industry (e.g. in the 1930s and 1960s respectively). In consequence, collective bargaining, although in highly different ways and content, has become the basic feature of typical "Fordist" regulation in the industrial relations of both countries. Nevertheless, the two models of collective bargaining, and more general industrial relations, have gone remarkably different paths, especially since the 1970s. The boom of the electronics industry, claimed by many scholars as the symbol of "post-Fordism" (Dicken 1998: 353-4), has marked the divergence. The industry boomed in the US and later spread to Germany, at a much faster pace than the automobile industry. It is true that the broad range of varieties in production and enterprises in this industry has weakened the role of traditional collective bargaining systems in both countries. Nevertheless, while it created a notorious union-free sector and the collapse of social contract in the U.S., in Germany the industry-wide collective bargaining was able to maintain the coherence of the economy and society much longer.

Therefore, I compare the two distinctive models of collective bargaining in the U.S. and Germany, and examine the institution-building processes of both models. Through the observation of both the automobile and electronics industries, this study attempts to summarize the key factors for the formation and functioning of collective bargaining throughout the rise and fall of Fordism.

At the same time, while taking general rules from other countries as reference, it is important to survey the special characteristics of industrial relations in China. To a certain degree, industrial relations is a country-specific system. For instance, strong labor movements, according to an intriguing research of Silver (2003), came along with the development of modern manufacturing and capitalist labor relations. She argues that mass production recreates similar social contradictions and accordingly increasing labor struggles wherever it emerges. Throughout the twentieth century, this norm proved itself, as shown in North America in the 1930s and 1940s and Germany in the 1960s and 1970s. However, in spite of the existence of modern manufacturing and capitalist relations in China, a strong labor movement has not emerged. Also, the system of collective contract came into being not through the pressure of workers. In this sense, China is an exception in the norm found by Silver.

Accordingly, collective bargaining is explored in the specific economic, social and political conditions of China today. This study is based on the investigation into production regimes at the factory level in both auto and electronics industries, and wage regulation at regional and national levels. The auto and electronics industries, as the leading industries of the twentieth and twenty-first centuries respectively, are now the core and strategic sectors in China. Although some low-end, low-tech, low-cost traditional sectors appear as the main image of China, many capital-intensive, high-tech and modern industries are quickly developing too. The conditions of the two leading industries may forecast the trends collective bargaining and industrial relations may take in the future.

Above all, this study takes into consideration both common patterns throughout history of industrialization, as well as the specific configurations of China. Besides, the current global industries and politics have provided new conditions for establishing collective bargaining systems than that of the post-war era. It is uncertain whether China may follow the global trend of the demise of Fordist wage regulation or welcome the return of Fordism, namely relatively regulated and effective collective bargaining. In any case, we have to expect that the regulation itself, the actual process, and the driving forces behind it, may be very different from those in the past. This study attempts to find perspectives that combine the advantages of collective bargaining models in both the U.S. and Germany and avoid their fundamental flaws, particularly excessive trade-offs in concessionary bargaining. On this basis, I try to identify the essential problems of the existing collective contract system in China, and explore a future model that fits into both general tendencies and the specific conditions. In any case, the principles of collective bargaining, such as shop-floor control and above-enterprise coordination, shall not be forgotten. Fundamentally, the labor history of the U.S. and Germany illustrates that collective bargaining has always been a systematic process of institution-building driven by the efforts of collective labor, rather than a unilateral policy from top down.

A note on methodology and resources

This study is a qualitative analysis of collective bargaining and industrial relations, supported by selective quantitative data from both official sources and field study. Primarily, an extensive analysis of the existing literature provides a general framework of the historical development of industrial relations, especially collective bargaining in both the U.S. and Germany. The automobile and electronics industries - two representative industries of Fordism - are selected to illustrate the dynamics of production regimes and regulation modes. Moreover, case studies[3], complemented with statistical data and previous labor studies of the two industries, have been conducted in representative Chinese cities in order to position collective bargaining in the broader context of industrial world and in the national and international labor polities.

Historical materials have been mainly collected through library and media research. In order to trace the historical development of collective bargaining, previous literatures on production regimes, collective bargaining patterns, and general industrial relations systems in the U.S. and Germany are referenced. In addition, direct contacts with several companies and trade unions in Germany also help to clarify the current debates and challenges on collective bargaining.

As in the case of China, general information about automobile and electronics industries has been collected, such as the proportions of FDI and employment in the national economy. The two leading industries - the automobile and electronics industries, in terms of employment, investment, industrial values and exports, apparently are of extraordinary significance in exploring the China model of industrial relations.

Moreover, case studies from both industries are selected from China, including a broad range of companies - ten in the automobile industry and sixteen in the electronics industry. The author attempts to cover at least three typical cases in each representative category of enterprises, following the distinctive industrial structures respectively. Thus, there are auto assemblers and part suppliers, and a more complex combination in the electronics industry. From the perspective of ownership types, I have included global brand name multinationals, joint ventures, no-name contract manufacturers, private small suppliers etc., from Europe, America, Japan, Taiwan and Mainland China. Besides, this selection covers the three core industrial clusters - Beijing and Tianjin, Yangtz River Delta, and Pearl River Delta - in North, East and South China with distinctive local features. In practice, interviews in each factory were arranged with human resource managers, trade unionists, and workers whenever

---

3 The field study was conducted in a joint research project funded by Hans Böckler Stiftung. Detailed case studies have been published. See: Lüthje, Luo, and Zhang, 2013

possible, through existing contacts with Chinese universities and labor experts. In some occasions, interviewees were former classmates or acquaintances of the author, which provided a more open atmosphere in speaking about certain problems and concerns. At the same time, on-site observation of work processes, including the division of labor, polarization of skills, and work organization were also conducted, which show the features of production flow and working conditions, as well as the wage structure, job appraisal scale, and training system. This method was effective in evaluating the reliability of interviews. Beyond that, several conversations centered on the question of collective bargaining were arranged with trade unionists, engineers, and government officials, which added different perspectives in the policy debate.

As the outcome of the field study, profiles for each company have been documented. In terms of production and work organization, one major question asks whether there are certain Fordist production features, such as assembly line, segmentation of work, the hierarchical division of labor, the polarization of skills, and the degree of rigidity. In addition, working conditions were another key part of the investigation, particularly wages. Relevant questions that were raised were: Were wages determined by collective bargaining, individual negotiation or management only? What was the role of trade unions or other forms of collective workers? Were the wage levels for similar occupations comparable in each enterprise, or each industry? What were the wage differences between manufacturing workers, engineers and managers? In summary, I present comparisons among enterprises within the same industry and between the two industries. I also examine how the impacts of the "country of origin" or ownership forms determine differences in collective bargaining.

Besides the production regimes, the actual status and future possibility of wage regulation and collective bargaining are evaluated in the broader context, such as the interaction between major players in industrial relations and the existing national and global labor polity. On the basis of both empirical research and previous literatures, the role of the state, both central and local states, and its relationship with capital are analyzed to understand the obstacles behind the policy-making and problematic implementation (e.g. the acquiescence of some local governments to employers' violation of labor rights). Moreover, the potential of workers in initiating and participating in the collective bargaining process is explored, apart from the often-criticized trade union. Even though industrial relations may be formed "on the basis of given conditions inherited from the past" (Lipietz 1987: 195), the struggle of people is the ultimate drive for change. Through a systematic analysis on production, social and political factors, the findings in the dynamics between workers, state and employers may illuminate the prospects of collective bargaining and industrial relations in China.

An overview of the chapters and main proposals

This study focuses on the status and prospects of collective bargaining in China with valuable lessons learned from the industrial relations systems in the U.S. and Germany. Collective bargaining is a core wage regulation that has shaped post-war Fordism in both countries. Its formation and effectiveness are closely linked to the production and accumulation regimes as well as the specific modes of regulations during historically specific moments in the two countries.

In the first chapter, the general theoretical framework for capital accumulation, labor relations, and socioeconomic transformation is established. Firstly, I review previous research on China. Most of the work, unfortunately, seems largely descriptive and rarely provides any clear answer to existing conditions and problematic implementation of labor law and policies. In consequence, several relevant theories and key concepts are examined, in order to provide a theoretical background for the following analysis. Finally, the regulation approach, a most relevant theory on capitalism, is employed as the conceptual basis. According to this approach, collective bargaining is one form of wage regulation. Collective bargaining is impacted by existing accumulation regimes while at the same time it should normalize the conflictual relations between labor and capital in the regimes. This study argues that an analytical model that examines the institution-building processes of collective bargaining should be based on the following three levels: production regimes in factories, policy-making at industrial and national levels, and the general influence from the global economy and politics trends. At each level, the interaction among four major actors - workers, trade unions, capital and state, both central and local states - affect the institutionalization and effectiveness of collective bargaining.

The second chapter, attempts to sort out common conditions at all above-mentioned three levels that have impacted on the formation of Fordist wage regulation. It also explores the key features of collective bargaining, through two distinctive cases of the U.S. and Germany. I show that both countries had developed Fordist wage regulation, namely, better pay and other working conditions through collective bargaining, which had assured the steady economic growth and industrial peace from the 1940s to the 1970s. However, due to divergences in production regimes and industrial relations systems, the outcomes were relatively better and longer lasting in Germany than in the US.

The review concludes that the final institutionalization of collective bargaining has resulted from certain conditions, including the labor-capital interaction within factories, economic and labor policies of the state, and global pro-labor political environments. Historically, collective bargaining had not appeared automatically. Rather, it was the result of long-term struggles and compromises between workers and employers under certain historical and social conditions (e.g. under the "New Deal" of the U.S. after the crisis of the early 1930s). Following the changes of industries and politics, especially after the 1990s, collective bargaining and the labor movement in both the U.S. and Germany have been transformed problematically. Their success and failure further illustrate the foundational aspects for collective bargaining, including relatively homogeneous production regimes, inclusive social security programs, pro-labor policies of the state rather than direct intervention, and a broad coverage and high-level coordination of the mechanism itself. Two factors are particularly essential today, namely institutional guarantee and workplace control against management prerogative, which not only make collective bargaining effective but also preclude its decline in the long run.

Industrial relations in China are addressed in the third chapter, with a focus on the new regimes of production in factories, and the evolution of wage regulation and particularly collective bargaining at macro levels. Varieties of production regimes in both the automobile and electronics industries have been shaped by many factors, such as the position in the production network, the ownership structure, the country of origin, and local government policies. Whereas the automobile industry is centered on leading whole-car joint ventures, there is a large segmentation, with a distinct new group of contract manufacturers, in the electronics industry. With a shrinking core workforce in the auto makers, more flexible production regimes are commonly seen with low base wages, high turnover rates, and no collective contracts or even trade unions. In the electronics industry, even in the leading brand name companies, employment security and wage stability are absent. The large segmentation among workers and individualized labor standards for different workers in different enterprises make it extremely difficult to set up a general contract through collective bargaining for an entire industry or a region.

The variety of production regimes in both automobile and electronics industries provide considerable challenges for collective bargaining. With only a few "model" cases of wage negotiations, labor standards have been largely up to unilateral management decisions, rather than mutually-agreed through collective bargaining. At the same time, the existing system of collective contract in China today is problematic not only in terms of the ambiguities of laws, but even more so in the implementation at the enterprise level.

The question of whether "Fordism is coming back" is explored in the fourth chapter. Although the mass production and work organization, which had given birth to Fordism, have been found in many factories in China today, some key elements of collective bargaining are absent. This chapter examines the reasons of such absence while at the same time it probes into the decisive forces for a new prospect of collective bargaining in China, from the perspectives of production organization, the relationship of the state and capital, and the role of trade unions and workers. Primarily, the peculiar history of China and the current global context carry significant weight in explaining the dysfunction of the collective contract system in China. As a whole, the global economy and politics seem not to be on the side of labor. The largely diverse production regimes at factory level, especially in the electronics industry, create barriers for labor collectivity. Moreover, the relationship between the Chinese state, trade unions, employers, and the often-forgotten role of workers, makes effective collective bargaining more difficult. At the same time, potential drives for change are also identified under the new industrial and political conditions (e.g. workers gain stronger workplace bargaining power in the lean production organization; and the Chinese ruling class has gradually shifted its policies toward a relatively pro-labor direction). In particular, although Chinese workers may not be able to re-compose themselves into a strongly-unified working class, their potential is on the rise as the major players in collective bargaining, indicated in the recent wage negotiation of Nanhai Honda.

The concluding remarks provide an answer to the question of whether Fordism is coming back to China, not only by comparing the industrial development of China to that in the post-war US and Germany, but by examining features of the workforce and labor polity. At present, I argue that the institutions and practices of collective contract system in China are flawed at large. It simply has not improved workers' wages and other labor standards. Nevertheless, the prospect for collective bargaining is considered on the basis of a thorough examination of Chinese industrial relations at the factory, industrial, and national levels under the global industrial and political trends. Effective collective bargaining is most likely to be an adopted model based on current industrial and political conditions in China, not solely via the rule making of the state, but also on the basis of institution-building from below. In particular, following the strike wave in the auto industry of early 2010, collective bargaining in China has entered a new stage, making the successes and mistakes of the U.S. and German experiences especially relevant.

Theoretical perspectives: labor relations and socioeconomic transformation in China

Industrial relations have increasingly become an inescapable topic in light of China's sweeping socioeconomic transformations. This study attempts to examine the statuses and prospects of collective bargaining within China's changing industrial relations. In order to do so, it is necessary to first overview the existing research and to introduce a theoretical framework that fits to the major questions of this study.

In the past, there has been a wealth of remarkable research on socioeconomic transformation, such as the collapse of planned economy and the establishment of the market, and the following changes of industrial relations in China. These scholars have provided on the ground facts and some meaningful insights. Nevertheless, previous studies on general wage policies and the mechanism of collective bargaining remain largely descriptive and rarely provide any clear answers to existing problematic statues of collective bargaining. Thus, this study attempts to offer a systematic analysis by referring to several theories and key concepts.

The structure of my thesis is as follows: I first introduce the Regulation Approach, a most relevant theory on capitalism, as the overarching theory of this study. The two principal concepts from this approach - mode of regulation and regime of accumulation - are accordingly applied to respective countries, the United States, Germany, and China. In order to flesh out the ultimate problems of collective bargaining in China, the historical experience of the U.S. and Germany are reviewed. In particular, the key factors that influence the formation and function of collective bargaining, especially in the era of Fordism, are explored and then compared to current conditions of China.

As the Regulation Approach shows, the mode of regulation is supposed to normalize and guide the conflictual course of accumulation. Collective bargaining is well recognized as one ideal type of wage regulation in capitalist development. Therefore, an effective mechanism of collective bargaining should lead to orderly labor-capital relations, at the same time, its formation and function are restrained by the existing regimes of accumulation and may also be inspired from the tension or defect of such regimes. In this study, the wage regulation refers to wage standards, collective contracts, bargaining rules, and labor law and policies at the macro level, whereas the regime of production is signified by the employment systems including production and work organization, personnel management, and labor relations at the factory levels.

1.1 Previous Research on China

A review on previous research on the topic of collective bargaining in industrial environments not only sets the starting line of this study, but it also reveals certain theoretical gaps in relevant scholarship. It is true that the rapid GDP growth, the relatively fast recovery from the 2008/2009 financial and economic crisis, the appreciation of the Chinese currency and so forth, are of considerable interests to scholars and analysts, both along domestic and international levels of analyses. At the same time, the industrial relations system is also drawing more and more attention.

Collective bargaining, as the key mechanism of adjusting labor-capital relations, has to be analyzed in the broader context of the fast-changing industrial relations in China. Given the economic, political, and social circumstances of China in the last decades, the focus and perspective of previous studies in this field have also shifted in different periods of time. In the past decades, there have been numerous studies centered on production regimes in certain types of enterprises and their workers, both individuals and collective labor. Furthermore, labor law and policies were observed by many scholars, including the legislation and implementation of collective bargaining and collective contract. These will be introduced in detail as below.

1.1.1 Workers in the socioeconomic transformation

The socioeconomic transformations of China, primarily symboled by the replacement of the planned economy by the market economy, has brought along new changes of economic positions and social identifies for workers. In the last several decades, many studies have looked at the status of Chinese workers within a particular type of factory or those in one region. Along with the large-scaled privatization of the economy, there has been great diversification of production regimes in enterprises with different types of ownerships at various stages of the economic transformation. Within different kinds of production regime, the production and work organization, and labor standards of workers have largely differed with time as well as from one factory to another. Further, the collective labor actions have also developed distinctive features accordingly.

Before and during the ownership reform predominantly in the 1990s, most labor studies in the mainland concentrated on state-owned enterprises (SOEs). As early as in the 1980s, Walder (1984: 13) used the term of communist "Neo-Traditionalism" to describe the work organization and industrial authority in SOEs. The "Neo-Traditionalism" model contained two key features. The first was the "organized dependence" of workers, economically on their enterprises, politically on the party and management, and personally on supervisors. The other was the "institutional culture" of the factory, including the patterns of association between superior and subordinate, the patterns of association among workers, and the strategies employed by workers to advance their interests. In the 1980s, tension existed at shop-floor among activist and non-activist, skilled and unskilled, permanent and temporary or local and migrant workers. The fragmentation within workers was mainly caused by the state policies. Despite the legacies of the SOEs today, such a communist model of production and work organization had faded out.

Subsequent studies began to focus on the dismantling of the old state ownership, increasingly on the booming private economy, and its army of migrant workers. During the transformation of public ownership or the privatizing process, many studies focused not only on the degeneration of workers' economic, political, and social status, but on the increase or even explosion of collective conflicts. The poor working conditions and violations of labor rights in private firms had been disclosed in public. Most private firms that mushroomed in the early stage of economic reform were typically labor-intensive, export-oriented, and small- and medium-sized in the coastal areas, especially in southern China. In the late 1990s, in Guangdong province an overtly coercive mode of labor control, infliction of economic penalties, proliferation of shop-floor conflicts, and the demise of the patron-clientalism were observed in factories. This was defined by Lee (1999) as "disorganized despotism" in the widely-marketized economy, transformed from Walder's labor regime of "organized dependence" in old SOEs. Former SOE managers could exploit the disorganizing impacts of reform, but workers came under coercive modes of labor control.

Besides everyday labor-management relations, some scholars also investigated into the peculiar organizations of work and life in factories as one aspect to look at labor polity in China. One example is the study of Ren and Pun (2006) on the massive factory dormitory in southern China. They argued that the dormitory system put strict control on workers. Such control was the tool of the capital to obtain maximum surplus value as well as of the state to achieve the goal of economic development while assuming minimum responsibility of labor reproduction. This resulted in the formation of the new migrant working class and existing labor relation.

In regard to collective labor, the segmentation of the workforce has always been the central topic, particularly the focus upon migrant workers. Currently as the backbone of the non-public economy, migrant workers were rural residents from the hinterland of China and rushed to cities for waged-jobs, particularly since the 1990s. As the "elite" of the countryside, those migrant workers, who first arrived in the cities, were usually at the bottom of the urban metropolises (Lee 1995; Li 2004: 129). With a combination of the new employment status and rural registration, migrant workers were called "the third social stratum" (Li 2004: 387-388). Based on survey data, Yao and Lai (2004) found enormous gaps on labor standards and working conditions between urban- and rural-based workers. About 70 to 80% of such gaps could be explained by the different levels of human capital and conditions of enterprises where certain workers were employed, and the rest were caused by discrimination on the basis of the rural residential identities of migrant workers. Due to different background and labor experience, migrant workers have developed distinctive perspectives on work and entitlement that is different from the view shared by traditional urban workers. For instance, regarding laying-off, migrant workers would think "it is not that unfair since it is also a process of winnowing out the incompetent", while former urban employees blame their situation on changes in the enterprise system or government policy (Lei 2007).

In consequence, both former SOE employees and migrant workers would go to the streets to protest, but for different reasons. Urban labor contention often sprouted as the decentralization of economic authority and welfare responsibility destroyed the old "social contract" of the planned economy, and subsequently former SOE workers became laid-off. On the contrary, migrant workers mainly opposed to the violation of their direct material interests, such as legally specified wages or overtime pay.

Such divergence has been best illustrated in the work of Lee (1998a; 2007). Through a thorough comparison of workers' protests in the old industrial base of the northeast China in 2002 and those in the South, Lee (2007: 35) identifies the two types of protests as "protest of desperation" and "protest against discrimination" respectively. In the rust belt, insurgents feared downward mobility, exclusion and betrayal since the "social contract" with the state was withdrawn, while in the sunbelt, law and legal mobilization played a dominant role as aspiration to upward mobility, exploitation and discrimination. Rustbelt workers held class and Maoist discourse, whereas migrant workers had never had any experience with socialist industrialism or Maoist class politics. Therefore, there was a conspicuous absence of class identity claims, usually subordinate to the claim of laborers' and citizens' legal rights (Lee 2007: 13). Nevertheless, existing protests at large are typically "cellular activism", characterized by legalism, localization, and decentralization.

In other research on labor protests during the restructuring of SOEs, Chen (2003a) observes that due to the existence of employees and workers' congress in SOEs, as well as the tolerance of the government toward such protests, most conflicts eventually dissolved. More importantly, most demonstrations were spontaneous, and workers had neither their own organization nor representative leaders. Thus, these "contentious gatherings" by no means reflected organized labor power (Chen 2003b). In addition, labor protests in China were unusually weakly linked with other social groups, especially intellectuals, in both strike waves before and after the establishment of new China (Perry 1994).

It is noticeable that besides these typical groups, which consisted of former SOE employees and migrant workers in the sweatshops of South China, there are still a large number of various types of enterprises and urban employees in between (Blecher 2002). With mixed identities within the range of public, private and quasi-public, those employees work in enterprises with different ownership structures, and have either urban or rural backgrounds. In fact, neither the type of ownership structure of the enterprises nor residential statuses of the workers could immediately determine their working conditions or characteristics of collective actions. Under the umbrella of economic globalization, particularly in light of the large influx of foreign investment, advanced technologies and modern management methods from abroad have fundamentally changed nearly all industrial fields, including those among the former SOEs and the export production zones of South China.

In a word, Chinese workers are largely individualized and fragmented by nature of enterprise ownership, citizenship, gender and so forth. Nevertheless, as Chang (1995: 16-20) mentioned, workers, as a social group, are forming a distinctive social stratum and displaying an increasing influence in the society. Many believe that China is entering a stage within which social conflicts in industrial relations will occur frequently.

Taking into consideration the extreme diversification of enterprises today, it would be beneficial to observe the leading industries within certain representative areas in order to tease out patterns of industrial relations. For instance, studies on manufacturing sectors, which historically served as the driving force of the labor movement and welfare reform in many industrialized economies, have been marginalized by Chinese scholars and attracted some attention only from the West (e.g. automobile industry: Sit and Liu 2000; Zhang 2008; and electronics industry: Lüthje 2002; and Ernst and Naughton 2008). This study focuses on automobile and electronics industries as the former has a strong SOE tradition in China, and the latter is dominated by non-public firms. Different production regimes and labor control are expected in factories of the two industries. In spite of these structural differences, individual labor relations and the emerging collective labor toward collective bargaining are examined cross various case studies.

1.1.2 Labor law and policies

While a production regime mainly reflects the labor-capital interaction at the factory level, labor legislations and policies are originated from a broader context. Policies often result from power struggles among different interest groups, which further impact institution-building and policy-implementation in practice. There have been many studies discussing the legislation process and the content of the law and policies, as well as the implementation of collective bargaining and collective contract. However, it is far from enough only to point out the ambiguities of labor law and the dysfunction of the existing mechanism of collective bargaining in China. More important research on the causes and solutions of those problems is yet absent.

In the course of the economic reform in China, the priority of state policies has apparently been given to economic growth, rather than social justice toward the disadvantaged groups, like workers. China's development path of low labor costs and export-led growth had been highly criticized by international labor and trade organizations (She and Fu 2001), because these policies have led to increasing inequality in public allocation of economic, social, cultural and informational resources (Lu 2002). In addition, the long-term preference by the state in promoting economic policies ahead of social or political reform has resulted in instability of the industries in China (e.g. Lee 2007). However, the 1994 labor Law was promulgated only 16 years after the initiation of the market reform. During the following decade, there had been no new other labor-related statutes at national level, with the exception of the revision of the Trade Union Law in 2001 and several regulations at the ministerial levels. As one response to the exploding waves of labor protests, in 2007 three national statutes, the labor Contract Law, the Employment Promotion Law and the Law on Labor Dispute Mediation and Arbitration, were successively promulgated.

The promulgation of labor laws in 2007 experienced wide opposition from employers as well as from some local governments. During the drafting of the Labor Contract Law, the voices of workers were mostly isolated and scattered, but some foreign or semi-foreign business associations, such as the Hong Kong SME association and European employers' association in Shanghai, collectively expressed their opposition against the new law in fear of increasing costs for enterprises. Moreover, several local governments joined in the opposition of implementing the same law and later in 2008 requested to suspend the adjustment of the minimum wages as a response to the world financial crisis.

In academic circles, there have consistently been many advocates of the free market policies. As early as the 1980s mainstream economists started to argue that low labor cost was the biggest comparative advantage in China (Wei 2004).

According to them, China should continue its role as the processing workshop of the world, while workers who served as the country's key supply of cheap labor remained at the bottom of the international production hierarchy (Han 2006). As for the Labor Contract Law, the typical opposition against it was that it would cause fatal effects upon economic growth and consequently end the continuous improvement of living standards for the majority of Chinese people.[4] The main argument was higher wages and legal payment of social insurances would lead to the close-down of many enterprises or force them to leave China. Another liberalist advocate of free market put forward that government intervention cannot improve labor rights. Accordingly, state intervention may harm small- and medium-sized enterprises and worsen the living and developing environments of their workers (Wang 2004). Even labor relation scholars hold different opinions toward the law. For instance, Dong (2006: 4, 9, 16) deemed that the labor standards in the law were too high. According to him, an alternative would be a "society-based" way of regulating labor relations by labor and capital, rather than legislation or the state authority. At the same time, state intervention and legislation were emphasized by others (e.g. Chang 2004b and 2008) based on the view that labor relations in China were completely unbalanced and labor rights were widely neglected and violated in enterprises.

In spite of these debates, many laws and mechanisms of industrial relations were nonetheless introduced by government officials. The system of collective bargaining and collective contract has been established in China as a tool of counteracting increasing social tensions among workers, management, and the state. In the early 1950s, collective contracts signed between employers and trade unions were experimented in a few private firms. Nevertheless, as the private sector was completely integrated into public ownership during the Great Leap Forward[5] and subsequent socialization movements, the dominance of industrial unions shifted toward region-based unions. In effect, collective contract was institutionally abolished. Only in the early 1990s, the issue of collective bargaining[6] was initially raised by the 1992 Trade Union Law, and

4 This is a well-known argument by an economist Steven N.S. Cheung in public speeches and on his blog in 2008, e.g. A boding of disaster - discussing new labor law for the third time, http://blog.sina.com.cn/s/blog_47841af7010088gh.html

5 The Great Leap Forward was an economic and social campaign of the Communist Party of China from 1958 to 1961. It aimed to use the vast population to rapidly transform China from an agrarian economy into a modern communist society through agriculturalization, industrialization, and collectivization.

6 In China, the terms of "collective negotiation" or "equal negotiation" are used instead of "collective bargaining", in order to avoid the confrontative meaning of "bargaining" (see 3.3.3 of this study). Without special notes, the three terms are interchangeable here.

then by the 1994 labor Law, which entitled the ACFTU to promote the system. There are also specific regulations devolving the territorial jurisdiction of local governments in order to deal with rising disputes on working conditions involving different types of enterprises (Zhao 2004).

Clearly, many agree that current policy-making has shifted toward a relatively pro-labor direction. However, the implementation of the law and policies is far from satisfactory. The system of collective bargaining and collective contract in China is problematic. At the beginning, collective contract was the result of ACFTU's persistent lobbying to the government and even to some enterprises. It regarded this system an active way of influencing labor conditions in large- and medium-sized enterprises (Chan 1993). Nevertheless, the function of collective bargaining and collective contracts has been widely questioned. Even the director of the legal department at the ACFTU, Mr. Liu, Jicheng, in an interview regarding the third amendment of the Trade Union Law by a leading business media, admitted that only 20% of existing wage negotiations may actually function.[7]

Scholars and practitioners regard the actual implementation of the labor law as even less desirable (e.g. Clarke et al 2004). Primarily, the content of existing collective contracts has not resulted from specific environments and rules of enterprises (Brown 2006). Contemporary collective contracts in China do not reflect the actual work organizations and labor practices. As clearly shown in a survey of SOEs (Taylor et al 2003: 251-252), there are three types of clauses. The first clauses relate to the terms and conditions of the contract (e.g. requirements of negotiators); the second are requirements that must be carried out by both sides. The last clauses outline the responsibilities of both sides and the duration of the contracts. As the major part of a collective contract, the second type of clauses accounts, on average, for 70% of the text, within which 60% are exact sentences copied from the labor laws, 20 to 30% refer to legal stipulations, and only about 10% are about labor benefits. In addition, there was no effective supervision mechanism in practice on employers' implementation of collective contracts (Wang and Zhao 2005).

Another major problem involved the process of reaching those collective contracts. In many cases, collective contracts were just the direct result of "quota" policies set by the ACFTU (Pringle 2005). For the majority of collective contracts, there was no collective bargaining in practice, or even negotiation (e.g. Feng 2005; Luo 2011). According to several empirical studies, so-called collective negotiations in China are just a way of obtaining consent from

7 21st Century Business Herald, Trade Union Law will be amended - wage negotiation may be raised to industrial levels, Aug. 19, 2010

employers (e.g. Taylor et al 2003; Guo 2004; and Clarke et al 2004). In many private enterprises which have signed collective contracts, employees do not even know the existence of collective contracts. Without actual bargaining, many employers just sign a copied contract together with union cadres when they anticipate pressures from local governments or higher-level trade unions (Guo 2004). In this sense, collective contracts were regarded as no more than an "ineffective byproduct" of labor relations laws (Taylor et al 2003: 206). As Clarke et al. (2004) also commented, the most positive effect of the collective contract system in many enterprises was merely to remind employers and trade union cadres of their respective legal responsibilities.

In addition, some scholars have noticed that there are problems with the existing law itself. For instance, there was no article explaining the process of collective bargaining, although the process of drafting the collective contract has been intensively described (Ye and Xu 2005). Besides, the right to strike, a necessary guarantee of equal and effective collective negotiations, has been omitted in Chinese laws since 1982. However, to leave out the right to strike from legal codes does not avoid labor-capital conflicts in reality (Chang 2003).

Apparently, the practice and content of collective contracts reflect deep-rooted problems that plagued the industrial relations system at that time. Subsequently, many scholars attempted to find out the underlying causes. For instance, some (e.g. Jiang 2004) regarded the economic and position-based dependency of enterprise unions on employers as one crucial reason for the exclusionary practices of the bargaining process. This is an important argument. However, the dysfunction of the existing collective bargaining mechanism is a more systematic and deep-rooted problem that should be analyzed on the basis of the changes of production as well as industrial relations. Apparently, whereas most previous studies correctly described the problematic policies and implementation of collective bargaining and collective contract in China, only a few have analyzed the root of these problems but few proposed any solutions.

1.1.3 The state-capital-labor relationship and "corporatism" approach

A further exploration into the state-capital-labor relationship is necessary to understand the operation of the law and actual practice of collective bargaining and collective contract. Besides workers, other major actors in industrial relations, namely employers, trade unions and the state have been fairly studied at both macro policy arena and at the factory level. In particular, the impacts of the state policies, with its continued control over social and political apparatuses and to a less degree over the economy, has been an important topic of study, especially in its relations with the emerging group of employers, as well as the ambiguous role of the trade unions.

Employers in China have their distinctive features. In 2003, there were 26.57 million private businesses, employing more than 200 million people and accounting for 1/3 of the national GDP (Wei 2004:11). However, there had not been a single homogeneous class of capitalists that shared common identities, interests, and behaviors, exerting a unified political impact upon the central government (Tsai 2005). Indeed, capitalists in China have different social and political identities, from which they draw upon different networks and resources. They also diverge in the types of grievances they have against the state largely due to their distinctive local business conditions. In particular, the political membership of the private sector has been remarkably fluid during the past two decades, such as a large group of "red-cap businessmen" or "official businessmen" [8] in the 1990s and a growing number of Communist Party members in the new century. In addition, there are no autonomous employers' associations or industry confederations comparable to Western countries. Rather, employers associations are officially sanctioned and licensed by the Chinese government. Even within the relatively autonomous foreign sector, the China Association of Enterprises with Foreign Investment along with its branches are run or involved by former or active foreign trade officials, who are charged with helping to implement, promote, and improve China's investment policies (Pearson 1994). Pearson called it "a dualistic mixture of state-domination and limited independence". Thus, unlike the conditions of bourgeois revolutions in Britain, US and France (Moore 1966), Tsai (2005) concluded that it was much less likely that China's capitalists would be at the forefront of systemic revolution. In fact, this is understandable considering that Chinese employers have not been excluded from the current authoritarian regime, nor their material interests were under threat.

In practice, collective labor organizations - the official trade unions - are under firm control of the state. The ACFTU is criticized for not being a real trade union as the representative and defender of workers. In the planned economy, trade unions were kept largely irrelevant (Chen 2003b). The "proletarian" ideology restricted the role of socialist trade unionists in working primarily for workers' material improvement during the Maoist period (Walder

8 The words "Red-cap businessmen" or "official businessmen" in China particularly mean either government officials involving in business themselves or those businessmen having a close relationship with government policy-makers. In recent years, the latter applies to more and more cases.

1984:126). Historically, the trade union acted as a "bridge" or "transmission belt" between the party-state and workers or welfare distributors, except during the Cultural Revolution when it was regarded as unnecessary and thus banished (Chan 2008:73).

After Reform, the obscure role of the ACFTU between the state and workers has not significantly changed. According to the labor laws and union constitutions, Chinese trade union represents the interest of workers as well as the interests of both governments and enterprises (e.g. Feng 2002:129; Tong 2005). Clearly, the ACFTU is not the interest representative of workers as trade unions usually are in the West. In addition, trade unions in China also have social functions, such as coordinating interest groups (Feng, 2005:12), or playing an intermediary role (Zhang 2001a:11). In the current market economy, the state, fearing mass protests within traditionally communist countries, continues to prohibit any form of independent labor organizations outside of the ACFTU framework. Nevertheless, the challenge in maintaining stability among workers and managers in the industrial workplace forced the state to open some space for trade unions, particularly in serving as an intermediary role in labor disputes and settlement negotiations (Chen 2003), through new laws and policies. Further at the enterprise level, the function of grass-roots trade unions is also highly restricted by their limited role in protecting workers. On the contrary, enterprise unions tend to be over-controlled by employers (Chang 2004a: 241).

As for the relationship between the state, employers and trade unions, "Corporatism"[9] is perhaps the most widely quoted theoretical concept among scholarly works in China. Schmitter (1974) divided state corporatism and societal corporatism. While state corporatism is mainly authoritarianism by setting up organizations externally in order to maintain social control, organizations in societal corporatism are built from the bottom up and given formal recognition from the state (Gerber 1995). Negotiations are emphasized in societal corporatism, and the key to this mode of corporatism is aimed to

---

9 The concept of Corporatism received dramatic academic attention in the 1980s, and again in the late 1990s, especially for places where the institutional basis for collaborative, bargained methods of policy making and conflict resolution seemed distinctly unpromising. Schmitter defines "Corporatism" as "a system of interest representation, in which the constituent units are organized into a limited number of singular, compulsory, noncompetitive, hierarchically ordered and functionally differentiated categories, recognized or licensed (if not created) by the state and granted a deliberate representational monopoly within their respective categories in exchange for observing certain controls on their selection of leaders and articulation of demands and supports". See: Schmitter, 1974

integrate the interests of labor organizations into decision-making, income policies and industrial production relations, which is also called "neo-corporatism" or "democratic corporatism".

In China, the approach of "corporatism" has been applied in several studies that address this matter (e.g. Unger and Chan 1995: 47; Zhang 2001b; Chen 2003). Zhang (2001b) analyses the trade union system as one type of social organizations in corporatism, which functions as an intermediary between the state and its constituency - that is, its employees. On one hand, the trade union is obligated to coordinate its members and to unify their dispersed claims. On the other, the representative status and right of the trade union are verified and protected by the state as the only organization for workers. Similarly, through studies on state intervention in the organization and operation of social associations, inspection institutions, funding resources, etc., Gu and Wang (2005) highlighted features of state corporatism that characterized the relations between the Chinese state and professional associations. Nevertheless, there are also contrary conclusions. For instance, White (1996) denied the existence of state, societal corporatism or civil society in China. According to his field study, White believed that since 1989 the state increased its dependence on the official trade union in maintaining labor peace out of the concern of social and political stability. The trade union may maintain its close relationship with the party and continue its monopoly over the representation and negotiation of labor interests. However, at the same time, its autonomy could only be realized within the restrict limitations of the law.

Moreover, another important applications entails the current status of state-society relations, particularly the question of whether China is developing away from "state" toward "societal" corporatism. The key among different types of corporatism is the state corporatism contains the least power from the bottom and lowest degree of democracy. Pearson (1994) categorized the interaction between the state and business association as "socialist corporatism", while Chen (2003) used the term of "state corporatism" . Besides, Unger and Chan (1995) described it as "regional corporatism", in comparison to other East Asian economies. In their work of 2008, state corporatism continued to hold sway in the operation of associations in spite of dramatic economic reform and social transition.

Nevertheless, many studies recognized that the pattern of corporatism has changed since the 1980s. They regarded economic liberalization and societal corporatism, rather than pluralism, as the most conceivable future. For instance, Gu and Wang (2005) believed that in countries emphasizing collective interests rather than individual interests civil society would not be able to rival the government. Instead, the state and society might mutually empower each other when the Chinese government would further change its direct commands on the economy and society. Guo (1999) similarly concluded, based on his research of labor policies in the mainland and Taiwan, that collective dialogue with the government and industrial democratization were the key methods in achieving societal corporatism. Moreover, Unger and Chan (2008) argued that even without political democratization, societal corporatism was conceivable in China. Societal corporatism might emerge as the state gave permission to autonomous trade unions in order to avoid another wave of social unrest after the 1990s (Chan 1993), or by integrating peasants and industrial workers from non-state-owned enterprises into the corporatist framework (Unger and Chan 1995), or possibly through the staff and workers' representative congress and by demanding direct elections for workplace union officials at the grass roots level (Zhu and Chan 2003).

It is true that some features of "state corporatism" fit well to the conditions of China. For instance, the exclusive interaction between the state and monopoly organizations easily impairs the political voice of smaller groups. Nevertheless, given the definition of societal corporatism as "the concomitant, if not ineluctable, component of the post-liberal, advanced capitalist, organized democratic welfare state" (Schmitter 1974), some necessary conditions for implementation are lacking in China. For instance, there is simply no full autonomy of employers' associations and especially of official trade unions, and democratic negotiations between the state and associations do not exist. Besides, adequate representation of employers' associations or trade unions remains a question. Therefore, the application of "societal" or "neo-" corporatism requires at least a full-scale political and social overturn, which looks rather distant for China. Further, the Corporatism approach attempts to generalize the relationship among the state, capital and labor, whereas in practice industrial relations in China vary largely from one industry to another and even from one factory to another. In this sense, a crucial examination at the micro levels, in a certain region or within specific establishments, is missing in most existing studies of corporatism.

To sum up, previous research has provided a general picture of the changing industrial relations in China. These studies investigated the conditions of workers in light of evolving production regimes, newly-built industrial relations mechanisms including the collective contract system, and the relationship between trade unions, employers and the state. Primarily, the regimes of production have transformed from Walder's "neo-traditionalism" in the 1980s to Lee's "disorganized despotism", particularly in south China. As various types of industries and enterprises continue to grow, the conditions of work among the majority of migrant workers contrast that with former SOE workers, in terms of citizenship, social and economic statuses. There is extreme diversification of enterprises in different sectors and regions today. However, previous studies concentrate either on the declining state-owned economy or on small private firms in south China, but research on the diversity of manufacturing industries and enterprises are widely absent. Furthermore, literature on the relevant laws and on the implementation of the collective bargaining and collective contract mechanism mostly focuses on practical questions, such as the necessity of legislation, the actual implementation, and the prevalent dysfunction of collective bargaining. Apparently, only a few have analyzed the roots of such problems and rarely has any solution been proposed. Lastly, studies on the state-capital-labor relationship reveal the firm control of the state upon the ACFTU, thereby revealing the close linkage between capital interests and the state. Among these studies, scholars show that the corporatist approach has outstanding relevance to China. They therefore emphasize a focus on the questions of whether China is a case of state or societal corporatism and how societal corporatism may emerge. However, this approach encounters limitations in the existing political framework in China and tends to overlook ongoing changes of industrial relations, especially at the micro levels.

1.2 Key theories and concepts

With the exception of the above-mentioned theories of the Corporatism approach, many major political and social approaches in the West remain unknown among academics, or unfamiliar in practice among industrial practitioners in China. Apparently, simply taking China as an exception through the discourse of "Chinese characteristics" is no longer convincing, while its economy and the life of people have greatly integrated into globalization. In order to trace the past and future industrial development of China, it is important to position China within the relations of the global economic, social and political history. Several relevant theories and concepts provide an appropriate context from which to compare China with earlier industrialized economies such as the U.S. and Germany. Those include the approach of "varieties of Capitalism" (VoC) in comparative political economy, and the concepts of "forces of labor" and "factory regimes", which will be addressed in detail as below.

1.2.1 Comparative political economy

Comparative political economy mainly looks at variations of economic and political institutions across nation-states. For many, the major approach is VoC, which is designed to identify the various types of capitalisms on the basis of different modes of governance. VoC not only compares the patterns of similarity and difference across nations, but also discusses the transformations among national political economies. So far, the dissimilarities of political economies among developed countries have remained the main focus. However, developing economies have rarely appeared in existing studies of VoC. In addition, "varieties" of capitalism are highlighted, whereas less attention has been paid to "capitalism" itself (Pontusson 2005: 164).

Soskice (1999) identified four interlocked spheres of production systems as important elements of the VoC approach: the organization of education and training, the nature of labor market institutions, the degree of financial intermediation, and stringency of competition policy. In another representative work from Hall and Soskice (2001: 1-68), a comprehensive introduction of the VoC approach was provided on the basis of the comparison with previous approaches in comparative political economy. The same study identified two ideal types of political economies based on the different way in which firms resolve their industrial or resource coordination problems - Liberal market economies like the American case and coordinated market economies as in Germany pose a comparative example. In reality, however, many nations are located between these two polar models.

Following this categorization, Boyer (2005) regarded the U.S. and U.K. as typical liberal market economies, which centered on free and private-firm governance, and Germany and Japan as coordinated market economies. Furthermore, in the light of the comparative structures of private hierarchy and civil society, Boyer sorted out at least four brands of Capitalism: market-led, meso-corporatist, social democratic, and state-led. If ranked by the degree of market orientation, namely the lineup from market, company, community to state, the U.S remains at the top of the hierarchy together with other English-speaking countries and Norway. Following them, Japan and Korea, characterized by the exchange of solidarity against mobility and conglomerate types of economic unit, belonged to meso-corporatist. Scandinavian countries were the flag-bearers of social democratic political economies, where frequent negotiations were conducted between social partners and public authorities concerning governing rules. In the least market-oriented group, there were most continental countries taking part in the European integration.

As for China, no matter how much the government insists that the economy operates as market socialism, many research, both international and national levels, have become skeptical toward this claim.[10] Still, some scholars (e.g. Arrighi 2008) regard China as a non-capitalist market economy. In the field of industrial relations, Chinese workers have no democratic control as those in capitalist societies, and the ruling communist party brings along legacies from the bureaucratic planned economy. Moreover, China may appear different from many other nations in terms of economic infrastructure and firm behavior, given the strong political background of Chinese capitalists as well as fierce internal competition among different regions. Nevertheless, other capitalist countries, such as the U.S., Germany, Japan, all have their own history, culture, and distinctive paths of economic development, and indeed there are no two single countries in the world that may share every common feature.

Most importantly, the key elements of capitalism are contained in the path of economic development rather than in pure ideology. Despite any phenomenon at the surface, any development path that fits within these key elements is capitalism. Summarized by Ten Brink (2010), capitalism is featured by: the horizontal axis of capitalist social relations, including increasing interdependence of socioeconomic processes, competition-driven accumulation etc.; the vertical axis of capitalist social relations, i.e. social stratifications, particularly vertical class polarization between property owners and property; monetary conditions that money or the capital turned into money plays in modern capitalism; the particular role of the state and the interaction between economic and political actors, typically, structural interdependence; and, the inter- and transnational capitalist system integration. As for other popular indicators, such as democracy, they may play a role but not as the most essential feature. These indicators can not apply to all capitalistic countries either.

Thus, the real question is China is developing what variety of capitalism. Following the five indicators summarized by Ten Brink (2010), China is identified as a new variety of Capitalist market economy - a "market-liberal state capitalism". It is a combination of the self-preservationist interests of the party-state and the objective of the market-mediated accumulation by capitalists. This model is also primarily characterized by a dynamic state intervention; by particular forms of competition and of corporate organization; by a specific

10 In general, Chinese scholars are cautious in talking about capitalism in China, at least on a theoretical level, although it is rather common during oral discussion and in on-line blogs. In particular, New Leftists believe the road of China towards modernism and democracy is a standard and typical process to capitalism, and thus all criticism in the West on capitalism can be applied to China. See: e.g. Lippit 1997; Information Center for Social Sciences at Renmin University, General theories on social sciences, 2006: 41

variant of corporatism; by strict regulation of money and currency relations; and by a particular form of conflictive-cooperative integration into the global economy.

In the study of Baumol et al. (2007: 60-61), China was dominated by entrepreneurial capitalism. In this study, capitalism is divided into four different types according to the leading force in the economy, such as state-guided capitalism, oligarchic capitalism, big-firm capitalism, and entrepreneurial capitalism. Entrepreneurial capitalism means entrepreneurship, basically new private start-up companies, as the driving force of the economy. It has powered the US economy toward a higher growth rate since 1990s and widespread in Ireland, Israel, UK, India and China. The best form of "good capitalism" claimed in this book is a blend of 'entrepreneurial' and 'big-firm' capitalism, although the precise mix varies from country to country, depending on a combination of cultural and historical characteristics (Baumol et al 2007:4). This explains why the China model of "incremental change", which encourages entrepreneurship while not necessarily privatizing all of its SOEs and banks at once, has worked far better than the shock therapy in Russia. So far, many SOEs in China remain in business with the support of continuing loans from state-owned banks. At the same time, the central government has also permitted provincial and municipal governments and individuals to launch their own enterprises. In this context, the seedlings of new enterprises have grown rapidly, and they began to play more and more significant role in the economy, which seems to fit the model of "entrepreneurial capitalism'.

In another study also with a focus on entrepreneurship, Huang (2008: xvi) defined "capitalism with Chinese characteristics", which resembles the most popular perception in China today. Similar to Baumol et al., Huang was strongly in favor of bottom-up entrepreneurship and regarded policies in the 1980s, which encouraged the boom of town- and village-owned enterprises (TVEs), as the genuine drive of the economic miracle. Nevertheless, although "capitalism with Chinese characteristics" also means a political balance between the entrepreneurial, market-driven rural China and the state-led urban China[11], Huang (2008: 43) held a distinct view from others that Chinese economy is a version of the state-led capitalism that characterized Latin America, rather than East Asian end. Huang emphasized that on the one hand, the policies since 1990s had favored urban heavy-handed interventionism, and a biased

11 The rural China began to develop industries on the basis of bottom up entrepreneurship and supply and demand in the market in the 1980s. At the same time, the economy of the urban China had always been in the tight control of the state and supported by the state both financially and policy-wise.

liberalization that privileges foreign direct investment (FDI) over indigenous private entrepreneurship, which contradicts the general view that Chinese state was to create a market economy based on complete private ownership. On the other hand, Huang believed the very success of the economy was indeed a function of indigenous private-sector development, financial liberalization, and property rights security. As a result, the income disparities had risen, and social opportunities available to the population to attain education and health had contracted since the 1990s. Thus, Huang concluded that the existing state-led policies could not work any longer, but a reorientation toward more liberal institutions was needed to achieve a sustained and welfare improving growth trajectory.

Apparently, the typologies of "market-liberal state capitalism", "entrepreneurial capitalism", and "capitalism with Chinese characteristics" largely differ in their theoretical background and perspectives, and the overly strong focus on entrepreneurship in the latter two studies remains debatable. However, the development path of China is undeniably in accordance with capitalism. Thus, the relations between the market, entrepreneurship, and the state should be further explored. Therefore, it is indicative to position China into the much broader trajectory of the global economic and political arena, of which, China has already become an inseparable part. At the same time, the limitations of VoC approach on industrial relations studies are obvious. Primarily, it regards the drive for changes as only coming from the structure, but in fact the interactions between firms, workers and the state not only shape everyday practice but also influence the policies and institutions at macro levels. Besides, the VoC framework has strongly focused on developed economies while China has not yet fit into this group. There might be more peculiarities than similarities when China is compared to developed nations. Thus, a more thorough theory, which takes into account both micro conditions and macro policies in the specific field of industrial relations, would better fit this research. The Regulation Approach is thus selected, which will be addressed in the section 1.3.

1.2.2 Forces of labor

The force of labor is not a new concept, but an enduring concept that attracts increasing attention within the processes of economic globalization. Throughout the history of capitalism, labor movements have all along pushed forward the evolution of the systems of industrial relations in different countries. In order to look at the institutions and functions of collective bargaining, the ultimate drive - the labor force - should be emphasized, which not only determines production regimes at factory levels but also shapes labor polity in the long run.

In his classic book *Capita'*, Marx emphasizes the inseparable nature of labor power and humanity at the point of production. In this sense, wage-labor is a fictitious commodity in the capitalist world, which is not only one object of "just" trade relations but it also contains "power". The capitalist relations, on the one side the capitalist, on the other the wage laborer, is far from "just". Capitalist production of itself reproduces the separation between labor-power and the means of labor and thereby constantly reproduces the conditions of exploiting laborers. In the history of primitive accumulation, great masses of men are suddenly and forcibly torn from their means of subsistence, and hurled as free and "unattached" proletarians on the labor-market. In this way, laborers were forced to sell their labor-power in order to live, and the capitalists could purchase labor-power in order that they may enrich themselves. Besides, the surplus-value that laborers create and capitalists possess is in substance the materialization of unpaid labor. The expropriation of the agricultural producer, of the peasant, from the soil, is the basis of the primitive accumulation of capitalism. Thus, the capitalist mode of production and accumulation, and therefore capitalist private property, have for their fundamental condition the annihilation of self-earned private property; in other words, the expropriation of the laborer. Accordingly, there were the long-term struggles of English working classes since the seventeenth century, in France in the eighteenth century, and nearly sweeping the entire Europe in the middle nineteenth century. This leads to his well-known conjecture that the fundamental contradictions of capitalism will eventually result in the end of itself, and working classes confronting capitalist exploitation play the role of overturning capitalism.

Similarly, Polanyi believes that labor, like land and money, are not a pure commodity, although it is essential factor of production. Nevertheless, rather than stressing the conflict between labor and capital, Polanyi (1944: 176-7) argued that the extension or deepening of the labor market - the market for "labor power" - is countered by the mobilization of the state and capitalists to regulate and constrain it, through a variety of mechanisms, including social legislation, factory laws, unemployment insurance, and trade unions. According to his theory, labor history follows a pendular movement between modification and protection. In the late nineteenth century and early twentieth century, globalization of markets produced a strong countermovement from workers and other social groups. In response to rising labor militancy and in the wake of the two world wars and a depression, the pendulum swung toward the de-commodification of labor after WWII.

Critiques of Polanyi (Silver 2003: 16-25) highlight his emphasis of labor polity from the perspective of "justice" but neglects the factor of "power". In light of his logic, an unregulated world market would eventually be overturned ‘from above’ even if those from below lacked effective bargaining power. Yet, the reality is not quite as promising. In the new wave of economic globalization since the late twentieth century, the hypermobility of capital worldwide has led to a “race to the bottom” along global production network and brought unprecedented threat to labor movements in both developed and developing countries. As Arrighi (1990) pointed out, the cost-cutting race of the late twentieth century proved once again that, according to the dictates of capital, all the members of the proletariat were interchangeable instruments of labor, regardless of age, sex, color, nationality etc.. However, so far there has been no apparent shift back to the “protection” stage in Polanyi's pendulum. In the end, the analysis still needs a return to Marx's standpoint of “power”.

In the field of industrial relations, the force of labor is fundamentally manifested in the bargaining power of workers. In his remarkable work, Wright (2000: 962) has identified two principal types of workers' bargaining power - associational power and structural power. The former originates from the formation of collective organization of workers, especially trade unions and political parties. The latter comes from their location within the economic system, which further divides into two subtypes - the marketplace and workplace bargaining power. Marketplace bargaining power is directly from tight labor markets, indicated by special and high demand skills, low unemployment rates, and the capability of workers to leave the labor market and live on non-wage incomes. Moreover, workplace bargaining power is possessed by a particular group of workers at strategic locations within a key industrial sector. Usually for workers who are enmeshed in tightly integrated production processes, the stoppage of work in key positions may cause far larger loss. For instance, production lines have to be completely shut down if one part of work stops, and even more so in enterprises applying just-in-time delivery of parts.

In the study of Silver (2003) on labor power, she includes a global narrative of labor unrest over the past 130 years. Using the example of the automobile industry, Silver found an interesting phenomenon that the relocation of production by capital to geographic locations with lower cost and more controllable labor was always followed by rising labor militancy in new locations. This is because mass production tends to recreate similar social contradictions wherever it has grown, and, as a result, strong and effective labor movements have emerged in virtually every site where Fordist mass production expanded rapidly (Silver 2003: 41). Along with the transnational flight of the automobile manufacture, this norm proves itself firstly in North America in the 1930s and 1940s, in northwestern (and then southern) Europe in the 1960s and 1970s, and in rapidly industrializing countries, such as Brazil, South Africa, and South Korea in the 1980s and 1990s, with the only exception of Japan.

Indeed, this norm may not look so mysterious if one considers the nature of labor-capital conflict and the sources of labor force. For the sake of profitability, industrialists after the WWII mainly adapted the strategies of relocation, automation and rationalization. One important criteria in investment relocation involves cheap and preferably docile labor, besides political stability, a booming market, and hard and convertible currency. However, labor-capital conflict is embedded in an inherent tension between the legitimacy and profitability of production, which is first shown by the basic contradiction between higher wages for workers and more profits for employers. The introduction of work organization and labor process to the new site again raised such conflicted interests, and sooner or later, workers demand better labor standards with increasing bargaining power. The result is the recreation of militant labor movement in new sites, although the struggles of workers may be expressed in different ways and in different places, depending on the composition of the workforce, the development of social movements, etc.. In a word, relocation had only geographically shifted the contradictions from one production site to another, but was never able to permanently eradicate the problems of profitability and labor control (Silver 1995b: 173-85).

Japan however was one notable exception to this norm. The problems of the Japanese labor movement itself, particularly the destruction of communist-led militant trade unions, may explain the absence of substantial labor unrest at the stage of economic boom in the 1960s and 1970s. Besides, the well-known "lean production" method, which has been selectively emulated in many sectors, has sustained this generally quiet tone of Japanese labor movements. In this highly flexible production system, the "lean and dual" model offers employment security to a core labor force in exchange for cooperation, while at the same time creates a large buffer of less privileged workers without the same rights and benefits. At the time, the rural workforce in Japan including wives and daughters of male workers acted as the lower-tiers to a core labor force, which relieved the contradiction between the core and peripheral workforce (Okayama 1986).

Furthermore, whether this norm can be applied in the future is uncertain, as dramatic changes have been and are taking place in the new century, especially due to the widespread lean production, human resource management methods, and the emerging sectors, smaller-scaled enterprises and divided workforce among different industries and countries. One of the major obstacles is it is more and more difficult for workers to unite. New production and management methods, new sectors and new types of enterprises have largely segmented and divided workforces, which poses challenges to labor movements everywhere. However, the inherent conflicts in capitalist production have not changed, or even worsened in many cases. For instance, many American and European companies employ a "lean-and-mean" practice, which means lack of employment guarantee even for core workers. This may lead to massive complaint at new production sites. Accordingly, more attention needs to be paid to "achieving improved wages, security, and working conditions" than before (e.g. the case of Fiat, see: Camuffo and Volpato 1995).

The boom of the electronics industries, the leading capitalist industry of the twenty-first century, makes this picture more complicated. In particular, microelectronics was suggested by Peter Dicken (1998: 353-4) as the "industry of industries". Since the 1970s, this industry - through the "computerization of everything" - has had at least as profound an impact as the automobile in the twentieth century on the experience of everyday life and work (Silver 2003: 104). In particular, the invention of computers and microelectronics greatly facilitated the global networked production, so that the parts and components of one product (e.g. a mobile phone) could be produced in different parts of the world and only be assembled at the end in one factory. However, the high degree of automation in wafer fabrication, board assembly and so forth, along with the requirement of precision and quality in production, results in limited job creation. At the same time, the further de-skilling of manufacturing work (e.g. front-line workers only in charge of loading materials and unloading the final products out of highly-automated machines) has led to an enlargement of low-wage industrial proletariat. Some features, such as vertical dis-integration of production and the corresponding proliferation of sites of production and employers faced by workers, have segmented the working classes and made collective consciousness and actions less likely, which may resemble the environment of textile workers rather than automobile workers.

In addition, the relatively pro-labor political environment for workers' associational power in the nineteenth and twentieth centuries, resulted from the pressure of Communism and economic depressions, seems to no longer exist (Silver 2003: 165). At the time, facing depressions and wars, institutional experiments and accommodation of capital to proletariat (e.g. Keynesian package) shifted the waves of world-scale labor unrest from rising and becoming explosive to being stable or declining in the post-WWII period. Nevertheless, today labor movements are facing a world-scale crisis. Since the 1970s a combination of spatial, technological/organizational, and financial fixes seriously has weakened workers, allowing for an open assault by states and capital on core labor movements. In the 1990s, most of those Second and Third World labor movements that had been impressively strong in the 1970s and 1980s were in a crisis themselves. Further, whether the current crisis of legitimacy may raise the attention of the world's elite to livelihood and security as in the early part of the last century also remains unknown. In the meanwhile, labor internationalism, the struggle for the livelihood of all, is yet blocked by the high dependency of workers in developed countries on protectionism, mostly restriction on import and immigration (Silver 2003: 171-2; 177-9).

Whether China is another exception of this norm is a key question of this study. In the global scenario, China became one of the new sites for capital expansion in the late twentieth century. Now the automobile sector is one of the pillar industries in the country, since the production of both whole-car and auto parts has been growing rapidly. At the same time, the electronics industry is developing at an unprecedented speed. As Dicken (1998: 357) described, China "came from nowhere" to become the world's largest maker of televisions in 1987. Along with the steps of industrialization, whether China would begin another new cycle of spatial relocation and militancy attracts much attention. In the last three decades, the dismantling of the planned economy and SOE system has provoked widespread waves of labor unrest from workers whose established ways of life and livelihood are being overturned. For example, there were 30,000 demonstrations in the first nine months of 2000 alone (e.g. Li 2001), most against job loss and unpaid wages and pensions.

In order to answer the question, the entire system of industrial relations in China should be examined. Two factors are crucial - the existing labor and production regimes at the factory level and the industrial and national policies. The aggregate bargaining power of workers is ultimately determined by both factors. As the relocation of production has also shifted the social contradictions of mass production, the problems raise the questions of what forms these social contradictions take in China; whether collective bargaining could accommodate such contradictions; and what forms collective bargaining would take.

1.2.3 Labor process and factory regime

The existing labor and production regimes serve one of the essential factors in determining the modes of power among major actors in industrial relations and particularly in the processes of collective bargaining. Until Braverman's book Labor and Monopoly Capital (1974), the question of the labor process has been largely neglected by Marxists, although Marx himself has first analyzed the labor process of Capitalism in his book Capital (Burawoy 1985: 41).

Braverman (1974) argued that control of the production processes lies at the center of all management systems. Taylorist scientific management was the method among American capitalists to control the labor process among workers, resulting in higher surplus value, weaker oppositional potential among workers and deskilling of front-line workers. However, although workers' capacity and power may be weakened, such power remained a threat to capitalist. When the employment conditions allowed or the degree of labor intensity exceeded the limitation acceptable for workers, the power might explode into industrial actions. In his work, Braverman did not explore the cause of such confrontation.

Influenced by Braverman, Burawoy (1979) refused that management could directly control workers. Instead, he argued that management needed to adapt to workers' struggle, thus making it necessary for managers to compromise and to submit some rights of workers. According to his research on a machinery multinational in south Chicago (Burawoy 1979: xii), once workers entered workshops, coercion alone could no longer explain workers' behaviors. He also argued that another factor, the consent of workers should be taken into consideration. Primarily, the productivity of workers depended far more on the active mobilization of workers' consent than on heavy-handed coercion. Moreover, the promotion ladders, within internal labor markets provided an incentive for workers' cooperation and loyalty, whereby detailed work rules and grievance procedures created a legal framework at the level of the firm for the purpose of resolving conflicts. Thus, Burawoy (1985) believed the factory regime of capitalism had shifted from "despotic", to "hegemonic", and then to "hegemonic despotism".

The "Despotic" factory regime is based on management's exploitation of the market and workers' total dependence on wages for their livelihoods; This regime s also characterized by overtly coercive disciplinary regulations through the institutionalization of wage dependence and the threat of job-loss. In contrary, a "hegemonic" factory regime is based on state interventions in forms of social insurance legislation, compulsory trade union recognition, grievance machinery and collective bargaining; This regime is characterized by circumscribed and regulated coercion and prevailing consent between labor and capital. The "hegemonic despotism" is no longer the despotism of managers to individual workers; Rather, it involves the "rational" despotism of capital flow to collective labor. The reproduction of labor became re-binding with the production process, not at individual level, but at the levels of the company, region or even state (Burawoy 1985: 50). In the process of globalization, competition from firms and/or countries with greater shop floor flexibility threatened the viability/profitability of hegemonic factory regimes (Burawoy 1985). However, some criticized that Burawoy ignored the impact of workers' struggle and capacity on factory power structure (Edwards 1986: 51-52).

The "factory regime" was another key concept in Burawoy's work, which linked state regulations of labor, such as legislation on contracts, minimum wage, social insurance, and collective bargaining, and the social reproduction of labor power - i.e., means of subsistence, daily and generational reproduction of the capacity to labor - to workplace control and workers' capacity for resistance (Lee 2007: 21). The idea was that the linkages between labor and management and among workers related to the broader political intervention in the regulation and reproduction of labor. Different labor relations did not just link the factory regimes to public institutions, but also to the types of different production models and organizations. Piece rate, internal labor market, collective bargaining and channels directed towards grievance resolution served as key features of the factory regime.

In his study on Russia and former socialist countries in the East Europe, Burawoy (2001) believed that the dismantling of the socialist camp did not mean the impossibility of realizing socialism. Rather, capitalism successfully exerted its potential and alleviated its own contradictions. Due to the rule of the world history, socialism did not have such a chance to consummate itself. Through the analysis on two comparable companies in the U.S. and Hungary, Burawoy and Lukacs (1985) overturned the stereotype of low-efficiency in socialist state-owned enterprises and proved that, under similar conditions, capitalist enterprises were not more efficient than socialist ones. In addition, in his numerous studies on Russia (e.g. Burawoy 1996; 2000), Burawoy referred to China extensively by stating that state has brought about successful accumulation and prosperous market economy whereas the neoliberal "shock therapy" in Russia only resulted in the failure of transformation of production, society and the state. Nevertheless, the actual conditions and struggles of workers in China were not seriously discussed in his study.

The successors of Burawoy have extended his research of "factory regime" to the situation in the Pearl River Delta (PRD). Through a comparative study on electronics assembly factories in Hong Kong and the PRD, Lee (1999) found distinctive features of factory regimes. In the process of dismantling the state socialism, the former system was abandoned, but the new market order had yet become mature. Hence a "gap" emerged in the rules of labor-capital relations. According to Lee, the neo-traditionalism by Walder no longer existed in state-owned enterprises in Guangzhou. Instead, the labor relations in privatized enterprises during the transition were characterized by "disorganized despotism". "Disorganized" meant that there was not enough interest coordination among different social groups, due to the lack of cooperation among support for various reform policies. Further, "despotism" included the institutional dependency of wage-earners on manufacturing work, coercive form of labor control, and collective anxiety of workers on their material interests and their spiritual acknowledgment toward such control.

Moreover, some scholars attempted to complicate the "factory regime" concept. For instance, based on their investigations on enterprises in mainland

China, Taiwan and South Korea, Nichols et al. (2004) distinguished three aspects of labor regimes: labor control, material support and contract. As the major finding, those labor regimes that featured long-term stability and relative privilege to workers (i.e. wages and other material support) were gradually destroyed in all cases.

It is fair to say that Burawoy and his followers have profoundly influenced the academic field of labor process and production regime. Many of their applications on China also gained valuable results. Nevertheless, most labor process studies focused on a rather narrow scope of the shop floor or factory levels. Thus, the main flaw among these studies is that they lack a systematic comprehension of capitalism as social relations involving not only the labor and capital but also the state.

Therefore, while applying those concepts, such as "factory regime" (or "accumulation regime" in the Regulation Approach) and "the forces of labor", to China, it is necessary to take into consideration the history of capitalism and labor movements. As clarified in the part on the VoC approach, China today is part of the capitalist world, no matter whether we call it "socialist market economy" or a new variety of capitalism. Consequently, the development path of other economies in the past may offer valuable lessons to China. At the same time, industrial and political changes at the global level from the post-war period up to now are worth researching, as both Silver and Burawoy have reminded us. Therefore, this study aims at a systematic analysis of changing industrial relations combining the factory, industrial and national, and global factors, by adopting several key words from previous studies as well as referring to the regulation approach as the overarching theoretical framework.

1.3 The Regulation Approach

This study takes the regulation approach as the basic theoretical framework. Importantly, the Regulation Approach fills in significant theoretical gaps in the field by systematically combining production processes together with social and political institutions at both micro and macro levels and by examining the linkages between existing accumulation regimes and the corresponding modes of regulations. This approach features two major concepts - the "mode of regulation" and the "regime of accumulation". Collective bargaining is recognized as one ideal type of regulation in capitalist relations. Therefore, an effective mechanism of collective bargaining should lead to orderly labor-capital relations, at the same time, its formation and function are restrained by the existing regimes of accumulation and may also be inspired from the tension or defect of such regimes. This is demonstrated in the representative studies on Fordism as below, as collective bargaining is the key of Fordist wage regulation.

Furthermore, I review previous applications of the Regulation approach on China, along with its weaknesses. At the end, the theoretical framework of this study is built up on the basis of the Regulation approach, integrated with the key concepts such as "force of labor" and "factory regime".

1.3.1 Major concepts

Inspired by Marxist Structuralist theories of the 1960s (Jessop and Sum 2006: 2), the Regulation approach was pioneered in the 1970s in France and refined in the 1980s (Amin 1994: 7). There were seven major schools in the 1970s and 1980s, mostly having similar concepts and pursuing similar objectives. At the time, this approach had gained remarkable international influence among scholars due to its explanation of economic growth in post-war epoch until the mid-1970s and throughout the subsequent crisis of Fordism.

The word "Regulation" (often misinterpreted as "reglementation"), originated from French language, means "a wide range of economic and extra-economic mechanisms in seeking to explain the 'regularities' of economic behaviour" (cf. Théret 1990a, from Jessop and Sum 2006: 14). As Koch (2006: 17) marked, the regulation approach is an attempt to bridge general theories of capitalist development with empirical research on employment systems and socioeconomic regulation. The goal of this approach is to show how these mechanisms interact to normalize the capital relations and guide the conflictual and crisis-mediated course of accumulation. Accordingly, this approach has the following four major goals (Jessop and Sum 2006; 18): 1) "to describe the institutions and practices of capitalism; 2) to explain the various crisis tendencies of modern capitalist and/or likely sources of crisis resolution; 3) to analyze different stages of capitalism and compare accumulation regimes and modes of regulation in a given period of capitalist development; and 4) to examine the social embedding and social regularization of economic institutions and conduct". To understand this, several key concepts and most relevant applications of this approach need to be addressed.

In order to explain the complex relationship between capitalist development and the accompanied social and political processes, many terms have been developed, such as "dominant industrial paradigm" or "labor process", "mode of development" (Lipietz 1987), and "mode of societalization" or "societal paradigm" (Jessop 1992). Among them, two fundamental terms are the "mode of regulation" and the "regime of accumulation".

Regime of accumulation (theoretical terms in Marx's Capital - a schema of reproduction) is defined by Aglietta (1979: 68) as "a form of social transformation that increases relative surplus-value under the stable constraints of the most general norms that define absolute surplus-value". In the definition of Lipietz (1987: 14), it is "the fairly long-term stabilization of the allocation of social production between consumption and accumulation". Concretely, a regime of accumulation includes norms pertaining to the organization of production and work, forms of exchange between branches of the economy, common rules of management, principles of income sharing between wages, profits and taxes, norms of consumption and patterns of demand in the market, and other aspects of the macro economy (Amin 1994: 8). Among all, the utilization of labor-power in production is the key, such as fixing of the legal duration of labor and wage determination, and socialized management of the reproduction costs of the wage-earning class like welfare (Aglietta 1979: 69).

A regime of accumulation may be primarily (or predominantly) extensive or primarily intensive, depending on whether capital accumulation is a means to expand the scale of production (with constant norms of production) or to further the capitalist reorganization of labor ('the real subordination' of labor to capital) by increasing productivity or the coefficient of capital (Lipietz 1987: 33; and Aglietta 1979: 71). In other words, an extensive regime of accumulation pursues the maximization of surplus-value, whereas an intensive regime is marked by utilitarianism and the seeking of a regular and rapid increase of profits. In the study of Lipietz (1987), for instance, the regime of accumulation which prevailed in the most advanced capitalist countries between the WWI and WWII was primarily extensive. In contrast, the post-war regime that had centered upon the growth of mass consumption was intensive accumulation.

Correspondingly, a mode of regulation includes "institutional forms, procedures and habits which either coerce or persuade private agents to conform to its schemes" (Lipietz 1987:21). In another definition (Nielsen 1991: 22), a mode of regulation is the set of internalized rules and social procedures that forms the long-term contractualization of wage relationship, including rigid control over redundancy, a regular wage increase indexed to prices and productivity, a vast socialization of revenues through the welfare state and so forth. In practice, the mode of regulation consists of a range of formal or informal "rules", including, law, state policy, political practices, business codes, bargaining rules, consumption cultures and social expectations. Those rules "regulate and reproduce" a certain accumulation regime. The state is the archetypal form of all regulation (Lipietz 1987: 19).

Generally speaking, the emergence of a new regime of accumulation is not a preordained part of capitalism's development, even though it may correspond to certain identifiable tendencies. It is also clear that not every mode of regulation is suitable for every regime of accumulation and a single mode can take the shape of different combinations of partial forms of regulation (Lipietz 1987: 34). Inappropriate regulation modes, which do not match or facilitate the accumulation, can cause minor or major economic crises. A minor crisis, also called "crisis in regulation", may be corrected within the mode of regulation. However, when major crises occur, it often means that the mode of regulation is not adequate to the regime of accumulation, either because the old regulation is blocking the emergence of a new regime, or because the potential of the regime of accumulation has exhausted, given the prevailing mode of regulation. The crisis of 1930s was the former example, when new forms of work organization - the Taylorist and then the Fordist revolutions - led to unprecedented rises in productivity, but the demand did not keep pace with the rise in productivity. Thus, it was a "a crisis of overproduction". According to Lipietz (1987: 43), the major crisis of the 1930s was either "the first crisis in intensive accumulation" or "the last crisis in competitive regulation". Moreover, in the 1970s, the development pattern that workers were only in charge of routine operation, but machines exclusively designed by industrial specialists became better and more advanced than before, and consequently productivity increased, had reached its limit. Profitability dropped uncontrollably. Finally, this crisis led to the turning point of divergent regulation modes in many industrialized economies, indicated by the general declining of Keynesian polices and the rise of Neoliberalism.

In a word, an integral economy comprises of an "accumulation regime and mode of regulation". In reality, the regimes of accumulation or modes of regulation are always the product of past struggles and are penetrated with present struggles. In consequence, in countries with similar degrees of economic development, the accumulation regimes can display remarkably different features and their modes of regulation may largely vary from one another.

1.3.2 Fordism and historical evolution

According to the Regulation Approach, the development of capitalism cannot be separated from the employment systems and socioeconomic regulation in a given period of time. Socioeconomic regulation should normalize the capital relation and guide the conflictual course of accumulation. Otherwise, it may block the accumulation and even lead to crisis. The epoch of Fordism and thereafter exemplifies such interaction between the mode of regulation and the regime of accumulation. Gramsci[12] provided insights into Fordism. This term loosely reflects the mass production methods and management rules pioneered by Henry Ford during the 1920s and 1930s. "Fordism" brought about the "golden age" of the Capitalism from 1940s up to the 1960s. As the representative model of mass production and collective labor regulations, Fordism represents the age of "intensive accumulation" with "monopolistic regulation" of the economy (Amin, 1994: 8). The Taylorist[13] reorganization of the labor process essentially makes the intensive accumulation in Fordism possible (e.g. Braverman 1974; Edwards 1979), through the intensification of work, the detailed division of tasks and mechanization to raise productivity, and various forms of monopolistic regulation to maintain the order.

In the analysis by Jessop (1991: 136-7), Fordism has four levels of meaning. Firstly, as a distinctive type of labor process, it involves mass production based on moving assembly-line techniques operated by semi-skilled mass workers. As a stable mode of macroeconomic growth (a regime of accumulation), Fordism involves a virtuous circle of growth. This circle is first based on mass production and productivity increases, which bring into income raises and mass demand growth. Further, profits increased based on full utilization of capacity and thus investment further improve mass production equipment and techniques. Moreover, as a mode of social and economic regulation (a mode of regulation), it includes the separation of ownership and control in large corporations with a multi-divisional, decentralized organization subject to central controls; monopoly pricing, union recognition and collective bargaining, wages indexed to productivity and inflation, and monetary emission and credit policies orientated to securing effective aggregate demand. Lastly, as a general pattern of social organization, Fordism involves the consumption of standardized, mass

12 Gramsci rejects the application of Fordism on socialism in so far as it separates the executive from the management, the particular consciousness of single tasks of the executors from the general consciousness of the sense, meaning towards which each task tends of the coordinator, rationalizer, manager. It is against that of the collective workers. See: Jessop, 1997

13 It is noted that Taylorism only symbolizes certain forms of work organization at the level of enterprises, rather than the description of any accumulation regime as a whole. Originated in the late nineteenth century, Taylorism emerged in the U.S. in engineering industries. The aim of "scientific management" was to combat the relative autonomy of jobs in old system. In the 1920s, such work organization became generalized in the US and, to a certain extent, in Europe. Based on far-reaching deskilling processes, Taylorism destructs traditional craft forms of workers' power and introduces efficient techniques of managerial control and supervision. See: Lipietz 1987: 35; Aglietta 1979: 113-4; and Hirsch 1991

commodities and provision of standardized, collective goods and services by the bureaucratic state.[14]

The fact that Fordism has a causal connection with the long upturn of the capitalist world in the post-war period is intriguing. Intensive accumulation took place during the interwar period among major industrialized countries, where extensive or exploitative means of capital accumulation had become incapable to sustain economic growth. The lack of mass consumption led to a crisis of capitalism in 1930s. This demand-side crisis was first counteracted by Keynesianism, which attempted to coordinate the maintenance of world demand. In the following several decades, changes in production and social consumption norms have given rise to the "golden age" of capitalism in the major industrialized world.

Fundamentally, Fordism is the ensemble of the mechanization-oriented mass production, collective contractual regulations on wages, mass demand or consumption-driven growth, and steady monetary and pricing policies at macro levels. Noticeably, Taylorist work organization, which signifies a strict separation between organization of production process (technical offices) and execution of standardized and formally prescribed tasks, is often regarded as a basic feature of Fordism. However, Fordism is not equated with the narrow concept of Taylorism.[15]

Further at the socioeconomic level, Fordism is characterized by compromises between capital and labor, so that shared productivity gains are ensured. The methods of determining wages reflect the nature and direction of a system of industrial relations. While the state forms part of the very existence of the wage relation, both capital and labor act on wage standards through continuous fighting and compromising. In Fordism, collective bargaining between capital and labor is the essential means in realizing the long-term contractualization of the wage relations. Such relations include rigid control over redundancy, a monitored increase in salaries as indexed by prices and general labor productivity, and a vast socialization of revenues through the welfare state assured a permanent income for the wage laborers (Lipietz 1997). In the era of Fordism, wages and salaries had been the drivers of consumers' demand in the domestic market.

---

14 The latter, the provision of standardized, collective goods and services by the bureaucratic state, also has a key role in managing the conflicts between capital and labor over individual and social wages, linked to the rise of Keynesian economic management and the universalist welfare state but neither element is regarded essential for the growth of Fordism.

15 For instance, Maschinenbau (Mechanical Engineering) in Germany is one typical sector with non-Taylorist work organization in Fordist economies.

The "reorganization" of labor mainly took place in a way that workers' control over their work is constrained by standardization of tasks and simplification of jobs. Instead of craft workers in the older system, semi-skilled workers, mostly rural migrant and newly entering the group of the industrial workforce, became the major labor force in factories. Meanwhile, supplemented with a higher degree of mechanization and automation, the work was intensified so as to enhance productivity. In order to keep workers in high labor intensity despite mostly repetitive jobs, capitalists began to pay "generous" wages. Most well-known case was Henry Ford's 'five dollars a day' offer at Highland Park on the eve of the WWI. Nevertheless, this policy in practice served a vastly different purpose. This scheme tried to subsume every aspect of the reproduction of labor-power, including the management of the workers' household budget, under a system of authoritarian productivism (Davis 1986: 108). Such a corporate welfarism operated as an anti-union strategy in practice.

In contrast, the Fordist wage regulation, which secured the growth of mass consumption in the long run, had resulted from the "social contract" agreed upon between collective labor and capital, which in turn was achieved through long-term negotiations and mutual compromise. A primary example is the case of the U.S. At the peak of the labor movement in the 1930s and 1940s, Fordist regulations took form. The 1940 collective agreement between General Motors (GM) and the United Auto Workers (UAW) was regarded as the first Fordist regulation in a real sense (Davis 1986). From approximately 1940 to 1975, the U.S. had experienced Fordist wage relations. Such a "social contract" sustained the economic upturn until the neoliberalism and globalization became dominant in the 1970s. The first overall trend of wage increase decelerated in 1982, which was the first time in the last 40 years (Davis 1986: 142).

While Germany developed a Fordist mode of regulation later in the 1950s, it took a rather different form as that of the U.S. The German labor movement after the WWII was re-organized as a unified trade union body covering all ideological and political wings under one umbrella. The two-channel representation by trade unions and works councils was re-established by the Works Constitution Act of 1952, and was subsequently amended in 1972. Under this system, collective bargaining took place at above the enterprise level, usually between industrial unions and employers' associations. The conditions laid down in collective agreements were consensual. Besides, the agreements cover a huge number of enterprises and workers, so they garnered public attention. Such a mode of regulation has given Germany a different path of economic upturn, social coherence and industrial relations.

In fact, Fordism may develop distinct forms in countries with different economic and social conditions. Only several other countries have all basic characteristics of Fordism as in the U.S. Indeed, the American version is just one variety of Fordism. The forms of which Fordism takes depend on the development path of the specific country (e.g. the extent to which new norms of production, consumption and management of wages relations were invented or adopted). As some scholars categorized, Britain was a so-called hindered form of Fordism and Canada exemplified a permeable Fordism (Jenson 1990), dependent on the U.S. both in natural resources and commercial relations.

After the 1970s, the real divergence between the U.S., Germany, and many others occurred. The U.S., Britain, and France, where the market dominated and workers' distrust on employers overflew, chose a defensive way of flexibilization. On the contrary, Germany, Japan and Scandinavia countries, based on the trust and cooperative relations between labor and capital, were able to use intellectual capacity of direct labor in carrying out production processes. This is one example that the trust-based negotiated involvement outclasses the "flexibility" strategy at least in the following two decades, as a superior organizational principle and a more environmental friendly option. [16] In particular, the Japanese rationalization and "just-in-time" methods of managing the production cycle became widespread in the manufacturing world. The "responsible autonomy" (Lipietz 1997: 4), which means trade unions promised the choice of a solution based on negotiated involvement or commitment of workers, works especially well when putting new technologies into operation. This was called Toyotism at the time and labeled as "Lean Production" only in the 1990.

The concept of Post-Fordism or Neo-Fordism (Jessop and Sum 2006: 82,153) has become widely known since the late 1970s. New models of production focus on either the particular production models, such as Toyotism and Sonyism, or the international division of labor between industrialized and newly industrializing countries, such as "Periphery Fordism" or "Imposed Fordism" in Latin America, and Exportism in East Asia (Jessop and Sum 2006: 153). Those models were in contrast with the original models of Fordism in the sense that they had been not developed in the core of the industrialized world but imposed by external force, or highly "export-oriented" rather than focusing on domestic consumption. At the time, a number of major industrial economies started to suffer from declining profitability and subsequently the new wave of globalization took off. With different significance in different nations, the crisis

16 In terms of the greenhouse effect, capital-labor relations has clear implications. The hierarchy of environment-friendly countries is as followed: Scandinavia (the Alpine arc), Japan, other European countries, NICs, least developed countries, with the striking exception of U.S. as both rich and "dirty". See: Lipetz 1987: 34-35

of Fordism was caused by several major factors (Nielsen 1991: 24), including declining productivity gains as a result of the social and technical limits of Fordism. Workers protested against existing work organizations, thus challenging the ability to balance ever longer and more rigid production lines. A growing social expenditure also led to inflationary pressures and distributional conflicts. Moreover, the consumption pattern gradually changed towards a greater variety of use values and could not easily be satisfied through mass production methods. Last but not least, the expansion of mass production led to increasing globalization of economic flows, which made national economic management increasingly difficult.

In this context, Japanese capitalism invented "Toyotism" that proclaimed to be able to translate the skill of its producers, both manual and intellectual, into productivity (Lipietz 1987: 136-137). By far, it is regarded as one widespread, if not the most important, type of Post-Fordism after the 1970s. Toyotism stands for flexible manufacturing technologies with technologies that aimed at stripping all non-value-added activities from the production process. To match lower-volume production, Japanese added more flexibility to production by lowering minimum efficient scales of operation in each phase of the manufacturing process, replacing large machines with several small ones, attaching special jigs and fixtures to general-purpose equipment, perfecting quick die changes and machine set-ups, and assembling several different models on the same line. Similarly, to reduce the capital costs of rapid expansion, they cut down inventory and work-in-progress as far as possible. The Japanese assemblers deliberately stimulated the creation of networks of specialist suppliers networks clustered around the main factory, which frequently spun off to form their own organization (Sachse 1988). In this way, the dense cooperation in engineering and quality control could also be facilitated. Not surprisingly, this profitable "best practice" rapidly prevailed among most large-sized enterprises worldwide.

Nevertheless, some key elements of the Japanese model have been widely neglected by western or other imitators. In particular, the employment security that Toyota provided for core workforce, though a rather small percentage of its total workforce, is an exchange for workers' loyalty to the goals of extreme flexibility and efficiency in production. Besides, another key element - team work - is absent in the real sense. Some doubt that labor control occurs through a set of far more subtle and carefully contrived strategies than in Fordist factories, or it is no more than a means of exploiting workers both physically and intellectually (Lichtenstein 1995: 443).

Fundamentally, if looked at closely, many practices of "lean production" are only the modification or improvement to the Fordist models of production

(Wood 1991; Moody 1997: 86). Basically, most of the techniques, notably the labor-intensive assembly line along with the "scientific management" design of jobs through time-and-motion measurement, are associated with "Fordism". By further reducing non-value-added jobs and the rest time of workers, lean production is featured by an even higher degree of standardization and intensification of work. According to the 1991 Ernst & Young survey, 60% of firms questioned in the US use cycle-time analysis and 47% process simplification, while in Germany, where lean production had barely a foothold in 1991, the comparable figures were 47% and 34%. Apparently, Taylorist methods actually increased with lean production. Further, the production chain is decentralized and archaic forms of work organizations, such as contracting-out, casualization, old-fashioned speed-up, and the lengthening of working time, are frequently deployed. Lean production is later referred as "management-by-stress". The propagandized "autonomy" is not real. Conformity, rather than creativity, of workers is the goal of standardization of work and management control of the labor process. Thus, as Moody (1997) commented a decade ago, from being a "new way of working" that promised a more humane workplace, lean production has been revealed as a system of brutal work intensification and a means of by-passing or undermining unionism.

So far, although many doubt the existence of a single representative regime and regulation mode in Post-Fordist era that could be generally recognized as comparable to Fordism in its own time, a new order has emerged since the mid-1970s. In this new order, new methods of production are based on microelectronics, flexible labor practices, a much reduced role for trade unions, a new and sharper division between core and peripheral workers, a reduction of state intervention, a greater degree of individualism and social diversity, and a new relation between production and consumption (Bonefeld and Holloway 1991: 1). As the "first-wave" Newly Industrializing Countries (NICs) such as Brazil and South Korea were becoming less competitive as wages began to rise, a second stage of relocation has been directed towards what the OECD observer (1982) called "the new wave of industrial exporters": Malaysia, the Philippines, and China.

1.3.3 Previous applications on Asia and China

The majority of previous research focused on the varieties of accumulation regimes as well as regulation modes in early industrialized countries, and, in the NICs. This could be interpreted by the development of the Regulation approach in the West, which originated in France, and whose fundamental purpose was to explain the systems of Capitalism. Asia, with the exception of Japan, had been left out of the scope of capitalism for very long time. Nevertheless, the rising of early NICs in the late 1970s, later on of other Southeast Asian countries, and today particularly of China attracted increasing attention.

Asia has no formal blocs, thereby contrasting to the conditions in Europe or America, where European Union or North American Free Trade Agreement respectively exist. In particular, Asia lacks regulation over general consumers' demand. Each country maintains its right to apply external adjustments, protectionism or parity adjustment. Besides, political tensions always exist, for instance, between China and Japan/ North Korea (Lipietz 1987: 33). Moreover, throughout Asia, there has been heterogeneity of technological paradigms, which may restrict the industrial development of countries at the bottom. In the late 1970s, Japan, as the first developed country in the whole region, led the way of developing Toyotism. In the next place, Hong Kong, Singapore, Taiwan and South Korea became the second-tier of implementing this industrialization process. Then Malaysia, Thailand and Philippines followed suit.

It is noticeable that in South Korea wages were still very low before the 1980s, although big corporations boomed, the economy grew rapidly, and both assembly lines and integrated corporations emerged. These conditions contradict the popular belief that Fordism is supposed to involve both mechanization and a combination of intensive accumulation and a growing market for consumer durables (Lipietz 1987: 79). The lack of "institutions of wage negotiation" in South Korea was the general explanation for low wage standards. However, the establishment of such institutions firstly requires internal class struggles. This is proved by the fact that the lack of wage negotiation in South Korea changed only after students and workers went to the streets, thereby promoting the radicalization of the labor movement there.

A few research has also tried to apply the Regulation Approach to China. Lipietz (1997: 8) categorized former socialist countries, particularly former Soviet states, and China, in their Socialist time as "unsuccessful Taylorism" in light of their technological levels, import-substitution strategy and the corporatist way of organization. According to Lipietz, during that period, the tenure system in the Soviet Union and industrial sector in China contained more rigidity than in Fordism. When such rigidity led to a crisis in the late 1970s and encountered fierce blame, those countries thus became in favor of flexibility and "rationalization", to different degrees. Moreover, right after the economic reform in 1978, China, similar as India, was followed a classic form of "primitive Taylorism" (Lipietz 1997: 9), particularly in some labor-intensive sectors, such as electronics and textiles. The generally oppressed wage levels and cruel working conditions, especially collectively-owned enterprises, at the time may confirm such an argument.

Nevertheless, there have been large varieties and diversification of enterprise ownership, local labor policies, and industries in China as the reform has deepened. For instance, Chinese SOEs have very different labor regimes from those in small and medium private firms. In a recent research (Lüthje, Luo, and Zhang 2013), the concepts of regimes of production have been further broadened and applied to major manufacturing enterprises in five key industries in China. On the basis of extensive field study, five generic types of production regimes have been identified: State bureaucratic, Corporate bureaucratic, Corporate high performance, Flexible mass production, and Low wage classic.[17] This typology has illustrated the various forms of production and work organization, personnel management and labor relations at the factory level in China today, thus the concepts of production regimes are employed in this study.

Generally speaking, the applications of the Regulation approach on China before the early stage of the reform were rather over-simplified and, as stated above, have become largely out of date. Especially in the last two decades, the dramatic changes have led to the fact that China has gone beyond, or at least is moving beyond, the old concepts such as the NIDL.[18] The current development in certain industries in China may appear as a new form of Fordism under the circumstances of a developing country, in which the institutions of wage negotiation have not generally taken effect. In spite of a growing aggregate purchasing power and expansion of the domestic market, the average social wages remain very low, and income inequality is remarkable. A vast market and a labor force freed from its old peasant loyalties are not in themselves enough. If there is no significant expansion of worker and peasant purchasing-power, markets will remain restricted to the ruling and middle classes created by the export economy, which was in any case limited, also sociologically stratified and resistant to the consumption of standardized articles. In this sense, the short-

17 For more details on the typology of this study, please see the appendix.

18 It is noticeable that the idea of New International Division of Labor (NIDL), which was influential in the late 1970s and 1980s, has been proved remarkably wrong. It was the fact in the last several decades, industrialized economies relocated low-end and low-skilled work to periphery regions, which were labeled as "peripheral Fordism" in the 1970s. Nevertheless, this approach believed that those periphery regions would end up with a "bloody Taylorism" or other failed forms of Fordism (e.g. Lipietz 1987: 61), due to the impossibility of transferring technology and lack of market. An obvious case against this idea is South Korea. "Exportism" is proved to be a successful accumulation model. Until now, the national economy of South Korea and its multinational corporations are developing the same as those in the early industrialized economies.

comings of wage regulation, apparently failed to match the expansion of production, may lead to a crisis of overproduction as the one in the 1930s. Apart from this, labor conflicts and social tension have increased. Thus, it is important that a latecomer country does not just attempt to industrialize by using Fordist technologies, but also learn from its mass consumption norms and social labor processes. It is the right time to ask whether the current accumulation and production regime in China resembles that of Fordism; are there some elements of Fordist wage regulation, particularly strong collective bargaining, in certain industries or regions; if not, what conditions are missing and how similar regulation could successfully form in the future.

These questions would be investigated through the Regulation approach. This study focuses on the wage relations particularly through collective bargaining. As the Regulation Approach shows in detail the development of capitalism cannot be separated from the employment systems and socioeconomic regulation in a given period of time. The regime of accumulation is signified by the employment systems including production and work organization, personnel management, and labor relations at the factory levels. At the same time, wage regulation involves the de facto wage determination process, wage-related labor law and industrial policies, and to a lesser degree, the industrial, managerial and political trends at global level that impact on the decision-making power of major actors in industrial relations. As the general principle, the latter - wage regulation - should normalize capital relation and guide the conflictual course of accumulation.

Collective bargaining is regarded as one ideal type of wage regulation for adjusting industrial relations. In this sense, its formation and development is determined and restrained by the current regimes of accumulation, but may also be precipitated by the tension or short-comings of such regimes. Moreover, an investigation into the existing wage determination process and wage policies can reveal how much collective bargaining operates in practice. Most importantly, the institution[19]-building processes of collective bargaining ultimately result from the interactions among workers, trade unions, capital and state officials through everyday factory work-life and through social and political discussions. Accordingly, this study examines factors at three levels: production regimes in factories, existing policies and policy-making at industrial and national levels, and the general influence from the global economy and politics. Together, those

19 The term 'Institutions' should stand for 'all the patterns of behaviour into which individuals must fit under penalty of encountering organized resistance' - including not only legal institutions such as property rights or contract regulations and the agencies engaged in their generation or enforcement, but also informal norms, conventions and customary types of behaviour. See: Schumpeter, 1950/ 1991: 438.

factors decide whether the institutionalization of collective bargaining would be possible in China.

In the following chapter, the historical experiences of the U.S. and Germany with regard to the formation and function of collective bargaining would be explored first. Both countries had developed Fordism, albeit in different forms, with the core Fordist wage regulation - collective bargaining. In history, different economies have developed a variety of Fordism that originated from specific social and political conditions, thereby forming specific class alliance based on different socio-economic factors. Through a review on the U.S. and Germany, this study attempts to sort out common features at all three levels that have helped shape collective bargaining. Such features would be compared to those of today China, in order to find out the fundamental causes for existing problems as well prospects for collective bargaining in China.

Collective bargaining in the U.S. and Germany: The rise and fall of Fordist wage regulation

This chapter places China within the broader historical development of accumulation regimes and regulation modes that set the stage for world capitalism. Before delving into the problem of China, two distinctive cases - the United States and Germany - are analyzed to show common factors that have led to the formation of collective bargaining and also impacted its social impacts.

This study examines the history of industrial development in the U.S. and Germany, with a particular focus on the period between the two World Wars. It was not only this time when post-war Fordism had taken form, including the institutionalization of collective bargaining, but this period also marked a profound impact on the different structures and functions of the systems of industrial relations up to the present day. Thus, the country cases starts from comparing their distinctive institutions and functions of collective bargaining. Moreover, the original causes of such two distinctive models - the similarities and differences of industrial, social and political conditions in the process of institution-building - are carefully analyzed. In the two historical cases, the inter-linkage between the mode of regulation and the regime of accumulation at historical certain stages is further clarified. Lessons are drawn from the advantages and disadvantages of the two collective bargaining and industrial relation systems, which is in large part mainly determined by whether they facilitate or block the development of intensive accumulation regimes, typically machine-based mass production at the time.

2.1 Two systems of industrial relations

Throughout the golden age of Fordism, high wages and industrial peace, achieved through collective bargaining, have largely led to the prosperity in the U.S. and later in Germany. Nevertheless, industrial relations systems in the U.S. and Germany differed from one another. Whereas the U.S. is well known for its market-oriented business unionism or no union at all, Germany has been praised for the cooperative labor-capital relationship - "social partnership". Business unionism is exclusively centered on the economic interests of the limited group of trade union members. In contrast, the social partnership in Germany is a comprehensive system that the majority of employers and workers decide together a large range of labor-relevant issues, including wages and other labor standards, and social matters, at both industrial and enterprise levels. A detailed comparison of the two systems will follow.

It should be noted that industrial relations are anything but static systems. The US indeed had a glorious labor history back in the early of the twentieth century, featured by strong industrial trade unionism. As for Germany, the social partnership has also continuously evolved. The tradition of industrial unionism and strong contractual labor-capital relationship, and the German "high-road" model, unfortunately, have been coming close to the end since the 1990s, as a result of both industrial restructuring and the decline of workers' mobilization at workplaces. In particular, the hypermobility of capital and highly-segmented workforces in the globalized production networks have presented common challenges to labor movements in both Germany and the U.S., as in elsewhere of the world.

In this chapter, I compare the differences of collective bargaining in the two industrial relations systems. This analysis illustrates what factors are necessary for effective and functioning collective bargaining. At the same time, this study records dramatical changes of production processes, work organizations, management methods in factories, and economic and political circumstances at national and global levels since the Fordist era, especially after the 1990s. It is also worth to looking into the question of how those tendencies are challenging collective bargaining and jeopardizing labor movement in different nation.

2.1.1 Collective bargaining in comparison

Collective bargaining has become institutionalized as the major mechanism of determining wages and other working conditions in both the U.S. and Germany in the post-war period. Nevertheless, in the distinctive contexts of production regimes and industrial traditions, the developmental paths of collective bargaining in the U.S. and Germany have largely diverged. The typical market-oriented individualized wage-setting mechanism in US and a classic German mode of industry-wide wage negotiation have not only differed in the methods of determining labor standards but the two models also featured opposing principles of industrial relations.

In the U.S., the Fordist wage regulation had come into being since the 1940s, and in Germany mainly it developed since the 1960s. Collective bargaining, central to Fordist regulations, has involved different levels of centralization in the two countries, particularly the major actors involved, the modes of governance, the scopes of content, and coverage, etcetera. Due to those differences, collective bargaining has accommodated economic changes and upheld social cohesion in the post-war Germany. However, this is not the case in the U.S.

The experience in the U.S. featured wages and benefits that were negotiated at the national level between industrial unions and large companies. For example, in the automobile industry, bargaining would typically start from the big three, GM, Ford and Chrysler, thereby setting a precedent for collective bargaining in other enterprises in the same industry. Thus precedent would then be imposed by trade unions on others actors in the industry, through strikes if necessary, or through multi-employer master agreements (Moody 2010: 7-9). Standards established through precedent often spilled over to related sectors, and thus benefited other groups of workers. In this way, the wages of mass workers may increase, and the mass products coming out of the Fordist factories could be consumed. Therefore, a virtuous cycle of production and consumption was able to be sustained.

However, this model of collective bargaining has never been applied to the majority of workers in all industries. The individual company-based bargaining as well as the internal competition and segmentation among trade unions has limited the influence of collective bargaining. In consequence, it has failed to achieve a major goal of collective bargaining - setting up a non-wage competition for employees and employers at large. Instead, Ford's principle of corporate welfarism, which is based on paternalism as a replacement of industrial relations, in the example of the automobile industry, has become dominant. Strong employment opposition to trade unionism has been well known in the U.S. and in the 1970s and 1980s it has finally helped destroy the "social contract" of Fordism that the labor movement had striven to achieve after the wars. Since the 1980s, lean production, such as the flexible manufacturing system of GM, rapidly spread throughout American industries.

At the same time, American managers emphasized hierarchy, obedience, and strict division of labor in their respective workplaces. They drew a hard line between the prerogatives of management and responsibilities of labor, between the authority of the foremen and the rights of their subordinates (Lichtenstein 1995: 443). Their highly-propagandized Human Resource Management (HRM) is in practice a unilateral managerial device based on individuals and cooperation. It was designed to justify new production methods like lean production by taking over the traditional fields of industrial relations, such as working time, pay and dismissals. In the concept of HRM, employees have no control, and their trust solely rests on experiences with managerial decisions. The fast-evolving HRM methods, such as job evaluation, performance-based bonus, created increasing competition among workers. In addition, "employee relations", which emphasize the human-based management and employees' loyalty while ignoring the conflicted interests between labor and capital, are propagandized with great efforts as a substitute to industrial relations. For instance, GM made a sharp distinction between industrial relations, in which it bargained with the UAW, and "employee relations", as specified by a separate department that competed with the unions for the loyalty of those same employees. This is often true in American subsidiaries set up in other countries as well.

In the U.S. model of collective bargaining, the ultimate problems have been the lack of industry-wide coordination and of a universal social security scheme. In the early of the twentieth century, a remarkable absence of a socialized wage relationship based on universal social security by the state was present in the U.S. challenging any strong advocacy among workers, except among academic and professional circles. In practice, without employers' associations as the counterpart to industrial unions in collective bargaining, wages were negotiated only through individual companies. Given the large union-free and unregulated labor market, working conditions like work time are for the most part acquired informally through individual negotiations with supervisors (Berg 2008). At the workplace level, stronger rank-and-file and local unions have shown to be militant, able to grasp certain aspects of managerial control. However, in places with weak representation or no union at all, workers simply have no voice in determining their labor conditions. In a sense, the fact that multiple topics regarding nearly every aspect of work are all regulated in union contracts leads to a great likelihood of conflicts at shop-floor level. For example, local unions often had to choose between higher wages and a better health care program. At the same time, a comprehensive social security program, particularly a public healthcare system, had never become a reality at above the company level.

Comparatively speaking, the German model of collective bargaining is much more centralized and comprehensive. It has a model of centrally coordinated multi-employer bargaining at the regional and sectoral levels. Wages are negotiated for one sector within a single or a conglomerate of federal states (*Bundesland*). For example, the sector with the strongest interests in world market competitiveness, such as the metal industry, sets the tone for pay rounds in Baden-Württemberg, between *IG Metall* (Industrial union of metalworkers) and *Gesamtmetall* (Employers' Associations for the Metal and Electrical Industry). On the *IG Metall* side, the negotiations are conducted by bargaining commissions, whose members are elected at the local level. They represent the most important companies comprising of the largest member of members. This "pilot" agreement has a role of setting the precedent for further bargaining rounds in other federal states and other industries (e.g. Kenworthy 2000: 42; Koch 2006: 45). Apart from this, single-employer bargaining have been conducted by smaller firms, with notable exceptions such as Volkswagen (VW)[20] and Lufthansa. Nevertheless, single-employer contracts have a limited coverage, e.g. only 8% of West German employees in 1998 (IAB, 1998), and the agreements often modeled on standards in industrial agreements. Industrial agreements could be extended to all enterprises of the same industry[21], although there has never been a statutory income policy. On the whole, differences among regions are small, due to close coordination by trade unions and employers associations. Differentiation among industries might vary according to the economic performance of the very sectors. Furthermore, trade unions should not strike when the industrial agreements are still valid. Bargaining rounds are often accompanied by warning strikes or short-term strikes, which demonstrate the trade unions' ability to mobilize workers as a functional prerequisite of the industrial bargaining system (Müller-Jentsch and Weitbrecht, 2003:19).

Moreover, the content of German collective bargaining is highly focused, typically concentrating on wages, and more recently on working hours. In the cases of the automobile and electronics industries, *IG Metall* distinguishes four main categories of collective agreements: agreements on wages, salaries and trainee pay, non-wage agreements, agreements on wage and salary systems, and collective agreements on special problems.[22] In practice, the levels of collectively bargained wages are set by skill levels, which is based on workers' formal qualification. The classifications of workers usually serve as one key issue of debate, but vocational training and skill level continue to be the major

20 Volks Wagen has never been one part of the industry-wide metalworking agreements, however, VW agreements follow the general outlines of the metalworking agreements.

21 The Tarifvertragsgesetz (collective bargaining law) can authorize the Labor Ministry to declare collective agreements as generally binding. In this way, the power of trade unions is less strongly linked to the sheer size of their membership, thus they are less forced to attract members by following a confrontational course towards employers. Also, there is less adversarial capital-labor relations, which is critical for a skill- and trust- intensive production model. These are in contrast to the American model.

22 Agreements on wages, salaries and trainee pay determine the pay increases according to the rising cost of living and ensure that workers receive their share of productivity gains. Non-wage agreements concern such issues as weekly work hours, length of holiday, termination of employment, extra pay for overtime, etc.. Agreements on wage and salary systems determine how blue- and white-collared workers are classified on wage and salary scale, the principles of remuneration such as piecework, etc. Agreements on special problems include the payment of Christmas bonuses and early retirement, the conciliation procedures, etc.. Wage increases are generally agreed for 12 months, and the rest are valid for several years. Source: IG Metall website, der Branchen Metall-Elektro, Textil-Bekleidung, Holz-Kunststoff und der Informations- und Kommunikationstechnologiebranche.

criteria of worker classification.[23] The wages for each category of employees are clearly written in the agreements, as minimum standards. In practice, large corporations may pay 20-25% higher than those standards. In recent years, working time has become the second major issue in bargaining, including agreements on daily, weekly and annual time schedules, holidays, time corridors etc. In addition, the last part of collective contracts contains miscellaneous questions, such as arbitration procedures, pension funds, and vocational and further training (Müller-Jentsch and Weitbrecht, 2003: 31-35).

Through collective bargaining, the German trade union has won a number of other victories besides wage, salary and trainee pay increases. These victories include a reduction in working time from 48 weekly hours in the early 1950s to 35 hours from 1995; an annual holiday of 30 working days; holiday pay and Christmas bonuses; continued payment of wages to workers on sick leave; guaranteed earnings and protection against dismissal for elderly employees; and collective agreements on early retirement and employment guarantee.

The most important result of collective bargaining is that wages are effectively taken out of competition, since a huge number of enterprises and workers in Germany are covered in the same agreements. In 1999, collective bargaining covered nearly 90 percent of all West German employees (WSI 1999). In this way, companies are forced to compete on a high skills/high productivity/high value added basis. Additionally, this model avoids internal competition among workers, while simplifying the management of workers to a certain extent.

To sum up, in contrast to the uncoordinated bargaining and company-based agreements in the U.S., the "one general contract" bargaining in Germany seems to be a better model, especially in maintaining social and economic coherence. It has a medium level of centralization, wide coverage, and indeed allows for a certain amount of variation in wage increases across the economy. In contrast to "neoliberal" assumption that decentralized and deregulated labor markets are most adaptable and responsive to external shocks, certain modes of coordination proved to be superior in this regard. From 1971 to 1996, because of the highly-coordinated bargaining model, the growth of labor costs in Germany not only adapted most quickly to external shocks, but also showed the highest responsiveness to unemployment, inflation, and productivity growth. At the macroeconomic level, wage coordination may improve the ability of countries to adapt rather quickly and smoothly to changing economic conditions.

---

23 In the past, the classifications of blue-collar, white-collar, technicians and foremen were all different, but now there are unitary schemes.

2.1.2 Major differences of industrial relations

To an important extent such contrasting models of collective bargaining reflects the differences between two industrial relations systems in the U.S. and Germany, which are marked by a strong individual orientation on the one hand and a coordinated labor-capital relationship on the other. Without considering the broad industrial systems of industrial relations as well as the continuous evolution of the bargaining models, one is very likely to over-emphasize the advantages of the German model. In fact, both systems have developed distinctive features that contain their respective advantages and flaws. Trade unions, employers and state actors in each system have just followed specific strategies, which result in divergent labor practices.

When the U.S. model of collective bargaining first developed, it was at the peak of the labor movement during the 1930s and 1940s. Industrial unions, with representatives of United Auto Workers' Union (UAW) in the automobile industry, became the drive for Fordist wage relations. UAW signed the first collective contract with GM in 1948. In the mid-1940s, the trade unions reached a peak when more than 40% of the labor force became union members. At this time, relatively extensive solidarity was realized for the first time in nearly two centuries.[24] Nevertheless, the U.S. system of industrial relations had been marked with internal conflicts and defects of the labor movements (e.g. between industrial and general unions) at the first place.

After WWII, industrial relations were featured by a union system in which skill-based craft unions survived and industrial unions were rivaled by general unions. A pluralist principle dominated, which allowed the co-existence of different types of trade unions. It is said the so-called "decline of the U.S. labor movement... happened at its best time" (Davis 1986). Since the mid-1950s, union density declined dramatically, roughly 40% to 1980, and the decline has continued up to the present. An important reason was that the labor movements of the 1930s and 1940s failed to unify the American working class on either the economic or the political planes. It rapidly shifted from mass mobilization toward a decentralized business unionism. Indeed, the contests among trade unions have been ongoing since then. The watershed was in 1935 when the craft-based American Federation of Labor (AFL) expelled six unions that helped form a more radical union - the Congress of Industrial Organizations (CIO)

24 For instance, the Workingman's Movement of the 1830s had never developed more than preliminary level of political self-consciousness (Hugins 1960). Even later in the nineties, the trade unionism was reminiscent of the 1850s that the working-class dissension and fragmentation remained intense as Protestant was again mobilized against Catholic, white against black, and native against immigrant.

(Abel 1976). In the first half of the twentieth century "exclusive jurisdiction" was granted a bargaining monopoly to the AFL, which awards one of its affiliates an exclusive franchise to organize a certain occupational or industrial territory, free of competition from other unions.

Since then, the labor movement had put direct economic interests as its top priority. Trade unions became top-down 'business' or 'service' unions, resembling little of the fighting spirit it demonstrated during previous decades. Business unionism, rather than organizing and mobilizing the majority of the working class, divided the working class at large and led to the de-mobilization of American trade unions (Davis 1986). The U.S. working class is often said to be 'disorganized', as the majority of workers do not belong to any trade union, and increasingly 'depoliticized'. Mass workers became indifference to politics, and the idea of an American "end of ideology" in the 1950s became a consensus between labor and capital.

The targets of business trade unions became narrow and exclusive, with a focus on the interests of its white, male members in the industrial sector, while neglecting the development of a more inclusive welfare state. On one side, even in the same unions, workers increasingly were divided along skills and races. In the case of UAW, the skilled workers were increasingly disenfranchised by industrial unionism after 1960s, as the pride and social consciousness that had once made them as union pioneers gradually brew resentments (Lichtenstein 1995: 414-5). On the other, the deep racial antagonisms divided the working population, and progressive America failed to find a way to bridge the gap between the divided white and black populations. Along with the changing employment structure in the late 1960s, which includes increasing unemployment and part-time or season workers, the privileging of while male workers not just severely weakened the bargaining power of trade unions, but also isolated labor union activities from the flourishing anti-racialism and gender movements in the 1960s. The leaders of UAW, not to mention other trade unions, were slow to understand the importance of a radical shift in race relations that were transforming society at that time. Without organizing the majority of workers, including most activist elements of the black community, trade unions had no choice but to increasingly accept concessionary bargaining in the 1980s, which by nature created even more segmentation among workers. For instance, trade unions, in the fateful auto settlement of 1984, abandoned the unemployed within the inner cities in exchange for temporary security for senior/white workers. Unfortunately, as unionized labor has become an privileged group among the majority of resentful, low-wage workers, income inequality within the working class has reached levels unseen for more than two generations. For instance, when the tractor company Caterpillar took on the

UAW in the early 1990s, managers found that years of deindustrialization and wage stagnation had generated a huge reservoir of eager "replacement workers" whose residual commitment to their working-class neighbors had long since been extinguished in their desperate scramble to hold on to their houses, cars, and dignity (Lichtenstein 1995: 441).

In addition to individual workers, different trade unions competed with each other, as demonstrated in the early split between AFL and the CIO. The UAW and the craft unions split also has never really ended (Sachse 1988). The rivalry continued since the establishment of the CIO in the 1930s. Nevertheless, the differences among trade unions have become fewer. For instance, the 2005 split in the AFL-CIO involved a disagreement about which leadership model to choose, either the old-style business unionism practiced by many AFL-CIO leaders or the new 'corporate' unionism practiced by some of the Change to Win federation's outspoken founders. The latter, indeed, relies more on partnerships among corporations and offers workers weak organizational and "shallow power" (Moody 2007). Even effective joint shop stewards committees were often unable to overcome inter-union rivalries within multi-union companies and failed to develop coherent policies due to the lack of unity among trade unions (Tolliday and Zeitlin 1986: 99).

Moreover, U.S. employers are traditionally hostile to collective labor. Anti-union strategy of employers is "deeply ingrained in American ideology" (e.g. Locke et al. 1995). Therefore, industrial relations have been directed towards deregulation and individualism, rather than worker collectivity. For instance, the domination of company unionism features no legal protection against the replacement of strikers, thereby enabling anti-union strategies. Employment at-will is the major feature of the US labor market, and the mainstream often reviews employment relations primarily as an economic transaction between relatively equal parties, reflecting the country's liberal market economy.

Throughout the twentieth century, capitalists had invented a variety of management methods to replace industrial relations. American employers have attempted to establish workplace cooperation without unions, often accompanied by a conspicuous shift of responsibility for labor relations from the traditional industrial relations staff to a newly created and rapidly growing HRM function (Strauss 1984). In particular, job evaluation, since the 1920s[25], has been one way for employers to keep wages low and to keep the weaknesses of the union under the Fordist social contract most visible. Although HRM was sold as 'science' in order to gain legitimacy, it is a tool used by management to control

25 Four major job evaluation methods were in existence by the end of 1926: ranking; grade description; factor comparison; and point factor.

wage-setting practices and to restrain wage increases, instead of collective bargaining. HRM sets wage rates 'for the job' on the basis of internal hierarchies and external market wage surveys. Many employees challenged claims of the objectivity of job evaluations. For example, in an early labor economics textbook originally published in 1951, Lloyd Reynolds (1971: 263) argued that "it is not possible to 'measure' the relative worth of different jobs with the precision and impersonality of a thermometer". In their manual, What's Wrong with Job Evaluation, the International Association of Machinists believes job evaluation pitted workers against one another, jockeying for better ratings within the system. In this way, organized labor's unified voice in opposition to management is undermined. As mass production replaced craft production, employers sought to pay their workers on the basis of deskilled job content. In spite of some early resistances job evaluation became widely accepted in the 1950s, which marked the eventual acquiescence of labor to management as well as the transformation from the peak of militant unionism in the 1930s toward business unionism. It is analogous to the relinquishing of workers' right to bargain over the technical relations of production, as codified in the proliferation of 'management rights' clauses in the US (Gordon et al. 1982). Workers were no longer involved in the design of the production process (Taplin 1995). In return, they received job security and a share of the dividend that resulted from increased productivity. Thus, even though their economic status was improved through an increasing social wage, workers in effect became dis-empowered at the workplace.

Facing offensive employers, those already problematic trade unions chose to retreat instead of fight, so union leaders made concessions and "partnered" with corporations (Moody 2007). Ironically, the response of the AFL-CIO to the marginalization of unions was a growing commitment to the development of a more partnership-oriented attitude toward management and more performance-oriented work organizations (Jensen 2006). Shop-floor militants were able to build limited organizations in face of managerial resistance in the 1940s and 1950s. Nevertheless, because of the New Deal policies like the Wagner Act, they were able to consolidate shop-floor organizations effectively when management refrained from confrontation and favored accommodation in the war period and in the late 1950s. In another word, the temporary truce of offensive employers since the end of the World Wars and shortly after then was the result of pro-labor policies of the government.

Partly, CIO's dependence on support from government agencies was due to the overwhelming power of business opponents. Unfortunately, since a consolidated labor party is largely absent in the U.S., it took too long for trade unionists to find out that the Democrats were the poorly served as the appropriate political party that could speak for labor and the liberals (Lichtenstein 1995: 442). Indeed, after the electoral success of Theodore Roosevelt and his Democratic Party, the expansion of the federal state' s role and enactment of the rights provided to workers have detrimentally affected the labor movement. In particular, whereas the Wagner Act of 1935 empowered workers by giving them the legal right to organize unions, its applications, interpretations, and amendments simultaneously diminished the collective capacities of workers by setting highly-restrictive legal conditions for collective activities. Three years after its passage, the same law assured the employer's right to continue production in spite of a strike. This diminished the effectiveness of the strike, reduced the likelihood of its occurrence, and limited its legitimate forms (McCammon 1990). As Lichtenstein (1995: 442) pointed out, since the inter-war period leading up to the 1960s, the trade unions had missed several important chances for shifting their support on the left side.

Since the 1970s, the government has largely withdrawn from supporting trade unions. A neoliberal succession was reshaping the Democratic Party's power structure, marginalizing labor and minorities. It was clear that 'the people', in the expansive Rooseveltian sense, no longer determined 'what is good for America' (Lichtenstein 1995). The government supported the view that increasing corporate productivity, at the price of downsizing and lower wages, was necessary for nations to compete globally, and became uncommitted even to the defense of the reforms that workers achieved during the post-war period. In particular, the countermeasures of the US during the 1970s crisis, was an opposite case to Germany, which shifted in favor of flexibilization and deregulation. This has not just proved to be a less successful strategy for capitalist development, especially in traditional industries like the automobile industry, but further weakened the union movement.

As a result, the problems of trade unions since the 1980s led to the decline of bargaining power, the collapse of social contract, and the breakdown in social dialogue, as well as ideological attacks on unions from employers and political parties (Kochan 2012). Collective bargaining is an exemplary case of the continual decline of the labor movement. As early as in the 1950s, relocation of industrial production to the South had destroyed collective bargaining, because the South was largely union free. By the 1990s, the crisis of the labor movement had deepened at a global scale. Employers aggressively attacked unions and demanded cuts in wages, benefits, and other labor standards. New strategies were made, particularly a shift toward flexibilization and the expansion of its "bottom line" calculations by searching for low cost sites with least resistance of organized labor. In practice, companies have not only re-designed machinery and production processes, but also taken measures to improve flexible employment, personnel deployment and outsourcing. Moreover, the collapse of Keynesianism in the US has given the way to neoliberalist policies.[26] For example, the firing of 11,000 striking air traffic controllers by Ronald Reagan in 1981 gave strike-breaking an official approval.

Under the pressures of flexibilization at the national level and the "race to the bottom" at the global level, trade unions in the US have initiated an era of concessionary bargaining, beginning with the concessions made by the UAW as part of the 1979/80 Chrysler bailout plan.[27] The concessions came primarily through the heavily unionized industries, the automotive and steel industries. Since the early 1990s, the UAW began to accept the divergence of wage standards between the Big Three, e.g. the 1996 bargaining with GM (Moody 1997:109). Wages in auto part factories were taken out of the collective bargaining sphere by granting GM the right to pay at the local "prevailing wages" to the top one-fifth of UAW members in a given area or of the top one-fifth of companies in that area. This formula breaks the sixty-year-old practice of a single union standard within the Big Three auto companies.

The piecemeal, but rapid, means of going "lean" in industrial production makes resistance and union control over the process more difficult. As relatively well-paid union jobs become threatened, unions often make trade-offs between the security of those jobs and other conditions. For instance, one result was the dismantlement of workplace union rules and restrictive practices, which were achieved through struggles in previous decades. Speed-up and lengthy hours, reduction of the workforce, became prevailing policies of management in American factories. For instance, in the GM Saturn factory, many UAW unionists thought that the model of consensual decision-making process and its associated teams as a "milestone in the advance of the UAW toward industrial democracy" and believed that "the union plays a key role in all aspects of the decision-making process". However, this model was actually based on

26 Neoliberalism is featured by the policy of dismantling much of the national regulation of economic life throughout the capitalist world in favor of market governance, a process referred to as "reform" or "liberalization". See: Moody, 1997: 43

27 When Chrysler almost went bankrupt in 1979, Douglas Fraser, then the UAW president, deployed the rhetoric of Walter Reuther's WWII "equality of sacrifice" campaign to convince skeptical autoworkers that the survival of the company depended on UAW agreement of a new labor contract to cut wages and benefits well below those of its competitors. In return for a loan guarantee, the Carter administration scrutinized every move by Chrysler management, and the company even put the UAW's Fraser on its board of directors. This bargain temporarily breached management's well-guarded "prerogatives", but it also generated a wave of "concession" bargaining, even among profitable companies. See: Lichtenstein, 1995: 440

competition and, along with the eclipse of the union system of shop representation, deprived workers of the ability to resist a subtle form of speedup. Moreover, the social contract collapsed as individual firms abandoned collective bargaining, cost-of-living protection, and employment security. By the 1990s the UAW found that it could not organize the new Japanese and German plants, and halt the de-unionization of almost the entire auto parts sector. Unionism thus became a synonym for wage reductions, plant closures, and lost strikes.

Nevertheless, the "war zone" (Moody 1997), characteristic of Central Illinois, had spread to other parts of America by the mid-1990s, as indicated by strikes and struggles from Staley to the Detroit News Agency and Yale. They also involved contract jobs in Los Angeles' construction sites, building service, and waterfront trucking industries. Some ended with partial victories for workers. After the drastic 1987-96 downsizing in GM, the series of local-level strikes, centered on lean production methods, such as staffing levels, subcontracting, and health and safety, had swept GM from 1994 through 1997. Apparently, it is not that workers no longer needed their representation. Rather, they could not find a reliable channel within which they would collectively negotiate with the prevailing social and political context at that time. Without reinvigoration of the grass-roots collectivities, it is unlikely that trade unions can dramatically reassert their clout within the economic and political system in the U.S.. One vital strategy for American trade unions, suggested by Moody (1999; 2007), is to develop new links and alliances with other civil society movements and political organizations.

To sum up, the labor and trade union movements in the US had their heyday in the 1930s and 1940s, but since then some key features of trade unionism have declined. The largely decentralized system of corporate-based collective bargaining and business unionism, in which trade unions represent narrow and privileged interests have disconnected themselves from racial, gender and other social movements, leading to ineffective business associations and trade unions in carrying out unified agreements. On one hand, the hostility of employers has been traditionally strong and even manifested after 1978. Their invention of anti-union strategies or of substitutions to industrial relations has never ceased. On the other hand, trade unions have developed a focus on narrow economic interests among certain working groups exclusively. This closely relates to the de-politicized trend or "end of ideology" in the 1950s. The isolation of trade unions and union members results from the deep racism and political antagonism in the society, which becomes inseparable from the question of a genuine trade union reform. Accordingly, within the segmented working class, distrust and even resentment towards trade unions and their members prevail, and the top-down business unions are increasingly unable to mobilize the majority of workers. In consequence, trade unions have to accept the hegemony of managerial authority in workplaces and lose job control which had sparked their early organizing drives. In addition, in the absence of a genuine labor party, trade unions have been over-dependent and improperly relying on the Democratic Party for too long. In practice, current social and political trends and established institutions have been largely on the side of employers.

The German system of industrial relations had been highly praised in comparison to the American model. This German model was established in the post-war economic and political restructuring in the 1960s. Further, the settlements of several major strikes in Germany by industrial unions during 1970s and 1980s pushed several innovations to the local model of industrial relations. These improvements include working conditions and work organization - under the rubric of "humanization of work life"[28] - in 1971 and "protection against rationalization" in 1978 (Streeck 1981). Nevertheless, many factors contributed to the long and accelerated path of union decline in the U.S., including changes to certain occupations (e.g. more white-collar workers) and industries (e.g. the emergence of many non-union electronic enterprises) after the 1970s as well as challenges to trade unions to represent those new employees. Such industrial changes have also impacted the German system.

Industrial relations in Germany are fundamentally characterized by a dual system. At the sectoral level, collective bargaining (*Tarifvertragssystem*), centered on wages and duration of collective contract (*Flächentarifverträge*), is conducted between strongly organized employers (in employer associations) and employees (in unions). At shop-floor level, workers have the right to participate in management of the companies they work for, so-called "co-determination" (*Betriebliche Mitbestimmung*[29]). Works council is the organ of operational codetermination. This dual system acknowledges the very existence of

---

28 'Humane design' of work organization primarily means the reduction of division of labor, particularly between planning and execution. Apart from eliminating or reducing stress, work loads, monotonous assembly-line work, and so on, the concrete demands focus on three points: 1. the creation of meaningful and comprehensive work content granting the individual worker a broader scope for taking action and making decisions, and allowing the integration of mental and physical demands made on workers, in other words, diversified jobs; 2. the development of group work, for which numerous individual aspects are defined, such as the number of group members, the wage structure, the exact definition of tasks, etc.; and 3. all aspects of these demands for the design of work forms and work organization include co-designing training for such jobs.

29 The original meaning of "Mitbestimmung" is much broader than co-determination. Nevertheless, the co-determination at shop floor is far more important today. See: Walther Müller-Jentsch, 2003: 39-56

competing social and political interests and requires a balance of power between capital and labor, which was also true in the "neo-corporatism" regime of the 1970s. Furthermore, often referred to as "social partnership" , this centrally coordinated system has a high degree of institutionalization, including vocational training and economic policy discussions at all levels, and jurisdiction (Müller-Jentsch and Weitbrecht 2003:19). Through legislation and collective agreements, regulations and their associated institutions guarantee a complex of legally enshrined employee participation rights (Tüselmann and Heise 2000: 162-175). In this way, " *Tarifautonomie* " (autonomy of bargaining) is up to both sides of industry, namely employers and collective labor, whereas the involvement of the government is limited.

Industrial unionism is the principle of union organizations in Germany. It is encompassing, neither split by political divisions, nor fragmented into general, industrial, and craft unions. Both blue-collared and white-collared workers are organized into one trade union, covering the entire economy including the public sector and civil service. At the enterprise level, "one plant, one union" is applied (Streeck 1984: 9). In order to avoid inter-union competition, only one trade union is allowed to exist in each plant, and all plants in one industry should have the same union in principle.[30] In addition, the labor movement was re-organized as a unified trade union body covering all ideological and political wings under one umbrella, *Deutscher Gewerkschaftsbund* (DGB, the Confederation of German Trade Unions). Such an encompassing structure of unionism in Germany was closely linked to the historical background at the time. After the downfall of the Nazis, the lesson for the labor movement was to overcome the ideological divisions. Accordingly, the German trade unionism abandoned its traditional political divisions and thus formed the joint organization, regardless of workers' political membership. Nevertheless, it is noted that German trade unions at times rigorously excluded Communists and left-wing trade union militants from the office and membership - as in the seminal crackdown on the KPD in the 1950s and the exclusions of leftist opposition groups in the 1970s.

In general, German trade unions have been stable. For the DGB, the only change in 40 years since its establishment in 1949 was to admit a 17th affiliate, the *Gewerkschaft der Polizei* (GdP) in the 1970s. The membership of DGB unions rose from 5.5 million in 1950 to 8 million in 1980s (Müller-Jentsch and Weitbrecht 2003: 21). It had avoided a membership crisis until the early 1990s,

30 This is a general principle, but there are exceptions. Most recently, the Federal labor Court permitted several unions in the same company, which is already the case in some companies, e.g. Lufthansa and the Deutsche Bahn. In addition, for a long period, there has been the DAG for white collar workers.

when the German unification led to financial difficulties among various unions (Streeck and Visser 1998). The wide coverage of sectoral agreements and stable union density (around 40% overall between 1970 and 1990) gave labor organizations substantial influence over working conditions.

Works councils are a German innovation of industrial democracy. They are the "shop-floor" organization representing workers, as the establishment-level complement to sectoral collective bargaining by industrial unions. Similar to industrial unions, works councils are encompassing, representing all employees except executives, and putting forward all kinds of requests. Works councils were firstly legislated in February 1920.[31] According to the Works Constitution Act of 1972, they were legally established by the express wish of the workforce in all firms with at least five employees, and works councils are elected every three years. Necessary expenses for the works council office fall on the employer.

At the enterprise level, works councils have the legal rights to information, consultation and joint decision-making on a wide range of subjects, including negotiating works agreements with employers. In practice, works councils have the most leverage in co-determination on social matters, such as wages, working hours, holidays and monitoring of performance, and to a lesser degree on personnel matters, such as recruiting policy and dismissal, personnel planning, in terms of change of work process, working environment, and financial matters and alternations. According to Koch (2006: 45), works councils in companies with more than 500 employees have functions that are more extensive. Furthermore, in large enterprises, elected workforce and trade unions are represented on the supervisory board to serve as a supplementary mechanism for works councils. An empirical study showed that plant-level co-determination

31 Although works councils later became accepted by all sides of the society later, it is noticeable that the original responses were commonly opposition. On the side of the workers, there has been found “neither desire nor capacity to co-operate with employers; and but little understanding of the requirements of industry”. Also, the Councilors are to a great degree hampered by division of loyalty—on this side to their duty on the Council, on that to the Marxian doctrines concerning class war; they are hampered further by lack of the education, experience and time necessary for acquiring practical knowledge of the organization and problems of modern business; and, being elected year by year by their fellow-workers, find natural difficulty about taking a line of action which would tend to lose their support. On the employers' side the real root of a dislike which seems to be often effectually obstructive is opposition to the Works Council's right to inspection of their financial position. See: Notes And Queries, June 16, 1928, p431-2, The Works Council: a German Experiment in Industrial Democracy. By C. W. Guilleband (Cambridge University Press. 16s. net)

reduced personnel turnover, improved the use of flextime, and brought about higher wages and productivity among workers (Dilger 2003: 127).

In general, German trade unions represent workers at industrial levels, and works councils represent workers mainly in the workplace. Industrial unions are exclusively endowed with the rights to collective bargaining and monopoly over strikes[32], while works councils are in charge of co-determination at firm- and establishment-levels. This structure has essentially limited the power of trade unions to mobilize on workplace issues - a fundamental determinant in social stability, which differ from countries with workplace based collective bargaining like the U.S.. At the same time, works councils and trade unions in Germany are interdependent from each other. To a certain degree, works councils are the workplace organizations of industrial unions. Legally speaking, all workers are entitled to vote and to participate in elections, but in practice 80% of all works councilors are elected from candidates nominated by DGB.

In addition, as distributive bargaining agents, works councils have a limited role in that they only negotiate enhancements to collectively-agreed pay rates and induce employers to pay above those rates. Indeed, such externalization of wage conflict is a major guarantee for works councils to function. In this way, works councils and management can aim at achieving consensus (Müller-Jentsch 2003: 39-56). Over time, they have developed a consensual, high trust/low conflict relationship, characteristic of a micro-corporatist productivity coalition (Windolf 1989). Since works councils have no right to strike but have a "serious commitment to consensus", the procedure of co-determination is closer to problem-solving negotiation than to distributive bargaining.

Employers in Germany have over time accepted the principle of industrial consensus, rather than absolute managerial prerogative. Industrial relations and

---

32 Industrial tribunals take the view that only trade unions may call strike action and that such action may be taken only over the issues involved in the negotiations. The decision to take strike action rests with the Executive Committee. However, it may only take a positive decision if a secret strike ballot has been held in the collective bargaining zone in question and if 75% of IG Metall members have voted in favor of strike action. These provisions ensure that a strike is called only in exceptional situations, and that principle remains valid today.
The trade unions must always be able to calculate the consequences of taking strike action since IG Metall has to fund strike pay for all its members who are called out on strike in a given area or who are locked out by employers. An example is the strike of 1984 in the metal industry of Northern Baden-Württemberg/ Northern Baden and Hessen. In this case, an agreement concerning the reduction in working hours from 40 hours per week to 38.5 hours could be negotiated only after seven weeks of strike. Source: IG Metall website, der Branchen Metall-Elektro, Textil-Bekleidung, Holz-Kunststoff und der Informations- und Kommunikationstechnologiebranche.

HRM, regarded as a most important department for managing industrial relations in the majority of companies, have integrated. This cooperation includes works council's codetermination rights. Rather than a unilateral domination of HRM as in the U.S., the legal mandatory institutions of industrial democracy - works councils - reflect collective voice and resolve conflicts. Additionally, workers have certain control over works councilors via their voting rights and their trust relies on the participation of works councils in managerial decisions.

Moreover, a majority of employers are organized in employers' associations, BDA (*Bundesvereinigung der Deutschen Arbeitgeberverbände).* BDA covers almost all private sector employers, including 75% of eligible firms that represent 80% of all employees in the private sector in early of the twenty-first century (Müller-Jentsch and Weitbrecht 2003: 19). Firms have relied on their associations for a wide range of services. As early as in 1905, employers' association in Germany already had a highly developed and centralized structure. In fact, the original goal of employers' association was not to conclude collective agreements, but rather diminish the socialist unions' influence on the workforce. It took a long time for employers to recognize the socialist unions as legitimate spokesmen for the workforce. In the aftermath of the WWI, employers' associations were assigned the responsibility of representing business in collective bargaining by a union-employer agreement promulgated by the national government (Müller-Jentsch and Weitbrecht 2003: 19). At present, similar to DGB, BDA no longer plays direct role in collective bargaining, but has substantial coordination capacities (Tüselmann and Heise 2000).

Importantly, the German state, which has no strong tradition of industrial policy, clearly shows its unwillingness to directly intervene in industrial relations after the WWII. At the early stage, the governments had been engaged in building the contemporary industrial relations system, including legalization of works councils and policy making in the labor market, which involve labor exchanges, unemployment, social insurance, industrial hygiene, courts trying labor cases, etc. In principle, the Bismarckian social insurance legislation had laid the groundwork for the full-fledged corporatism of Weimar as well as the "social partnership" in West Germany (Steinmetz 1993). Nevertheless, the right to bargaining independent from government influence (*Tarifautonomie*) was established in reaction to the strong involvement of the state in collective bargaining practices during the Great Depression, when government-imposed arbitration and emergency orders became subject to massive working class mobilizations against the state. Consequently, legal intervention was not direct but designed to strengthen the role and the organization of the "social partners" - the trade unions and employers' associations, and allocate responsibility to them for effective self-governance. In the post-war era, the powerful Federal Ministry of Economic Affairs followed a liberal supply side policy with the aim of safeguarding the functioning of the market through free international trade and promotion of domestic competition. Thus, the trade union and the employers' association generally lacked the capacity to lobby for protective-selective intervention. Even when the crisis reached its peak in 1974, the government only prepared a range of regional labor market measures to relieve possible mass unemployment (Streeck 1984). At the same time, as a result of the well-established institutionalization and long-term practices of industrial autonomy for workers and employers from the state, the state' capacity for direct intervention became limited both vertically and horizontally (Streeck 1997).

Moreover, the Federal Labor Court has established a wide range of criteria for associations representing parties in collective agreements.[33] The labor court, usually composed of a professional judge specializing in labor law, one representative of trade union, and one from employers association, has jurisdiction over both “individual labor law” and “collective labor law”. This court sets important precedent for case law. Also, the Federal Constitutional Court plays a dominant role in all areas of collective labor, which shapes the basic structure of collective labor law by verifying decisions of other courts as well as legislative Acts.

The modern system of German labor law had largely developed during the World Wars, when governments steadily interfered in industrial relations. The most important act at the time was the Auxiliary Service Act of 1916, which was also called the Magna Carta of German labor, for it made possible the great development of trade unions from 1916 to 1932. During the Weimar period (1919-1933), the system of collective bargaining was growing rapidly, and the core features of today’s labor law were developed. Most important acts include the Act on Works Councils of 1920, which was sometimes referred to as the archetypical example of a modern corporatist system of labor control, the Hours of Work Act, the creation of a specific system of labor courts in 1926, and the

---

33 There are seven major criteria. 1) the association has to be created for an indefinite time (not ad hoc association); 2) the requirement of a corporate structure (organized in a way which guarantees its continuity even if members leave the association); 3) it is independent from the opposite side (experience from the Weimar period - not ‘yellow unions’; 4) members of the associations may only belong to one side, whether it is the employees' side or employers' side; 5) an employees' association may not be confined to one plant but must exceed this scope (as 3); 6) it must be independent from the state and from political parties; and 7) inner structure of the association, to guarantee that members are able to influence the association’s activities (this is why the requirement of democratic organization was established). See: Weiss 1989: 122-123

Unemployment Insurance Act in 1927 (Chamberlin 1942:19). Nevertheless, there is now no special union act. Major issues of industrial relations, including arbitration procedures, are regulated by collective agreements and court orders. In practice, the freedom of association is the only labor right in the Constitution, which has been fully recognized as the leading principle of collective labor law since 1918 with the only exception of the Nazi period (Weiss 1989:186).

Since the late 1970s, the industrial restructuring and neo-liberal political trends have also impacted on German system of industrial relations. In a sense, the Fordist welfare state has been largely replaced by a post-Fordist, neoliberal workfare state in different forms (Jessop 1994; Lipietz 1994). While the crisis of accumulation hit on Germany in the early 1990s, capitalists began to demand drastic changes in the production regimes. Although internal relocation has never been an option in the automobile and electronics industries until 1990, manufacturers increasingly forced their suppliers and subcontractors to adopt lean methods leading to "reductions in investment, direct labor, floor space and set-up time". Flexibilization, as suggested in new work and management methods like lean production, is required by employers not only on work but also on wages and labor relations. Cost reductions are cited by German managers as the top reason for outsourcing (e.g. Hendrix et al. 2003). Some companies, like T-Mobile and Daimler Chrysler, win concessions in-house by threat of spinning off or outsourcing. As a result, a more stratified labor force has developed, shifting employment from industrial sectors to the service sector and increasing the numbers of white-collared workers and young workers who have no experience of unionization (Jensen 2006). In addition, since the mid-1990s, some of the largest German companies, especially those in internationally competing sectors, have changed from the tradition of "stakeholder economy" towards more Anglo-American style of shareholder orientation, which values economic interest much more than before (e.g. Jürgens/Rupp/Vitols 2000). Although there is no sign that shareholder value companies attempt to put an end to co-determination, it drives works councils towards efficiency orientation and increasing conflicts between industrial unions and works councils at micro levels (Höpner 2001).

Noticeably, those challenges nearly ended the German model, especially after the 1990s. The crisis of Fordism in the 1970s, featured with declining profitability, led to a growing exodus of employers, especially smaller-scaled enterprises, out of employers associations. Organizations and services, such as training providers, also have replaced trade unions. The unification of Eastern and Western Germany directly caused large fluctuation of trade union membership[34], even though the unification itself was successfully peaceful. The first great eastern labor conflict since April 1993, also known as the first major collective bargaining conflict in eastern Germany since the Weimar Republic, became a test of will and staying power among collectized workers (Turner 1998: 9). A growing belief emerged among observers that the socially embedded economic institutions were no longer assets but liabilities for future performance. A less-regulated, Anglo-American version of capitalist economy, which in a short time earlier had appeared hopelessly in decline, grew in popularity. Since the mid-1990s, the German model of industrial relations, which boasted a tradition of coordinated collective bargaining and a remarkably robust trade union movement, had come under unprecedented stress.

This development changed the traditional power balance between capital and labor, as well as between industrial unions and works councils. A direct result was the general decline of the German trade unions in the 1990s, which faced with the impact of German unification, along with deep changes in the economy. This included the decline of manufacturing and the rise of service, the re-organization of large firms, and privatization of industries which undermined the strength of public sector unions. Entire new sectors emerged from technological changes, featuring more precarious employers (Streeck and Visser 1998). Even in the metal industry where trade unions were most powerful, in 2001, 62% of employees in west Germany and 28% in east Germany worked in member companies of the Gesamtmetall, a decline since 1991 from 68% and 54% respectively (Schröder and Wessels 2003: 671). Along with the declining membership and heterogeneity of interests among workers, trade unions have a declining pattern-setting capacity in collective bargaining.

Consequently, toward the end of the 1980s, concessions among trade unions to the demands of management gradually undermined the Fordist wage regime. There was a rollback of in-plant worker participation to their legal minima, even in large firms with strong union presence. There were highly visible defeats in union strongholds, such as the lost metal industry strike in 2003 (Schröder 2002), and concessionary agreements on pay and work time at Daimler Chrysler, Siemens and VW. Moreover, while all the automotive assembly plants and the large leading mega-suppliers were included in the metal industry agreement, their subsidiaries, parts suppliers, service subcontractors and temporary agencies were covered only by a variety of sectoral, firm-level and plant-level agreements. The latter normally contained much worse labor standards than the metal

34 The 8 million of DGB union membership rose to 12 million after unification, then suffered from massive losses, largely due to the dramatic de-industrialization of eastern Germany. See: Müller-Jentsch and Weitbrecht, 2003: 21

industry agreement. According to IG Metall's analysis, every auto maker except for Porsche reduced its per cent of in-house value-added between 1989 and 1998, and the overall figure declined from 41% to 35% (Caprile 2000). In this way, enterprises dodged the general industrial agreements that demanded higher labor standards. As a result, the working class became segmented.

Accordingly, the flexibilization of wage-setting and the decentralization of industry-wide wage bargaining practices became new trends in Germany. Membership among industry-wide agreements shrank as growing numbers of firms, especially smaller ones, began leaving employers' associations. This pattern has increased wage inequalities in industries and opened up a loophole in regulation that previously existed but a much smaller scale. In the meantime, wage bargaining has been increasingly decentralized. There is some degree of decentralization in industry-wide wage agreements, such as "opening clauses"[35] and PECs (Pacts of employment and competitiveness)[36], which allow for phased wage increases in companies facing temporary economic difficulties, in which has affected primarily the automobile, electro-technics and engineering sectors. In addition, collective bargaining in many traditional union strongholds has shifted from sectoral to individual plant level, which usually means less bargaining power for workers. For instance, VW, one of the exceptionally large companies with its own collective agreement, reduced 20% weekly work hours and 10% of annual wages of workers during a crisis in 1994. Later in 2001, it hired 5000 unemployed workers at lower contractual wage rates. Workers also have to guarantee perfect quality in products, which they must compensate through unpaid overtime work in case of production defects (Müller-Jentsch and Weitbrecht 2003). Moreover, details on wages and work hours are more and more regulated through work agreements at plant level between works councils and individual employers. There has been proliferation of so-called variable pay

---

35 Major types of opening clauses include: 1) hardship clauses, e.g. wages are reduced in exchange of job security if enterprises justify economic hardship; 2) location clauses for new investment; 3) entrance pay clauses. The company can pay less if employing young or unemployed workers; 4) option clauses. Enterprises decide to completely/partially carry out collective agreement; 5) corridor clause, mainly on flexible working time; 6) competition clauses. When collective agreements from different industries conflict with each other, social partners at enterprise level have the right to choose lower standards; 7) suspension or postponement clauses; 8) branch clauses. In a large industry with multiple branches, e.g. public service, branch-specific contracts can supplement or substitute collective agreements. See: Müller-Jentsch and Weitbrecht, 2003: 35

36 e.g. the 2004 "Pforzheim Agreement" in metal sectors stipulates that as long as the enterprise increases or stabilizes employment/ rises new investment/ enhances competitiveness, it can deviate from regulations in sectoral agreements. However, trade unions may demand external validation of the situation of the firm. Jürgens et al, 2006

regimes, in which workers are paid individually for their performance rather than on the basis of fixed positions in the division of labor.

In addition, further trade-offs have been made in concession bargaining. Moderate wage increases or wage restraint is often accepted in lieu of employment guarantees or extension of employee participation rights. As a result, real-wage growth in Germany has ceased to follow the productivity increase since 1993. Gross wages in 2009 decreased for the first time after the wars by 0.4%. Moreover, unions have observed segmentation of the working class (e.g. the exclusion of a number of unemployed from rising real wages in the 1990s). In particular, the effects of outsourcing became more disruptive. In many cases, outsourcing served as an alternative to other concessions that would directly affect the pay and working conditions of the core workforce. Early research on the auto industry in the late 1980s and early 1990s found that unions and works councils incorporated major subcontractors into industry agreements (Turner 1991). However, subcontractors, subsidiaries and temporary agencies often have no collective bargaining practices. In a few cases, they are covered by different firm-level and sectoral agreements that lay out lower labor standards. Such practices of avoiding higher labor standards in the general IG Metall contracts was legally difficult for employers before. As increasing numbers of employers have moved jobs to those subcontracting firms, they have introduced new organizational boundaries across the production chain and disrupted traditional bargaining structures. Thus, there is increased variation in wages and working conditions between subsidiaries, suppliers, service providers and agency workers, thereby exerting further demands for concessions (Doellgast and Greer 2007). Also, these developments have challenged worker representatives to coordinate the sector as a whole, yet easing employers' abilities to introduce variation in labor standards for different groups of workers.

Therefore, as diversity in production regimes grows, both the coordinated wage negotiation and workplace-level workers' participation in the German model have eroded. On the side of trade unions, significant trade-offs have been made, including wage moderation and constraint on working time, like the 1984 contract of *IG Metall*.[37] Sadly, those trade-offs have not lead to more jobs. At the same time, organizing efforts in the private and service sectors, particularly

---

37 In 1984, IG Metall launched a national strike over a general reduction in weekly working time to 35 hours with full pay. With partial success that different sectors agreed to between 35 to 37.5 weekly hours, flexible working time was one condition from the employers, including variation in working time in response to product demand and variation across types of workers. Basically, IG Metall abandoned the aim of a general and quick reduction of the weekly working time. It became the opening to shop-floor related flexibility schemes.

groups of engineers and white-collar workers, have only met with limited to marginal success. In particular, white-collar workers have outnumbered blue-collar workers since the mid-1980s, but union membership has not reflected this increase. In 2001, 70% of the unionized workforce still consisted of blue collar workers, who were recruited from traditional industries and from the public sector. At the same time, the influence and power of works councils has increased substantially, as more and more members are delegated from industrial bargaining to work agreements at workplace levels. The decentralization of wages results not only in bargaining costs, but may destroy the harmonious high trust/low conflict relations between management and works councils. Given the intermediary nature of works councils, one direct result of those work agreements is the flexibility and differentiation of labor standards (Koch 2006: 45). In fact, the power imbalance among works councils presents a rather lopsided picture. This pattern applies to large-scale enterprises with strong works councils, but the majority representing economically weak industrial branches or enterprises or small firms, may not succeed in this task even with the help of union counseling, and may do worse without it. Furthermore, the crucial informal solidarity linking industrial unions with works councils has been broken (Herrigel 2008). For instance, during the "hostile takeover" of Krupp by Thyssen in 1997, IG Metall demonstrated against it, but the works councils did not even attend (Höpner 2001).

Employers' associations are losing their traditional strength too. In the past, firms relied on employer associations for a wide range of services. The labor movement used leverage from this bottom-up/top-down coordination to win gains in well-organized industries and regions, such as the automotive plants, which then extend to poorly organized work sites, like electronics plants (Turner 1991). Recently, there has been a growing exodus of employers from employers' associations. Consequently increasing numbers of firms and workers do not directly participate in the construction of industry-wide wage agreements, although they often remain oriented toward such agreements (Artus 2006). Furthermore, as many smaller members leave, local employer associations establish non-union affiliates in hope of retaining members in order to help companies cope with labor law and human resource issues without binding them to a sectoral agreement (Schröder and Silvia 2003). Alternative private service providers began offering works councils training and advisory services, as seen in Rossmann in 2001, often replacing trade unions in this capacity.

Apparently, the German model of industrial relations has come under crisis. Streeck and Thelen (2005:4) define the tendency as " changes within continuity" . Similarly, Müller-Jentsch and Weitbrecht (2003: 37) regarded the new trends in industrial relations as controlled decentralization and regulated flexibilization. At the same time, others (e.g. Vitols 2001) argue for a "hybridization" of the political economy, with an emphasis on exogenous influences combined with path-dependent processes. Most importantly, they all share the idea that the change in Germany is a gradual and path-dependent process.

As a whole, Germany has an comprehensive, legally regulated and centralized industrial relations system. Characterized as a "coordinated" (Hall and Soskice 2001) model, this system has two levels, industry-wide collective bargaining and co-determination at plant levels. Through this system, the age-old goal of "taking wages out of competition" has been achieved. German unions are featured by the absence of religious or political divisions, joint organization of blue- and white-collar workers, and limited inter-union competition.[38] Unions are exclusively entitled with the rights of wage bargaining and strike monopoly. The other actor of collective bargaining - employers' associations - have been well-established. In dealing with labor-capital issues, autonomy in the bargaining process is the major principle, since the state is refrained from intervening in industrial relations. Thus, it is a "neo-corporatist" pattern whereby trade unions and employers' associations assume, in a variety of ways, a quasi-public status under which they exercise delegated regulatory authority with strong legal facilitation (Streeck 1987).

In light of these common challenges since the 1980s, the different systems of collective bargaining, and industrial relations in general, led not only to different levels of sustainability among the systems, but also to distinctive alternative labor strategies. Both models have been greatly impacted by current tends in flexibilization, deregulation and decentralization of industrial processes. Nevertheless, German trade unions remain to be the most important actors in asserting political reforms whereas American unions are in accelerated decline. The turning point of the U.S. trade unions was when they failed to organize the majority of workers at the peak of labor movement in the 1930s and 1940s and further gave up their control over production process. In Germany, no reversal to the former Fordist welfare state seems possible as long as the challenges to collective bargaining continue. However, the collective bargaining model, as one part of the encompassing and relatively centralized industrial relations system continues. Both collective labor and the BDA have been aware of the political risks inherent in an untamed decentralization process, and have

38 Interunion competition existed only for white-collared workers - between the DGB and a breakaway white-collar union, the DAG - and for civil servants, where the DGB competed with the Deutscher Beamtenbund (DBB). Nevertheless, in both cases, DGB has advantages in the numbers of membership. In addition, "one plant, one union" is applied at workplaces in order to avoid multi-unionism.

demonstrated their willingness to adapt, or to revitalize, collective bargaining processes to the new socioeconomic environment.

2.2 The development of collective bargaining

The birth of collective bargaining has historically emerged only through labor struggles within certain production regimes. Since then, the practices have only been gradually accepted and institutionalized by the state and the interests of capital. Despite different systems of industrial relations, both the U.S. and Germany have developed systems of collective bargaining Furthermore, both systems are continuously changing. Industrial development, featured by specific types of work organizations, division of labor, hierarchy of skills, control over work, management styles, etc., often triggers these transformations in industrial relations. It is worthy reviewing the different paths in order to tell their advantages and disadvantages respectively.

Firstly, the production systems in the factories have impacted on labor-capital relations and accordingly the formation of collective bargaining. In the historical epoch of Fordism and its aftermath, industrial relations and collective bargaining in both the U.S. and Germany have evolved closely following the development of two industries - automobile and electronics. Labor movements have always been shaped by the features of industries and the corresponding production regimes.

A key feature of Fordism featured semi-automatic assembly-line mass production within the American automobile industry. Specifically speaking, Frederick Taylor and Henry Ford took the lead in the revolutionary changes that finally made mass production possible. At the turn of the last century, scientific management designed by Taylor outpaced control of the production process by craft workers, through the fragmentation of work into detailed parts and the precise coordination of production scheduling in order to eliminate any superfluous motions and to ensure maximum speed. In this way, the Taylorist division of labor passed the knowledge and skills of craft work into managerial hands, thereby de-skilling workers. In 1913, Ford completed the transfer of control with sophisticated machines. In this way, fragmented work processes could be re-integrated into a totally rationalized mechanical system. In a typical Fordist factory, specialized machines and assembly lines controlled every move of de-skilled workers through the clever machinations of industrial engineers or designers (Gartman 1998). Alfred Sloan from GM enhanced Fordism through innovations in marketing and organization in the 1920s and 1930s (Thompson 1999). Fundamentally, Fordist production was characterized by specialized machines, largely standardized products, a de-skilled workforce, and tight control on work process by management.

Since its early stage, such a production system had provided both demands as well as conditions for collective labor struggles, which eventually led to the development of collective bargaining. Primarily, work organizations in Ford's factories were highly rigid and hierarchical. In the pre-union auto factories, as in other mass-production industries including rubber, steel and electrical goods industries, workers' experience had been pervasively insecure and subject to arbitrary managerial discipline (Tolliday and Zeitlin 1986: 110). The Fordist mass production turned human subjects into abstract, calculable, uniform things, and mere objects in a totally rationalized system controlled by and for others. Workers experienced their work, including the timing and spacing of the production process, as a merely alien whose work discipline was entirely imposed on them from outside (Marx 1887). Unsurprisingly, after the machine-based production was introduced around 1913, Ford encountered a wave of worker resistance in the forms of absenteeism, turnover, and threatened unionization (Gartman 1998).

At the same time, the force of labor had escalated in Ford factories, which provided the fundamental condition for collective labor actions. Two types of workers' bargaining power are identified by Wright (2000), which are structural power and associational power. The structural bargaining power describes workers in the economic system, which includes two subtypes - marketplace and workplace bargaining power. In Ford factories, increasing levels of automation and de-skilling of work had replaced craft labor with semi- or un-skilled workforce and reduced workers' control of their own work. Compounded by increasing numbers of immigrant or rural workers in the labor pool, workers' marketplace bargaining power weakened.

Nevertheless, workplace bargaining power increased for Ford workers who are enmeshed in tightly integrated production processes. The factories were gigantic, though workers and machines were densely arranged. Along the supply chain, the interruption of work by wage-earners in key positions along the assembly line may cause far larger loss than before. When one key part of work on assembly line stops, production may have to be completely shut down. Furthermore, the massive employment of unskilled workers with similar background, mostly former peasants or immigrants, resulted in easy organizing, especially within and around factories. As a result, the associational power of workers enhanced based on the formation of collective organizations, especially trade unions. As Silverly (2003:19) commented, the 'advance of industry', featured by new production methods, may weaken the marketplace bargaining power of workers, but it tends to increase both workplace and associational bargaining power. Noticeably, in the U.S., the strong control of workers at the grass-roots level contributed to the strong industrial union movement in the 1930s and 1940s.

The case of Germany contrasted from the American experience, which started from the emergence of the automobile industry. Fordist mass production took hold in Europe only after the World War II (Lipietz 1987; Piore and Sabel 1984). Germany, together with other parts of Europe, faced the monumental tasks of not only building democracy but also modernizing industry after the war. At the time, Ford's mass production was championed by the German government as the model for capitalists to emulate. In early of the post-war period, VW, Ford and Opel became mass producers. As early as 1925, Ford set up its German subsidiaries in Berlin, and in 1929 GM took over Opel in Rüsselheim (Streeck 1988; Katzenstein 1988: 6). Launched during the WWII, VW in Wolfsburg turned into the German version of "Ford".

Nevertheless, the German automobile industry always has its peculiar characteristics. Primarily, the production and the market had never been as unified as the mass production lines in the US. Traditionally, with widely varying taxation structures, income distributions, and road conditions it was impossible for any single producer in Germany to dominate the market or for any single design philosophy to prevail. This fragmentation of the market left ample space for more specialized manufacturers of luxury cars, such as BMW and Daimler Benz, to grow alongside the mass producers. In the early stage of post-war period, VW, Ford, and Opel were engaged in mass production, whereas South German craft production, such as BMW, Daimler Benz, Audi, NSU, Porsche, and others, always co-existed, especially after the collapse in 1963 of the Bremen company, Borgward. In addition, although the initial products of Fordist factories before 1960s were standardized, functionalist, and repetitive, as the Austin Seven and Morris Monor show. Rising incomes in Germany during the 1960s led mass producers to offer a wider range of models in order to maintain shares in an increasingly diverse national markets (Sachse 1988). Thus, the strong specialist tradition in Germany blended into mass production, including high product variety, flexible specifications, and a strong emphasis on quality engineering and manufacturing (Streeck 1988). Such diversification of products requires a wide range of technologies and skills, while the workforce may have certain control on their work processes.

Besides exemplifying a tradition of craft production, the German automobile industry has also been characterized by remarkable traditionalism, which means high integration of production, operation of giant plants, and diversification which extended only into closely related sectors. The supply base entailed primarily domestic sourcing, due to the traditional priority given to product quality. Apart from quality control, the purpose of domestic sourcing was to enable close cooperation between research and development, as demonstrated by the long-standing alliance between Daimler Benz and Bosch, as well as short supply lines, similar to the Japanese "*Kanban*" than to the "world car" philosophy. Kanban is a scheduling system to control the logistical chain for just-in-time production. As high efficiency is desired in the flow from logistical chain to the point of production, the optimal stock should be zero. South German producers easily accept the zero-stock purchasing policy. However, the major difference that sets German auto makers apart from Japanese competitors can be explained by the high degree of vertical integration of production. German producers have a high proportion of in-house value-added, and a preference for "making" parts and components by themselves rather than "buying" from outside. Moreover, the German model is also known for the pursuit of a particular kind of engineering excellence. With high investment in R&D and a long trial and testing period before marketing a technical innovation, the costs of new products are often higher than in other countries, with a longer production time. For instance, Daimler Benz is famous for "the better second" (Streeck 1988), which means its products often enter the market slower than other similar products but with better quality. All these strategies have cultivated a domestic supply base of small artisanal firms that rejects cross-national cooperation. Even in the 1980s, when production abroad increasingly became an alternative to protectionism and vulnerability to the fluctuation of exchange rates, the German auto industry, with the exception of Ford and Opel, lagged behind their competitors. Domestically-produced parts and components remained the primary option. In addition, banks also had tremendous influence on large firms, especially on major auto makers, e.g. bank representatives on their supervisory boards. Thus, the financial strategies were rather conservative, while current profits and Hausbank credit were important sources of capital in lieu of equity (Streeck 1988).

Consequently, these features of the German automobile industry - traditionalism of production, competition within the quality-controlled domestic supply chain, and conservative financial strategies - have brought along a unique context to the development of industrial relations. The key was industrial consensus among workers and management in building up labor-capital cooperation and social partnership in the post-war era. Accordingly, the well-known strategy of "high wage/high quality/high skills/high investment"[39] was

39 Also called "diversified quality production" (Wolfgang Streeck), or "high quality incremental innovation" (David Soskice).

developed in Germany together by industrial capitalists and trade unionists, with the support of banks and state.

The principle of this "high wage/high quality/high skills/high investment" strategy was non-price-competitive. It explained the successes of the German industries and its economy, especially the auto and machinery industries after the 1970s, when collective bargaining and the labor movement in the U.S. as a whole declined. Later in 1986, the output and domestic sales of cars in Germany exceed that in 1971, the peak before the crisis of profitability in the 1970s. Additionally, the upsurge in employment in the automobile industry spiked in the 1980s (Streeck 1988:15). At the same time, workers were provided with one of the highest wages, shortest working hours, the most generous holiday packages, and benefits in the industrialized world (Bundesministerium fuer Wirtschaft 1998).

It is fair to say that the differences in the U.S. and German collective bargaining systems have originated from and further reflects the two distinctive production regimes. Capitalism in the U.S. is well known for its extensive use of labor, activity- or performance-based wages, managerial prerogative, shareholder orientation, deregulated labor market, and welfare system. In contrast, Germany has intensive use of labor, ability-based payment, capital valorization through the optimization of technological based in work processes, stakeholder orientation, high levels of employers' contributions to public funds, re-regulated labor market and welfare system with high level of state expenditure (e.g. Koch 2006: 37-40; Tüselmann and Heise 2000:162-175).

In consequence, German production regimes in the post-war era were rather homogeneous in the automobile industry and, to a lesser degree, in the electronics industry. The regimes of production in both industries had similar kinds of work organization, production process, and wage determination. This feature has greatly facilitated the industrial bargaining processes and the application of general collective agreements. In practice, the general collective contract applies to all enterprises in the same sector in an entire region, and between regions and sometimes even among industries with centralized coordination. Apart from wage standards and recently working hours set by such a sectoral collective bargaining, social insurance is also provided by state programs. This leaves a rather limited space for negotiation on other working conditions between works councils and individual employers.

Comparatively speaking, while the automobile sector in the U.S., particularly auto makers, remained relatively standardized throughout the 1950s and 1960s, it has changed dramatically since this period. Relocation of parts supply production, along with the advent of non-union transplant factories, mostly from Japan, resulted in massive non-union regimes in the U.S. since the

1970s. Moreover, the production regimes in electronic factories have been highly diversified. In particular, a dramatic change in the U.S. occurred in the 1970s, whereby non-union regimes grew in the auto parts supply factories, and even more so in its electronics industry. By the late 1950s, as the uniform mass products from Fordist factories could no longer meet the increasingly diversified demands of consumers, automakers had began to offer a wide range of structurally and mechanically different cars: compacts, intermediates, personal luxury cars, muscle cars, pony cars, etc. (Gartman 1998). Such diversity severely taxed the Fordist mass production system. The expansion of factories and machines for different types of cars began to tie up capital in inventory, and fluctuating volumes of orders slowed down production and created coordination problems. By the late 1960s, Fordist work could no longer be further divided, and machines could not be further specialized. Thus, productivity growth slowed and profits lagged. The Fordist economy fell into crisis during the recession of 1973 (Aglietta 1979; and Lipietz 1987). In general, although in a couple of traditional large US companies, actual labor standards may be close to the results of collective bargaining, it is full of uncertainty and insecurity for workers in the increasing numbers of smaller firms, in terms of wages, employment and so forth.

Manufacturing in the U.S. began to decline following the 1970s crisis. The early practices such as tightening discipline, trimming workforces, and forcing the rest of workers to labor harder, proved to be rather counter-productive. For instance, in GM's Lordstown plant, young workers launched an unusual strike against the speed and monotony of the assembly line. Ultimately, U.S. automakers invented Japanese lean production to further their goals of production relocation and flexibility. In a search for cheap, non-unionized labor, corporations shifted production out of the industrial Midwest and Northeast to the American Sunbelt as well as offshore, abandoning industrial cities and leaving millions of unionized blue-collar workers unemployed. The professional-managerial class that engineered the restructuring processes experienced a rapid windfall of profits, leading to a growing income inequality across American cities. During the 1970s, the organization among the working poor and minorities rapidly declined. At the same time, the new middle class comprised about 23.8% in 1977 (Davis 1986: 213), which included a sub-bourgeois, a mass layer of managers, professionals, new entrepreneurs and rentiers, who benefited from the degradation of job creation and erosion of mass consumption norms.

In the electronics industry, the production regimes were even more diversified and wage regulation more flexible than the auto industry. The non-union sector further expanded in the U.S. The 1970s marked a turning point, wherein new information and communication companies boomed in the US. With the remarkable development of Silicon Valley, new companies with narrow specialization emerged, which focused only on design or marketing but got rid of actual manufacturing. The representatives were chip firms like Intel, AMD, or later Apple, Microsoft and Compaq in the PC industry. These are typically non-union companies. In fact, even the first generation of electronic companies in the U.S., OEMs such as General Electric, Westinghouse and IBM set up non-union subsidiaries in some South states as early as the 1950s. In addition, contract manufacturers, the largest companies in the electronics industry after the 1990s, are union-free, just as their numerous small- and medium-sized parts suppliers. As the tendencies for vertical dis-integration and production relocation proceeded, the electronics industry continuously created new decentralized sectors in urban settings.

As a result, the labor movements in the U.S. have been further weakened since the 1970s. For instance, those non-union Silicon Valley companies champion for corporate paternalism in modern capitalism (Luethje 2002), which involves extended systems of corporate values, human-oriented management, incentives and bonuses, etc. The modern company paternalism is conditional, and company generosity to employees is ultimately an anti-union stance by demonstrating the excess of union organizing. Since the 1970s, wage rules were modified and decreased. In the automobile industry, a divergence emerged between local practices and involvement by the UAW and workers in increasing participation in corporate and shop-floor decision-making. Under the growing pressure for cost reduction and greater flexibility, major trends in the US automobile industry after the late 1970s featured decentralization[40] and de-regulation. At the same time, many firms abandoned the strategy of following the wage standards in pilot collective bargaining and increasingly relocated from traditional industrial cities to low wage, non-union locations in less-developed regions. Many also downsized and outsourced production to low-wage suppliers.

In a word, collective bargaining in the U.S. has coexisted with trends toward decentralization and deregulation, along with a large non-union sector in the South, increasing union-free companies and industries, and the hollowing out of industrial manufacturing overseas to low-wage countries. Overall, workers have weaker bargaining power, since few are union members. Additionally, wherever there are trade unions, increasing numbers of workers must face production

---

40 Decentralization denotes the organizational side of the disintegration of hierarchically structured corporate complexes: the reduction of the in-house range of performance, the transfer of competence from central instances to executing units as well as the strengthening of autonomous action and own responsibility of organizational units. See: Sauer 1999

relocation. In this way, the "pattern" bargaining between trade unions and large firms, including Ford and GM in the automobile industry, has less influence upon the entire industry. In addition, while trade unions exclusively focus on the economic interest of its limited members, a majority of non-union workers are left out. In the 1970s and 1980s, involuntary part-time jobs and non-union sectors have spread extensively, which were excluded from the terms set by collective bargaining. During the time of the Reagan era overall trends towards wage increases decelerated for the first time in 40 years, while labor standards declined since 1982. In this sense, the post-war social contract did not apply to the majority of workers in the U.S., thus leading to its eventual collapse since the late 1970s.

In contrast to the U.S., the non-union option was not possible for German car makers and electronics firms until after 1990. In Germany, wage levels in collective agreements are theoretically applied to all workers. In addition, there s no regulation governing the rising numbers of part-time workers in the U.S., whereas in Germany they are involved in tripartite bargaining and entitled to additional welfare payments in both the auto and electronics industries.

Furthermore, another core feature of Fordism was the collective contractual wage relations that guaranteed demand and mass consumption. On the one hand, work organization and technological processes, particularly Taylorism and mechanization, ensured gains in labor productivity; On the other hand, social products are allocated between capital accumulation and consumption (purchasing power of wage laborers) in the form of collective bargaining (Aglietta 1979: 116).

In fact, the origin of production regimes is closely linked to not just industrial tradition and development, but also to socioeconomic and political regulations within which the labor history was made. Henry Ford's "Five-dollar day" marked new type of consumption that was closely tied to the initiation of mass production. The motivation for his scheme was to find new consumers for all the goods manufactured from his mass production lines. Only the working class was large enough to provide the requisite numbers at that time. Turning workers into consumers entailed raising their wages and persuading them to buy their means of livelihood, as opposed to producing them at home. Ford began this transformation of workers to consumers in 1914. This scheme doubled the wages for most of his workers. However, to be eligible, workers had to participate in his social engineering program, which involved attending church, learning English, and embracing "American values". Ford undertook paternalistic investigations into his workers' domestic lives in order to encourage a lifestyle shaped by the stable consumption of durable goods, as well as to cajole workers to spend their wages the 'right way' (Gartman 1986; Meyer 1981).

Nevertheless, this "Five Dollars a Day" scheme is indeed very different from the Fordist wage regulation. The offer of high wages by welfare capitalists like Ford was no more than a tool of stabilizing and integrating the workforce that responded to lack of market demand and workers' resistance inside the factories (Sachse 1988). Within the rigid mass production system, disciplined labor was an essential. High wages and mass consumption were originally encouraged to induce and motivate disciplined labor. This schema tried to subsume every aspect of the reproduction of labor-power, including the management of the workers' household budget under a system of authoritarian productivism. Over the long run, it was rather "a transitory form of remuneration". Such a paternalistic measure of giving high wages, which was sometimes referred to as company "welfarism", was by no means secure or sustainable. It could easily change when workers adapted to the production system or when competition for capital intensified. Gramsci cited the "ideology of high wages", which meant that the high wages were a means for creating social consensus in order for individuals to adapt to new methods of production and work. Pure coercion was combined with "persuasion and consent" to assure an optimal period of habituation. Once the "average type of Ford worker became the average type of worker in general", high wages would decrease, thereby highlighting the instabilities of this program (Rafalski 1988: 46).

In fact, the Fordist model of wage increases and mass consumption was later strengthened by labor movements. By demonstrating their collective capacity and labor militancy, workers won not just the legal rights to organize, bargain, and strike, but they also pushed for the general acceptance of these rights among capitalists. In the 1930s and 1940s, labor movements reached its peak in modern history of the US. During this period, trade unions developed a collective bargaining system that underwrote the wages of all workers, particularly the UAW. Under the pressure from the labor movements during the 1930s, as demonstrated in mass strikes at the GM Flint plant, the collective contract which pioneered the Fordist wage regulation (also known as "The Treaty of Detroit") was signed between the UAW and GM in 1948. This collective contract marked one significant step by the industrial union movement in institutionalizing an uniform, nationwide wage pattern. The GM strike programme, before reaching the agreement, also made a strong appeal to public interest groups as part of the emerging Keynesian consensus by claiming that a substantial boost in mass purchasing power would be necessary to avoid a post-war depression (Lichtenstein 1995). Since it was signed, such formulaic mechanisms were enacted to set wages in collective contracts, including an annual improvement factor and a cost-of-living adjustment (Katz 1986: 283).

Starting with this collective contract, the Fordist wage regulation, a "social contract" in a real sense, came into being. Through collective bargaining, parties set wages at the corporate and industry levels, and local work-rule bargaining was bounded through limits imposed by the national union. In this "pattern bargaining", a precedent of wage and benefits was set at a company before it is then imposed upon other companies in the same industry through strikes or through multiemployer master agreements (Moody 2010). In terms of grievance resolution, local and national unionists were involved. As a result of collective bargaining over fair wages, the aim of income equality had been achieved. By 1945, the family income of the bottom two-fifths of the population had increased by over 60%, more than doubling that of the remaining population. From 1948 up to 1979, collective bargaining and collective agreements set wages among Big Three companies, namely, GM, Ford and Chrysler. A stable and relatively centralized bargaining structure was realized during the next quarter century.

Last but not the least, collective bargaining in the U.S. became institutionalized through government policies during the New Deal era. The Great Depression indeed marked a turning point. By the late 1920s, the market for consumer durables in the U.S. saturated. By 1932 one-quarter of the labor force was unemployed, and total manufacturing production had dropped by nearly half (U.S. Bureau of the Census 1975). The economic crisis unleashed unprecedented mass protest. Before this background, the importance of mass consumption, which originated from an increased purchasing power among workers, began to serve as one indispensable factor in surviving the financial crisis. An interventionist Keynesian state emerged to implement both social spending programs and fiscal and monetary policies that sustained aggregate demand (Aglietta 1979; Piore and Sabel 1984). At the end, with the advent of the New Deal and expansion of collective bargaining, stable and rule-governed institutions were set up to overcome wage competition, and the potential market was enlarged and accumulation accelerated.

The New Deal introduced broad changes in the political and economic statuses of mass workers in the U.S. Policies and legislations also helped to balance the power between labor and capital. In particular, the National Labor Relations (Wagner) Act, passed by the Congress in 1935 and affirmed by the Supreme Court in 1937, provided the most significant changes to the legal foundations of present-day industrial relations. This act granted workers the legal rights to organize trade unions, to bargain collectively, and to strike. This was at a time when employers still held strong oppositions against collective bargaining. In addition, this act established the National Labor Relations Board (NLRB), a federal agency, to act as a formal mediator in industrial disputes.

Nevertheless, the promise of social peace and confirmation of managerial initiative in the Treaty of Detroit also had a profound impact on the internal structure of the UAW and the character of industrial relations (Lichtenstein 1995: 140, 145 and 176). Most importantly, a compromise was made in which the trade union gave away control of shop-floor work procedures to management (Davis 1986). Additionally, divisions increased between union members and non-union members. Long-standing non-union sectors in southern U.S. maintained links to racist political regimes in those states. Even at the peak of the labor movement, the US working class failed to unionize the majority of workers and protected the diversified production regimes. In this sense, the decline of the American labor movement started from these problems.

In contrast, the institutionalization of collective bargaining and industrial relations system in Germany was in general a top-down process. The success of the upmarket strategy, in which wages continued to increase, employment was guaranteed, and comprehensive vocational training was provided, should be attributed to the industrial consensus between labor and capital. This consensus was supported by the state and banks. As a result, the system cultivated a highly-skilled workforce with positive attitudes and full adaptability toward new technologies and innovations, as well as stable high trust alliances between capital and labor (Müller-Jentsch and Weitbrecht 2003: 19). For instance, extensive vocational training programs had been set up by all parties. As sector-wide collective bargaining set the uniform wage standards for all employees, firms have no incentive to divide young skilled workers from each other through mutual outbidding (Soskice et al. 1997: 43-45). Hence, they would train young apprentices without fearing that attractive wage-offers would lure young workers away from them later. This greatly facilitated the high human capital investment in the majority of companies (Tüselmann and Heise 2000). In another example of organizational flexibility, employment security was guaranteed by legislation. Collective agreements associated with the high costs of dismissal created external labor market rigidities, and the emergence of internal labor markets made sure new jobs were primarily given to current employees. Therefore, modern concepts, such as broad job content and a reintegration of conception and execution, perfectly fit the German industrial strategy. In practice, trade unions, represented by IG Metall, have also advocated de-Taylorization of work organization since the 1960s.

Although the dual system of industry-wide collective bargaining and workplace-level works councils had already existed during the Weimar period, it only became a success story in the aftermath of the WWII. As a matter of fact, collective agreements already existed in the second half of the nineteenth century. In the 1890s, the widespread of Socialist and Communist thoughts to

Germany aroused political debate among trade unionists and politicians. The key was whether to choose socialist labor movement or collective agreements within the Capitalist framework. This debated eventually led to a shift from revolutionary to reformist strategy. The labor movement began to emphasize on welfare-oriented improvement for workers and social reforms within the capitalist framework. Since then, participation and democratization of all areas of society, including the economy, had become new key words. This resulted not only in a new attitude towards collective agreements, but also a new understanding of the necessity of workers' participation within enterprises. During the war period, the groundwork for collective bargaining was renewed and modified. The coal and steel industries in the Ruhr region began with pilot projects in German industrial relations. As the Fordist mass production was emulated in Germany, industrial relations did not completely copy the U.S.. Rather, a dual system represented by industrial bargaining and plant-level co-determination is a combined result of the traditional craft and new mass production methods, which was specific to the labor history in Germany.

Streeck (1988:14) noted that "Nowhere else has the West German industrial relations system performed better than in the automobile industry, and no industry has in the past contributed more to the evolution of the system than autos". The German automobile industry has been highly unionized. IG Metall is the major union of the sector. Almost all large employers are members of the Gesamtmetall and serve as signatories to sectoral agreements. At the same time, works councils are organized at the factory level and increasingly at the European and international levels. One legal task for works councils at the factory level involves the supervision of the implementation of industrial agreements. In the automobile industry, works councils have increasingly become the center of trade union organization in the workplace (Streeck 1988). Works councils have a "serious commitment to consensus" (Müller-Jentsch 2003: 39-56). When the Trade Act was amended in 1891, which firstly introduced the initial legalization of works councils, trade unions strongly opposed it. Only after a shift toward a reformist strategy, the labor movement reconciled itself to the works council structure (Weiss 1989: 27-29).

Moreover, the state and the law also have played a significant role in industrial relations, under the pressures from the internal labor movement and the Russian revolution at the time. In the context of German industries which had been discredited from the Nazi era,Germans faced threat of nationalization. Strong co-determination emerged to institutionalize cooperative and strong labor-management relations. The national government promulgated a union-employer agreement, stipulating that management not only approved the introduction of the works councils system but also accepted trade unions as representative agents of the working class in determining wages and working conditions. The same agreement also assigned employers' associations the responsibility of representing businesses in the collective bargaining process (Müller-Jentsch, and Weitbrecht 2003). With regard to works council, the organizational assistance provided by the state played a key role in its institutional developments. In the 1951 Works Constitution Act (Betriebsverfassungsgesetz, amended in 1972 and 2001), the legal status of works councils system was finally confirmed. As for employers, although their early agreement was initially merely tentative, they soon accepted it.

The German approach in dealing with the 1970s crisis diverged from the American experience. Whereas American manufacturers endeavored to seek flexibility not only in products, but also in wages and labor relations, the German strategy of "high wage, high quality, high productivity" reaped its benefits. For a long time, German model was praised as the exemplary case, when the US automobile industry went through its chronic decline, especially in the 1980s.[41] Strong trade unions in Germany imposed restrictions upon management through industrial bargaining and co-determination. Such restrictions indeed helped firms to embark on more demanding and, in the long run, more successful adjustment strategies (Streeck 1988; Katzenstein 1988: 46). Besides, by 1975 West German wage levels surpassed the US average (Davis 1986: 195). The high wages and labor costs were well compensated by high workers' skills, high organizational flexibility, and accordingly high productivity. From the late 1980s till early 1990s, the German system of industrial relations had driven the industrial boom which led to a stable and peaceful environment.

Nevertheless, the German model has recently confronted crisis as well. As the production regimes became more diversified after the 1990s, coordinated wage negotiation and workplace-level workers' participation gradually eroded. Significant trade-offs have been made in collective bargaining, including wage moderation and constraint on working time, but unfortunately many trade-offs did not lead to more jobs. In addition, organizing efforts in the private and service sectors among engineers and white-collar workers have only met with limited to marginal success, although white-collar workers have outnumbered blue-collar workers since the mid-1980s. At the same time, more clauses in sectoral collective agreements give exceptions to enterprises, and more and more subjects have been delegated from industrial bargaining to works

---

41 For instance, the German experience was especially influential on the thinking of the Dunlop Commission set up by the Clinton administration to propose reforms to US employment relations. See: Marsden, 2008

agreements at plant levels. Consequently, informal solidarity linking industrial unions with works councils has eroded (Herrigel 2008). Due to the intermediary nature of works councils, decentralized work agreements may lead to flexibility and differentiation of labor standards (Koch 2006: 45), high bargaining costs, and damage of the labor-capital trust relationship. Furthermore, the shrinking employers' associations also weakened industry-wide collective bargaining.

In a word, the combination of industrial tradition and mass production methods have brought about a new application of Fordism in Germany, as featured by cooperative labor-capital relations and social partnership. The economic boom led to the rebuilding of German capitalism to rise among the top three internationally competitive economies in the 1970s, apart from the U.S. and Japan. At the same time, it also made wage increases for workers possible for employers. Most importantly, the continuous struggles for an increasingly stronger labor movement had accelerated the profit-distribution. Since the end of the 1950s, high wages and stable employment were realized through sector-wide collective bargaining in post-war Germany, set by industrial trade unions and followed by works councils at factory level. This German model had sustained up to the 1990s. Since then, the global industrial trends of flexibilization and decentralization have also impacted on Germany, although the changes have been taking place in a step-by-step form with certain control and regulations.

To sum up, the two divergent cases in US and Germany demonstrate that collective bargaining has played an essential role in inducing disciplined labor and in sustaining mass consumption during the golden age of capitalism. It is significant not just to acknowledge the positive role of collective bargaining for the economy and people in the society, but also to remember the achievement of this system was accomplished primarily because of the long-term struggle of workers and trade unions. Noticeably, the early institutionalization of high wages by several welfare capitalists differed from the wage policies characteristic of Fordism. Evidently, an encompassing wage scheme with steady increases could not be achieved only through the "good-will" of capitalists. Most importantly, collective bargaining is initiated and finally institutionalized following the lead of strong industrial unionism. From the labor side, mass mobilization of workers is achieved through class struggle and radical democracy. Moreover, certain economic and political circumstances remain decisive, such as the necessity of mass consumption and the support of Keynesian government policies. Such policies can only emerge from situations where the prerogative of capitalism over the production process and society in general is seriously questioned. Nevertheless, distinctive differences exist between the U.S. and German models of collective bargaining, which lead to divergent industrial strategies, as demonstrated by contrasting resolutions to the crisis of the 1970s, and the disparity of economic and social stabilities at large.

2.3 Valuable lessons

Production regimes impact socioeconomic and political regulations, yet at the same time, they are the direct result of such regulations. Proper regulations must normalize the capital relations and guide the conflictual and crisis-mediated course of accumulation. From the historical experiences of the two country cases, valuable lessons can be learned. Primarily, some general factors are found in common at the early stage of the formation of Fordism and its wage regulation. Production methods as well as workers' bargaining power at the factory level, and policy-making at industrial and national levels has shaped the institutions and functions of collective bargaining. Moreover, the historical experiences of both countries, particularly their distinctive industrial relations systems in the post-war era, and the common challenges faced by labor movements since the 1990s, may enlighten other countries to establish well-functioning collective bargaining processes that adapt to their respective contexts.

2.3.1 Common conditions in the formation of Fordist wage regulation

The formation and institutionalization of collective bargaining both in the US and in Germany was essentially driven by collective labor. From mass production to lean methods, labor-capital conflicts have consistently characterized daily production and work organizations. Employers doggedly pursue increasing profit rates. Ultimately strong labor movements initiated struggles within factories and then instituted collective bargaining as national policies. Consequently, the state accommodated the claims of labor through legislation, policies, etc., which was eventually acknowledged by employers to different degrees. In the meantime, the national and global economic and political environments had been rather favorable for developing Fordist wage regulation.

At the factory level of both countries, the Fordist model of mass production in the automobile industry had brought about conflicts as well as a growing collective labor force. The Fordist work organization is typically marked by a rigid hierarchy, a Talyorist division of labor, and strict labor control. In this rationalized system, work is divided into standard simple tasks. Unskilled or semi-skilled workers are employed, and control rests completely upon the hand of management. As a result, work is simplified, repetitive and intensified, and consequently workers feel pervasive stress and insecurity.

In the process of establishing Fordist wage regulation, the force of labor is essential, including workers' structural power and associational power, as identified by Wright (2000: 962). Primarily, production regimes determine workers' location in the economic system and thus their structural power, including marketplace and workplace bargaining power. In Fordist production system, labor's marketplace bargaining power was weak because firstly the systematic decomposition of skills had marginalized craft workers. Consequently, unskilled industrial workers can be easily substituted. In addition, the labor markets were flooded with former peasants and recently proletarianized immigrants, who were mostly unskilled workers without previous experience of unionization. Given the oversupply of labor market and the difficulty in organizing the new workforce by trade unions, workers' workplace bargaining power weakened. In 1941, 43% of all employed Americans were blue-collar workers and four million out of fifteen were migrants, mostly from the rural South of the country, and from Eastern and Southern Europe (Lichtenstein1995: 176). In the 1950s and 1960s, the majority of immigrants in Germany were from other part of the Europe, such as South Italian, Spain and Turkey. It is noted that open immigration was outlawed in the U.S. in the 1920s, which helped stabilize the U.S. working class and contributed to CIO victories in the 1930s (Silver 2003: 27).

More noteworthy is workplace bargaining power. Since assembly-line-based production is tightly integrated and highly dependent on the continuity of the production flow. Workers can gain strong power through strategic work stoppage. This was the case in Ford factories around 1913. Thus, Ford began to offer generous wages and welfare schemes together with discipline programs, in order to avoid further resistance. During the heyday of the labor movements, the 1930s in US and 1960s and 1970s in Germany, spot strikes, rolling strikes, and lightning strikes were conducted. All these new forms of strikes involved only small numbers of people and short time of work stoppage. They achieved maximum disruption by targeting the most sensitive links in the production network. In consequence, the role of unions rapidly expanded during these periods of time, and workers were able to put limits on management prerogatives to get wage increases.

Another type of labor force - associational bargaining power - is the foundation of labor movements, and collective bargaining. Collective force originates from labor organizations, especially trade unions and sometimes political labor parties. In early Fordist factories, the massive employment of unskilled workers with similar background, mostly former peasants or immigrants, led to effortless labor organizing within and around the factory (Silver 2003: 19). In both countries, the first generation of immigrants hardly protested against the harsh conditions of work and life. However, the second generation became the backbone of militant struggles which later "succeeded in radically transforming relationships within the factory and within society" (Silver 1993).

In particular, industrial unionism played a key role in both countries. Organizing all types of workers in the same sector has always been a priority since the late 1940s in Germany. In the U.S., industrial unionism was reborn in the Fordist integration of mass production (Lichtenstein 1995: 57). At the time, the new forms of technologies and organization attacked craft standards and chipped away at the "consent" of the "labor aristocracy", inducing skilled workers, to reach out to growing ranks of unskilled workers. In this context, trade unionism became more aggressive and less sectional. Overall, the formation and expansion of strong unions enhanced the associational power of workers and attempted to voice workers' demands for determining wages and other conditions through collective bargaining.

This sense of solidarity and class consciousness has played a central role in the making of labor history, in both the U.S. and Germany. Before the early twentieth century, communist and socialist ideologies widely influenced labor leaders and posed great pressure on capitalist states. When the debate of 1890s finally shifted from revolutionary to reformist politics, collective bargaining became institutionalized by governments, as a less militant way of balancing the labor-capital power. As in the case for the US after the Great Depression and Germany during Weimar Republic and the post-war era, it also served as a tool for realizing the mass consumption required by intensive accumulation. In Germany, the basic institutions of corporatist and Fordist regulations, as well as the Works Council system, were established in the 1920s. In the Weimar period from 1919 to 1933, German workers were highly conscious of class divisions and were politically organized by the Social Democratic Party (SPD), the Communist Party and other left-wing working class parties. In the U.S., socialist groups in 1912 did not unite the working class or coordinate trade-union strategy with socialist philosophies. The basic institutions were established much later, at the wake of Roosevelt's National Labor Relations Act, but also in a period of "class struggle".

However, the qualitatively different levels of class consciousness between German and American labor movements had become less obvious after WWII. The breakdown of the German labor movement in 1933 nearly ended working class radicalization. In the aftermath of the wars, Communism and socialism also lost favor in Germany. The post-war German system of industrial relations was largely the result of top-down policies that emphasized cooperative and labor-management relations. Restriction of shop-floor militancy was imposed from above, as they were written into the laws and regulations codifying a social partnership between organized labor and capital. The imitation of Fordism and the co-determination system made the labor-capital relations much less adversary. In the U.S., the shop-floor power had given way to a reformist union leadership. The dissension and fragmentation of the labor movement was intense. One phenomenon was the anti-communism trend among top union leadership (e.g.Davis 1986; Lichtenstein 1995). The US labor movement missed another chance in the 1930s and 1940s to unify the working class, and a 'disorganized' and increasingly 'depoliticized' working class became reality in the 1950s. Accordingly, the narrow focus and economic orientation of trade unions has limited the functions of collective bargaining.

In a broader context, global politics beyond the purview of industrial relations are a critical factor in determining workers' bargaining power and patterns of labor unrest at the national level over time. In the late of nineteenth century and early twentieth century, the ideas of communism and socialism influenced many labor activists. Growing labor militancy intertwined with growing nationalist agitation, particularly in response to the 1917 Russian Revolution. In the U.S., the social democratic movement eventually gained its position as quasi-labor parties, and high wages and welfare were accepted to legitimate its ruling. In Germany, the 1890s political debate finally led to a shift from revolutionary to reformist strategies. Participation and democratization of all areas of society became the new key words, and labor movements agreed to collectively bargain in order to reach compromises with management within the framework of capitalism. In other words, the global political transformation opened the space for setting up mass consumption and developmentalist social contracts at the national level. Thus, more labor-friendly international environment appeared in the post-war period. Nevertheless, since the 1970s, a labor-unfriendly neoliberalist regime, including cutting of dismantling of social safety nets in many countries, had largely replaced Fordism. The global industrial and political circumstances have changed dramatically, which had soon ended the social contract in the U.S. and exposed the German model to crisis after the 1990s.

2.3.2 Major implications for effective collective bargaining

It is important not only to review historical experience, but also to put it into use. Based on the advantages and disadvantages of the U.S. and German models, it is clear that collective bargaining relies upon external factors, such as the diversification of production regimes and a broad array of social and political institutions, particularly national social security programs. It also depends upon internal features, such as the coverage and governability of collective agreements. We could learn important lessons from the past. At the same time, since industrial and political circumstances at the national and global levels have changed dramatically in the last few decades, the applications of historical lessons also need to be adapted to specific contexts today.

At the factory level, one of the major differences in industrial relations between the U.S. and Germany during the post-war era was the degree of diversification among production regimes. As the German experience showed, homogeneous production regimes could facilitate the functioning of bargaining as well as the application of a general contract within an entire industry. Compared to the auto industry - the representative of German industrial relations, electronics factories have always been diversified in production, work organization, working conditions, and labor relations. Nevertheless, even during the heyday of Fordism, there existed significant differences between Germany and the U.S in both industries. In the U.S. the diversity of production regimes has always been more varied. This diversification was a major reason that explained why collective bargaining in the U.S. existed only between single employers and trade unions, while coordination at above-company level became increasingly difficult. At present, both industries are vertically disintegrated, albeit to a lesser degree for the auto industry, while production regimes have been fragmented. This transformation in the types of production regimes offers an even greater challenge for collective bargaining in countries undergoing industrialization, including China where factories of a whole production network, from leading brand name companies down to low-cost contract manufacturers at the bottom exist. As a result, a general industrial contract would be more difficult to apply, but at the same time, higher-level coordination of labor standards among different enterprises becomes even more urgent than ever.

It is also noted that workplace power is critical for collective labor. The shop-floors were originally sites of strong militancy, particularly in the U.S., where the workplace-based collective bargaining proved to be effective at the beginning. Unfortunately, workers' mobilization was later curbed, and the unions surrendered workers' power to control shop-floor negotiations. The 1950 Treaty of Detroit was also the historical deal that promised social peace and confirmed managerial initiative. Excessive negotiations had been made in regards to high wages and increasing productivity. Sophisticated union leaders such as the head of UAW - Walter Reuther - sought to incorporate demands over workplace issues such as production standards into their bargaining strategy, albeit to a limited extent (Tolliday and Zeitlin 1986:112). Some rank-and-files leaders set up work rules that restrained managerial prerogative. However, most have been removed under employers' offensives in recent years. Trade unions de facto relinquished the right to bargain over technical relations of production, as codified in the proliferation of 'management rights' clauses (Gordon et al. 1982). In return, unionized workers received job security and a share of profit dividend that resulted from increased labor productivity. As a result, unions and their few members had only limited and contractually based participation in business decision-making, and thus were dis-empowered at the workplace. For instance, in the auto industry, conflicts over the pace of work and production standards became the most recurrent local union grievances, and became the issue that created the most tension between rank and file and higher-level union officials.

Similarly, in Germany, the promise of social peace and the rise of managerial power became the basic flaw of post-war collective bargaining. According to German law and collective agreements, negotiation did not permit any substantial intervention in the technological and organizational design of work processes. In the late 1960s and early 1970s, massive strike waves and labor radicalism centered on Fordist mass-production industries were sparked by factory speed-ups. Nevertheless, related laws and regulations imposed restrictions on shop-floor militancy. Social partners were in principle responsible both for improving industrial organizations and for workers' well-being. The dual system of industrial bargaining by unions and the co-determination by works councils essentially limited the power of trade unions in mobilizing workers on workplace issues. Since works councils had no right to strike but merely served a legal obligation to "serious commitment to consensus", their relationship with employers indeed became almost a consensual productivity coalition. Co-determination is probably the least controversial mechanism in German industrial relations.

The divergent paths of the U.S. and Germany in labor movements and their collective bargaining practices demonstrated the vital role of solidarity. For a long time, Germany embraced a comprehensive industrial unionism and sectoral wage bargaining, whereas the U.S. was dominated by business unionism as well as uncoordinated and decentralized collective bargaining dominated by individual enterprises. In Germany, this system facilitated the post-war industrial boom and social stability up to the 1990s. Even when the changes of production, industries, and politics problematized collective bargaining and labor movements in the two countries, the demise of the two systems occurred at different speeds and followed divergent paths. In the U.S., large segments of the working population were left out of the union bargaining and the strong shop-floor dominance was surrendered by a reformist union leadership. As a result, the post-war social contract was overturned overnight by capitalists and by the state. In a way, the German model survived the 1970s crisis much better than the American one. However, since the end of the post-war economic boom, the corporatist deal making has become increasingly segmented, between unionized core workforces and unemployed, precarious workers. [42] Accordingly, coordinated sectoral wage negotiations and workplace-level worker participation gradually eroded. Nevertheless, German capitalists did not question the principles of the post-war labor system. Rather, the demise of the German model occurred incrementally through "changes within continuity". Simply put, on the one hand, as collective bargaining system became the key to the success of German industries, capitalists willingly adapted and revitalized the new socioeconomic environment. On the other hand, capitalists and their associations are aware of the political risks inherent in a process of uncontrolled decentralization process. Thus, a simple break from the past is not desired by industrial relations actors in Germany.

Moreover, regulations set at industrial and national levels helped to balance the power between capitalists and laborers. In the U.S., the Wagner Act of 1935 endowed workers the legal rights to organize trade unions, to bargain collectively with employers, and to strike. In this way, trade unions, particularly the UAW, institutionalized collective bargaining that underwrote the wages of all workers in the 1940s. In Germany, it was Neo-corporatist regulation that responded to the economic crisis of 1975 and the industrial unrest of the late 1960s and early 1970s. Policies during both periods promoted rapid industrial expansion which attempted to overcome the crises caused by market failure.

In particular, Germany established institutions to facilitate the self-governance of capital and labor. The SPD, usually regarded as the labor party of Germany, allowed more political space for trade unions to defend workers' rights, especially before 1933. However, after the breakdown of the labor movement in 1933 due to the rise of Hitler and the Nazis, new institutions were introduced "from above" with little working class participation. After the wars, the dangers of "total state"[43], featured by over-intervention and direct command by the state, not only led to deliberate reduction of the state power in the management of the economy, but they also changed the labor movement. In particular, a strong degree of co-determination was given to institutionalize cooperative and labor-management relations through national policies. Working

---

42 This is a major criticism raised by critical Marxists in Germany, such as J. Esser or J. Hirsch since the 1980s.

43 Lessons were drawn not only from the Nazi disaster, but also from the failure of the parties of Weimar that were held responsible for having paved the road for Hitler.

class radicalization nearly disappeared, and trade unions, instead of focusing on ideology or politics, emphasized welfare-oriented improvement and social reforms for workers within the capitalist framework. In consequence, the conflicting interests between capital and labor somehow accommodated the self-governance structure as regulated by the state.

Among public institutions, a national social security program is one of the factors that set Germany and the U.S. apart. Germany is well known for its comprehensive system of social insurances, especially universal health insurance. Thanks to this system, collective bargaining is largely exempted from verbose and complicated details pertaining to workers' benefits. Instead, trade unions are able to fully concentrate on wages and other direct working conditions when negotiating with employers.

On the contrary, the U.S. never developed a national schema of social security. In the wake of the 1930s crisis, the New Deal left out social welfare and a safety network. As a result, American trade unions bargained on every tiny detail of pension and health insurance, which could be seen from the volumes of American collective agreements. These agreements contrasted from Germany, which had only a few pages in the contracts. On one hand, the content of collective bargaining led to the possibility of more conflicts, while on the other hand, it added the extra burden upon enterprises. Often trade unions had to make concessions in other important aspects like wages.

It should be noted that although legislations and policies are important, the role of the state and political parties should not be the decisive factor in industrial relations. In Germany, after state repression on trade unions from 1875 to 1890, alliance between unions and the SPD became mutually beneficial. In the post-war era, a decentralized federal state 'moderated' rather than intervened in the economy and the labor market (Thelen 2004). Nevertheless, this pattern cannot be labeled as "Americanization". Rather, it served as a compromise between economic "liberalism" - Ordoliberalism[44], and the aliberal, corporatist Bismarckian welfare state, which was reconstructed in the 1950s. The social insurance programs and labor-related laws helped to stabilize a system of industrial self-governance and thus established a system of coordination within a "liberal" market environment (Manow 1999). The

44 It is a school of liberalism that emphasizes the need for the state to ensure that the free market produces results close to its theoretical potential. The theory was developed by German economists and legal scholars in the late 1920s and early 1930s as a reaction to the world economic crisis. Although it is generally understood to "have laid the intellectual foundations for the free market economy in mid 1948" and have been since then served as "the quasi-official credo of West Germany's economic policy", it was much less liberal than it is normally perceived.

insurance-principle of the welfare state put a premium on guaranteed employment and offered labor and capital the opportunity to externalize adjustment costs without endangering the coordinated model. Thus, this model could function without much state interference.

At the same time, the labor movement should not become over-dependent on the state. In the U.S., the trade unions have wrongly counted on the Democratic Party. The state has often opposed collective labor. For instance, the Wagner Act of 1935 granted workers basic legal rights, but also limited the effectiveness of strikes by allowing employers to hire replacement workers and by regulating the ability of unions to picket and to levy union fines. In fact, this act altered the frequency and form of strikes by fostering an concession of workers' no-strike pledge for an employer's agreement to arbitrate disputes. The Taft-Hartley Act, which passed over President Truman's veto on June 23, 1947, gave "encouragement and new weapons to anti-labor employers".[45] Besides its unique detailed regulation of the right to strike, the specifications of the bargaining process continued to evolve since then.[46] In a word, labor law since the New Deal diminished and substantially constrained workers' collective power. In this context, collective bargaining with a narrow focus on economic interests, restricted the social and political strategies once advocated by the Left (Lichtenstein 1995).

In addition, the mechanisms of collective bargaining models in the two countries have certain distinctions. One key of the German model is its coordinated standards for wages and working conditions that covered the entire sector of a region. Only this can achieve the original goal of collective bargaining - which aspired to "take wage out of competition". A wide-ranging solidarity and a broad focus of bargaining, not limited to the economic interests of members, are indispensable. In the beginning, industrial unions set better pay and working conditions through collective bargaining (e.g. in the automobile industry the UAW in the US and IG Metall in Germany). Nevertheless, industry-wide bargaining later facilitated the success of the German model, whereas U.S. collective bargaining became limited to single employers and featured a lack of coordination at higher levels. In Germany, strong labor associational power took the form of comprehensive industrial unions with social and political visions. The differences of ideologies and the distinctions between blue- and white-collar

45 This law required union leaders to sign anti-Communist affidavits, the prohibition against secondary boycotts, the enactment of section 14b allowing states to prohibit the union shop, and the ban on foreman unionism. See: Lichtenstein, 1995: 261

46 Only in the U.S. are there judicial principles of majority rule, exclusive representation, and representation elections, as well as the specific determination of legal forms of representation, the nature of bargaining unit, etc.. See: Davis, 1986:116

workers were irrelevant in the post-war union movement. However, American trade unions have been entangled with ideological and racial problems. They failed to form an organic bloc with Black liberation, organize the South, and defeat the power of Southern reactionaries in the Democratic Party. Moreover, political segmentation of the proletariat and middle strata confounded these problems. As a result, American trade unions have stuck with their maintained exclusivity with white and male members and de-collectivized a majority of workers. Furthermore, the goal of German unions was not only to increase wages, but also to enhance the social position of workers and to protect their health (e.g. "humanization of work" and "protection against rationalization" have been major goals of IG Metall since the 1970s). In the U.S., in the 1930s and 1940s, trade unions were militant in setting up workplace rules and other forms of constraint over management. However, soon after that, collective bargaining became a means of exclusive protection over a limited number of union members.

To sum up, the rise of collective bargaining systems in both countries had commonalities, such as strong collective labor born out of conflicts in Fordist mass production and organized industrial unions. Additionally, under the pressures of global political ideological rivalry, post-war governments issued relatively pro-labor policies, primarily for the sake of aggregate demands and economic development.

Today both the labor movement and policy making bodies in China may learn from the advantages of collective bargaining in the U.S. and Germany, whereas the shortcomings and negative consequences, namely, the segmentation of the workforce and cleavage in societies, should be avoided. Primarily, the well-known German model may serve as the "lesser evil" for China. In spite of the top-down building of the system and highly bureaucratic unions, at least the basic rights of workers are institutionally guaranteed. At the same time, the workplace-based bargaining in the U.S. also has its merit in that it was built from the bottom up and gave stronger shop-floor control and democracy to workers in many cases.

More specifically, homogeneous production regimes are favorable for collective bargaining, so that the early experiment may start from industries with less diversified production regimes like the auto industry. Furthermore, since global production networks and lean methods have nearly ended the possibility of homogeneous production regimes, a broad coverage of collective agreements as well as coordination on wages and other labor standards may facilitate the balance of industrial relations and class and social coherence. Such coordination is essential in reaching the designated purposes of collective bargaining.

At the same time, institutional guarantees and workplace control are essential in collective bargaining, not only to enable efficiency but also to preclude the possibility of decline in the long run. As for institutions, the role of the state is crucial in providing labor right legislation, a comprehensive national social security program, and also regulation for the necessary principles and procedures for collective bargaining. Workplace bargaining power is the ultimate guarantee that collective bargaining would not simply yield to concessions when workers face the continuous rationalization strategies of capital. The biggest flaw of the post-war Fordism was concessionary bargaining, in which trade-offs were made between high wages and the confirmation of management prerogative or between high productivity and employment security. Today capital is increasingly vulnerable to disruptions in the production flow, especially in the just-in-time parts delivery system.[47] Consequently, further integration of production and new logistic methods have increased workers' bargaining power. Workers' mobilization, by democratic unions at the shop-floor level, is the catalyst for effective collective bargaining. Ultimately, individual workers have to realize their source of power in labor-capital relations can only originate from solidarity. Solidarity with other workers and other segments of the working class, and even other social movements, would strengthen the labor movement and increase workers' associational bargaining power.

---

47 For instance, the Dayton strike in 1996 lasted seventeen days and closed down all but one of GM's assembly plants in the US, Canada, and Mexico. The New York Time, The General Motors Strike, Published: March 23, 1996, http://www.nytimes.com/1996/03/23/opinion/the-general-motors-strike.html

Industrial relations and new regimes of production in China

Many aspects of early capitalism, such as assembly-line-based mass production, insecure employment, barely sustainable wages, lengthy work hours, and stuffy workshops, are found in China today. Does this necessarily imply that China is going through the same development path, as what U.S. or Germany had in the early twentieth century? I argue that a simple 'yes' or 'no' answer to this question would be far from the reality.

The historical experiences of collective bargaining in the the U.S. and in Germany were initiated and shaped by production regimes in the factories, by state laws and policies, and by the global politics and economy. Fordist wage regulation ensured steady economic growth and industrial peace during the golden age of capitalism. However, due to divergences in both production regimes and industrial relations, the economic and industrial outcomes were better and more stable in Germany than in the US.

In order to compare China with the US and German models of industrial relations and collective bargaining, a systematic analysis is necessary. First, I examine the general working conditions in China's factories, including capitalist strategies on production and work organization, as well as de facto labor standards. I focus on the automobile and electronics industries to illustrate these conditions. I further analyze wage regulation and collective bargaining within the historical and current political and social circumstances. In addition, I describe the new trends in global production and polity, including the unprecedentedly mobile capital, the dominance of neoliberalism, and the labor-unfriendly development. On this basis, I compare the current status and potential future of collective bargaining within China's changing industrial relations with the historical experiences of the U.S. and Germany.

3.1 The automobile and electronics industries

The automobile and electronics industries have dramatically transformed everyday working lives of people at different historical periods time for more than one century. These two industries of the past two centuries have developed under distinctive economic and political circumstances. The life cycles of these industries in different economies have shaped labor movements and thus industrial relations world-wide. At the same time, the changes of industrial relations have also affected the development of each industry in specific ways.

The automobile industry was first developed in the late nineteenth century and early twentieth centuries, while the electronics industry began to boom only in the 1970s. Centered in the U.S., the first expansion of the automobile industry occurred from 1910 to 1950. The second major wave took place in Western Europe with a fivefold growth from 1950 to 1960. This growth doubled by 1970 (Altschuler et al. 1984, quoted from: Silver 2003: 50-51). When the electronics industry grew in 1970s and 1980s, the remarkable boom occurred in Silicon Valley. The electronics industry developed at a marvelous speed and brought dramatic changes into the industrial world and everyday life. New work organizations, new production models and new management methods prevailed. These innovations affected or weakened labor movements ever over time.

At first glance, the automobile and electronics industries, as representative sectors of Fordism, share common features such as mass production, advanced technologies, and capital-intensive. Primarily, the organization of work is subject to market and product strategies. The automobile industry transitioned from a standardized mass market to less homogeneous markets since the 1960s. This became possible because of the flexibility of micro-electronic technologies and equipment, such as robotics and computer-automated tools with which machines can be reprogrammed and quickly adapted to production changes. In fact, microelectronics was suggested by Dicken (1998: 353-4) as the "industry of industries", among the broad range of electronics subsectors such as computer service, software, telecommunication and other networks, and equipment manufacturing. Silver (2003: 104) also commented that the semiconductor industry had profound impacts on everyday life and work, through the "computerization of everything", including automobile and textile production.

Furthermore, other similarities are found in the two industries in regards to work, production and management methods. At present, Fordist production organizations in most large manufacturing factories which feature assembly lines and strict division of labor exist in many industrialized and newly-industrializing countries, in spite of subtle variations. Besides, since the early 1990s, lean production has become another cross-industry convention after Taylorism. For instance, different cars with distinctive colors and models can be produced along the same production line. Further, "module production" enable standardized parts and components to be produced for different final products, sometimes by different enterprises, and put together in the assembly plants at the final stage.[48] As a result, global networked production has created cross-border relocation at an unprecedented scale through outsourcing and subcontracting, use of temporary labor, and the expansion of secondary sectors and periphery

48 e.g. in GM-Opel, a same component like chassis can be used for different car models.

workforce. To a large degree, the standardization of work and flexibility in lean production has fragmented the industries production processes.

At the same time, differences exist between the two industries, including the products' life cycles, technological processes, speeds of innovation, physical differences of semi- and final products, etc.. In regards to industrial relations, both industries were traditionally characterized by vertical integration, which covered all procedures from design, manufacturing, marketing, even to after-sale services. Since the 1970s, the critical difference between the two industries has lied in the degree of vertical dis-integration that results from the new organization of work and production methods.

Vertical dis-integration is typically defined as the creation of new intermediate markets in a previously integrated production process (Jacobides 2005: 465). Primarily, the changes include the shift of production or service work from vertically integrated hierarchies to networks of two or more organizations. In the automobile and electronics industries, especially before the 1950s, production was located in one foreign nation mainly for the purpose of producing for that nation's (or adjacent) markets. However, since the 1970s, a new type of globalized production has begun to rely more and more cross-border production. In both the automobile and electronics industries, parts and components are mass produced in lower-cost countries and transported "back home". In addition, some studies (e.g. Doellgast and Greer 2007) also include subcontracting production to a separate firm, the creation of independent subsidiaries and use of temporary agencies for staffing into the types of vertical dis-integration. The entire electronics industry has become widely dispersed geographically due to outsourcing and subcontracting networks. Since the 1980s, the spread of lean production methods and its just-in-time parts-sourcing strategy has been redirected toward a spatial re-concentration of production, as the proximity between assemblers and suppliers reduced transaction time and costs. This pattern is seen particularly in the automobile industry where the parts and components are often bulky and heavy.

This trend has divergent impacts on the two industries, partly due to the physical differences of the products they offer. The automobile industry is still dominated by a traditional way of integration whereby nearly all procedures are done within the integrated enterprises of the whole-car makers with the exception of parts and components. The production of parts and components, however, rely on massive outsourcing which has given birth to numerous small- and medium-sized suppliers with widely different working conditions. In general, the structure of the automobile industry remains simple, with the whole-car makers in the center surrounded by a number of parts and components suppliers.

On the contrary, massive vertical dis-integration has been taking place in the electronics industry, since its manufacturing and service are less restricted by space or time. A large variety of electronic firms along the production network are characterized by different work segmentations at dispersed locations. This vertically dis-integrated production system has been referred to as the "Silicon Valley system", or "horizontal computer industry" (Grove 1996), or "Wintelism" (Borrus/Zysman 1997). Starting from Silicon Valley in the 1980s, a new brand of companies emerged, specializing in hardware- and software-products for the PC sector, computer servers, internet equipment and mobile computing devices such as laptops or handheld digital assistants. Chip companies like Intel, AMD, or later Apple, Microsoft and Compaq in the PC industry are representative companies. Most of them produce only key components like microprocessors or software operating systems (Lüthje 2001: 165). Over time the production system becomes increasingly "modular" with each standard parts and components being purchased from open markets and to be assembled and configured in various ways.

Additionally, many formerly Integrated Device Manufacturers (IDMs) began to focus only on narrow filed of the value chain, mostly design and production development or marketing, and became "fabless"[49] by getting rid of all manufacturing functions. They increasingly sub-divided their business to new branches or subsidiary firms. Many IDMs outsource or subcontract service and production to suppliers, or sometimes set up logistics service companies within the same corporation group. Many of them also began producing in regions with lower wages, more disciplined labor or looser regulations.

Furthermore, the outsourcing of previously-integrated manufacturing processes, as opposed to the outsourcing of parts and components production in the automobile industry, has enabled Electronics Manufacturing Service (EMS) companies, such as Foxconn and Flextronics, to become the largest manufacturing companies in the industry. This new type of subcontracting networks proliferated in the 1990s, which is now called "contract manufacturers". They provide integrated manufacturing services for brand-name companies, including all elements of manufacturing from product engineering, assembly, configuration, to distribution logistics and repair services (Lüthje 2002). Acting as transnational "network builders", they have increasingly become the centerpiece of globalized production networks. Either through building gigantic industrial parks or through integrating various mid-sized plants

49 "Fabless" describes semiconductor companies without their own factories. Many semiconductor brand names got rid of the fabrication of chips, thereby becoming the first to separate the design of chips from their manufacture.

in one region, contract manufacturers have become the core of the "re-integration" of manufacturing, though they generally operate without the same brand recognition as their clients. At the bottom, traditional small-scaled subcontractors continue to exist as suppliers of cheap standardized parts for contract manufacturers and brand-name companies.

In a word, whereas the automobile industry can be divided into two parts: whole-car makers and parts suppliers, the picture of the electronics industry is much more complex. Due to massive vertical dis-integration and "re-integration" from below, there is a wide range of electronics enterprises: IDMs, "fabless" design firms, small- and medium-sized parts suppliers, and contract manufacturers. In addition, quite a number of start-up companies, with enormous investment from venture capital, play an important role in developing cutting-edge technologies for certain components or market niches. Noticeably, the number of venture capitalists in the technological revolution has led to speculative investments among countless competitors. Compared to the relatively stable auto industry, there is more uncertainty within the complex electronics industry. Such differences account for the diverse patterns in the labor movement and industrial relations of the two industries.

In China, the segmentations of the automobile and electronics industries at global level continues. The two industries are leading the way in the industrialization process, not only in terms of economic growth, but also in the development of industrial relations.

First of all, manufacturing continues to be the dominant sector in the global economy, especially in China. As Moody (1997: 47) argues, globalization is anything but a "post-industrial" process, as the proportion of manufactured products in total merchandise trade has risen from 52% in 1952 to 73% in 1988. Although services surpassed goods in total trade since the late 1980s, the alleged drive toward a post-industrial world is still urged by the industry itself (e.g. Dicken 1998). As China serves as the "world factory", the proportions of industry and of manufacturing in the national economy are even more significant. In terms of the Gross Domestic Product (GDP), from 1978 to 2008 the proportion of the secondary industry remained more than 40% (See table 1). Since 2000, the percentage of industry (or manufacturing) in GDP has slightly increased, along with the proportion of manufacturing-related service in the tertiary industry. Moreover, the secondary industry alone employs 21.1 million workers, which account for 27.2% of the national workforce in 2008. The majority, about 90% of those employees, remain in manufacturing, according to the second national economic survey of China in 2009.

The automobile and electronics industries have been two key pillars of manufacturing in China since the reform. According to the 2009 statistics yearbook of the National Bureau of Statistics (See Table 2), there were 76,000 and 132,000 enterprises with legal entity in transportation vehicle manufacturing and electronics manufacturing in 2008.[50] Besides, the two industries had 5.773 million and 13.236 million employees respectively.[51] At the same time, the industrial outputs of both industries in 2009 are 6.6% and 14.6% of the national sum, and capital assets are 7.2% and 11.1%. In 2008, major automobile enterprises had a fixed capital of 1184.688 billion RMB, and those in the electronics industry had 1927.292 billion RMB. In addition, the development of one industry also brought "spillovers" to the rest of the economy. For instance, in 2001 the automobile industry alone accounted for 5% of employment in manufacturing and 6.1% value added[52]. According to national statistics, the production of each car create on average 2.5 jobs in China.

Moreover, the outputs and sales of both industries have expanded rapidly in the last decades. Until the end of 2003, the annual production of autos had been 30 times of that in 1978, according to the Almanac of China's Automotive Industry 2005. According to the second national economic survey, a total of 9.306 million automobiles were produced in 2008, including 5.038 million passenger cars. In terms of domestic sales, from 2002 to 2006, the average annual increase of auto sales was more than 36%. During the global financial crisis in 2008 and 2009, auto makers continued to expand turning China into the largest auto market in the world in 2009. This expansion created a new global record of more than 18 million cars produced and sold in 2010.[53] The sum of auto output and sales reached 13 million for the first time. In addition, the market is likely to grow further as the GDP per capita in many cities of China has reached 3000 US$.[54] More than 80% of cars are now sold for private use.

---

50 Data are quoted from the No. 2 report of the Second National Economic Survey, released on Dec. 25, 2009 by the survey group of the State Council and the National Bureau of Statistics. In the categories of the statistics, "transportation vehicle industry" stand for automobile industry, at the same time, electronics industry is the combination of the "electric machinery and equipment manufacturing" and "telecommunication, computers and other electronic equipment manufacturing".

51 For automobile industry, if calculating its supplying sectors, such as steel and rubber, the total relevant workforce will be 20 times more. E.g. In 2002, there were 1.57 million employed by the automobile industry, and 31.9 million workers by all relevant sectors.

52 It also demanded 5-6% of the total steel production, 80-90% of petroleum, 14-16% machine tools, 50% of tempered glass, 45% of tire, 15% of engineered plastics , and 15% of paint (CATARC, 2001).

53 The Ministry of Industry and Information Technology of the People's Republic of China, 2010 Report on the Economy of the Automobile industry, January 18, 2011

54 According to the experiences in industrialized countries, as the GDP per capita is between 3,000 to 10,000 US$, the consumption on cars increases the fastest.

Thus it is reasonable to expect growths in private auto consumption if incomes increase among ordinar households.

At the same time, in the electronics industry, value added from 2000 to 2006 increased from 184.5 to 722.9 billion RMB, nearly fourfold (See table 3). The statistics from the Ministry of Industry and Information Technology show that in 2010, 998 million cell phones, 246 million PC, 118 million color TV, and 90 million digital cameras were produced. In terms of sales, in 2010, electronics companies above designated size[55] had a revenue of 78 trillion RMB, a 29.5% increase from 2009. Particularly, electronics manufacturing above designated size had 16.9% growth in industrial value added and 25.5% increase in sales.[56]

Since the 1950s, the Chinese state has been making great efforts to develop the Chinese automobile industry. In the beginning, the former Soviet Union supported China in developing the industry. The First Auto Works (FAW) was thus founded in 1953. After the breakup between China and Soviet Union, the Dongfeng Auto Group (formerly the Second Auto Works) was established in Hubei Province in 1969. By the middle of the 1960s, five automobile factories had been built and several models were put into production. Nevertheless, up to the end of the 1970s, the major focus had been on large, heavy or special-purposed vehicles, such as trucks, lorries and jeeps. In a word, the early efforts of the state were politically-oriented to display the advantages of Socialism in industrialization, which featured the emphasis on heavy vehicles rather than passenger cars.

Expansion of the industry occurred only after the implementation of the reform and open-up policy in 1978, marking the beginning of decentralized policies. The government continued to list the auto industry as a pillar industry of the national economy. However, the intervention of the government through industrial policies and regulations remained strong in spite of the abandonment of direct command. Since 1978, several policies paved the way of industrial development. In 1986, the central government shifted from the strategy of self-sufficient and specific-import (producing domestically to meet its own needs and only importing specific types of vehicles from other countries) to the cross-border import-substitution one, marking the start of macro level coordination by central authorities. In 1992, the government began to promote large-scale restructuring of the industry to create economies of scale, a move that was reflected in the 1994 auto industrial policy promulgated by the state council.

---

55 A term in Chinese statistics, which means enterprises with an annual sales over 5 million RMB

56 The Ministry of Industry and Information Technology of the People's Republic of China, 2010 Report on the Economy of the Automobile industry, January 18, 2011

Again, in 1998 state-guided mergers and takeovers created a "national team" of auto makers. Until 2003, 80% of the government investment had been used in 13 large enterprises, and the three corporation groups - FAW, Dongfeng and SAIC Motor- had concentrated more than 70% of car production (Xu 2003). During this phase, there was a new wave of equipment modernization and technological innovations, mainly through the implementation of international production standards. In the 1990s, the total number of automobiles produced in China grew ten-fold. After years of integration and expansion, there was a severe overcapacity of production. China today is committed to expanding exports.

Similarly, the electronics industry also benefited from government support. This industry underwent growths and down-turns due to political disturbances before 1976. The boom came after 1978, particularly in the late 1990s and the early twenty-first century. Back then, only a handful of former SOEs produced television and small-sized home appliances. The period from 1977 to 1982 was a transition period for important industrial adjustment policies, although industrial growth continued to fluctuate. Afterwards, it experienced an explosive growth rate. Similar to the auto industry, the electronics industry also went through a transition from military use toward market-oriented civil products (e.g. color TV project in 1984). Because of this policy shift and the economic reform, the electronic industry developed higher quantity and quality of parts in the 1980s. The high dependence on color TVs finally changed in the early of 1990s as the telecommunication and computer sectors boomed at 40-50% annual growth rates. In the mid-1990s, the strong emphasis of the government on electronic and information project accelerated the production of the electronics components. During this period, foreign equipments and investment were first permitted to enter the domestic industry, which soon bolstered the industry. In spite of the 1997 Asian financial crisis and global recession in the early 2000s, the industry has grown at an annual growth rate of higher than 25%, according to the Electronics Industry Yearbook of China. So far, the industry clusters around the Yangtz River Delta (YRD) and Pearl River Delta (PRD) with continuous policy and research support from the government. At the same time, China has become the world largest markets for computers, telecommunication equipments, consumer electronics, and networking facilities. Indeed, China slowly integrated itself into the global electronics industry, while in the process rapidly developed its own domestic industries.

In recent years, support from the Chinese state remains strong in both industries. In the automobile industry, for instance, one major program in the huge government "rescue package" is to cut car purchase taxes and to provide easy credit and incentives for developing low-emission and clean energy-powered cars in order to stimulate domestic consumption in the 2008/2009 crisis. Similarly, the long-term development of "TD-SCDMA", the 3G telecommunication standards, would be impossible without the backing up of the government both financially and technologically.

At present, both automobile and electronics industries feature a mixture of public, private and foreign enterprises. It is estimated that about 70% of the national economy now relies upon the private sector, which is greater share than those of some European countries. Along with the deepening of economic reform, restrictions on foreign investment have been loosened gradually. Government attention has also increasingly focused upon high-tech FDIs. However, there are different ownership structures in the two industries, particularly the role of FDI and foreign firms.

In the automobile industry, FDI plays an essential role. At the top, auto assembly is now dominated by foreign-sino joint ventures, which require that the local enterprises own at least 50% of shares. There are core members of FAW, Dongfeng, SAIC Motor and Changan groups, and another nine major producers including Guangzhou Honda. According to government policies, a foreign auto maker can have at most two joint ventures in mainland China. As early as in 1983, an American auto maker and Beijing Automobile manufacturer set up the first joint venture - "Beijing Jeep". Following this step, many global auto makers began to set up joint ventures in China, particularly after Deng's south tour in 1992.[57] For instance, VW has joint ventures with both FAW and SAIC Motor, and Toyota has also two joint ventures - FAW-Toyota and Guangqi-Toyota. Honda has both Guangzhou Honda and Dongfeng-Honda, and a whole-car factory in Guangzhou that exports all its products, which is not restrained by the quota. On the Chinese side, the structure is more complicated. Since 1984, SAIC Motor has established joint ventures with auto makers from Germany, U.S., Japan, UK, France, Italy, etc. In the case of Dongfeng, it has joint ventures with Citroen, Peugeot, Nissan, Honda, Kia, etc..

By now, major global players have all established their presence in China and competed fiercely on the fast growing domestic market. Essentially, the automobile industry mainly produces nationalized models for mass consumption in the domestic market. In 2010, 544,900 cars were exported, a very small proportion in comparison to the national output of 18.26 million and sales of 18.06 million in the domestic market.[58] The joint ventures mostly use the brands

57 Deng, Xiaoping's tour to southern China marked the beginning of a new era that market economy and private property had been ultimately confirmed and ideologically justified in China.

58 The Ministry of Industry and Information Technology of the People's Republic of China, 2010 Report on the Economy of the Automobile industry, January 18, 2011

and models from the foreign side, then produce and sell them in China. Some specific designs of these models such as the length of cars may change by following Chinese consumers' preference. As a whole, the overseas brands accounted for more than two thirds of total domestic market shares.[59]

Favorable FDI policies, such as two-year exemption and three-year reduction on taxes for sino-foreign joint ventures and foreign-owned firms, reflect the government strategy of using investment as a means of economic development. At the same time, there are also restrictive policies. Firstly, policies require a local content requirement of production. The government expects a spill-over effect on the domestic industry which can benefit local businesses. Besides, the maximum-equity regulation implies that MNCs can not develop vehicle assembly and engine manufacturing in China in forms of takeover or branch plants. In addition, the joint-venture structure forces the FDI to subject to Chinese corporative rules and management policies. Debatingly, such regulations may grant workers better wages and welfare. Whereas the production and technologies have been adapted to international standards, the style of personnel management remains highly characterized by Chinese SOE-style management practices.

Compared to joint ventures, domestic producers largely lag behind these leading joint ventures in technologies and in the global market. While foreign investors exchange technologies for a piece of the Chinese market, several local brands have gradually become whole car makers, such as Chery, Geely, and BYD. However, the auto industry constantly develops new technologies in safety, pollution control, energy-saving, etc.. Thus, although the continuous absorption of foreign investment and technologies has led to a better manufacturing capacity of Chinese automobile industry, the gap between domestic producers and global brand names continues to grow. On the one hand, domestic firms depend on direct imitation of foreign technologies, but for a long time, the technologies provided by foreign partners in joint ventures have been mostly out of date due to the concern of technology-sharing by the foreign side. On the other hand, the national investment and policy support on R&D are insufficient so that national R&D centers are developing very slow. Besides, domestic enterprises are often too small-scaled to highly invest on R&D (Xu 2003). Therefore, they depend on foreign technologies because of their weak ability of independent development. This fact further lowers the possibility for them to cultivate such ability. So far domestic automakers have just started to enter the global market. Chery and Geely started working on their own brands in 2003, and more powerful state-owned auto groups quickly followed suit. In fact,

59 For instance, foreign JVs accounted for 78% market share in 2006, 81% in 2000

their target of lower end smaller cars proves to be successful. Since the government canceled restrictions on the production of small cars and the fuel price rose in 2006, all domestic brands benefited from the policies. Together they accounted for 26% of the domestic market, for the first time exceeding the shares of German, Japanese or other foreign brands.[60] In 2009, sales of private companies, such as Chery, Geely, BYD, Brilliance Auto and Great Wall, topped 4.58 million, 44% of nationwide sales and up 4 percentage points from 2008. However, their total exports in the first eight months of 2009 were no more than 200,000 cars, mostly to low-end markets in Algeria, Vietnam and Syria:[61]

In spite of the leapfrogging effect[62] in the short term, overdependence on foreign technologies and assembly-type of industrial development should be transferred to a new model that introduce and absorb foreign technologies and further develop and innovate independently (Ma 2005). This model has been proved successful in Japan and South Korea based on careful planning by the government. Both countries began to develop domestic auto industries through introducing and absorbing foreign technologies and 20 years later the governments encouraged the domestic industry to innovate technologies and create national brands. By 1980s and 1990s, automakers in Japan and South Korea became the leading players in the global auto industry. In fact, there are also plenty of successful cases in China following the same model, such as color TV and recently the TD-SCDMA 3G project in the electronics industry. Therefore, it is important for the government not only to establish higher standards to make the technological transfer possible, but it must also provide the favorable policies, necessary infrastructure, and technological support to domestic enterprises in order to facilitate their R&D and brand-creating activities. As an exemplary case, the Ministry of Science and Technology is investing in the hybrid-electric or fuel-cell vehicles. A few local producers have begun actively to engage in the new fields. Recently, as the global automobile industry undergone economic restructuring, Chinese automakers also relied on

---

60 China Industry Annual Report 2007 - automobile, State Information Center, http://ar.cei.gov.cn/web/Column.asp?CId3=292

61 Sohu Auto, Who will become the biggest auto enterprise, different situations in global markets., Nov. 19, 2009

62 The concept of "Leapfrogging": (Goldemberg 1998) industrializing countries can avoid the resource-intensive pattern of economic and energy development by leapfrogging to the most advanced energy technologies available, rather than following the same path of conventional energy development that was forged by the highly industrialized countries. Generally speaking, there are two types of "leapfrogging", either by skipping over generations of technologies, or not only skipping over generations, but also leaping further ahead to become the technological leader. See: Gallagher 2006

acquisitions to build product lines and to expand their manufacturing capacity, a case exemplified by Geely's decision to buy Volvo. Although domestic brands are still competing on a price basis with foreign cars, one day they may be able to close the skill and technological gaps with support from the government and qualified professional personnel returning from overseas.

Another important part of the automobile industry is the parts and components suppliers. According to statistics gathered in 2004, auto parts accounted for 21.3% of 946.3 billion RMB, the total output value of the automobile industry (See Table 4). As a whole, the auto parts sector is low-priced, small-scaled, and rather dispersed. In recent years, the tendency of production decentralization and a spatial shift toward coastal regions, with the strategic support of local governments, has resulted in several clusters of suppliers surrounding major whole-car makers. For instance, the YRD has formed a well-supported cluster of parts supply. In 2004, more than 30% of the output value in the Shanghai automobile industry came from auto parts, and this percentage in Zhejiang even reached to 60.7% (See Table 4). Comparatively, both the traditional industrial base of North East China and the newer center of Guangdong are less developed in auto parts. Guangdong, with the presence of three Japanese auto makers, had only more than 10 enterprises among China's top 100 auto parts makers in 2004. Since the Japanese auto makers are keen on increasing the ratio of local production and sourcing of parts and components, the next step for the region is to attract and to accommodate auto parts players.[63]

In contrast, the ownership structure of the electronics industry is highly mixed, whch includes SOEs, COEs (collectively-owned enterprises), shareholding enterprises, foreign- or Hong Kong-, Taiwan- and Macao-invested enterprises, etc. There is no dominant type of enterprises, such as the assembly joint ventures in the automobile industry. Noticeably, only since the mid-1990s, have FDI and foreign enterprises begun to enter China, albeit at a highly accelerated speed. By 2010, the revenue of domestic firms only accounted for 27.6% of the total industrial revenue. The target of the foreign electronics producers, in contrast to the automobile industry, focuses not only on the domestic market but also on exports. This industry is the largest export sector for China, in spite of a huge and booming domestic market. For example, the 2010 exports of electronic manufacturing products was 5.912 trillion US$, accounted for 37.5% of national exports.[64] Geographically, Eastern China used

63 The Greater Pearl River Delta Business Council, Industrial Restructuring in Guangdong Task Group, Report on Guangdong's Industrial Restructuring - Opportunities and Challenges for Hong Kong, June 2006

64 The Ministry of Industry and Information Technology of the People's Republic of China, 2010 Report on the Economy of the Electronics and IT industry, February 11, 2011

to be the most developed (e.g. 370.5 billion RMB investment in 2010), but Central and Western China are catching up rapidly, with the investment of 164.5 billion RMB and 64.3 billion RMB respectively. Moreover, the revenue and sales of enterprises above designated scale in Central China had grown 42.5% and 80.4%, and 46.6% and 55.8% in West China, in comparison to 27.3% and 51.8% in the East. As many enterprises are "going inland", provinces next to developed coastal areas, such as Anhui, Jiangxi, Henan, and Guangxi, had more than 35% increases in sales and output. In particular, Sichuan and Chongqing, in West China, increased 49.6% and 74.4% in sales.[65]

At the top of the value chain, many global brand-name companies have set up subsidiaries in China through FDI or outsource for lower-end manufacturing processes, but the foreign side largely controls R&D, design and brand marketing. In 2005, 88% of high-tech exports were made by foreign-invested enterprises. Since many traditional IDMs have gotten ride of manufacturing by spinning-off or downsizing in the past few decades, their branches in China often specialize in defined market niches. Following this trend, contract manufacturers have also emerged, who attempt to re-integrate the manufacturing process. The leading ones are mostly from Taiwan or America and have established gigantic industrial parks or factories in low-cost countries like China. However, there is one paradox: whereas they are highly capital-intensive and integrated, their workplaces are featured by de-skilled work, Taylorist division of labor and very low wages. Moreover, the domestic electronics firms, compared to the auto makers, have benefited more from FDI and foreign-invested enterprises than the auto industry. Successful development of capabilities and transfer of technologies have resulted from international networks of cooperation and competition. In particular, the capacity of rapid learning among leading Chinese companies enables them to catch up. In the research of Ernst and Naughton (2008), second tier enterprises in China, composed by former local state-owned, foreign-invested enterprises or domestic start-ups, dominate in the electronics industry. Among the top 100 IT enterprises in 2008 ranked by the Ministry of Industry and Information, Lenovo ranked number one with a total revenue of 146.2 billion RMB in 2007. In terms of profits and R&D investment, Huawei was the No. 1.[66] Rather than the "radical" innovation strategy of the government, they succeed in architectural or

65 The Ministry of Industry and Information of China, 2010 Official Report on the Electronics and Information Industry, Feb. 22, 2011, http://www.miit.gov.cn/n1129347 2/n11293832/n11294132/n12858462/13593391.html

66 China Electronics News, 100 leading enterprises in electronics and IT - Huawei, Haier and Founder rank the top 3, Nov. 11, 2008, http://www.cena.com.cn/Article/yaowen/ 2008-11-11/20081111104942_13843.shtml

incremental innovation.[67] Moreover, many smaller and entrepreneurial high-tech start-up firms, especially in the semiconductor industry, play a significant role. They are typically founded by Chinese returnees from the U.S., modeled on Silicon Valley and focus on a narrow market niche. Consequently, their management style and labor relations assemble many specialized brand name companies from the West to a certain extent. In addition, there are numerous small- and medium-sized suppliers, often the second- or third-tier parts suppliers or subcontractors, operating at low-tech, low-margin and labor-intensive basis. For instance, the PRD is dominated by Original Equipment Manufacturer (OEM). The local government has attempted to transform those OEMs toward Original Design Manufacture (ODM) or Original Brand Manufacture (OBM), which have more content of independent design or brand than OEMs, or to realize economies of scale through the establishment of clusters (Hu et al. 2005). In 2001, locations with the largest numbers of electronic employees are Guangdong, Jiangsu, Shanghai, Zhejiang, and Beijing.[68]

In a word, the automobile and electronics industries are representative of intensified industrial development in China. Similar to the global scenario, the major difference between the two is the vertically-integration of production among core automakers, and the disintegration and vertical re-integration by contract manufacturers in the electronics industry. This has created a contrasting picture of a top auto assembler-dominated value chain and a great diversity of electronics enterprises. This explains why the 2008/2009 global financial/economic crisis greatly affected the electronics industry. More importantly, such difference has profound impacts in the areas of industrial relations, such as labor standards and collective bargaining.

---

67 In the case of Huawei, while improving the cost, time-to-market, and performance aspects, it has developed equipment and solution packages that under-perform relative to established products in mainstream markets but satisfy the essential needs of operators at much lower cost. The strategic geographic expansion of Huawei also creates a successful path for other Chinese MNCs, firstly toward Southeast Asia, then Russian and Africa, and lastly Europe. See: Ernst and Naugthon 2008: 51

68 In 2001, the annual average numbers of the workforce in electronics and communication equipment manufacturing enterprises were 634009 in Guangdong, 207896 in Jiangsu, 114596 in Shanghai, 114496 in Zhejiang, and 70314 in Beijing. See: China Statistics Yearbook on High Technology Industry, 2002

3.2 Production regimes

The regimes of production at factory level are one of the key factors that impact the formation and functioning of collective bargaining, as proved in the labor history of the U.S. and Germany. Proper wage regulation and collective bargaining may normalize labor-capital interaction. At present, a variety of production regimes have emerged in China, combined with special configurations of local management styles and labor relations. The trends such as vertical disintegration and flexibilization of production and staffing are similar to the global level. Production regimes in the automobile industry are relatively homogeneous, especially among whole-car makers, whereas the electronics industry has highly diversified production regimes due to the trends of disintegration and vertical re-integration from below. Particularly, the latter trend has resulted in the emergence of contract manufacturers in China, which serves as the testing ground for this production model. Besides, the two industries in China also have specific features, such as the ownership structure and distinctive role of FDI, which have different impacts on industrial relations.

Accordingly, in order to analyze the problems and future prospects of collective bargaining in China, I examine the various production regimes including the models of production, work organization, wages, collective labor relations, etc.[69] The investigation is done among ten auto companies and sixteen electronics firms in three industrial clusters - the Beijing area, the Yangtz River Delta (centered on Shanghai, Suzhou and Nanjing), and the Pearl River Delta (mainly Guangzhou, Dongguan, Foshan, etc.). Representative cases are selected, including those from Europe, U.S., China and other part of East Asia. With a focus on the production regimes and modes of regulations, the major findings are summarized as below. All information is gathered from interviews, public sources and investigations I collected from the field. It should be noted that due to the limitations of research access and funds, the samples may neither be the most representative nor comprehensive description of the situations in China. The main purpose is to illuminate one perspective on production regimes using available resources among two leading industries in China.

3.2.1 The automobile industry

Production processes, work organization, management methods, and labor relations among whole-car makers, especially foreign-sino joint ventures, have

69 The field study is jointly conducted with another research project. The typology and case studies of individual factories have been published: Lüthje, Luo and Zhang, 2013

substantial influence on the rest of the industry. Independent domestic auto makers attempt to adopt the level of technologies and production processes of those joint ventures. However, management methods and labor standards in these joint ventures and domestic auto makers differ according to their locations, ownership forms, government intervention policies, and the influence of foreign investors. Along the lower levels of the value chain, there is a more complex structure. The first- or second-tier suppliers, mostly in the form of foreign MNCs or joint-ventures, have relatively modern production but lower labor standards than whole-car makers, while small- and medium-sized subcontractors at the bottom resemble the "classic" model of sweatshops.

The whole-car makers

The dominant production regime, as indicated in almost every major whole-car joint venture, follows the "corporate bureaucratic regime".[70] Since the industry' development for more than a century, the production has become largely standardized among major players.[71] In my survey, all auto makers from the U.S., Europe, and East Asia are equipped with world-class facilities, machinery, and technological processes. In particular, newer factories are more integrated with up-to-date rationalization concepts than older ones. For instance, they have single-floored factories that facilitate work flow and just-in-time delivery. They have multi-model production lines or flexible production systems[72] which produce cars with different designs and colors along a single assembly line. The emphasis on both quality and productivity is common among enterprises. Nevertheless, among leading European auto makers, the level of automation is usually higher, for the purpose of precision and quality control. At the same time, it can lower the physical intensity or overhead work among workers in some positions. In general, the level of manual work is higher in Chinese factories than in the foreign countries of origin, because the low labor costs and the large

70 For a detailed typology of regimes of production, please see appendix B.

71 The life cycle of products includes: the innovative stage, the stage of maturity and final standardization. Auto production was innovated by Ford in 1913; matured in Europe in the 1960s/70s; and standardized among NICs in the 1980s/90s. See: Silver 2003: 77

72 Flexible production systems are designed to automate multiple product line manufacturing, by intensifying and automating manufacturing processes; coordinating the automated processes involved in warehousing and materials transport to maintain a tight production path; and using computers to automate production preparation and production control. There are three types of flexible production systems: flexible automated lines; flexible production modules; and flexible production complexes

scale of the Chinese workforce enable flexibility in production and work processes.

The production capacities of whole-car joint ventures have expanded rapidly since their establishment (e.g. more than 12 folds in one Japanese auto makers in the last decade). With the exception of one or two export-only factories in a given industrial cluster, major factories target the massive domestic market. This was the major reason that in 2008 and 2009, production flows of most auto makers, particularly those with large shares in the domestic market, were stable. The only exception was one high-end producer from Europe, which underwent major restructuring. The domestic market has been growing particularly through favorable policies by the governments during the economic crisis of 2008. However, the crisis caused certain degree of fluctuation of employment in this industry. Before the Labor Contract Law took effect in 2008, many of these joint ventures used large proportions of temporary workers from dispatch agencies. If the production reduced due to shrinking orders, dispatched workers may be returned by joint ventures to agencies any time without any compensation to the workers. Nevertheless, because these temporary workers were not officially counted as the workforce of the joint ventures, this part of information for the period was not disclosed.

By far, joint ventures have provided a wide range of products, from economic cars to middle- and high-end ones. Most have established highly integrated production in their Chinese factories, ranging from stamping, body shop, manufacturing of engine blocks and gears, and the various stages of the car assembly processes, etc.. The only exception was a European-Sino joint venture, which has been confined to the assembly of completely knock-down (CKD) parts imported from Europe before 2010. In 2010, it announced that it would start fully integrated manufacturing in China. Nevertheless, the degrees of localization of parts and components manufacturing are different. Older joint ventures, especially one from Europe and one from Japan, have realized a high ratio of localization of parts production and even introduced new car models developed by local engineers. These two joint ventures ranked top sales in Chinese market. In other companies, engineers mainly engage in processing and maintenance work, but several R&D centers for new products have also been planned in the next few years. In a word, localized production and R&D are increasingly popular among Chinese enterprises, and will continue to do so in the near future.

Another distinctive similarity among those auto makers is the widespread application of lean production methods. Lean production instituted among many Japanese factories, particularly in newer factories established in the last decade. This model emphasizes flexibility and efficiency, namely just-in-time delivery of parts and components. Just-in-time delivery aims to reduce in-process inventory and associated carrying costs through signals or (kanban) between different points in the process, which tell production when to make the next part. It also features Andon line-control panels including the famous stop-button with which workers can stop the line, continuous improvement processes (kaizen), and moving parts supply bins along the assembly line, enabling workers to perform tasks while walking along the line. These features are also integrated among Western factories.

Nevertheless, some key concepts specific to lean production, which are supposed to set it apart from Taylorism, are less emphasized in practice, especially in Western factories. Most factories adopt the concept of work teams and groups. However, the team organization does not include any substantial features of self-directed group work. The actual functions are attendance check and holding meetings to discuss quality control and improvement. Only in several Japanese factories, there is a limited amount of job rotation within work teams. However, standardization remains the primary focus, and the possibility of job rotation is under the discretion of the group leaders. At the same time, the division between line workers and technicians seems less strict among Japanese factories than Western ones. For instance, preventive maintenance is often conducted by line workers in Japanese factories. In addition, the Continuous Improvement Program (CIP) collects suggestions of workers or work groups about production problems. In particular, some Western companies integrate CIP with industrial engineering in order to further rationalize production. Meanwhile, individual line workers may conduct one or more tasks, but their tasks are simplified and segmented. The tasks may be clearly described by standard work specifications at each position along the production line, which ensures the flexibility of line managers to easily substitute the work of any laborer. No substantial evidence is found to prove any intention of companies to create broadly skilled and relatively autonomous craft workers. As a whole, in spite of slightly different practices, the design of work organizations in all auto makers is highly standardized and intensified, and aims at high efficiency and cost-savings.

As for integration at the industrial level, the principle of outsourcing and subcontracting in lean production has become common practice. Service work in nearly all factories, including canteens, cleaning and security, has been outsourced to external firms. More importantly, the production of certain parts and components is outsourced from first-tier to second- and third-tier suppliers along the supply chain. A relatively new concept of "modular production" has become popular among newer factories. Before final assembly is conducted by the whole-car makers, all parts in a module have been produced and packed together so that all modules could be quickly assembled at the final stage. In China, hundreds of parts and components suppliers with different scales and technological levels have been emerging along with top auto makers. In a Japanese company, 72% of the outsourced parts and components are made in China and more than 50% are produced in the nearby area. As the tradition of Japanese companies, the key or high-end components, such as engines, are manufactured by suppliers co-owned by the foreign mother companies or joint ventures. In most Western companies, the selection of outsourcing partners is more flexible, although they tend to cooperate with local branches of well-established parts and components enterprises back in their home countries.

As for the workforce, whole-car makers mainly recruit operators or line workers from junior colleges and technical secondary schools. They are in oversupply, according to most interviewees. For this reason, finding skilled technicians and experienced engineer is relatively difficult, especially for non-Japanese companies that have a weaker tradition of recruiting fresh graduates through in-house training and promotion. Although the majority of manufacturing workers in joint ventures are urban-based male technical school graduates. Workers who are employed by factories built on the places of former SOEs often has an older average age than others. The reason is these factories often absorb a part of former SOE workers, who have already years of working experiences. In contrast, the majority of workers in Japanese factories are in their early twenties. Even within older factories, most worker are between 20 to 40 years of age. Moreover, dispatched workers, who are mainly comprised of migrant workers and new graduates from technical schools, work along production lines (e.g. 30% of all workforce in an European-Sino auto maker) in large numbers, particularly in SOEs. The wide use of dispatched labor not only directly reduces labor costs and responsibilities of the host companies, but it also deducts taxes by shifting labor costs into the accounting category of operation costs. Those workers are similar to their counterparts in other countries in regards to their low-pay and vulnerable to the fluctuations of labor market demands. In spite of doing the same work as regular employees, temporary or dispatched workers receive only legal minimum wages and thus have to work overtime (OT) in order to receive an extra pay. They are excluded from training programs and insurances coverage paid by the enterprises they work. Besides, in economic slowdowns, they may be returned back to the labor agencies anytime without compensation. Since the 2008 Labor Contract Law took effect, legally speaking, dispatched workers should be paid the same as regular workers for the same work. In top auto makers, the practice has been modified accordingly. Some begin to sign a longer-term contract with dispatched workers (e.g. two years), and others choose to only hire regular workers. However, the reality of most auto suppliers is far less promising.

Working conditions in factories of whole-car makers are relatively good. The workshops are clean and modern, but the labor intensity is generally very high. Extensive training system is implemented in order to improve the efficiency of work and technological flows. Training does not increase the wages of the employees automatically. Usually work intensity and individual competition are compensated by stable wages and comprehensive social benefits. The compensation system is based on the evaluation of workers' position and ability. For companies from Europe, position-based wages are common, and positions are assigned according to skills. In Japanese-sino joint ventures, wage systems follow the Japanese tradition whereby wages are determined by administrative levels and posts. Almost all new employees are in the same wage bracket which may change according to their performance. What is common for all Japanese and Western companies is that the regular base wages make up the major proportion of the total compensation, while the flexible part, usually including performance-based incentives and OT pay, accounts for less than 30% of annual income. Performance-based incentives account for a relatively small proportion in the Chinese context, though it is still bigger than that of their home countries. OT pay is extra but it tends to be low since major companies follow the restrictions of OT hours in national labor laws. The only exception is that the annual bonuses in a few Japanese and Western companies could be very high, which range from five months to more than ten months of regular wages. Moreover, seniority wage is now regarded as the hallmark of SOE tradition and has been replaced or combined with other long-term benefits, including pension. In general, the wage levels for workers with three to five years experience are a little higher than the local average wages. This is one major reason why the average turnover rates of operators in whole-car factories are very low.

Furthermore, other labor standards in all major joint ventures meet the minimal legal requirements. For instance, OT is limited to two hours per day and often there are short breaks in the morning and afternoon respectively. Five working days and two days of rest every week are usually followed, but workers during busy seasons need to work on Saturdays. In addition, social welfare is good too, which includes the social security programs - five basic insurances and one housing provident fund, and also complementary insurances, such as pension and medical care. In addition, there are other allowances such as festival payment, food and transportation subsidies. Since most workers are urban-based, shuttle buses allow workers to commute from other parts of the cities. In South China, free dormitories are provided in one or two cases for non-local production workers, and university graduates share well-furnished flats at low prices. In particular, most offer car-related subsidies and quota for purchasing cars come big discounts. However, for many line workers, it is still not possible for them to afford the very cars that they make with the wages that they earn.

Among all major auto makers, wages and other labor standards are not determined through collective bargaining, even with the presence of well-established trade unions or institutionalized collective bargaining in their home countries. Neither the German model of sectoral contract nor the model of single-company bargaining in the U.S. is visible. Wage standards have never appeared in collective contracts in China. In fact, wage grades and categories exist, but only as the concern of human resource management. Furthermore, there are no Fordist wage norms. Wage levels are determined in reference to market surveys by third-party consulting firms (e.g. different wage levels for the categories of first-tier cities, second-tier cities and so on), and the cost-of-living and wage guidelines established by local governments. As for individual employees, their starting wages are decided during the recruitment process, mainly based on technical skill and work experience. A certain percentage of well-performed employees may get wage raises based on their performance appraisals.

Since the most important labor standards are determined by management on an individual base, the function of collective bargaining and collective contracts is questionable. In practice, trade unions and communist party committees are well-established in all joint ventures, thanks to the SOE tradition. There are even trade union committees, branch unions and union groups in each department. However, in some cases, union officials hold management titles simultaneously. As typical SOE trade unions under the ACFTU leadership, one of their main targets is to carry forth "harmonious labor relations" in companies. For instance, a European company was continuously awarded city-level and national prizes for achieving such harmonious relations. On paper, the formal work of trade unions includes the following ten tasks: helping employees sign labor contracts, negotiating collective contracts, assisting workers in labor arbitration, mediating labor disputes within the company, occupational training, monitoring the enforcement of the law, inspecting work safety and health, intervening in case of risky working conditions, investigating violations of workers' rights, and negotiating with the employer in the case of strikes. In practice, the relationship between trade unions and management is very cooperative. Trade unions actively participate in production improvement programs. In some European companies, trade unions claim a good communication with unions in foreign mother companies.

In fact, collective contracts are signed by individual establishments. As early as in 1985, a European-sino car maker had initially signed collective contracts with its trade union. Usually, collective contracts are signed every two or three years, sometimes in Chinese and in English. Also, enforcement is reviewed by both parties every year. Nevertheless, the procedures of reaching those collective contracts do not contain real “bargaining”. Normally, HR departments draft the collective contract and send it to trade unions. Then trade unions collect suggestions and comments of workers, make revisions accordingly, and send the reports back to the HR departments. Both parties sign the draft if they agree to. In separate cases, official negotiations and informal discussions are held by representatives among laborers and capitalists. Normally, collective contracts only apply to regular workers of the company.

Collective contracts do not substantial clauses on wages or other labor standards. The content of existing collective contracts is usually general. In many cases, the specifications on working time, occupational safety and health, etc., merely reflect legal standards. As for wages, the principle, structure, and sometimes pay grades are written, but there are no specific data for each work category in any of the collective contracts that are available from the joint ventures. The exact figures of wages are only written in the individual employment contracts. In one collective contract, it is written that “the wage system of the company should be implemented, as they are designed by the human resource department”. At best, another collective contract states that “when the profitability of the company is good, wages should be increased; when it is not or in deficit, wages should not be reduced”. Festival bonuses and some minor benefits are specified in only two cases.

There are many reasons for the absence of substantial figures in collective contracts. From the perspective of HR managers in Japanese and Western joint ventures, a fixed increase may not be able to realized for years with low profit margins. In practice, the administration decides the wage system, and wage increases rely on the profit conditions of the company in the specific year. The flexible terms as specified in the existing collective contracts are preferred, because they do not exert any pressure upon the employers. Moreover, enterprise unions are usually accepted without any objections for two reasons. First, the trade unions believe that workers' rights are contingent upon the profitability of the company. Second, they regard their role not as overseeing administrative matters but simply enforcing the general guidelines as they are specified in the wage system. Apparently, most enterprise unions are not ready to negotiate the detailed wage levels for each work category with the managers through collective bargaining.

Nevertheless, trade unions in those joint ventures are not as negligible as it looks, even though collective contracts merely serve as formality. Each year, wages are negotiated during the bargaining process to decide whether to increase, maintain or decrease wages, depending on the operation of the whole company and the individual performance of workers. A committee, composed of representatives from the trade union, employees, and administrative members, participate in the discussions. Although trade unions understand the needs for compromise, they are sometimes persistent in maintaining wages and thus emphasize the importance of wages in retaining a quality workforce. In particular, trade unions among Japanese auto makers jointly calculate wage rates with managers, so that wage categories and remuneration standards for each category are fixed. Thus, those enterprise unions know the precise figures of each category. However, employees are not informed about them, since the public collective contracts do not include such information.

More importantly, wages are kept confidential from employees among most companies. By covering up such information, the companies primarily attempt to prevent employees' feelings of "internal inequality". Wage hierarchy is so high in Western auto makers that workers may feel unfairness if they compare their own wages with others in the company. The only exception includes East Asian companies that claim open information on wages thanks to a low wage hierarchy. Although European and a few traditional American companies have clearly-written collective contractual wages in their home countries, company management in China tends to regard wages as "top secret". This may be explained as particularities in Chinese management practices, as well as recent influences from popular management thoughts in the U.S.. The third part of this chapter will elaborate on this issue.

To sum up, on the side of production, all foreign-sino whole-car joint ventures have installed up-to-date machinery and technological processes in their Chinese factories. They plan for further development, including expansion of production and setting up R&D centers, in spite of different ratios of localization. In terms of work organizations, lean production methods are adopted in all major factories. With large-scale outsourcing and module production, whole-car makers mainly perform final assembly and quality control. At the same time, the country of origin, whether it is U.S., Europe, or Japan, has certain influence on labor practices. For instance, in some European joint ventures, practices such as time account and extensive pre-entry training have been introduced in China. In some companies, workers have very long work shift in a certain period of time, such as 12 hours per day or 70 hours per week, and then rest for another shift. Time account is used for such cases thereby the total work hours are calculated in a month or even in a year. Through time account, workers usually get holidays instead of OT pay for the extra hours they work in the shift. Additionally, European-style of pre-entry training is also practiced by two auto makers. They offer specific training to selected new apprentices together with Chinese vocational schools, similar to their ways in Europe. However, the numbers of foreign expatriates, both engineers and management staff, are rather few in most Western-Sino companies. On the contrary, Japanese companies retain a large proportion of managers from Japan (e.g. 50% in a new factory in South China), and thus the Japanese management style is carried out in China. Management is also distinctive among Japanese-sino joint ventures, which feature tight integration of management from Japan and China at each level. In most non-Japanese joint ventures, the foreign managers may be in charge of financial, marketing, and technical administration while Chinese managers oversee human resources.

Featured by a traditional "hegemonic" factory regime, those factories mostly recruit workers from both local and external technical schools. These employers offer relatively stable and competitive wages, well-regulated working conditions, comprehensive training in spite of high work intensity, and limited team work or job rotation, etc.. The overall workforce is relatively stable, and long-term employment is emphasized. As the bottom line, companies follow national labor laws. In most joint ventures, their wage levels meet medium levels of the market wages or higher. These levels have been suggested by consulting firms in light of wage guidelines set by the local governments. As for individual workers, their job positions and skill levels determine their incomes in Western joint ventures, whereas personal ability and performance serve as the wage criteria among Japanese firms.

With regard to labor relations, it is relatively well regulated, due to dominant state ownership[73] and roles of large MNCs as the foreign partners of the joint ventures. Generally speaking, labor relations are more or less adapted to Chinese characteristics of the former SOEs, such as relatively good welfare and well-established party committees and trade unions. Otherwise, the joint ventures have developed combined styles with influence from the country of origin (e.g. extensive channels of communication and negotiation in Japanese companies), rather than any traditional models that are copied from the different countries of origin. After the transition of former SOEs into joint ventures, former SOE employees have filled new positions after training or transferred to other companies within the same corporation groups in the nearby regions. Thus, the transition process was relatively peaceful. In particular, personnel management is often dominated by Chinese managers so some SOE forms of management remain. As in many SOEs, trade unions have a semi-administrative status and

73 Chin (2003) argues that a particular 'hegemonic regime' of labor control in the major auto joint ventures is resulted from the strong state intervention in regulating the employment relations.

the relationship between trade unions and management is very cooperative. Through ample consultation, trade unions have the right to consult on production plans and work-related issues. Additionally, many channels attempt to quell tensions between laborers and capitalists through trade unions or human resource management, so documented labor conflicts are very rare. Trade unions alight themselves with the state propaganda of "harmonious labor relations" by mediating between employers and workers. Managers and trade unions also follow legal formalities, including signing collective contracts.

However, the content of collective contracts merely copies legal requirements or states at the end of each clause that "the final decision is up to the management". For instance, wage rates, the single most important issue in collective bargaining among most industrialized countries, are not written in existing collective contracts. Only one collective contract mentions that "wages should not be reduced in case of low profitability". In addition, wage determination and collective contracts are limited within single enterprises. When asked about wage coordination with other companies in the same region, company unions show no interest. Apparently, the industrial union under the ACFTU does not play a role in determining labor standards, and the huge differences of wages and other standards among enterprises are not seen as a problem for major joint ventures because they are preferred among oversupplied university and technical school graduates. In fact, a single standard for the whole industry remains an illusion beyond the imagination of trade unions and many managers.

Besides those joint ventures, there are also a few domestic automakers, such as the private-owned Geely. Domestic automakers are making great efforts to catch up in the levels of machines and work processes of the joint ventures, either by taking over well-known foreign auto brands and parts companies or by recruiting overseas Chinese engineers or managers with working experiences in the global automobile industry. Indeed, some companies (e.g. Chery), belong to the same Chinese corporation groups as the joint ventures. Consequently, the transfer of technologies has upgraded the domestic industry. In addition, with strong government support, the independent R&D capacity of domestic companies is developing rapidly, although their total output and market shares still lag behind, especially in the field of high-end vehicles. The future of this industry largely depends on the indigenous development of domestic enterprises.

Work conditions and labor standards are relatively lower than in joint ventures. Most domestic enterprises, which are located in the inner provinces, offer lower wages, limited complementary benefits, and less modern working environments to their older workforce than more advanced counterparts. Former

SOE employees have been largely dismissed during the dismantling of SOEs in the late 1990s and 2000s, which targeted at "reducing staff and enhancing efficiency". The majority of the workforce are recently-recruited technical school and university graduates. However, the turnover rates in those enterprises are higher than in joint ventures due to lower labor standards and fewer opportunities of training and for workers to advance their career development. Retention of technicians and engineers is regarded as a big problem. A private firm called Geely invested in private technical schools, universities, and even graduate schools in order to educate its own workforce. By the end of 2009, 70% of its technical workers at the first line were graduates from its own schools, and 40% of the R&D staff.[74] In terms of labor relations, although trade unions exist in large companies, the practice of collective bargaining is not any better than that of joint ventures.

Automotive suppliers

Under lean production management, there is extensive use of temporary or dispatched workers along the production lines. At the same time, the manufacturing of parts and components may be outsourced or contracted to suppliers for the sake of higher efficiency and cost reduction. The latter has become particularly popular in China after the promulgation of the 2008 Labor Contract Law, which restricts the regular use of dispatched labor. Consequently, the conditions for employers in suppliers are inferior, compared to the well-paid "core" workers in the whole car makers.

Among major industrial clusters, numerous parts and components suppliers have been established alongside auto makers. For instance, surrounding VW factories in Jiading - one district of Shanghai, there are more than 200 auto parts suppliers, which contributed the industrial output of about 100 billion RMB in 2011. Nevertheless, supply chains for Japanese auto makers differ from those in the West. In general, Japanese companies often own the direct suppliers of key parts and components like engines. In China, such suppliers either belong to the joint ventures or wholly owned by Japanese investors. Except for a few key-tech suppliers, suppliers for other parts and lower-tier subcontractors differ greatly from the auto makers in terms of wages and working conditions. Western auto makers have never adopted lean methods fully. With no tradition of owning suppliers, European and American auto makers often purchase parts and components from first-tier suppliers, which are multinational corporations or joint ventures with established cooperation from their native countries.

74 Sina auto, Li Shufu: no Geely without the innovative model of talents, May 25, 2010, http://auto.sina.com.cn/news/2010-05-25/1926606161.shtml

Sometimes they also purchase parts from Chinese SOEs. Those large- or medium-scaled first-tier suppliers have relatively decent labor standards. Nevertheless, along lower hierarchies of the supply chain, especially among the second-tier or third-tier no-name factories, conditions are much worse. As a whole, a "lean-and-dual" model plausibly fits to the industrial structure in China. Local workers enjoy stable and higher-quality employment within the whole-car makers niche, and to a lesser degree in some first-tier suppliers. At the same time, the majority of migrant workers at lower parts of the supply chain must endure low wages, long work hours, unfavorable working and living conditions from their small- and medium-sized employers.

In both non-core suppliers for Japanese auto makers and lower-tier suppliers for others, the majority of workers are former peasants from less developed regions. As their specific products, and consequently the technological levels and work flows are so divergent, the workforce and employment are also different. In some joint ventures between foreign MNCs and local or township governments, the skilled workers, especially in mechanics, are treated better than unskilled line workers. Nevertheless, by and large, in contrast to the conditions in the whole-car makers, where workers have certain, albeit limited, control on work process, sometimes job rotation, and possibility to learn a certain spectrum of job-specific skills, the work in suppliers is feature by Neo-Taylorist organization and repetitive and simple tasks.

Wages, also other working conditions, are decided by management. Only in several cases of skilled workers and technicians, individual bargaining is involved. For the majority of unskilled line workers, any engagement or voice in decision-making is absent. Work stoppage or slow-down occurs every now and then, usually to show workers' dissatisfaction to their working conditions or management despotism. Even though collective actions often manifest through passive resistance, strikes or open protests are not rarely seen among the lower-tiered suppliers. These workers usually demand incremental changes, such as night-shift allowance and meal subsidies. In most cases, workers simply walk off from their jobs. Therefore, as a result of their low pay, lengthy work hours, harmful working environments, lack of training or career development, etc., a very high turnover rate is almost a norm. Indeed, the most common form of workplace resistance is "voting by the feet".

Although collective bargaining is a just, effective method of solving tensions, it has not been implemented in most suppliers. Indeed, many larger suppliers especially in the YRD have established trade unions, with the exceptions of Taiwanese- or Hong Kong-owned firms. However, those trade unions are often ineffectual since HR managers are also the union chairpersons. Collective bargaining and contracts are nearly unknown in their daily practices.

What is worse, the well-established trade unions of whole-car makers show no interest in standardizing wages at local or industrial levels. Coordination of collective bargaining along the supply chain is rarely seen as a task for the trade union. In fact, the whole-car makers may receive wage-related information from its first-tier suppliers and in a few occasions Japanese auto makers even intervened in collective labor conflicts of their suppliers. However, there is no any type of intervention of auto makers into the everyday labor practices of their suppliers. In particular, the trade union in one Japanese joint venture clearly states that different wage levels between the main company and its suppliers are just and necessary under the existing production system. In practice, it is possible that the first-tier suppliers refer to the wage levels of whole-car makers in order to adjust their own wage standards, though they usually lower the wages. However, management and trade unions of the whole-car makers usually demonstrate little interest in the wage levels among the second- or lower-tier suppliers. Along the supply chain, trade unions have no any form of coordination over working conditions. Fortunately, wage coordination along the supply chain has been put on the agenda of Guangzhou federation of trade unions, in the aftermath of the 2010 strike wave, which started at a Honda parts supplier in Guangzhou.

At a broader level, the existing industrial unions are not effective. Below the ACFTU are trade union federations at the provincial levels, which operate above industrial unions. There is complex administrative division among different trade unions. First, there are different union segments among assembly plants and parts suppliers within the auto industrial unions. Second, the investor who holds the largest share of a supplier company becomes the primary decision-maker in matters concerning the supplier union. Thus, as the whole-car makers do not usually dominate the share of the suppliers, trade unions in the whole-car makers have no direct authority over the supplier unions. Last, fully-foreign-invested or private enterprises should be monitored by the trade unions of the specific district or the community or street sub-division. In other words, there is no formal devolution of responsibility in the monitoring or in intervening upon issues concerning parts suppliers by trade unions among the whole-car makers.

Thus, since collective contracts are signed by individual companies in China, labor standards primarily depend on the specific conditions of the company and the bargaining capabilities of enterprise unions against their employers. At the best, district trade unions attempt to regulate the wage levels of the suppliers in some industrial parks in order to ensure that the wages do not fall below the legal minimum standards.

Summary

In the absence of any form of substantive collective bargaining or coordination at the above-establishment level, labor standards such as wages, working time and so forth are strongly enterprise-dominated. There are certain divergences among major whole-car makers, between Western, Japanese ones and domestic private firms, and huge polarizations along the supply chain. Unfortunately, collective contracts, where they do exist, are only signed in individual enterprise and often remain a formality.

Along the supply chains of most European or American auto makers, wages decrease commensurate to positions along the production chains, which organize hierarchically by assembly plants, first-tier suppliers, to lower-end parts suppliers. The gaps in wages and other working conditions in China are wider than in the U.S. and Europe, especially between urban employees in assembly plants and rural workers as dispatched labor or in suppliers' factories. On average, the annual incomes at the bottom of the hierarchically segmented production chain are one third or a half of those at the top which include assembly plants. Moreover, social benefits in auto makers are high, and they are equally distributed to manufacturing workers and office clerks. After the 2008 Labor Contract Law took effect, nearly all auto makers have abandoned the extensive use of dispatched labor. However, the majority of parts and components suppliers employ temporary or dispatched workers who often receive minimum wages, no employment security, and almost no benefits. For instance, in one former SOE that produced car engines, both regular workers and dispatched labor performed the same work, but the former group earned double of the wages of the latter group. In addition, Japanese auto makers clearly split core and periphery workforce along their supply chains. While all Japanese assembly plants emphasize good wages and benefits, comprehensive training, and employees' loyalty, their suppliers, including those that are fully-owned suppliers from the same corporation groups as assembly plants, employ a large proportion of dispatched labor or interns who receive much lower wages and have lengthy work hours. This contrasts the decremental trends of wage declines along Western supply chains.

Currently, the conditions in the automobile industry show some degree of instability. The policy of "same work, different pay" between regular workers and dispatched labor is a sensitive problem among workers, particularly after the 2008 Labor Contract Law entitled dispatched workers this right. Labor disputes, in the form of arbitration, court cases, or open protests, have increased in frequency as dispatched workers have become gradually aware of their legal rights and oppose the injustice they endure in their everyday work lives.

Another danger is veiled as the "lean-and-dual" model of Japanese auto makers, which has been increasingly perceived as unjust by "peripheral" workers. This model has largely explained the successes of the Japanese automobile industry in the postwar period that averted a major wave of labor militancy (Silver 2003: 69-73). It offered employment security for a core labor force, while the periphery was mainly female family members who are related to the core workers or temporary workers from the countryside. However, in the case of China, the close connection between core and periphery as demonstrated in postwar Japan does not exist. Rather, the lasting dual policies on urban and rural divided based on the household registration system (*Hukou*) among citizens in China have created wide gaps in incomes, education, and social identities. Dispatched laborers employed by suppliers consist of mostly migrant workers. There is no close relationship between these rural migrants and the urban-based technical school graduates. Whereas migrant workers are temporary dispatched labor, urban employees often have regular contracts. Although some auto makers offer to promote temporary workers to permanent status, the majority of migrant workers lack the opportunities of career development, promotion, wage increases, or adequate training. In this context, social divisions and inequalities between migrant workers and the long-term workforce may trigger conflicts along the supply chains. In addition, authoritarian management and the strict hierarchical divisions between Japanese and Chinese employees in typical Japanese companies make the conditions even more unbearable. The 2010 strike wave exposed the instabilities of the Japanese production model and management style. The fact that the walkout of workers in one supplier led to the complete shutdown of all four Honda assembly plants in China,[75] which in total produce 3,000 vehicles a day, also reveals the increasing workplace power of workers in a so-called seamlessly-integrated lean production system.

Last but not the least, although the higher wages and good welfare produce a group of "workers aristocrats" among whole-car makers (Lüthje 2008), some workers still quit from these assembly plants because of the high labor intensity and fierce competition among them. High work intensity is perhaps one of the top reasons for workers' resignation. Additionally, some employees complain that wages have stagnated in recent years, while high wages involved high productivity and large proportions of OT pay and shift allowances. At the moment, the relative generosity of management in whole-car makers have

---

75 There was extensive coverage on this by both foreign and Chinese media. e.g. economic observer, http://www.eeo.com.cn/industry/real_estate/2010/05/29/171354.shtml; the Wall Street Journal, http://cn.wsj.com/gb/20100610/bch091243.asp; and Reuters, http://www.reuters.com/article/idUSTOE66803020100709

diverted tension through various communication channels for the benefits of continuous production and quality guarantee. Nevertheless, there is no longer absence of open protests among auto workers in China.[76] If the imbalance of power between managers and labor collectivity continues, labor problems, such as the high work intensity in the whole-car factories and low wages in suppliers, may eventually result in serious unrests.

3.2.2 The electronics industry

Compared to the automobile industry, the electronics industry features a more diverse range of production regimes. Basically, this industry has many sub-sectors that produce variegated assembled products, including computers, cell phones, network solutions, consumer electronics such as air-conditioners and refrigerators, etc., as well as a variety of parts and components from high to low end, such as wafers, memory chips, acoustic parts, printed circuit boards, connectors and cables. For each type of parts and components, the organization of the production process also involves various suppliers and assemblers.

Apparently, there is nothing in this industry close to the dominance of whole-car assemblers over the automobile production chain. Quite the opposite, many electronics assembly factories often employ less advanced technologies with much lower labor standards than companies that specialize in particular parts and components. In a sense, differences in labor relations are largely up to the positions of products in the value chain as well as the production organizations, but no longer limited to the forms of ownership, the locations, nor the scales of enterprises.

Production regimes rely on the nature of product, the workforce, and the organization of the company. A trend since the late 1970s is that many former fully-integrated manufacturers have spined off or outsourced manufacturing. Among many reasons, the liberalization of the financial markets and government policies have threatened the traditional trade unionism and "social contracts" in the U.S. and Germany. Companies respond by increasingly specializing in narrower and often more profitable fields, such as design and marketing. At the same time, manufacturing, especially most technologically-complicated and investment-demanding processes, has shifted toward their subsidiaries or spinning-offs in lower-cost countries like China. Additionally, more production is entirely outsourced to external "one-stop-service" providers, such as contract manufacturers and chip foundries. Accordingly, many of those

---

76 As some scholars (e.g. Zhang 2008) pointed out before, the auto industry in China has been relatively calm while other industries had large numbers of strikes and protests.

now "fabless" brand names still dominate the production network as they distribute orders and control prices in the production network, although such dominance has become much less direct compared to the integrated manufacturing in the past.

In China, the electronics industry is the most important exporting sector and has a fastest growing domestic market. Multiple players are present, just as in the global scenario. At the top, the number of traditional IDMs is decreasing, while new IDMs emerge from Asian countries which have no history of industrial unionism or "social contracts". Following IDMs, there are specialized global brand name corporations, mostly resulted from spinning-offs. A number of Chinese MNCs have emerged from former SOEs or COEs. At lower tiers of the value chain, there are a handful of contract manufacturers with the largest sizes in the industry, and numerous medium- to small-sized no-name-suppliers or subcontractors at the bottom.

Global brand name multinationals

Notably, the number of fully-integrated brand name companies has decreased. Formerly dominant market players, such as Siemens, Philips and AMD, have gone through dramatic restructuring by continuously getting rid of non-core businesses. As a consequence, the traditional "Corporate bureaucratic" production regime in those companies, which feature secure employment, stable wages and decent working conditions rarely exists today. In the global electronics industry, the subsidiaries spin-off from those traditional companies as newly-built smaller-sized global brand name MNCs. There is another group of enterprises with similar degrees of integration as traditional IDMs but younger. Nevertheless, the traditional IDMs are now experimenting with new production and management methods, whereas the younger group of integrated enterprises are predominately in some Asian countries that lack a long history of labor-capital struggles or "social contracts". Thus, existing production regimes have diverged from the past. This trend is reflected in their Chinese subsidiaries. As a result, the production regimes of leading global brand names in China are a combination of "Corporate bureaucratic", the traditional IDM style, and "Corporate high performance", which features increasing importance of performance in determining wages and other labor standards.[77] As the number of the former is very few, the majority are increasingly closer to the latter.

In most smaller-sized new MNCs from the West, the production system remains to be highly integrated, and the output and value-added are tremendous.

77 For details of the typology of the production regimes, please refer to the Appendix B.

Vertical disintegration is the trend at industrial level, which means, compared to traditional IDMs, these new MNCs have a narrower focus within niches of the technology market. Such a focus, on the one hand, may encourage further specialization and productivity within a specific field, yet on the other hand this fragmentation leads to highly unstable production that are vulnerable to the fluctuations of market demand. Because they only produce a very small range of products, such as acoustic chips, even a temporary decline of orders from large buyers may seriously impact their production flow. As a result, even though many of such companies are still leading players, their very existence can be jeopardized by a major downturn in the global market. In fact, a large proportion of products made by their Chinese factories are exported to Asia-Pacific, North America, and other parts of the world. Thus, a global recession, like the one in 2008/9, dramatically reduces export demands on their products, which may close one part of the production lines or even the entire factories. For instance, several well-known brand name companies had to file for bankruptcy, while a few shut down in early 2009 due to a loss of more than 50% of their global orders. In other cases, factories had to slow down production, or to arrange training, equipment maintenance, and annual leaves for workers when their production stopped. Only until late 2009, global orders began to recover and domestic market boomed, with the assistance of the government's 4 trillion RMB stimulus package.

As for the production system, their products, such as chips and acoustic parts, are technologically complicated and serve as key parts of the final products. For these reasons, many European and North American brand name companies have highly-automated capital-intensive processes for the purpose of stable quality and continuous productivity. In those factories, the proportion of manual assembly work is very small. Most technologies are state-of-the art, and work organization emphasizes relatively high-skilled workforce. Thus, those companies are often cited as the exemplary case of industrial modernization within the regions or of the industrial parks where they are located. At the same time, high automation changes work conditions by requiring employees to inspect the functioning of these machines. With a few exceptions in European factories in China, the division between technicians or engineers and operators is highly strict. While most technicians or engineers have college or university degrees and the high skills to oversee computerized programs, operators perform simple tasks, such as loading materials, monitoring results, and unloading products. Normally, operators have nothing to do with maintenance, but only cleaning the machines. Consequently, they do not even need to know how the machines function. Apparently, semi-skilled workers with relatively short training periods are able to perform most of the operation tasks.

Normally machines run 24 hours a day and 7 days per week, while operators work in shifts for 12-hours or 8-hours each. The work environment is mostly modern and clean. In case of noise or heat, necessary protections are available. In addition, chairs with back are seen in workshops, which are very different from many labor-intensive electronics factories where workers have to stand during work. Individual work stations are typical, which seem workers may have more autonomy over their work than in machine-controlled assembly lines. However, this cannot be automatically interpreted as a higher degree of workers' control over work, if there is no certain type of workers' involvement or democracy at workplaces. In fact, workers often have strict quota that measure the quantities and qualities of their products.

Manufacturers apply lean production methods, including all typical features such as the stop-buttons, *Kanban*, CIP, TPM (total productivity management), and work disciplines, like "six Sigma" and "5 S". Nevertheless, only in one enterprise, the concept of team work is well implemented. Operators, through self-management team at shop floor level, have a certain degree of autonomy on daily operation and are also provided with the possibility to learn multiple skills. Nevertheless, this arrangement is completely carried out by HR, and the enterprise trade union plays no role at all.

These factories are positioned between global brand name companies and contract manufacturers along the production network. Just-in-time delivery upholds the highest precision in delivery and production schedules. In many cases, these factories also outsource production to local suppliers to take advantage of their low price and easy access, although key parts are completely imported. Generally speaking, outsourcing is not very common, simply because those smaller-sized MNCs are already a "spin-off" of former integrated companies. Their production has been highly specialized, and no much room is left for further disintegration.

In terms of the workforce, there are only very limited numbers of expatriates, but the majority are from China. Almost all employees are regular employees, especially along the manufacturing lines. After the 2008 Labor Contract Law took effect, long-term contracts (e.g. 3 years) were signed between individual workers and company management. According to Article 66 of the Law, dispatched labor may only be hired for temporary, complementary or substitutive positions. In practice, most operators are young graduates from technical schools and have no local city Hukou (Residential registration). For newly-hired operators, pre-entry training often takes one month or two while technical skills are taught on-the-job. However, in one small-scaled European-owned high-tech company, fresh graduates are not welcomed. Rather, two to three years working experience before entry is a basic requisite. It is noticeable that in all companies, numbers of the workforce fluctuate according to market trends. With their factories have been established in China, enterprises have experienced rapid growth in both production and employment. However, during the 2008/9 crisis, many companies have reduced their workforce to less than a half while a few tried to keep their core workers by reducing their wages to minimum pay. As the economy began to recover later, southern China experienced a wide labor shortage.

A typical wage system for operators includes base wage and performance-related bonus. For European companies, there is also one month extra pay at the end of the year - "the 13th month pay". Skills and positions are the criteria for base wages. No piece rate is found in any of my case studies. Generally speaking, the flexible portion of labor compensation, excluding OT payment, is relatively low (e.g. less than 30%), compared to the rest of enterprises in this industry. Nevertheless, performance has become increasingly important. Performance orientation is not only emphasized in corporate culture but is also integrated in wage systems. In two cases, performance bonus accounts for more than 30% of the annual income. Every year, the performance of individual employees is reviewed, and accordingly salary levels are adjusted. It is one of the major divergences between those specialized companies and traditional integrated ones.

Usually, OT is not much, because most companies follow the law strictly. The general lack of OT in Western companies is actually regarded by many operators as a disadvantage. In practice, operators, usually whose homes lie far away from their work bases, count their OT pay to get by, whereas engineers often prefer regular work schedules to balance their work and home lives. In some cases, "Integrated Calculation of Working Time" is adopted for operators, which means in busy seasons or in case of urgent orders OT may possibly exceed the legal monthly limit of 36 hours. This calculation makes it easier for companies to arrange flexible working time, but workers no longer receive extra pay for their OT hours during busy seasons. Instead, they have more holidays when there is less demand of production.

In a few cases, there is also retention pay, but not in a form of traditional seniority-based wage. Rather, incentives or a bonuses, which range from 5 to 10% of monthly base wages, are given to those who have worked in the company for more than a number of years (e.g. 10 years in one lighting enterprise and 2 years in a typical spinned-off high-tech company). Moreover, other benefits are normally good, such as transportation allowance, meal subsidy, sports club membership, and education assistance program. Canteens are mostly available, as are shuttle buses. In addition, almost all factories located in the South provide dormitory to the majority of their operators. For instance, in a typical factory in south China, eight to ten operators live in one apartment with two rooms and one toilet. It is usually free of charge or at a very low rate. In other regions of China, dormitories are rarely available, and workers seem to prefer cheap places around the city, which makes it easier for them to socialize with friends. Older workers may also live with their children and parents.

On the whole, wage packages for operators are above market average in the industry, although in many cases operators only earn half of that of technicians. A clean and modern working environment is generally offered by larger corporations. As a result, it is easy for those companies to recruit operators. The average turnover rates are around 10% annually, which is distinctively lower than the industrial average, especially in the South. Despite some variations, the average length of tenure is longer than the average market figures.

Moreover, those companies have relatively stable industrial relations. They obey the law and, in many cases, are under the direct monitoring of their clients (e.g. through the Electronics Industry Citizenship Coalition code of conduct). With advanced HR policies, they are able to maintain a good working environment through offering stable income, encouraging employees' engagement, organizing comprehensive training, etc. Indeed, many companies have won national or local prizes as "best employers" or for "best labor practices" from the governments. Normally, individual or collective labor disputes are very few even during large-scale job cuts. This is largely due to the existence of relatively good communication channels, such as regular employees' meetings, hot-lines, and suggestion boxes.

Nevertheless, only a small proportion of these enterprises abide by the legal clauses that guide in the establishment of trade unions. These enterprise unions result from the fact that companies intend to fulfill the requests of local governments. Therefore, trade unions have been set up from the top down, which means they are initiated by or indeed belong to the HR department. Managers are also union members, except for a European-based company. In many cases, all employees are automatically counted as union members, although they may not even know the existence of the enterprise trade unions.

Collective contracts rarely exist. Even in the very few cases with such contracts, the agreements merely state the general rules and legal content. Company unions cannot even negotiate informally with management on wages, working time, performance appraisal or so. Trade unions have no say, since management unilaterally makes the decisions and at best informs unions about it. As in the case of auto makers, wages are determined by market data, gathered through purchasing reports by global consulting firms. Often, the medium level of the market data is the target of total wage packages. Sometimes the wage survey and guidelines from local governments are referred to, but not regarded as critical in wage determination by these companies.

In a word, those specialized Western MNCs are featured by world-class manufacturing, leading R&D capacities, modern and legally-regulated working conditions, and relatively skilled and well-paid employees. In this industry, they also have the best labor practices mainly through advanced HR policies. In a few cases, there are informal HR clubs in the industrial parks. HR managers from large firms organize such clubs in order to share information and to reach agreements on certain rules, such as no poaching talents from each other.

Nevertheless, for both enterprises and their employees, there are tensions in the production model and industrial relations, in spite of the current peace. A revealing case involves the bankruptcy of several companies during the crisis due to the vulnerability of companies with a narrow specialization to the fluctuating global market. Since orders shrank during the crisis, companies must close down and sell their factories, causing large-scale redundancy or wage reductions. In those cases, advanced HR policies could not have saved jobs, including those of managers themselves. Without any effective forms of employees' representation there are no economic safeguards for factory owners or their employees. In fact, although managers seem to have complete freedom in setting wages, individual workers often exert pressure upon management. For instance, a highly-skilled worker tries to get higher wages by threating of moving to another company. The increasing emphasis on workers' performance, as seen in most companies with "modern" HR policies, aims for higher productivity by increasing work pace and competition between individuals. Under such pressures, relatively skilled workers have begun to express their demands. Although at the moment most disputes on wages are on individual basis, work stoppage has occurred in some factories. With the absence of effective employees' representatives and collective bargaining, the most well-designed HR strategy cannot be a satisfactory solution to the potential conflicts.

Besides those specialized MNCs from the West, as mentioned above, there are also relatively new companies with integrated production. They originate from Asia (e.g. Samsung). As we have already seen in the case of Japanese auto makers, management style and hierarchical relationship in Asian integrated companies seem to be distinctive due to different cultural backgrounds. For instance, in Japanese, Korean and Taiwanese companies, the top management are usually dominated by those from the country of origin. On the contrary, in Western firms, localization rates of the workforce particularly among engineers and managers are surprisingly high. Such structures lead to different styles of control and HR policies on the side of management.

In general, technologies and manufacturing facilities in those enterprises closely resemble the conditions of Western MNCs, in spite of small divergences. For instance, machines from Europe are relatively more complicated and flexible, thereby more suitable for "low quantity, high mix" production. Nevertheless, most enterprises primarily use machines from Europe or Japan, depending on the specific production. Thus, the production system is similar. At the same time, labor standards, especially wages, are rather different. For instance, although the total wages for operators are more or less the same as Western MNCs in the same region, Korean and Taiwanese integrated manufacturers provide very low base wages and a constantly high amount of OT pay. In some cases, the proportions of performance-based wages and OT pay are about 50%. Even if some operators from rural areas are willing to earn more money through more OT, the lengthy work hours and constant stress become increasingly unbearable, indicated in extremely high turnover rate in this industry (e.g. 70% annual turnover rate in 2011). In particular, workers may easily get to know that similar jobs in Western companies nearby are paid with similar wages but require much shorter work time. Thus, they frequently job hop from one company to another. As a result, the turnover rates in Korean or Taiwanese MNCs are substantially higher, and employees tend to be less positive about their working experience than those in Western MNCs.

Newly-emerging Chinese MNCs

Chinese MNCs have emerged mainly as the result of successful transfers from former local state- or collectively-owned enterprises in the 1990s. The pioneers were several television producers that thrived in the 1980s. Later, some manufacturers of home appliances or customer electronics, such as washing machines, microwave ovens, air-conditioners and mobile phones, emerged, and today there are increasing numbers of high-tech firms in the field of computers, networking, and semiconductors. Nevertheless, the government actively supports the development of the domestic electronics industry through technological aid and public procurement. Much younger than many global brand name MNCs, the newly-emerging Chinese MNCs are exploring their ways in production and market. Although the high degree of vertical integration in those companies closely resembles to traditional IDMs, their high dependence in providing Original Equipment Manufacture (OEM) services results in the proliferation of relatively lower-tech production and low-cost labor practices. Accordingly, only a few domestic flagship firms in computers, networking and chip makers, such as Huawei and SMIC, reflect the regime of "corporate high performance", and the dominant production regimes fall into the categories of "flexible mass production" or even "low-wage classic".[78]

In terms of the products, those enterprises have first targeted domestic markets for low-cost products, such as TCL and Haier in home appliance electronics, or Huawei and ZTE in networking equipments. At the same time, many companies also provide ODM service as subcontractors for global brand names. After accumulating strength in technologies and capital, they have grown very large and often succeeded in building up their own brands within China. Furthermore, they attempt to expand their businesses in multiple fields and to enhance their exports to less industrialized countries. This strategy is the so-called "incremental innovation" (Ernst and Naughton, 2008: 51). Their wide range of products and a focus on the domestic market, during the 2008/9 crisis, have largely protected them from the up and down of global markets. Some of them temporarily suffered from the loss of ODM orders, but soon after the crisis, more ODM orders came back due to the closing of many foreign factories.

Chinese MNCs often employ highly integrated production, including R&D and sales channels. Machines and facilities are relatively modern and clean, especially in newer factories. However, the level of automation is not as high as Western MNCs, with a few exceptions in the semiconductor sector (e.g. a wafer foundry). In less high-tech sub-sectors (e.g. color TV and mobile phones), manual work is done in many positions, especially in assembly and testing. Production lines are commonly installed. At the same time, in newer factories lean methods are partly imitated. For instance, process improvement projects are designed and implemented in some factories, so as to shorten delivery cycle and to speed up supply delivery in response to consumer demands. This has resulted from the request of global clients, or the motivation of the companies to catch up to international standards.

In general, work and production organizations are largely Taylorist. The division of labor is strict and work for operators is segmented. Workers, mostly young females, sit one by one putting together parts or checking the products. The work is repetitive and physically demanding. Individual workers have no control over the speed of production lines. There is no job rotation in the factories. While unskilled workers may easily adapt to various jobs after brief training, the majority of the workforce are not technical school graduates from the urban areas but are migrant workers who usually have lower levels of education and skill.

This composition of the workforce partially leads to a very high turnover rate. Primarily, since most workers are recruited from the labor market or

---

78 For details of the typology of production regimes, see Appendix B.

agencies, often as dispatched labor, it is almost costless for companies to hire and fire them. For instance, after global ODM orders dropped during the crisis, large numbers of production workers (e.g. one third in one factory) were immediately dismissed. Then as orders and production returned within the timeframe of only a few months, even more employees were recruited than before. Wages and other labor conditions are not regarded among workers as the most attractive in this industry. This explains why job-hopping is prevalent among most migrant workers.

Labor standards, on the whole, are not as good as those in most Western MNCs. While newer factories have higher production stability and environmental sustainability, older factories employ large-scale manual labor on physically-demanding and hazardous positions. One exemplary case is in a national brand name lighting enterprise, where 143 workers were found with high levels of mercury poisoning in their urine that exceeded the legal limit, while nine workers were suspected to have with occupational disease of chronic mercurialism by the end of 2009. Management began to use solid mercury on all production lines only after these unfortunate cases were reported.

Moreover, working time is very long. For operators, work shifts on average last normally 10 hours per day and 6 days per week. Some managers admit that it is not possible to meet the legal maximum of 36 hours OT per month. According to them, each worker has to make as many products as possible due to the low margin of the products, otherwise the factories may have to close. They argue that the state should consider making an exception for electronic manufacturers, because the whole industry cannot meet current standards. In most companies, global customers have exerted pressure through factory inspections since a few years ago. Nevertheless, they allow OT limits of as high as 60 hours per week and each month 80 to 90 hours. Additionally, OT is often paid on the basis of a "pre-agreed" wage written in individual labor contracts, which is lower than the legally-required total income. As a consequence, many OT-related labor disputes have occurred, especially in south China.

Paradoxically, many workers oppose restrictions to OT work. However, if we consider the overall wage structure, OT payment often accounts for about a half of operators' annual income. It means the monthly base wages are set too low. Especially in South China, new operators may receive a base wage lower than local minimum wages. Thus, workers have to work OT to meet their subsistence needs. Besides, in some cases there is an individual-output-based performance bonus, which accounts for roughly one third of monthly base wages. In an extreme case of the "Lighting Champion of China", piece rate was introduced in 2008, among many small and medium firms in South China to undermine the legal minimum wages. This aroused a 6-days strike so the enterprise had to stop the use of piece rate.

Even though managers still regard total wages as relatively high in this industry, the employees widely recognize the instability of incomes. Admittedly, their wage packages are still better than those offered by less recognized companies in the same region. In many Chinese MNCs, operators have similar welfare as other employees, including social security[79], annual paid-leave, and company benefits, such as high-temperature allowance, meal subsidy and free physical examination. In South China, free or subsidized dormitory is usually provided for operators. In addition, social facilities and living areas in former SOE or COE factories are quite well-equipped, such as basketball playground, library, Internet bar, supermarket, hair salon, ATM and laundry room.

Given the high mobility of the workforce and frequent disputes on wages, labor relations in those companies are unstable. Domestic brand name companies attempt to follow legal requirements better than smaller firms in the same regions, but their efforts are far from enough. For instance, employers objected to the 2008 Labor Contract Law which specified open-termed contracts and required social insurances for migrant workers. Managers who lack managerial skills or advanced HR concepts often follow a authoritarian military-style control. In particular, on the shop floor, severe punishment upon workers for defects and forced OT are common. Without effective channels of communication, tensions are accumulated at different levels.

Enterprise unions have long been established, due to the SOEs or COEs tradition as well as the close relationship of those enterprises with local governments. The leadership of party committees and trade unions often overlap. Most or even all trade union cadres are only part-time, and in one case the union chairman is the vice president of the company, and the vice union chairman is the director of the HR department. They are clearly not the representatives of workers.

Thus, it is logical to expect that those enterprise unions play no effective role in industrial relations. According to them, both workers' feelings and company interests are important. This is shown in trade unions' excessive cooperation with the management. For example, a union chairman once rejected the highly-propagandized "Opening Factory Affairs"[80] by the upper-level unions

---

79 In China, the national social security system includes "five insurances and one fund", the aging, medical, maternity, unemployment and work injury insurances, as well as housing provident fund.

80 This is a democratic management system initiated by the Party, which requires enterprises to report significant issues to employees, such as issues relevant to the development of the enterprises as well as to workers' interests.

based on the reason that "business secrets should not be publicized". In many cases, there is even no clear distinction between the functions of trade unions and of HRM. As another union chairman states, "as long as it is good for the company, it does not matter whether trade union or the HRM is doing the management work".

In consequence, many enterprise unions abandon the option of collective bargaining. While the 2008 Labor Contract Law draws the attention of companies to trade unions, the result is no more than a few more signatures by the union chairmen. Collective bargaining has not even entered the agenda of many trade unions, because trade union cadres believe "the corporate culture of new MNC is good and flexible, but collective negotiation is too conventional for such companies to follow." Therefore, faced with the common problems of unstable wages and lengthy OT, enterprise unions have no voice at all. Their role is also widely absent in frequent individual labor disputes and occasional collective actions.

Those newly-emerging Chinese MNCs are backed up by the governments in order to upgrade toward brand name companies at national and even global levels. In this process, their labor practices lag far behind. In most cases, the low-skill, low-cost strategy remains[81]. Generally speaking, the common labor conditions are characterized by insecure employment, flexible wages, excessive work hours, authoritarian management, etc. Accordingly, the turnover rate is high and individual labor disputes happen frequently. While the company unions are not workers' representatives, there is no effective form of collective bargaining. Nevertheless, it is certain that individual labor disputes, court cases, and occasional collective actions will not stop simply because of the ineffectiveness of trade unions. More importantly, the Labor Contract Law has not only endowed the trade union a more visible role in the company though this formality has raised awareness for workers' rights. In practice, increasing numbers of workers resort to legal measures to solve their problems. Besides, the fact that large numbers of grudging young migrant workers working along the mass production lines and dwell in factory dormitories may easily arouse their consciousness at a broader level. Before the tensions develop into more devastating labor unrest, management, trade unions, and governments should seriously consider of more peaceful alternatives such as collective bargaining to quell workers' growing discontent over their dismal labor conditions.

---

81 There is one exception of a wafer foundry, where the management and the local government joint force to educate more talents through a comprehensive education and training system. However, this is a very rare case.

Contract manufacturers

Contract manufacturers are a relatively new but a rapidly emerging group in the electronics industry. As most Western MNCs increasingly shed their manufacturing and fab-less design houses, a new type of business - contract manufacturing - has begun to reintegrate manufacturing processes since the 1990s (Lüthje 2002). Contract manufacturers provides "one-stop" service, including important elements of product design, procurement, logistics and after-sales services with lower costs and shorter time responding to market. Their business is very unstable and price-competitive since their orders are strongly influenced by fluctuating demands of end-user markets and the services provided by different contract manufacturers are more or less the same. They have thus formed a "large-scale, low-cost and low-margin" model and the dominant production regime is "flexible mass production".

The sub-sector of contract manufacturing, including EMS and ODM segments, had revenue of US$347.3 billion in 2010, a 33.4% increase from 2009. Revenue is expected to continue to rise between 9% and 7% annually, reaching $472.3 billion in 2014. In particular, China accounts for more than 75% of aggregate industrial growth of electronics manufacturing in 2010 (Dinges, 2011). The top contract manufacturers are mainly America- or Taiwan- based, such as Foxconn (Hon Hai Precision Industries) and Flextronics. Foxconn is the largest company in the entire electronics industry. In seven years since 2000, it had grown more than 60% annually, according to the statistics of E-Business Journal of China (Dinges 2011) Besides, some Western MNCs have also set up new independent companies to manufacture particular electronic components. For instance, a European-based MNC which specializes in network communication is also involved in the final assembly of base stations for global market. Such assembly work is a typical EMS business. As it also arranges a large part of production to contract manufacturers, its own factories are not as big as the latter.

Contract manufacturers typically concentrates production in a strong vertically-integrated value chain among closely related factory networks (Lüthje 2002), typically in gigantic "industrial parks". Such industrial parks are often seen in PRD, a center of export production with a large low-wage migrant workforce and numerous small- and medium-suppliers. For instance, a factory site of Foxconn has more than ten multistory manufacturing buildings in several square kilometers. Extensive warehouse and loading facilities also exist inside the complex, which form the part of a "bonded zone" permitting on-site customs procedures. At the same time, the rapid expansion of the enterprises also relies on the takeover or merger of other EMS players. For instance, a takeover by Flextronics in 2007 involved more than 20 factories in China.

Typically, contract manufacturers perform high-volume assembly for a variety of leading global brand names. In a few cases, factories with newer technological processes also have "high volume, high mix", which means high volumes with increasing flexibility in product configuration, or even "low volume, high mix". For instance, in a factory in the YRD, multiple models of products (e.g. 7 or 8 modules) are made on one line and each day the production line may change many times, depending on orders. Their products are wide-ranged, including computers, data networking equipment, cell phones, game consoles, etc. Notably, the technologies in most areas follow the highest international standards in order to meet the strict requirements of global brand name customers. In addition, the outsourcing of less-profitable sub-assembly work to smaller subcontractors is a common means of reducing costs and improving efficiency. Comparatively, Foxconn manufactures all major non-electronic parts by itself, such as metal, plastic and cables, where as others like Flextronics subcontract most services to external suppliers.

Inside the workshops, hundreds of production lines run 24 hours and 7 days. Workers wear uniforms and necessary protective gear. Normally, they have to stand along the production lines in order to carry out tasks. Every day, there are two or three shifts. In the core manufacturing lines (e.g. printed circuit board assembly), work is fully automated. At the same time, final assembly including configuration and packaging involves manual labor. While the final assembly is mostly done by women workers, physically heavier work in metal and plastics manufacturing is performed by males. Accordingly, the work involves either loading/unloading materials from highly automated machine or assembly line work, both of which appear massively de-skilled. In large contract manufacturers, the division of labor is strict and the work for operators is simple. In general, operators have no control over work flow and must work fast.

In many factories, lean production and the just-in-time delivery system have been introduced. The storage of raw materials is close to assembly lines. Shop-floor based quality management is designed to support Taylorist production organization. The top-down work organization enforces rules for each workplace and oversees the standardization of work procedures. There is also another system - "Six Sigma", originally developed in Japan. In the shop-floor,this system consists of a simple set of basic rules of workplace behaviour, particularly about orderliness and timeliness.

Despite their large sizes and advanced technologies, contract manufacturers are essentially subcontractors. This means the share of profits for contract manufacturers is squeezed by part suppliers and final customers. Furthermore, due to the standardization and wide availability of products and technologies, competition among contract manufacturers is fierce. As a result, production commonly proceeds at the cost of low margins and massive volume changes.

As orders are shaped by market swings, employment insecurity is prevalent. One exemplary case is the 2008/2009 crisis when several export-oriented factories closed down. For the sites that survived, large-scale redundancies were common. The majority of the workers are line operators, who are typically migrant workers between 18 and 25 years old. Many European- or American-based EMS factories in eastern China hire technical school graduates. However, still a certain proportion (e.g. 30%) of the workforce rely on dispatched laborers who are either technical school graduates or migrant workers with some working experience. On the whole, the workforce in eastern China is relatively better educated and higher skilled than that in the south. This difference leads to relatively lower turnover rates in European-based factories.

Besides, labor standards are also different among European-, American- and Taiwanese-companies in eastern and southern China. Generally speaking, contract manufacturers share modern and clean working environment and relatively good wages. However, the wage structures are very different. In more traditional European companies, the proportion of position-based base wages is relatively high, although performance is also an important factor in total wages. OT is restricted within legal limits. As for Taiwanese factories, base wages are much lower, often slightly above local minimum wages, and no bonuses are directly related to individual performance. OT pay accounts for a large proportion of workers' wages sometimes even doubling base wages. In addition, there are huge pay differentials among mainland Chinese and Taiwanese engineers. In American firms, the base wages and other labor standards are somewhere in between of European- and Taiwanese-based ones. Although total wages are not higher than Taiwanese, leading American companies have a better reputation among workers. In the case of Flextronics, due to a slower integration process following rapid mergers and takeover of other companies, a particular problem is the high differentiation of wages and welfare among different factory sites. This has aroused several strikes claiming of "equal pay for equal work" among different sites of a company in eastern China.

Another distinction is training. As the composition of the workforce is different, more flexibility and multiple skills are preferred for further development in European-based factories. The same applies to job rotation and the development of internal labor market. In most factories from Taiwan or America, the opportunities of skill development are different for operators and higher-skilled employees. The pre-entry training for operators is only three to five days, and covers factory rules, company values, basic work procedures, and one week on-job-training. In addition, strict divisions of labor, heavy workloads, and long work hours result to the absence of skill incentives. Only in the propaganda of the companies, it is possible for operators to get trained and promoted to technicians. Operators often complain about the external recruitment of technicians and engineers, rather than internal promotion from below among themselves.

Massive dormitory buildings are another feature of contract manufacturers. Especially in Taiwanese or American "industrial parks", there are multistory dormitories, with several operators sharing one bedroom for free. Dormitory is regarded as one part of the compensation package in South China and workers who do not live in the dormitory can apply for a housing subsidy (e.g. 300 RMB per month for operators). In addition, shuttle buses during the off-work time and weekends are available since most huge-sized factories are located outside cities. Because of a strict management control over work processes and other special designs (e.g. in arranging the dormitories) in order to preventing collective association among workers, labor-capital conflicts have shown to employ rather passive and individualized forms, such as high turnover rates of employees or individual disputes.

Noticeably, unequal treatment by management toward regular and temporary workers is a norm. One major problem in European- or American-based companies lies in managers' discrimination of dispatched workers for the benefit of regular employees, whereas the majority of operators in Taiwanese ones are treated as dispatched labor. Usually dispatched workers receive legal minimum wages as base wages and only get OT payment on the top. They do not have regular wage increases or paid annual leave. In a few companies, there are opportunities for them to become regular workers. In fact, only a small percentage of dispatched workers can do so every year, depending on their performance and the recommendation of line managers. Moreover, employers commonly use interns from technical schools or colleges as operators or technicians. In one or two years of internship, they work the same as others but receive hourly wages, which are usually lower than the minimum wages. Furthermore, the hierarchy of wages and bonuses between operators and the rest - technicians, engineers and managers - is predominant.

Generally speaking, contract manufacturers generally follow the law, but there is often "flexible handling" of legal requirements. For instance, a common problem of the industry is work schedules. Contract manufacturers do not follow the monthly limit of 36 hours OT. Several factories in eastern China adopt the "integrated calculation of working time" policy on a quarterly or annual basis, which allows flexibility to set work hours beyond the legal limits. Meanwhile, factories in the South justify a daily OT of 3 hours according to the Electronics Industry Code of Conduct (EICC), a voluntary agreement on labor and environmental standards. This code of conduct requires much lower labor standards than Chinese laws. Thus, the amount of OT in a normal month is about 60 hours. However, this illegal practice is somehow accommodated by the local governments. In addition, the 2008 labor Contract Law was criticized by a few HR managers for incurring extra costs because they had to pay social insurance fees for all regular workers and to sign open-termed contracts for employees who have worked for more than ten years.

This focus on company-oriented corporate social responsibility (CSR) or business codes of conduct, as required by brand name clients, has largely substituted the role of trade unions. Indeed, many contract manufacturers have quickly established factory-based unions after the institution of the 2008 Labor Contract Law and the series of negative publicity on working conditions in select factories (e.g. Foxconn). Nevertheless, those trade unions are organized through the initiative of the HR department, rather by workers. The union cadres are HR managers or at least "good employees" that would not oppose management. Consequently, the only major change they enacted is merely a legal formality to go through, which in the case of redundancies during the 2008/9 crisis actually became a way of helping legitimate management decisions of redundancies and wage deductions. In reality, the main task of the unions is organizing recreational and sports activities. In several cases, trade unions also set up hotlines to communicate with workers or to participate in grievance settlements. Their ultimate goal is to build "harmonious labor relations", which is a very cooperative relationship between trade unions and management. With regard to wages and other labor standards, trade unions have no role. In some cases, compliance with EICC rules is seen as an important goal by trade unions.

Accordingly, collective contracts barely exist. In European-based companies with strong brand recognition, collective bargaining has not been written in the company's global guidelines, so it is also absent in their Chinese factories. As for Taiwanese- and American-invested companies, collective contracts are signed in several factories where labor standards have aroused concerns over work conditions. Nevertheless, both the organization of trade unions and the signing of collective contracts are merely legal formalities that can be shown to the public. Collective contracts have only general and procedural statements rather than substantial regulations. Nor there is anything that guarantees wage increases. As no law requires the details of collective contracts, no company plans to institute wage grades in collective contracts.

Wage grades exist in those companies. In the view of many HR managers and even trade unions, wages and collective contracts are completely irrelevant. Usually, companies participate in salary survey of well-known consulting firms and accordingly target their total wages at certain percentiles, mostly the medium level, of market prices in the survey reports. In this way, wage grades are decided. As for individuals, wages shall be within the scope of certain grades. For support technicians and engineers, wages are discussed between HR and individual applicants in the process of recruitment. For operators, since there is no specific requirement on skills or experience and most are recruited through labor agencies, the same base wage is applied in many cases. Only for a few skilled operators, wages may be discussed during job interviews. It is noted that wage information is considered confidential and it is sensitive or even not allowed to discuss among employees.

Interestingly, collective labor conflicts have been rare and individual labor disputes or court cases only happen occasionally in contract manufacturers. One explanation is that there are communication channels and grievance handling mechanisms in European and American companies developed by HRM, whereas in Taiwanese firms the carefully-designed work organization and dormitory system attempt to avoid workers' associational activities. However, strikes have occurred in a leading American company due to lower wages in a factory than in others of the same company. The 2010 wave of suicides in Foxconn involving 13 employees has aroused concerns over work conditions in China and globally.

In a word, contract manufacturers fall mainly in the category of "flexible mass production" regime. On the one hand, they have advanced technologies, modern machines, highly integrated and flexible mass production, lean type of logistics, standardized work, and strict division of labor. On the other hand, the majority of the workforce consists of low-skilled operators with low wages and high turnover rates. Comparatively, European-based factories have a better-educated workforce, more emphasis on internal training and stable wages than other enterprises. Thus, they have lower turnover rates and better reputation among workers. This can be explained either by the concern for brand image or the local industrial environments, since most of them are located in well-regulated industrial parks of eastern China. As for American companies, the HR policies are flexible (e.g. hiring and firing of mostly migrant workers). Although many factories in the East have achieved remarkable upgrading in specialized low-volume production or planned to transform toward ODM after a wave of mergers and takeovers, such changes have not resulted in sustainable upgrading of skills or more employee participation. Taiwanese companies, which resemble American ones, are featured by low base wages, very high OT proportion, authoritative management, and strict hierarchy between operators and other employees.

In all contract manufacturers, major risks exist. Overall high turnover rate, occasional individual conflicts, and lots of complaints by employees on Internet forums show the lack of employees' loyalty and the instability of company-based HRM policies. In eastern China, most European- and American-companies use large shares of dispatched labor. The separation of a relatively stable core workforce from temporary workers saves costs and increases flexibility for the factories. However, the inequality in daily work and life may potentially lead to unrest. Moreover, Taiwanese companies in southern China offer all migrant workers with low base wages and lengthy work hours. Importantly, the recent changes in Chinese labor law have impacted all contract manufacturers. Although trade unions and collective bargaining remain pure formality, there are signs of positive impacts of legal regulations on working conditions. This situation may be replicated if there is some legal regulation on contractual determination of wages and pay grades. At the same time, employees have increasingly developed legal awareness of their rights. Since wages remain to be low, work hours are long and other basic labor standards remain unpleasant, the numbers of individual labor conflicts have increased. Collective bargaining is urgently needed, though for the moment most managers and workers have not yet realized this.

Low-end suppliers and subcontractors

There are two main types of subcontractors: one type describes suppliers within the large corporation groups, typically Japanese family corporations, and the other encompasses a huge number of external suppliers that operate in the low-end sector of the global production network in terms of technology, costs, and profit margins. The former type was established during the 1990s within state-planned industrial parks of eastern China, whereas the latter group mushroomed in the PRD after 2000.[82]

Within the first group of suppliers, ownership is either wholly-owned by the foreign companies or by joint ventures that involve small shares from local governments. In the cases of joint ventures, foreign companies still dominate capital and management. These suppliers produce specialized parts for other companies in the same corporation groups. Among most Japanese MNCs, parts and components are purchased from suppliers that are owned by the parent MNCs rather than by external providers. In those small- and medium-scaled suppliers, equipment and production flows are specialized but they are not necessarily the most advanced. Production lines are not common. Rather, work is mostly done by individual stations. In particular, a large proportion of work is

82 For instance, Guangdong province accounted for 47.87% of air-conditioner production nationwide from January to October of 2010, and 53.20% of home water heaters. See: the Consumer Electronics Industrial Analysis Report of 2010, http://www.made-in-china.com/actives/guide/111/184404/Consumer_Electronics_201101.pdf

manually (e.g. sub-assembly) done by migrant workers from all over China. Since the production can be easily substituted within individual operations, the threat of relocation is very likely to win compromise from the local governments and trade unions, thus negatively affect the wages and other labor standards.

Generally speaking, legal standards are followed by most suppliers among MNCs. Wage structures are different among Japanese enterprises, but they usually have base wages and performance-based incentives. Performance is evaluated every month and accounts for 30% of monthly pay. OT is regulated by local governments due to the recent changes of national law and policies, so the percentage of OT pay relative total income has reduced from 40-50% to 10%. In addition, there are half-a-year or year-end bonuses, ranging from one to three months wages. As for welfare, enterprises pay legal social insurances and housing fund for workers. There are also festival benefits and various cash bonuses, especially for model workers. Also typical in many Japanese firms, the wage hierarchy between operators and engineers is strict. For instance, the base wage for operators is about 1.5 times the legal minimum wage, and engineers get 3 or 4 times of this amount.

Besides developed logistics and transportation, another advantage in mass-producing in China is low labor costs. The workforce is usually very young, low educated and unskilled migrant workers, who are mostly female. Migrant workers are regarded as having weak self-awareness of protection. In case of dissatisfaction, for example when the OT was reduced to lower than 36 hours per month thus lowering their income, so they just leave their jobs. This passive way of "voting by their feet" partly explains the high turnover rates in the industry. In addition, compared to those in southern China featured by excessive OT and massive dormitory, companies in eastern China do not provide high base wages though the living costs, including rents, are higher than in the south. There is no seniority-based wage or retention plan for operators, except skill-based allowances for a small number of skilled operators (e.g. in product inspection). Thus, such companies are not attractive for potential employees. Many managers in eastern China complain about not finding enough operators.

It is particularly interesting that several Japanese suppliers in eastern China have been recommended by local trade unions as having best models of wage negotiation, one of which was even praised by ACFTU[83]. Trade unions have been set up since the establishment of the factories, and collective contracts were firstly signed in Japan-China joint ventures and one factory fully-owned by Japanese. Wage negotiations are conducted at least once a year. Since the

83 More details of collective bargaining in Japanese suppliers will be discussed in the following section.

atmosphere of such negotiations is cooperative, there has been no much disagreement over wages. In a few collective contracts, specific figures lay out what percentage of revenue should be distributed to employees as bonus. These are regarded by the ACFTU as good cases of wage negotiations compared to other companies in China.

The group of "external" suppliers from other parts of Asia, Europe, America and also mainland China fill the low- and mid-levels of the electronics manufacturing world. They specialize in mechanical parts, cell phone chargers, cable and connectors, etc.. Those are parts of the final products - computers, mobile phones or other consumer electronics of well-known global brands. Some suppliers completely export their products in order to avoid Value Added Taxes and then re-imported to sell on the domestic market. Besides, many others export most products to Southeast Asia, Mid East and other less developed regions. In contrast to Japanese suppliers, the general picture is a "low wage classic" regime despite divergences in size, location, and ownership.

Larger companies produce small parts and do sub-assembly for ODMs and contract manufacturers, whereas smaller ones only assemble small components or accessories with imported parts. Thus, the production varies from large-scale machinery to primitive assembly by hand. In particular, most of the simple manual jobs (e.g. putting two pieces of metal together) in small factories no longer exist in high-wage countries. In several large companies, the manufacturing of a set of parts is even highly integrated "in one roof", similar to that of contract manufacturers. They have relatively high degree of automation and machines are in charge of physically-demanding or high-precision work. With a small proportion of high-skilled workers in mechanics, tooling or pre-processing shops, where individual work stations are installed, most low-skilled workers are female laborers along production lines. As such work is normally simplified, it takes only one week or so on-the-job training after a worker is recruited from the labor market. In many cases, the content of training involves learning factory rules and safety procedures including how to use a fire hydrant.

Labor protection policies are better implemented in larger enterprises, perhaps due to their higher visibility than in smaller ones. Nevertheless, due to the nature of electronic products and low level of automation, many workers are exposed to poisonous or harmful materials. Most male workers are employed in such positions. Besides, the temperature inside workshops is often very high, especially in southern China where most of those subcontractors are concentrated. Air conditioners are installed in some factories, but they are rarely turned on in order to save electricity cost. In one European supplier, workers have heat stroke in workshops as early as in April. In addition, noise is another problem due to the wide use of air-winding machines. Earplugs are necessary but not all factories enforce workers to use them.

In the short term those suppliers may survive as they are now, especially when labor costs remain low. However, in the long term, a more sustainable way of development is indispensable. As many larger companies have developed rapidly, a few have begun to brainstorm long-term strategies. Lean production, 6 Sigma and other concepts are introduced in some larger suppliers, but mostly as formalities. In one Taiwanese company, a new production organization aimed at developing its workforce was introduced in early 2009, with the guidance of a former manager of a brand name Japanese MNC. In the plan, production lines were reformed into "cell production", in which each cell was composed of a certain number of workers and everyday production targets were assigned to each cell. Job rotation was possible. Besides, when the production volume was small, changes of the cell content could be frequent. Nevertheless, this was a special case. Due to the favorable environment of the well-regulated industrial park in eastern China, the transformation process seemed to go more smoothly than others.

Since most subcontractors have very low profit margins, economies of scale often matters. In past few years, some large companies have been expanding at an explosive speed, whereas many small- or micro-sized ones closed due to fluctuations in market demand. Small subcontractors tend to have a narrow focus on a few products or high dependence on one or two biggest customers. What is worst, the small subcontractors have no direct contracting relationship with brand name MNCs. Sometimes there are more than three- or four-layers between the MNCs at the top and these small subcontractors. Therefore, in case of the bankruptcy of MNCs, suppliers were not even able to claim for any compensation. Besides, the unstable currency exchange rates and rising costs for raw materials are blamed by small enterprises for their financial difficulties. They also accuse the 2008 Labor Contract Law.

Consequently, employment also fluctuates in those companies. Generally speaking, most of the workforce originate from outside of large cities. These enterprises recruit workers from all over the country, sometimes technical school graduates but more migrant workers at their 20s. Direct labor is the majority of the workforce (e.g. 80%). In assembly workshops, sometimes 90% are female. As a whole, the composition of the workforce, regardless of company size, may change every day due to a highly flexible hire-and-fire employment policy as well as very high turnover rates (e.g. 12% per month). Loyalty from employees is impossible. For instance, during the 2008/9 crisis, one fourth of the employees in a company voluntarily left after orders dropped 40% and wages went down accordingly.

Working conditions are apparently below average in this industry. Normally, the work intensity is quite high and working time is very long. In one case, there is a strict rule that workers along the production line need the permission of supervisors to use the toilet or drink water, and only one worker can go at a time. Besides, it is almost impossible to ask for a sick leave. Thus, there are cases when sick workers faint in workshops when they were forced to continue work. Moreover, a 12-hours day or night shift is common, which requires at least 3 hours OT every day. In many factories, the average working time may exceed 260 hours or even 300 hours a month, which is far higher than the legal limit of 36 hours. There is one day off per week or per month in large companies, but smaller companies do not offer any day off.

The wage system usually includes base wages, performance incentives and lots of OT. In spite of high turnover rates and labor shortage from time to time, there is no retention plan for operators. In most Taiwanese companies in eastern China, the base wage for new operators is the local minimum wage, but the total monthly income may double due to excessive OT. Wages may increase every year. There are strict divisions between different positions with associated base wages. It is possible for operators to be promoted to the position of supervisors within a span of several years, although this case is rare. The performance of groups is evaluated and then bonus is distributed to groups according to headcount. Further, there is also year-end bonuses, which are often based on work positions. Several kinds of allowances, free work meals, and low-rent dormitory, are provided. In addition, social insurances are mostly paid for all workers since the early of 2008. However, employers complain that the contribution ratio is too high.

In the southern China, the wages, especially base wages, in most factories are even lower. The base wages barely meet local minimum wage standards. Usually, the monthly income is 1.5-2 times of local minimum wages, but workers have to work on average 3 hours OT per day, including weekends. Piece work rate is adopted in some factories in order to dodge the minimum wages or legal OT pay. Besides, many operators were given social insurances only because of the stricter regulations in recent national law. As for the contribution to social insurances, 12% of employees' net income is paid by employers and 8% by workers themselves. In addition, meals and dormitory are provided for free or are subsidized in order to attract migrant workers. However, the quality of meals is poor and dormitory rooms are uncomfortable since they are shared by 8 to more than 20 people in one room.

Apparently, the 2008 Labor Contract Law had a positive impact on labor standards in those suppliers, especially in the South. Many improved their labor practices (e.g. to register the entire workforce, to pay taxes and social insurances, and to pay wages and OT) according to legal standards. For this reason, many employers complain that the law increased their costs. Nevertheless, the limitations in law enforcements marks a drawback in the labor struggle. First, it is not well implemented, especially in smaller enterprises. For instance, many workers only have short-term contracts (e.g. for only one year). Some labor contracts contain illegal clauses, such as a penalty on absence. Second, work time is too long. In many companies, the regular schedule is 3 hours OT every day and workers have no holidays at all. In small suppliers, managers frankly admit that they cannot afford to meet legal minimum wages for their employees, fulfill legal OT payments, or uphold standard work hours. In fact, local governments in southern China and less developed areas in the East mostly turn a blind eye on such situations. Even more, some local governments allow companies to use low-paid interns and lower OT calculation. Furthermore, the labor contract law could not solve the root cause of low labor standards and job insecurity. The problems result from the bottom position of those small subcontractors within the global production network, which means their profit margins are squeezed and production flows completely depend on a few major customers. Potentially, the low labor standards will continue unless workers, international organizations and government leaders cooperate in changing the profit relations, particularly by increasing the liability of brand name "clients".

It is expected that trade unions and collective bargaining simply do not exist among those suppliers. There is no much pressure from the local governments to institute trade unions and collective bargaining, perhaps because the focus of ACFTU is still on non-unionized brand name MNCs. In one Taiwanese company, workers' congress exists in place of trade unions. Labor representatives are elected from each department and they hold a meeting once a year to discuss labor-related issues (e.g. change of benefits). At the same time, no HR policies are in effect. Rather, authoritative management is common among companies of different sizes. In particular, many foreman and direct line leaders are promoted from operators but because they usually have no management experience, they are often harsh to workers. In some foreign- or overseas Chinese-invested companies, top management is dominated by non-Chinese nationals. It is almost impossible for operators to directly communicate with them due to language problem barriers.

In consequence, inhuman working conditions and repressive management polices have led to frequent labor conflicts among low- to medium-end suppliers. In particular, the awareness of workers' rights enhanced after debates concerning the labor contract law in 2007 and 2008. Increasing numbers of workers have begun to appeal to the law when management violates their rights. Indeed, the numbers of lawsuits have increased including some involving groups of workers.

Summary

The electronics industry has a complex composition of production regimes, and large differentiation in labor standards and industrial relations. Electronics manufacturers are highly integrated into the global production network and range from specialized Western brand name MNCs, Asian integrated producers, newly emerging Chinese MNCs, gigantic contract manufacturers, to small- and medium-sized suppliers and subcontractors.

Due to segmentation, enterprises vary in their working conditions. There are modern and clean workshops, HR policies and highly-skilled workforce among global brand names. At the bottom, there are classical sweatshops, abusive supervisors and unskilled female migrant workers in subcontractors. In particular, the development of contract manufacturers has brought along a massive "re-integration" of manufacturing from below. They use high technologies and are capital-intensity. However, contract manufacturers also feature Taylorist work organization, de-skilled work, and extremely flexible wages. Occasionally severe incidents occur in contract manufacturers, such as the suicidal wave in Foxconn. Among suppliers, a handful of Japanese firms are rather unique. They have extraordinarily coordinated labor relations, built on extensive communication channels and wage negotiations. Nevertheless, their collective bargaining is still highly limited within the existing production network and the current legal framework in China.

At the same time, there are similar problems among different types of enterprises. Primarily, fluctuations in production flows are commonly caused by the industrial restructuring since the late 1970s. Many traditionally fully-integrated global brand name companies become narrowly-focused on specialized products, through spin-offs, contracting-out and setting up subsidiaries. Besides, there are hierarchical supplying relationships along the value chain, with the global brand names on the top. Consequently, hiring and firing, along with the market fluctuation, is universal in this industry. In companies along the upstream of the production flow, dispatched labor ers have no security of employment. At lower-tiers of the supply chain, all jobs in contract manufacturers and lower-end suppliers could be temporary.

This is accompanied by another problem - extremely high turnover rates of employment. In specialized Western MNCs, employers have begun to use HR policies, internal labor markets, grievance procedures, and extensive training programs, to cultivate the cooperation and loyalty of the relatively higher-skilled workforce. However, for the majority of enterprises, even though managers often complain about the difficulties in recruiting enough operators or technicians, they have not taken any effective measures like wage increases to attract workers. Paradoxically, in some highly "flexible" enterprises, the high turnover rates are regarded as a good thing because employers do not need to pay legal severance compensation when workers voluntarily leave. Unskilled migrants are not deemed to be valuable assets of enterprises, but rather they are regarded as disposable. In particular, their wages remain very low and unstable, especially in assembly factories and subcontractors. On the one hand, this has been a pull-factor for global assembly and production firms to China. On the other hand, no matter how much the short-term profit is, such a structure keeps the majority of work simplified, the products labor-intensive, and the workforce low-skilled. These conditions obstruct attempts to upgrade the industry and the national economy.

A key factor that is absent in each scenario is the role of collective labor or trade unions. The presence of trade unions is rare in Chinese electronics industry, except in former SOEs or a few foreign MNCs. Accordingly, collective bargaining and collective contracts barely exist, with the exception of a couple of Japanese-dominated joint ventures. In large enterprises, HR policies or CSR are used as the substitute for industrial relations. However, the effect of such unilateral rules is only modest, given profit-seeking interests and the weak monitoring of labor standards.

In consequence, the electronics industry is highly segmented into different categories of enterprises, and flooded by strict divisions of labor, lengthy work hours, flexible employment of low-wage/low-skilled migrant workers, and occasionally severe occupational safety incidents caused by harmful working environments. Industrial relations are very unstable, since there are growing numbers of labor disputes, both individual and collective. They also take the form of passive resistances such as quitting, as well as active strikes. In order to change such situations and seek sustainable development, the characteristics of this industry should be taken into consideration. On the side of enterprises, external pressure is critical. For instance, since most consumer electronics are image-conscious, brand name MNCs and their direct suppliers often behave as good corporate citizens by following national laws and policies. Following this logic, expose of the unequal relationships along the supply chains of brand name companies may improve labor standards among lower-level suppliers and subcontractors. Besides, the implementation of labor law seems to rely on the whims of local governments, which have led to different conditions in various regions. The situation is more complicated among workers. Since trade unions are rare and ineffectual, workers' resistance to their repressive conditions remain largely individualized. Nevertheless, some distinctive features of this industry, such as employing high numbers of migrant workers and accommodating them in massive dormitories, may provide the base for labor collectivity. Since recent changes in labor law have enhanced workers' consciousness of their rights, they may realize their common concerns of labor standards and working conditions and eventually take actions together with each other.

3.3 Wage regulation

Whereas the production practices may have become increasingly similar in different locations around the world, the industrial relations of each nation still vary largely from each other. Wage regulation is not just one part of production organization, but is also at the center of industrial relations. Typically in Fordism, a social consumption norm and collective bargaining guarantee regular wage increases. Furthermore, wage regulation may also guide the direction of future development. The market-based wage-setting mechanisms in the U.S. and a German model of industry-wide bargaining show two distinctive principles of labor-capital relations.

Among all types of wage regulation, collective bargaining, regardless of its forms in various social and economic conditions, has been a key mechanism since the very beginning of the industrial revolution, particularly after the WWII. Historically, the institutionalization processes of collective bargaining in the U.S. and Germany have certain elements in common. In both models, collective bargaining resulted from long-term labor struggles led by industrial unions, and was institutionalized by the strategic choice or compromise of the state and capitalists under relatively labor-friendly global environments. Nevertheless, the functions of collective bargaining after its establishment can be very different in the two models. Its role in a specific economy depends on the specificities of the production regimes and industrial relations. At the same time, production and industrial relations may also be re-shaped by the degrees of governability and coordination of collective bargaining.

In this section, I investigate the existing forms of wage determination in China. I then trace the development path of these forms, before and after collective bargaining has been legislated. Last, I provide brief profile of wage regulation, particularly the status quo of collective bargaining in China.

3.3.1 Forms of wage determination

Among various enterprises in the global production network, from the top global brand name MNCs to the low-end subcontractors at the bottom, the processes of wage determination and wage levels are different within each production regimes. In the absence of any industrial or regional coordination, wages and other labor standards vary from enterprise to enterprise and from industry to industry. According to my field study wage determination in China may be divided, not exclusively, into three major categories, based on the form and degree of employees' involvement.

The first category includes the majority of companies, whereby wages are unilaterally determined by management. This is an arbitrary decision-making process. In most enterprises, workers are regarded as a commodity or production factor, rather than a "human being" . Employers, usually the managers, decide wage categories and levels for all workers. This has become the dominant and, in the view of many managers, most practical way of determining wages in a market economy (Lüthje et al. 2013). This field study has found that most employers and even professional human resource managers have no idea or no intention of learning what collective bargaining really is and they regard their unilateral power to determine wages and labor standards as given. Besides, there is a deep-rooted practice in setting specific wages for specific companies, specific positions, and specific workers, which follows the influential American HRM concepts since the beginning of the economic reform. This practice makes above-enterprise coordination in labor standards even less likely.

Normally, the data from market surveys, which are purchased from large consulting firms at expensive prices or conducted by companies themselves, have become the major tool for the management in determining wages (e.g. 50 percentile of the market prices in a first-tier city). It is impossible to verify all such data. Companies have complete freedom in handling wage structures and standards. Thus, the result is a wide diversification of wages. Empirical studies show that wages for the same type of workers are uneven between two companies of similar sizes, comparable products and proximate locations. In such cases, job hopping is an undesirable but unavoidable fact in many enterprises.

The only constraint, especially for the vast number of non-public enterprises, is the legal minimum wage. Other rules, such as wage guidelines issued by local governments, have no binding force. Since the beginning of the market reform, enterprises have been granted a high degree of autonomy in wage distribution. In theory, the legal minimum wage standards are supposed to be the bottom line, but in practice they are used by many enterprises as the criteria for base wages of manufacturing workers. As many enterprises today have no or low skill requirements on the workforce, employees' wages barely meet minimum wage requirements. Additionally, there are high proportions of performance-based wages or OT pay, which threaten the stability of their income for the majority of workers.

The second category of wage determination involves certain forms of negotiation at the individual level, which mostly involve an employee and his/her supervisor or the HR manager. As commonly seen during the 1980s reform period (Walder 1984), individual negotiations frequently occurred in SOEs. Today in the huge non-public sector, employees with higher skills or special expertise may demand better pay. Nonetheless, the results are often worse than their expectations, since the power of individuals is limited in a largely surplus labor market like China. In addition, many managers lack foresightedness towards the issue of workers' retention. Therefore, managers may simply recruit replacement workers or threat to do so, in order to end individual negotiations by workers.

For the majority of workers, the two categories of wage determination I outlined above are dominant in China. The individualization of labor relations has become the mainstream in China. In the first place, it is not easy to organize trade unions in many enterprises, as well as to bargain with employers. Some managers believe the reasons they set up enterprise unions are either legal formalities or coercion from upper unions that simply collect union membership fees from them. In a very small proportion of enterprises with SOE connections, such as JVs and former SOEs, trade unions have been established and collective contracts have been signed.

Without a collective organization, manufacturing workers in China, who are mostly comprised of un-skilled or semi-skilled migrant workers, have little institutional support to put forward their requests. Thus, individual workers' scope of negotiation is restricted. As a result, management has almost unlimited freedom in determining wages. Especially after the reform, the new orientation toward flexibility and rationalization have rapidly dominated many industries. Wages and other standards are determined by individualized performance-based HRM. However, HRM lists only unilateral rules, pitting workers against each other not only within the same enterprise but also between companies, industries, and even different countries.

There is simply no role of workers in the process. In fact, most low-skilled workers can be easily replaced at very low training costs and little efforts. Retention of front-line operators is not desired by employers. Even with a migrant labor shortage (e.g. in PRD since 2004 and particularly after the large redundancy during the 2008/9 crisis), wages have certainly increased within recruiting advertisement, but these increases were still not attractive enough to retain workers. In practice, migrant workers often have no choice but to leave a factory if there are disputes over wages. Consequently, the high turnover rates, in the auto suppliers and the entire electronics industry, clearly evidence that wages are too low or too unstable. For instance, in a large-scale survey in the electronics industry in 2007[84], 65.2% of all targeted employees regard compensation as the most important reason for high employee turnover, followed by low development opportunities.

The last but most important category is collective bargaining, which unfortunately has not taken hold in the contemporary history of China. Some leading enterprises, especially those with a history of public ownership, have tried to sign collective contracts either voluntarily or under external pressure. For the majority of Western companies, which have the best tradition of collective bargaining in their home countries, HRM has nearly eliminated any alternatives. Exemplified by American companies, the emphases on linking wages to performance and of pay differentials have become common practices among most Western MNCs, including European companies traditionally with centralized wage bargaining (Wächter et al. 2003: 96). The older version of integrated MNCs featured by strong collective bargaining and traditional unionism does not exist in China. Most of HRM concepts mirror the policies of modern paternalism, for which non-union American electronics companies from Silicon Valley in particular have become famous (Luethje 2001).

By only looking at the numbers of collective contracts, one might have over-optimistic impression. By the end of September 2010, 1.408 million collective contracts had been signed in China, covering 2.439 million employing units and 185 million employees[85], a significant increase from the 1.247 million collective contracts signed by September 2009. At the same time, among a total of 13 million enterprises, more than 10 million were small to medium-sized, where regional and industrial bargaining has gradually been recognized. According to the ACFTU, up until September 2009, there were 150,000 regional collective contracts that covered 962,000 enterprises and 41.975 million employees. In addition, 990,000 sectoral contracts covered 307,000 enterprises and 18.868 million employees. In particular, there were 512,000 wage contracts for 902,000 enterprises and 61.776 million employees.[86] The statistical data from the Ministry of Human Resource and Social Security seemed a bit different, recording more than 700,000 effective collective contracts covering nearly 100

84 Ccid net, Consulting, 2007 Survey, http://news.ccidnet.com/art/3157/20080521/145427 1_1.html

85 People's News, The "two universal" activity of the trade union in 2010 achieved good results, January 19, 2011, http://acftu.people.com.cn/GB/13771665.html

86 Xinhua Net, data released by Mr. Zhang, Jianguo, the director of collective contract department at the ACFTU, The ACFTU interview on how to implement "rainbow" plan, June 04, 2010, http://news.xinhuanet.com/politics/2010-06/04/c_12181248.htm

million employees[87], but the number of collective contracts was still very large. However, given the total employment of 780 million at the year end of 2009[88], more than 60% of employees were still not protected by any form of collective contract or special contract.

The ACFTU, as written in the revised Trade Union Law of 2001, emphasizes the "equal negotiation and collective contract system". Besides, the same law stipulated the legal responsibilities of employers for refusing equal negotiations without legitimate reasons, breaching collective contracts, and infringing labor rights. Furthermore, in 2004 the Regulation of Collective Contract was promulgated by the Ministry of labor and Social Security[89], which not only explained the system but also expanded the content and scope of collective contracts. So far the governments of 31 provinces (including autonomous regions and municipal cities) issued specific documents on the collective contract system.

However, those stunning numbers do not reflect the genuine function of collective bargaining. The effectiveness of collective contracts relies on the representative of the organizations that sign these agreements. Unfortunately, most of those agreements are the direct result of "quota" policies set by the ACFTU (Pringle 2005). In fact, the director of the legal department at the ACFTU, Mr. Liu, Jicheng, publicly admitted that only 20% of existing wage negotiations may be effectively carried out.[90] According to many scholars and practitioners, the actual implementation is even less satisfactory.

First, the content of collective contracts is problematic. It is usually not linked to the specific environments and rules of enterprises (Brown 2006), and does not reflect the actual interaction between laborers and capitalists. In many cases, the collective contracts in different enterprises have the same form and the content is merely a copy of labor law clauses, or are sample contracts issued by local government or trade unions at higher levels. According to a survey on SOEs (Taylor et al. 2003: 251-252), there are three types of clauses in these collective contracts. The first are clauses related to terms and conditions. The

87 China.org.cn, Online press conference on the work of the Ministry of Human Resource and Social Security, Mr. Yin, Chengji, spokesperson from the Ministry, Jan. 25, 2011,http://www.china.com.cn/zhibo/2011-01/25/content_21803701.htm?show=t

88 National Statistics Bureau of China, 2009 Statistic Report on National Economy and Social Development

89 The Ministry of Labor (before 2003) or Ministry of Labor and Social Security (2003-2008) has been renamed as the Ministry of Human Resource and Social Security since March 11, 2008

90 21st Century Business Herald, "Trade Union Law" will be amended - wage negotiation may be raised to industrial levels, Aug. 19, 2010

second are clauses that stipulate duties to be carried out by the signing parties. The last are clauses that outline the duration of the contracts. A major part of the collective contract entails the second type of clause accounts, on average, for 70% of the text, within which only 10% are about labor benefits and the rest only copy or refer to the labor laws. The same survey also shows that successful claims by employees are mostly backed by legal stipulations. Otherwise even reasonable requests by trade unions can be rejected by employers. Similarly, I have found from my field study that the content of collective contracts remains very general. On the one hand, there are almost no specific figures on wages or other labor standards. On the other hand, many contracts clearly show the management prerogative in determining labor standards. After some copied legal terms, such as "wages should be adjusted according to the consumer price index", it is noticeable that sentences like "the final decisions should be made by the General Manager" are added to the end.

This is easier to understand when one recognizes that the majority of collective contracts are agreed on without real "bargaining" (Feng 2006); that is, there is no process of sufficient negotiation and bargaining between the parties. "Bargaining", which means employees and employers express ideas and then negotiate, is the key to the system and probably the only way to effectively reach agreements. In reality, employers in China are typically characterized by individual-orientation, short-sighted management and weak legal awareness. Most of them, especially in non-public sectors, resist collective bargaining. In their opinion, any potential for successful bargaining is unwelcome. Although the law stipulates that "governments at the county level and above have the authority to correct the misbehavior of employers if they refuse to bargain without due cause", in practice this has never happened. What is worse, enterprise unions are dependent on employers for wages, and union officials usually hold positions or ranks within management (Jiang 2004), which makes them unable either to bargain against employers or to gain the trust of workers.

As a result, collective bargaining in many enterprises is initiated by upper level unions rather than enterprise unions. Negotiation is conducted by collective negotiation instructors rather than by labor representatives from the specific enterprises. This makes negotiation operate like formal meetings than legitimate bargaining. Moreover, these negotiations are primarily governed by management. Several studies have found that so-called collective negotiations in China are merely ways of obtaining consent from employers (e.g. Taylor et al. 2003; Guo 2004; and Clarke et al. 2004). In other cases (Luethje et al. 2010), the HR department in companies with public ownership or JV background would draft the collective agreement and send it to the enterprise union. The union may then make revisions after collecting workers' suggestions through union groups.

If parties agreed, the contract becomes final. In the majority of private enterprises, the processes of signing collective contracts involve even less negotiation. Usually, employers just sign a copied contract together with union cadres when they feel under political pressure from local governments or upper unions (Guo 2004). In most instances, employees are not even aware of the existence of collective contracts. Thus, although the numbers of collective contracts have grown rapidly[91], they are "ineffective byproducts" of labor laws, produced out of formalities similar to top-down administrative tasks (Taylor et al. 2003: 206). The most positive effect of collective contracts, as Clarke et al. (2004) comments is that they remind employers and union cadres of their respective legal responsibilities.

Noticeably, during my investigation, I have identified some relatively effective cases of collective bargaining. These cases could be divided into three main types: wage negotiations in Japanese-Chinese joint ventures; sectoral collective bargaining in eastern China; and collective bargaining following successful strikes. It is fair to say that each type has their obvious limitations and thus it would be very difficult to endorse them on a broader scale. Nevertheless, these case, especially the third type, may be the very first step of the institution-building process of collective bargaining in China.

The first type is collective negotiation within the existing legal framework. In eastern China, several Japanese-owned or Japanese-sino joint ventures were selected as model cases of collective bargaining, one of which was even praised by the ACFTU. This case is a joint venture with a small share from the city government. Since this joint venture was set up in 1994, it already practiced wage negotiation. Three negotiations over annual wage increase, annual bonus, and workers' welfare are conducted every year. Trade unions collect data before negotiations. The beginning of each negotiation entails introductions from the chief representatives from both parties who are usually the general manager and the union chairman. Then labor representatives consult with union committees and reflect on their opinions. After several rounds, the representatives of both sides sit down and start formal negotiations on a primary draft. All workers are involved and labor representatives discuss the draft of wage agreements.

The wage agreements state that wages should increase at least once a year. In the last years, the average increase rate has been more than 10%. The principle is that wage increase should be in line with the average profitability

91 The numbers of collective contracts officially registered in the labor administration had grown from 69,000 in 1996, the first year of spreading this mechanism, to 703,000 in 2009. Source: Annual reports on human resource and social security 1992-2009, http://www.molss.gov.cn/gb/zwxx/node_5436.htm

that each worker contributed. Average profitability per capita is used in place of labor productivity, because the complexities of calculating labor productivity overburdened workers. Average profitability seems more visible than labor productivity to workers.[92] Another figure in the formula is Consumer Price Index. The prices of food are taken into consideration. In addition, local minimum wages and average wages at provincial and city levels are also referred to. In addition, the wage agreements also contain other considerations. For instance, every worker is guaranteed several days of on-job training with fully-paid wages and bonuses. As for work hours, the legal requirement of the city is applied. The trade union has certain control over OT hours of each worker. Every day a name list of workers who will work overtime on the day should be given to the union representatives in each department and only if they agree, the list can be reported to the HR department.

This case is no doubt very unique. First, this case demonstrates a clear presence of the Japanese style of management. The management style has strong Japanese characteristics, such as paternalism and "complete obedience". The management is dominated by Japanese general manager, vice president, and the head of financial department. In spite of differences of China and Japan in cultures and trade union traditions, the consensus of "harmony" and "cooperation" leads to a friendly environment for union recognition and collective negotiations. In particular, wage negotiations are regarded by the top management as a way of motivating workers. Besides, there are extensive communication channels designed to promote the cooperation between labor and capital, which also facilitate collective negotiation. The "internal constitution" of this company includes a wide range of industrial democratic mechanisms, such as workers' congress, opening factory affairs, and labor-capital dialogue. At least once a year in the workers' congress, the general manager updates the production and operation situation to workers. In addition, there are also other forms of information exchange among management, the trade union, and workers' representatives, such as tea gathering and annual top-level meetings between managers and workers. At a broader level, the determination of wages in the company relies on internal information and communication among representative Japanese companies in the same industrial park and the same corporation group in a given city. Nevertheless, enterprise trade unions do not have such coordination among each other.

92 As a matter of fact, Japanese internal suppliers like this company receive raw materials from outside of China and export all products back, so it is very hard to calculate the actual profit in between.

Besides the special features of Japanese management, this case is also unique in other aspects, such as the charisma of individual union chairmen (Xu 2003) and the exclusion of the trade union from deciding work organization. Most importantly, collective bargaining in this company resembles more a mechanism of communication and consultation than a process of joint decision-making. Management still has the final say on almost every issue discussed in the negotiations. Nearly any success achieved by the trade union is already written in law, and employers do not accept any requests beyond the legal standards. For instance, if individual workers want the trade union to stand on behalf of them to argue against the employer on dismissal, the union may intervene but the final say is in the hands of the administration. The union chairman admitted that workers' real wages still could not meet their subsistence needs. Thus, collective contracts simply ensure that the minimum standards in the laws are enforced. In fact, they have not improved labor standards above the legal minimum.

Consequently, although this case could be called a model example of collective bargaining to a certain degree, it would be very difficult to further develop or popularize this model in similar enterprises, particularly in regards to claiming higher wages or intervening in work organization. Indeed, in the prevailing low-wage low-end production network, it is not easy for workers in individual firms, especially lower-end suppliers, to receive sufficient wages or to intervene in work organization if without any above-enterprise coordination.

The second type involves several cases of sectoral bargaining in eastern China,[93] which have also been highly propagandized by the ACFTU and its local affiliates. Those cases have a lot in common: the sectors are all pilar industries of the towns; there are a number of small enterprises in the same labor-intensive and low-tech industries; etc.. Before sectoral bargaining took place, workers in the majority of the enterprises had very low piece rates and lengthy work hours. Thus, there were very high turnover rates and frequent labor unrest, including workers appealing to upper governments. This had caused employers' collective complaints and local governments' concerns. In this context, the local trade unions or newly-established industrial unions, with major support from local governments and upper unions, began negotiations with employers' associations particularly on the pricing of each separated work procedures. The outcomes seemed to be quite effective for stabilizing the local industries.

93 E.g. Wool sweater industry in Wenling, http://news.sohu.com/20080414/n256268471.shtml; Luhe garment sector, http://cmqfyc.acftu.org/template/10001/file.jsp?cid=387&aid=4026; and Pizhou wooden board sector: Workers' Daily, http://www.sxgh.org.cn/particular.aspx?id=8091&parentID=33

In the cases of Wenling, Luhe and Pizhou, the sectoral collective bargaining has involved the highly visible role of the local governments and upper unions. In fact, the bargaining has been initiated by the local governments and upper unions. Thus, some suspect the governments try to set up political models. At the same time, the power and resource allocated from top-down by the governments and upper unions cannot easily be copied in other places. Therefore, such sectoral collective bargaining would be difficult to be promoted in a broader scope. In addition, these collective bargaining practices have mainly taken place in smaller towns with traditionally-developed industries that employed the majority of labor and created the most industrial value for the regions. Consequently, the instability of the very industries could cause huge concerns for the capital and especially local governments and finally make them take actions. However, the importance of a single industry in these small town is unlikely to occur in bigger cities or more open regions like South China.

The last type, in contrast to the first two types, does not fall strictly within the existing legal framework. They are not connected to official unions or part of the formal collective bargaining system. This form of bargaining is directly initiated by workers during or after successful strikes. A few cases have occurred. Unfortunately, this has been mostly a one-off process or temporary in nature, and rarely becomes institutionalized.

As the representative case of the 2010 strike wave in the automobile industry, the Nanhai Honda strike also marks a turning point in collective bargaining. Since workers in the Nanhai Honda parts factory demanded collective bargaining during their strike action in June 2010, this company has conducted three rounds of collective wage negotiation by early March 2011.[94] For the first time, collective bargaining immediately following the strike was a process that involved participants from outside the factory, including a deputy of the National People's Congress and a well-known labor law professor from Beijing. To a certain degree, the voice of workers was not well organized, since employees' representatives even were divided among themselves and the final agreement was not voted by employees' congress. In addition, although the bargaining reached a collective agreement in the end, many workers were not completely satisfied. The reasons for their dissatisfaction were that some employees failed to receive as much wage increase as others. For those who received, their raises were not appended to base wages as they expected but only under "special bonus". In Chinese industries, base wages are more or less the stable income, but "special bonus" may be canceled by the companies any time. Nevertheless, in the next two rounds of collective bargaining, workers had

94 There is a very detailed report on this case. See: Kong 2012

gradually learned to collect evidence for their demands and become better prepared for the negotiations. One reason that explains their progress in preparation was that they were allowed to elect their own union group leaders and new union committee members, albeit not the union chairman. Further, workers became involved in all through the process of collective bargaining. It should also be noted that in the last negotiation workers' delegates also referred to wages in a brand-name assembly plant nearby. It is a clear sign that workers no longer only look at their own specific problems, but have access to information of other workers and other companies.

This is a different case from others in the past. Apparently, it is no longer a singular process. If the attitudes of the local governments remain relatively positive toward such economic disputes, collective bargaining is expected to go on. Contrary cases were seen in the same strike wave in northern China, where some local governments still oppressed strikes. No collective bargaining occurred after these strikes. In order to make sure this case serves as the stepping stone for collective bargaining in China, institutionalization of collective bargaining at the enterprise level would be necessary. Later the institutionalization should be extended to industrial and national levels. At the same time, workers should never cease to develop their strength in the negotiation. Too much compromise can not reach harmony or win-win situations. For instance, the compromise in the first round of wage negotiations resulted to unsatisfied wage scheme for many workers. As a result, workers demanded another round of collective bargaining very soon. Rather, sometimes saying "no" is helping both sides to reach longer term stability.

In a nutshell, enterprises and workers have not used collective bargaining as the major way of determining wages and other labor standards. The existing collective bargaining and collective contract system has failed to fulfill the goal of the government that labor and capital can solve problems with full autonomy, and the expectation of trade unions that industrial conflicts must be transformed into legal procedures. Apart from the majority of unsubstantial bargaining and collective contracts, a few recent cases of wage negotiation have shown that the beginnings of the institution-building process for collective bargaining are present. In order to establish essential institutions in China, I analyze the flaws of the existing regulations - wage system and collective bargaining mechanism.

3.3.2 The development of the wage system

The existing wage system in China is derived from a complex interaction of market forces, government regulation, and social and cultural assumptions. As

Boyer (1990: 38; 2002: 74) defines, the wage relation is a "set of legal and institutional conditions that govern the use of wage-earning labor as the workers' mode of existence". It refers "to the type of means of production; the social and technical division of labor; the ways in which workers are attracted and retained by the firm; the direct and indirect determinants of wage income; and lastly, the workers' way of life". Clearly, wage relation is far more than a mere economic relation, but connecting individual work to the social and economic status of workers, and further to the production model and legal regulations at the macro level.

Generally speaking, the wage system since the planned economy has not experienced dramatic revolution. Rather, it has been defined more closely as "changes within continuity". Before 1978, the wage system had been defined by several key policies, including the 1958 Labor Wage Regulation and wage policies in the Cultural Revolution. The original design was to adapt the model of Soviet Union at that time. This system had been carried out from 1956 to 1978. It was featured by strong direct command of the paternalistic state in all aspects of the economy. Based on the logic of unified interests of individuals, collective and the state, the central government made wage plans on behalf of all employees, and the local governments and enterprises were only the executives of the plans. The bureaucracy decided the proportion of the gross returns to be delivered by each SOE under the heading of centralized net income. The same applied to the sum of all SOEs as to each enterprise: the bureaucracy decided what proportion of the total budgetary income would derive from the centralized net income of the state sector, and the headings and other channels for the rest of the state income. Much of the same applied on the expenditure side. The right of income disposal belonged to the bureaucracy (Kornai 1992: 73). In general, strict limits were placed on the total wage bill, the amount of payable wages in one enterprise were controlled in the form of annual wage plans, commanded by the government. The money was "earmarked" in the sense that "investment money" could not be converted into "materials money" or "wages money", or vice versa (Kornai 1992: 203). Regardless of profitability of an enterprise or the performance of employees, the enterprise had no right to pay wages above the prescribed standards.

Within factories, until early 1980s, the wages of most workers had been divided into eight levels, according to the complexity of work and the degrees of skill. Level one was paid the lowest wage and level eight the highest, equal to engineers. Wage hierarchy was low, since the highest pay was 2.7 to 2.9 times of the lowest. Nevertheless, wages were set so low since wages only guaranteed a basic living for the people and moral and political rewards received a higher priority over money. The social reproduction of labor could not sustain.

Consequently, there was another important aspect of wages - employment-based welfare. In order to show the benefit of socialism and to meet basic needs of labor, enterprises had to bear excessive welfare burdens, such as employing more than enough just to create jobs for urban residents, providing free or almost-free housing for employees, and running hospitals or clinics and schools. In the official ideology, such welfare was all "granted" by the state. As the wages did not account for the true social costs of free or heavily subsidized consumption, labor appeared unrealistically too "cheap".

The reason of setting such low wage levels for employees was to promote as much investment as possible in the national economy. This strategy was greatly propagated in all socialist countries at that time. In order to legitimate the Party's ruling, economic growth had become the major, if not the only, focus. Accordingly, surplus capital and resources had been allocated by the top leadership to fulfill the tight investment plans at the expense of limited consumption. With the effective control on price level and wages, the planned economy was capable of controlling whether nominal wages, the price level, and ultimately real wages rise, stagnate, or fall (Kornai 1992: 224).

However, such a wage system did not achieve the predetermined goal of industrialization by maximizing investment. Rather, the results were low motivation at work, redundant staff and an excessive welfare burden on the enterprises, and an inert and unbalanced economy. Primarily, the bureaucracy under socialism was neither a real owner nor "employer". Rather than profit-seeking capitalists, they were obliged to enforce wage discipline and labor discipline. This easily led to a misuse of power and disordered corporate governance. Besides, almost all urban citizens were expected to get a job and redundant workers could not be dismissed. Thus, internal surplus became a common problem in all public units. Together with the equalized wage system, in which working hard and good performance were not appreciated in form of material incentives, many employees did not work to the best of their ability.

Since 1978, the reform had begun. One key principle was to separate the "politics" from "economics", which was actually a structural requirement for the stable reproduction of any capitalist society (Hirsch 2000: 110). More exactly, the command of state apparatus in the economic realm was replaced by a less direct way of intervention. In other words, the dominating force of the economy had shifted from the governments' administrative control toward enterprise-based market adjustment. In the market economy, the major actors of labor relations were no longer the state and employees, but capitalists and laborers. Thus, the unified interests between individuals and collective no longer existed. Dramatic changes occurred as the life-long employment system dismantled, including the enforcement of the labor contract system, competitive recruitment system, and socialization of the welfare system, such as setting up social security programs and marketizing the housing system.

This reform has not been done all at once, but followed a series of steps with major disruptions and regressions from time to time. For instance, there was a remarkable difference in policies between the 1980s and 1990s. In the 1980s, there were more complex changes than a partial relaxation of political control. One such change involved increasing informal negotiation between workers and managers over wages (Walder 1984: 241). In the mid-1990s, in spite of a re-centralization trend, economic policies became more open. For instance, the state policies started to allow large flows of FDI into industries.

After all, the fixed eight-grade wage system in the planned economy was completely overturned. The most critical wage regulation for the market economy was issued in 1988 - the "Regulation on the Changes of Operation System of Enterprises". For the first time after the establishment of the People's Republic of China, this regulation entitled non-public enterprises the full autonomy of determining wages. Basically, there were two systems that resulted from this law. In the fast-expanding private sector, position- and skill-based wages were first carried out and soon became popular. At the same time, the SOEs were still subject to state control, either through the binding of wages and profitability or the total wage amount. They followed the "two 'lower' principle" which stated that the increase of total wages of enterprises should be lower than the profit growth and the average real wage should increase slower than labor productivity, which is in direct contrast to the Fordist wage norm.

As a whole, there are obvious differences but also continuities between the wage system in the planned economy and after the reform. In all types of working units, the wage structure in the planned economy was base wages plus bonuses, including year-end bonus. In governments and enterprises, the base wages were the same for employees with the same education background and years of work. Only the bonuses varied according to the profitability of each working unit. After the reform, different wage systems were applied to civil servants, employees of semi-public institutions, and of enterprises. For civil servants, wage grades decided wage standards, on the basis of individuals' positions and levels. Semi-public institutions used a similar wage grades based either on positions for administrative or academic titles. Performance-based wages were also introduced, firstly among teachers and then expanding to hospitals and scientific research departments. In the last group of enterprises, the principle was that the enterprises had full autonomy in determining wages. Although the total wages of SOEs remained under the authority of the state, private- and foreign-invested firms enjoyed increasing autonomy and developed a focus on performance appraisal of workers. The role of the state in the private sector was to guide them indirectly, through minimum wages and some non-binding documents such as industry-wide wage reports and wage guidelines. In addition, most bargaining on wages in the planned economy existed only at the vertical levels between the state and the managers. After the reform, the pressure on wages rose as employees become bolder in speaking out and making wage demands, and the bureaucratic resistance to such pressures weakened.

Today the wage system usually includes base wages, which are still based on the older principle of guaranteeing the basic living of employees, performance-based wages (either individual-, collective-, or the whole enterprise-based), and bonuses. The wage systems in SOEs are not too different from those in non-public enterprises. If we compared today's wage system to the old system in the planned economy, the wage structure has been basically consistent and the levels of base wages continue to be low. However, the degrees of wage diversification have become much higher.

In the majority of enterprises, such as auto suppliers and most of the electronics industry, wages have become so flexible that during the crisis, the first thing many enterprises did was to deduct wages. Base wages are usually low and flexible pay accounts for a high proportion in total income. Only the base wage is fixed. Because the flexible portion of wages is related to work load and quantity, when fewer orders lead to less work, enterprises could easily reduce workers' wages, sometimes to less than a half of their regular income. Even under normal circumstances, the wages for individual workers may fluctuate from month to month depending on the fluctuations of market orders. Evidently, this wage system has given employers tremendous flexibility, and thus risks and cost burden are largely shifted to workers.

Unfortunately, even if we assume that the very low base wages were inherited from the planned economy, welfare benefits, which had made the old system viable, are unmistakably absent now. In fact, the maintenance of low base wages in by employers was originally a way to avoid paying high taxes. Since 1988 income taxes have been charged on the basis of total wages with only a few exceptions. After 1988, enterprises began to consider the possibility of cost reduction through dodging legal social insurances premium, OT pay, or severance compensation. Many enterprises still paid those fees on the basis of base wages or minimum wages, in spite of the legally-stipulated basis of total wages. More importantly, the HRM concepts from the U.S. strongly influenced the labor practices of enterprises in China since the mid-1980s. At the time, both practitioners and academia were seeking for an alternative to the largely-equalized wage system in the planned economy. The emphases of the American-style HRM on individual performance and incentive perfectly fulfilled their expectations. Since HRM regards performance as such an important factor in wages, it often sets a low level of base wages. Besides, a large proportion of flexible pay is purposely designed in order to gain the effect of encouragement. In this sense, the similar form of wage structure today as that in the past is an unsurprising coincidence of both legal costs avoidance and adaptations of the American HRM model.

The HRM influence also applies to many enterprises where wages are intentionally kept confidential, going so far as to even be forbidden from employee discussion. At the same time, this fact indicates the very existence of a wage hierarchy within the enterprises, which employers are attempting to cover up. The only exception is a few Japanese auto makers, which typically have a lower wage hierarchy among their core workforce. Thus, Japanese auto makers allow their employees to have general wage information of their colleagues. The non-transparency on wages in a majority of enterprises has become much more than a way of keeping business information. It is a strategic HRM policy that conceals the truth that may trigger feelings of "internal inequality" among many employees, thus threatening the existing unilateral wage determination.

Therefore, as seen in the three categories of wage determination in the field study, the involvement of employees, especially collective labor, is mainly absent. Laws and policies after the reform entitled enterprises with the full autonomy in determining wages. This is very different from wage determination in advanced capitalist economies where this practice is mediated through collective bargaining at company, sector or national levels. Even the highest wages for workers in China, primarily those who labor in foreign enterprises or joint ventures, have not kept pace with the cost of living. Besides, the gaps among different industries, between urban and rural residences, and between different interest groups have worsened over time. Moreover, income polarization is aggravated by the wage hierarchy between workers and managers. The wages of managers are usually 20 times higher than that of workers, especially in SOEs (Ren 2010). A study finds that 21% of managers in Chinese enterprises were paid fifteen to fifty times higher than employees and 15% in FIEs were paid fifty times more (Brown 2006). Further, the large proportion of non-monetary or gray income for public employees and the dual system of urban-rural division exacerbate the income gaps.

In particular, low wages for the manufacturing workforce have become universal practice. For the vast group of migrant workers (e.g. in the PRD), the average monthly wage was 380 RMB in 1995, 700 RMB in 2003 and 893 RMB in 2006.[95] This is not only considerably lower than local average wages, less than 30%, but even below the local minimum wages, given the fact that up to 50% or 60% of the total income is OT payment. Even in many brand name MNCs, either advanced HRM policies or highly-propagandized CSR are under the auspices of continuously low wages, not to mention those at lower positions of the value chains. Based on the low wage strategy, some displays of corporate generosity (e.g. free dormitory and well-equipped living areas commonly seen in the South China), only reflect the fact that an increasing number of migrant workers do not work for a wage alone but also for the promises of becoming urbanized individuals. The offers of free dormitory and living facilities may arguably compensate their feeling of unfairness, but has nothing to do with actual improvement of working conditions or job security.

This low-wage development path has led to undesirable consequences. First, there is a generally low skill level of the manufacturing workforce, which is not equivalent to the improvement of labor productivity. According to a report from the Ministry of Human Resource and Social Security, among more than 70 million industrial workers, the numbers of technicians are slightly more than 1 million, far below the average ratio of 20% to 40% in industrialized countries. In consequence, “made-in-China” mainly means labor-intensive, lower-end and low-tech products, or in many cases, high-tech products but with core design and technologies controlled outside China and a strictly limited input from Chinese workforce. Therefore, contrary to the “high-wage/ high-skill/ high-quality” model in Germany, the vicious trap of China is “low-wage/ low-skill/ low-value-added”. Moreover, the general high turnover rates and frequent labor disputes can be interpreted as a lack of employees' loyalty and their unwillingness to cooperate in the long run. Accordingly, a cooperative relationship between management and labor, which makes the Japanese type of production system appealing (Shimokawa 1986: 233), is unlikely in today’s China. Workers' aspirations, experiences, interests, and subjective willingness to work always influence the concrete labor process. In this context, any innovation or industrial upgrading would be extremely difficult. Furthermore, the low wage model has aroused several major waves of labor unrest throughout China in the last years, with the representatives of laid-off SOE workers in the north and migrant workers in the south (Lee 2007). The recent slew of suicide cases at Foxconn and the Honda strike in 2010 have also exposed the dark side

95 People's Net/ First Financial Daily, Survey on working environment in PRD: female workers get less than 1 rmb for 1 hour overtime work, June 27, 2006, http://news.xinhuanet.com/society/2006-06/27/content_4755027.htm

of low wages, which are argued by Chinese media and Internet forums as a sign that the era of rock-bottom wages in China no longer rules (Yang 2010).

However, it remains to be seen whether the current "success", such as the 30% wage increase promised by Foxconn and the collective agreement signed between Honda and their workers, will be actually implemented and will last in the long term. Thus, it is time to pay more attention to wage guarantee institutions like collective bargaining. Notably, although the wage system in the planned economy has largely lost favor, some positive experiences could be drawn from it. Compared to the high diversification, flexibilization, and polarization of current systems, the low hierarchies and relative transparency of wages (e.g. the eight-grade wage system for production workers) have their merits in stabilizing the workforce and inducing cooperative labor relations. Clearly, collective bargaining is the mechanism that could potentially improve the current wage system. Over the last decades, changes have occurred at every aspect of industrial relations, which primarily involved the introduction and implementation of collective bargaining.

3.3.3 The formation and status of collective bargaining

Collective bargaining has played a significant role in industrialized economies and continues to take the lead in industrial relations of many countries, even under globalization and neoliberalism (e.g. Vissel 2005: 31). Collective bargaining is a process of dialogue and negotiation between laborers and capitalists within a balance of power. These negotiations produce collective contracts, which contain improved labor standards as well as regulations about collective labor relations. However, in China collective bargaining has not genuinely functioned, despite more than fifteen years in legislation and sky rocketing number of collective contracts.

There has been a rather comprehensive series of laws and regulations on collective bargaining, but particular ambiguities in the laws obstruct this mechanism's effectiveness. Although collective contracts used to be signed in SOEs and cooperative enterprises between 1949 and 1958, this practice was completely abolished until the 1980s. Since the reform in 1978, the large-scale dismantlement of traditional SOEs, combined with a growing low-wage sector, have led to waves of strikes and protests among formers SOE workers in the north and among migrant workers in the south. A collective bargaining and collective contract system has the potential to rationalize new forms of labor relations and to maintain industrial peace. Thus, collective bargaining has again drawn attention from trade unions and the state. For example, during the 1980s, collective contracts were signed in a number of joint ventures. In the 1990s, the right to collective bargaining was granted by national law and policies.

The first law that laid the legislative groundwork was the 1992 Trade Union Law. According to the second part of Article 18, "Trade unions can represent employees to sign a collective contract with the administration of the enterprises or institutions. The draft of a collective contract shall be submitted to and passed by the employees' congress or all employees." In the amended Trade Union Law of 2001, the right of collective bargaining and signing of collective contracts are again emphasized as trade union rights, and Article 20 legitimizes the support from unions at higher levels. In light of the laws, negotiators from the labor side should be selected by enterprise trade unions or elected by employees when there is no union presence within the enterprise. Both the laborers and capitalists are obligated to accept requests for collective negotiation. Otherwise the governments at above county levels could order correction or punishment, according to the Article 53 of the 2001 amended Trade Union Law. In case of any disputes over the implementation of a collective contract, trade unions can first appeal to labor arbitration and even go to court.

The implementation of collective contracts is mainly based on the 1994 Labor Law, which is the most fundamental law in the field of labor relations. It is the highest level of law with regard to collective bargaining and contracts, and, for the first time, it provides relatively comprehensive regulations, including the content of collective contracts, major actors, legal effect, and resolution of disputes. Firstly, Article 33 states that, "Employees can sign collective contracts with enterprises with regard to wages, working time, rest and holiday, occupational safety and health, and insurances and welfare." The same Article is also written that, "In enterprises without established trade unions, representatives elected by employees can sign collective contracts with enterprises". The following Articles, 34 and 35, are concerned with the effectiveness of collective contracts. Signed collective contracts can take effect only after they are reported to the labor administration and the latter has no opposition within 15 days. A legally-signed collective contract applies to all employees in the entire enterprise, and labor standards in any individual labor contract should not breach those that are stipulated in the collective contract. Furthermore, Article 84 of the law regulates the resolution of two types of disputes regarding collective contracts. The local labor administration can organize both sides to come together for settlement in case of disputes over the signing of collective contracts. In the case of disputes about implementation, each party of a collective contract can apply for arbitration, and appeal to the court within 15 days if they are unsatisfied with the award.

The Collective Contract Provisions, which are the concrete rules for implementing this system, were first promulgated by the former Ministry of Labor and Social Security and took effect from January 1, 1995. In 2004, this regulation was abolished and replaced by a new version. The new Collective Contract Provisions provide more detail about the content of collective contracts, the parties of bargaining, legal procedures, the terms and effectiveness of collective contracts, inspection by the labor administration at above county levels through the labor inspectorate, and dispute resolution procedures.

In the Labor Contract Law, which took force from January 1, 2008, as many as 11 articles mention collective contracts. It contains major improvements to the mechanism, which at least show increasing attention to its implementation. This is the first time that provisions for special collective contracts[96], and for sectoral and regional collective contracts were written in a national law, although the ACFTU has begun to promote such contracts since 1996[97]. Special collective contracts, as referred by Article 52, include those on occupational safety and health, protection of female workers, and wage adjustment. Moreover, according to Articles 53 and 54, sectoral or regional collective contracts can be signed in construction, mining, catering, and other sectors at administrative levels below the county[98] seat, and apply to all enterprises and employees in a specific sector or region. Since these industries usually involve medium and small enterprises with low union density and poor working conditions, such regulations are important in defending labor rights.

The terms stated in the 2008 Labor Contract Law are taken more seriously. In case of disputes on labor standards as stated in individual labor contracts, collective contracts must be followed, particularly when there are no fixed terms or unclear standards. Additionally, Article 75 gives the labor inspectorate the right to check relevant materials in collective contracts. This right was written into the law for the first time. Lastly, the role of trade unions is given more weight by this Law, particularly in establishing collective bargaining mechanism at the enterprise level (Article 6) and in dealing with relevant disputes (Articles 56 and 78). Interestingly, this law confirms the stipulation as stated in the 2001 amended Trade Union Law that in enterprises without established trade unions

96 Those contracts were mainly written in the ACFTU documents, except the 2004 Collective Contract Provisions issued by the Ministry of Labor and Social Security

97 e.g. in 1996 the ACFTU, the labor ministry, and China Enterprise Confederation - China Enterprise Directors Association issued a document together that allowed industrial unions to sign collective contracts for employers from different enterprises.

98 The word "county" is used to translate the Chinese term xian (县). On Mainland China, counties are the third level of local government, coming under both the province level and the prefecture level and above the town and village levels.

the "upper union"[99] shall guide employees to elect representatives in order to sign collective contracts. In case of disputes, "trade unions" can legally require enterprises to assume responsibilities of conducting collective bargaining, or "trade unions" can apply for arbitration and appeal to the court. Notably, former statues state that those were the rights or obligations of "employees" or "labor representatives".

In recent years, special collective contracts have been separately emphasized, especially wage negotiations and contracts, particularly since wages have become a key issue in Chinese labor relations. The Proposed Regulations on Wage Collective Negotiation of 2000 has provided some content and procedures on wage negotiation. Furthermore, a new Wage Regulation has been on the legislation agenda of the State Council for three years. Until late 2011, there has been no clear sign of official promulgation. However, once it is promulgated, this regulation will become the wage law in China with the highest legislation rank. The draft includes detailed clauses on wage distribution and negotiation. However, given the strong opposition from employers and the fact that it has been repeatedly revised, it is unlikely that this act alone can bring real reform to the current system of collective bargaining.

In a word, China has a relatively comprehensive range of the law and policies on collective bargaining and collective contracts (See Appendix B). Major principles are in accordance with international practices. The laws clearly stipulate the principle of territoriality and procedures of handling collective negotiation-related disputes in different types of enterprises (Zhao 2004). Nationwide, governments or relevant departments of all provinces (including autonomous regions and municipal cities) have issued special documents on collective contract.

At the same time, the law and policies in China also have distinctive features. The law is not effective in providing guidance in collective bargaining. New laws and rules introduced the idea of negotiated bipartite or tripartite decisions. Bipartite negotiations involve laborers and capitalists, whereas the state is also a major player in tripartite negotiations. These were very new concepts for the majority of enterprises in the 1990s. Nevertheless, some forms and procedures of the mechanism have special characteristics, such as the focus on collective contracts rather than bargaining, inspection of signed collective contracts by the labor administration and silence on the right to strike. These features have, at least partly, contributed to its diversified and unsatisfactory implementation.

---

99 "Upper union" usually refers to the union at one administrative rank higher than the existing one. As mentioned in an earlier footnote, in China there are "grass roots" unions and three levels of "upper unions", with the ACFTU being the highest.

Primarily, the word "bargaining" has never appeared in the law. Rather, the term "negotiation" is used. According to administrative interpretation, this is to alleviate the strong sense of confrontation associated with the word "bargaining", and the legal meaning of "negotiation" is in fact identical to that of collective bargaining (Peng 2003). Of greater interest is the use of the terms, "collective negotiation" (*Jitixieshang*) and "equal negotiation" (*Pingdengxieshang*). The Ministry of Labor and Social Security continually uses "collective negotiation" in Collective Contract Provisions and several other administrative regulations, whereas the ACFTU has adopted "equal negotiation" in all of its documents since 1995. The 1994 Labor Law and 2001 amended Trade Union Law, the two most key pieces of labor legislation in China, use "equal negotiation". Only in 2008, did the term "collective negotiation" appear for the first time in national law in the Labor Contract Law.

The difference between "equal negotiation" and "collective negotiation" is far more than just a matter of language. It indicates the divergent attitudes and behavior of the ACFTU and the labor Ministry. The interaction between the two is complicated. It does not always consistently facilitate cooperation. Because acting collectively is the means through which labor seeks to change its disadvantageous status in comparison to capital, it is the fundamental basis of "collective" labor relations. However, the term "equal negotiation" highlights equality on the surface but neglects the "collective" aspect. Some union cadres still believe that "equal", in this sense, means a comparable legal status between labor and capital. Nevertheless, without the legal recognition of "collective" labor, equality can only be hoped for. In practice, trade unions currently rely on administrative enforcement, rather than mobilization of collective labor. In consequence, such collective bargaining is anything but equal. Often the decision-making falls under the authority of employers. This problem is apparent in existing collective contracts. On the side of the labor Ministry, the insistence on using the term "collective" and its confirmation in the 2008 Labor Contract Law shows its aim to endorse the cooperation between collective workers and capitalists in improving labor relations. To a certain degree, it also indicates the dissatisfaction of the labor ministry with the current achievement of trade unions in collective bargaining. Nevertheless, this does not mean that the Chinese trade union is considered negligible by the government. Rather, certain agreement has again been achieved in this respect. Although the term "equal negotiation" as advocated by the ACFTU was abandoned, the 2008 Labor Contract Law emphasizes the role of trade unions as the official, if not exclusive, labor representative in collective bargaining.

Another distinctive feature of Chinese law is that there is no single article explaining the process of collective bargaining, although collective contract is extensively described (Ye and Xu 2005). The fact that the legislation emphasizes the "fruit" – collective contract – but neglects the "tree" that bears the fruit – bargaining – has led to the enforcement deviating from the original intention of policy-makers. Given the fact that China had no serious experience with collective bargaining, the idea of a democratic decision rather than unilateral prerogative was unfamiliar to most enterprises in the 1990s. This gap in policies may frustrate many practitioners, especially since today's trade unions and enterprises depend on the law in daily operation, or at least use the law as justification to achieve their implicit goals. For instance, many grass-root unions find that it is hard to bargain since there are no exact legal stipulations as to how the process should be carried out. Consequently, collective bargaining is usually conducted in the form of consultative meetings and varies greatly in content, procedures, and outcomes.

As partial compensation, the government's department of labor plays a special role in certain legal procedures, which unfortunately has not helped much in practice. First, any collective contract at county and above levels can only take effect after it has been reported and inspected by the labor administration. Nevertheless, given the fact that this system is still in the course of development, the existing contracts do not carry much substantial content. Another role of the labor administration is to "mediate" disputes related to collective contracts. As for disputes about existing contracts, the law allows legal procedures such as arbitration and a lawsuit. However, for disputes relating to signing a new collective contract, the law requires the labor administration to coordinate and mediate between trade unions and employers. Usually, the result is an "agreement on coordinated settlement" and none of the third parties, no matter whether it is the labor administration, the arbitration agency or the court, has the right to order both sides to "go back to the bargaining table". Thus, if mediation fails, there is no further procedure to follow, forestalling any further possibility of collective negotiations.

Furthermore, one core labor right, the right to strike, is not explicit in any law in China. While the right to strike is necessary to guarantee equal and effective collective bargaining since it is the most effective means through which workers can impose economic pressures on employers, Chinese laws have omitted this right since 1982. However, leaving out the right to strike in law does not avoid strikes in practice.

Strikes are nothing new for Chinese workers. They occurred in the early 1920s and frequently take place in factories today. The numbers of individual and collective labor disputes related to wages have increased dramatically in recent years, both in passive ways through high turnover rates and in active means including strikes. At the same time, since the right to strike is not actually forbidden by law (Chang 2005), strikes may be tolerated by the state[100]. In this sense, the example of Germany may be revealing since the law on industrial action almost exclusively is judge-made law (Weiss 1989: 132). Precedents are set on the basis of actual cases rather than following written legal clauses. In this sense, the absence of the legal right to strike may not prohibit workers' actions.[101] Given the dependence of official unions on the state and employers, compounded by the fact that strikes rarely involve them, it should be more cautious in advocating for legislation on the right to strike (e.g. Chang 2005). If the legislation grants the right to strike exclusively to the official trade unions, which is very likely that if this current trend continues (e.g. an emphasis on the role of trade unions in the 2008 Labor Contract Law), the majority of existing and potential strikes may be claimed to be illegal. The bottom line is that a law shall not become a constraint rather than a means of worker empowerment.

Finally, even if collective contracts are signed, there is no effective mechanism for supervising employers' implementation (Wang and Zhao 2005). The labor administration has the legal obligation to check and monitor the implementation. Labor inspection, the most important function of the labor administration, is now supported by huge resources and a large labor force. However, since there are enormous numbers of enterprises in China, it is impossible for the labor inspectorates to oversee the labor practices of all enterprises (e.g. one labor inspector for every 1000 enterprises). Furthermore, because the system of collective bargaining and collective contract is highly decentralized at enterprise or establishment level, the process is, to a large degree, up to the control or influence of employers on grass-root trade unions, symmetry of information, supply and demand of the labor market, etc.. In fact, trade unions, which operate on behalf of workers, would be the more effective facilitators of collective bargaining and inspectors of collective contracts. However, no matter how much effort the ACFTU has put into policy-making with the government or the amount of pressure it has exerted upon employers, the lack of mobilization at the grass roots level is the fundamental defect of this system. Workers, who are supposedly the major actor, are excluded from the bargaining process. As a result, the existing collective bargaining is too close to "consultation" or state-induced "concertation", which demands too much compromise from workers.

---

100 E.g. the government's response to the recent strikes proved that it is at least tolerating workers making collective claims. See: Katherine Ryder, China's labor market: Valuable asset or economic albatross? December 23, 2010, Fortune Chinese, http://www.fortunechina.com/business/c/2010-12/23/content_46296.htm

101 People's Daily, Wage Regulation will be promulgated within 2010, wage negotiation system receives the most attention, May 30, 2010

In practice, the diversification of wages and the various outcomes of collective bargaining are closely related to the fact that collective bargaining is dominantly conducted within individual enterprises in China. There is a lack of coordination of wages and other labor standards among enterprises. The level of bargaining should be determined by the circumstances of the particular country, conglomerate, company, employer, union federation, union and employee (e.g. ILO freedom of association committee). In China, the production regimes and labor relations vary from enterprise to enterprise and from industry to industry. For instance, the average annual wages for workers at the bottom of the auto supply chain are one third or a half of that of workers in the assembly plants at the top, not to mention differences in training, social benefits and employment security. The principle of "same work, same pay" between regular workers and dispatched labor has also remained a baseless notion. However, enterprise unions find themselves in a dilemma whereby they depend on employers both financially and in terms of employment, which makes them unable either to bargain against employers or to gain the trust of workers. Although there are many good samples of collective contracts drafted by provincial and municipal trade unions, but they hardly have influence on collective contracts concluded at the enterprise level. Only in recent years, have sectoral and regional collective contracts come into existence. At above-enterprise levels, the industrial union has dissolved in China since 1957, and has been replaced by a merged "industrial and regional" union structure. Although industrial unions have been re-established in many places, and some meetings about the role of industrial unions have also taken place since June 2008, industrial unions remain largely underdeveloped and inactive.

Theoretically speaking, collective bargaining is the solution to the economic and political challenges facing China, since it serves as the key to improving labor skills, stimulating domestic consumption, overcoming the obstacles of innovation and industrial upgrading, and stabilizing the workforce and calming labor unrest. Problematic implementation of the law and policies is rooted in and constrained by the interaction among the major actors of industrial relations. As shown above, the liberalized and increasingly Americanized style of management has jeopardized the status of Chinese workers and collective labor. Referring to the historical experiences in the U.S. and Germany, an effective collective bargaining should have certain conditions.

Fundamentally, collective bargaining in both the U.S. and Germany was at the initiative of industrial trade unions with a broad solidarity. Later collective bargaining became somehow accommodated by capital and the state, and it was finally institutionalized in both countries. In other words, collective bargaining was originally not a legal mechanism and could not be introduced from top down by the administrative power of the state as we have seen in China where shop-floor power is absent. Workers' solidarity and mobilization along shop-floors is the only and the essential source of effective collective bargaining, while the institutionalization may guarantee the continuity and stability of collective bargaining in the long run. The compromise of state and capital is unlikely to come about without the strong bargaining power of workers.

It is fair to say collective bargaining and collective contract in China is not only problematic in terms of its origin and function, but it also faces adverse environments today. At the first glance, the global industrial development and politics operates to the detriment of workers' protection. Besides, the largely diverse production regimes at factory level, especially in electronics industry, segment the working class and make sectoral or regional collective bargaining more difficult. At the same time, the relationship between the Chinese state, trade unions, employers, and the often-forgotten role of workers, differs from that in industrialized countries which features a relatively balance of power from the labor and capital and a mediating role of the state. Nevertheless, in a fast-changing economy and society like China, it would be too rash to deny any possibility for change. In the U.S., the "Fordist" integration of mass production set the stage for the emergence of the CIO and the rebirth of industrial unionism (Davis 1986: 57). China may also have a different future. Accordingly, the potential catalysts for change are explored in the following chapter, which surveys the impact of current industry and production trends on industrial relations in China as well as the specific roles of the state, employers, trade unions and workers in the polices and practices of collective bargaining.

Wage regulation in China: Is Fordism coming back?

This chapter compares the experience of collective bargaining in China in order to uncover the key aspects that differ from the effectiveness of collective bargaining and wage regulation processes in the United States and in Germany. I draw these comparisons through analysis of current global economic and political environment, industrial and production trends, specific development path of China, and the state-capital-labor relations within the industrial relation system of China. I argue that the successes in the Chinese model of collective bargaining and industrial relations mainly depend on whether this model is able to normalize the capital relations in existing accumulation regimes as well as to develop a fairer society.

Furthermore, this chapter explores the institutionalization of collective bargaining in China. As history shows, the institutionalization of collective bargaining must result from the combined endeavor of all major actors in collective bargaining - workers and trade unions, employers, and state. As the global economy as well as the development path and industrial relations of China have largely varied from those of the post-war US and Germany, general observations cannot determine the successes of collective bargaining in a specific country today. In particular, the social institutions that organize, regulate, and motivate production and consumption, must be taken into consideration. For instance, while trade unions today face globally similar economic pressures and social changes, they often respond in different ways (Boyer, 1995). This is clearly demonstrated in the different strategies of the German and U.S. Labor movements in response to the 1970s crisis. Accordingly, this research assumes that national economic, social and political characteristics do matter.

Therefore, the peculiar history and tradition of China and the current domestic and global context carry great importance, which explains why collective bargaining has not worked in China. Below, I refer to the industrial history of the American and German automobile and electronics industries in order to examine three main aspects of the industrial relations system. First, global trends in industries and labor movements set the unfavorable social, political and ideological environments for Chinese workers, featured by declining international labor movements, the dominance of pro-capital neo-liberalism, and the end of Communist ideology and working class. Second, the production regimes within the factories lay the groundwork for everyday relations between employers and industrial workers. Third, national policy-making is a combined result of the power struggles among the capital, labor and the state. In this way, the fundamental problems of collective bargaining are identified, and the decisive forces for an ideal model of collective bargaining in China's changing industrial relations are explored.

4.1 The new global context of China's development

A nation's collective bargaining practices are shaped by certain economic, political and ideological contexts at the global level. When it comes to China, both the global environments and the development path of the country diverge from those in the U.S. and Germany after the WWII. In fact, not only has the global industrial and political context dramatically changed since, but China has also grown at an unprecedented rate because of its vast size. Since industrial relations are an often nation-specific, China has to seek its own way out rather than simply repeat any forgoing path.

4.1.1 The new global environments

In general, the global economy and politics have been very different from those during the post-war industrialization in the U.S. and Germany. To a large degree, the pro-labor policy trends in industrialized economies at the time have no longer existed. Instead, the period after the decline of Fordism in the 1970s had witnessed a highly globalized market characterized by overproduction of industrial goods, and world-scale flows of capital, resources, products, and information. At the same time, neoliberalism has become dominant, which largely reduces state intervention. Ideological divisions between the two worlds in the Cold War have been debatably removed in the political realm, although from time to time it is still used as a reason for protectionism in the global market. Labor movements have declined. Overall, the world has presented new challenges for industrial relations in many countries.

In history, world politics have been central in determining the conditions surrounding workers' bargaining power and labor unrest. During the end of the nineteenth century and the first half of the twentieth century, the states depended on citizens to join the army or to work in warfare programs to mobilize a nation's resources for war. As a result, workers succeeded in pushing their governments toward a rapid expansion of workers' labor and voting rights.

By the end of the WWII, substantial world-wide political-economic reforms solved the chaos of the preceding orders. Apart from establishing global trade regimes, nations developed mass consumption norms and developmentalist social compacts. In light of world depressions and wars during the early 1920s and 1930s, experiments that attempted to accommodate capital to proletariat (e.g. Keynesian package) stifled the waves of world-scale labor unrest in the post-WWII era (Silver 2003). As capitalists began to realize that repression alone was a very unstable form of rule, the post-war tripartite pacts between capital, states, and trade unions successfully accommodated labor strength and quelled labor militancy. This was the case in both the U.S. and Germany.

Nevertheless, labor movements around the world, including those in industrialized countries, faced world-scale decline since the 1980s (Silver 2003: 165), as marked by shrinking union membership with the exceptions of Canada and the Scandinavian countries. In the U.S., Keynesian polices were generally abandoned in the 1970s, and the government ended the support of collective bargaining.

Collective bargaining faced constant pressure from employers' anti-union measures in each country. Indeed, opposition toward collective bargaining never ceased. For instance, in many countries which belong to the Organization for Economic Co-operation and Development (OECD)[102] during the 1960s and especially the 1970s, the moderation of real wages was urged since it was "necessary to increase or restore international competitiveness and profitability" for each country (Flanagan et al. 1983: 29). This concern intensified in the following two decades. As a result, wide-spread decentralization occurred in industrial structure and industrial relations, as some industry-wide and other multi-employer bargaining in the U.S. and elsewhere gave way to additional company- and plant-level contracts (Flanagan 1999). Furthermore, in the case of Germany, the trend of de-regulation (*verbetrieblisch*), which allowed individual enterprises to dodge the general collective agreements through exceptional clauses, also undermined the effectiveness of industrial-level collective bargaining and traditional stakeholder orientation, although the old system had been trying to accommodate such changes. In a word, the period since the 1990s was characterized by a labor- and development-unfriendly regime in which social contracts were abandoned from above and social safety nets in many industrialized countries were either cut or dismantled.

Such changes were initiated by a combination of spatial, technological, organizational, and financial fixes. One crucial feature is linked to the

102 OECD was established in 1960 by 18 European countries plus the United States and Canada. The aim was to create an organization dedicated to global development. Today there are 34 member countries from North and South America, Europe and the Asia-Pacific region, including advanced economies and emerging countries like Mexico, Chile and Turkey. Its mission is to promote policies that will improve the economic and social well-being of people around the world

flexibilization and vertical dis-integration of production, which was implemented particularly through the development of microelectronics. As the products and market differentiated since the era of Fordism, capitalism has been practiced through a vast, decentralized, global network. Although globalization has been anything but new, the new round of globalization since the late of the twentieth century has been at an unprecedented scale. It is true that, for example, trans-oceanic immigration already took place at massive scale at the end of the nineteenth century, and from the 1930s to the 1990s[103], capital had continuously migrated from established factories to new geographical sites which offer cheaper workers with little labor collectivity. Today, production networks span every corner of the world as far as it is profitable for their investors. This global network is still dominated by large corporations that subordinate localities to their calculus of exploitation, but the locus of corporate power is more diffuse and hence less easily identified (Amin and Malmberg 1994). The "globalization" of the new financial markets link all enterprises together.

Moreover, the organization of management never ceased to challenge labor movements, especially today within the global networked production. In the automobile industry, for instance, Ford transferred the production from skilled to de-skilled occupations. Furthermore, in order to enhance productivity, capitalists intensified the work pace of machines. Today, the capitalists adopt new methods. One example is the wide use of job evaluation in nearly all industries, an integral part of the transformation of the militant U.S. industrial unionism of the 1930s toward an era of business unionism. By emphasizing individual performance, job evaluations were originally used to deter industrial union organizing and to limit wage increases following unionization. Within the system, workers are pitted against one another, who must jockey each other for better ratings, ultimately undermining their unified voice in opposition to management. Moreover, Human Resource Management (HRM), which is in practice a unilateral managerial device based on individuals and cooperation, was also invented in the U.S. to facilitate new production methods like lean production. Lean production, originally developed by Japanese auto makers, emphasizes efficiency and flexibility on all aspects of the production and personnel, which leads to intensified work pace, lengthy working time, extensive outsourcing and subcontracting, etc. Although HRM emphasizes the empowerment and participatory among workers of lean production, many programs that defines the HRM model are simply a means of cost reduction for management. The concept of "benchmarking", which compares the business processes or performance to the best practice of the industry, is used to find the

103 Such an international escape route broke up between 1929 and 1958

quickest, the cheapest, and the fastest techniques and production practices (Moody 1997: 89, 91). In countries with a strong tradition of unionism and collective bargaining like Germany, HRM is originally seen by workers as a management tool that is now well accepted and used by works councils. However, in the U.S and other countries influenced by the U.S., like China, HRM is regarded as the exclusive representative of advanced management. In general, the weak or even lack of unions' resistance to such managerial strategies has jeopardized the role of collective labor in determining wages and other working conditions.

Within factories, the composition of the workforce in industrialized countries has changed, following the transformation of production and the deskilling of occupations. The proportion of the skilled, male and manual workers is declining, but there is a rise of service and white-collar classes, and a general "feminization" of the workforce. In the new composition, the traditional basis of trade unionism - blue-collared manufacturing male workers - has declined, whereas trade unions in many industrialized economies find difficulties in organizing white-collared and female workers. Accordingly, wage cuts and redundancy in old manufacturing bases and also profit squeeze along the value chains have been common consequences.

It is noted that most changes were domestically driven by endless efforts of capital to improve productivity for higher profitability rates (Lichtenstein 1995: 442). In the 1970s, the rise of East and Southeast Asian economies emerged out of the need for industrial relocation, stemming from over-investment and production over-capacity in the West, particularly the U.S. China is perhaps the largest economy among the newly-emerging economies. Since the 1980s, as competition for private investment intensified among low-cost regions, local governments offered the most "favorable" environments at the expense of labor standards, thereby initiating the so-called "race to the bottom". Additionally, the interests of capital transformed many labor processes through advanced technologies of automation. As Moody (2007) argued, the replacement of people by machines was the biggest cause of unemployment in manufacturing. Much of the job and income losses among workers in the U.S. was not the direct result of the export of capital or jobs, per se, but of a combination of neoliberal policies and cost-cutting efforts (Moody 1997: 41, 53).

Unfortunately, while economic globalization has freed capital, workers remained to be restraint by geographic locations and immigration regulations of different countries. The relocation of production, the advancement in information technologies, methods of contracting and sub-contracting along the global supply chains, and consequently the decline of traditional labor movement led to disempowerment of workers. Furthermore, a new level of competition among workers emerged at cross-industry and even cross-border levels. On one hand, many "core" jobs that offered long-term employment, high wages, and union protection, were destroyed in the industrialized countries. Industrial unionism and collective bargaining which shaped labor markets and offered a higher standard of living for workers were undermined under globalization. On the other hand, millions of newly-proletarianized workers emerged in the locations that provided favorable conditions for industrial expansion in both developed and developing regions. Workers at different geographic sites faced same employers at the top of the value chain. In this context, solidarity rather than antagonisms took precedence.

However, the roles of trans-national labor movements remain limited. Today major international economic and trade organizations are dominated by the neoliberal policies that stem from the US. This is similar to the economic integration process of the European Union. The European social dialogue is often regarded as one remarkable progress, which includes discussions, consultations, negotiations and joint actions at cross-industry level and within sectors involving employers and trade union organizations, and sometimes also public authorities. However, social dialogue covers only limited fields of social policy and explicitly excludes wages (Article 137 and 139 TEC). As a whole, although attempts have been made to internationalize the trade union movement, these attempts have never been really convincing (Jensen 2006). Labor movements are still fundamentally connected to nation states.

Moreover, the ideological division between the two worlds vanished from the political realm. As the debates and practices of Socialism and Communism came to the end, labor-capital conflicts had also shifted toward an image of social partnership. Surplus-value production became unquestionable. Consequently, the idea of "working class co-operating with their masters toward the maximization of profit and the consequent redistribution of such surplus value" became the center of modern economic policy (Jessop 1997). In addition, comparing the 2008/9 crisis with that in the 1930s or 1970s uncovers the mismatch of accumulation regime and regulation mode again. However, at least the dominant ideologies and political measurements of stabilization in 2008 and 2009 obviously depart from those in the past (Schmidt 2008). Since the 1970s, neoliberalism became the mainstream ideology. At the same time, fiscal and monetary policies were redirected to the supply-side of the market, supporting corporate competitiveness and military buildup. The New Deal of the 1930s, which stimulated mass consumption by workers rather than further investment by capitalists, did not take place in the recent crisis.

At the international level, liberal institutions, with representatives from the World Bank and International Monetary Fund, persist in implementing fewer regulations in order to promote free trade. Unfortunately, the prediction of neoclassic economic theory predicting that free market policies and globalization will equalize wages and bring the benefits of industrialization never happened.

Overall, the Fordist welfare state has been replaced by a neoliberal workfare state (Jessop 1994; Esser and Hirsch 1994; Lipietz 1994). Again, this pattern produced the move towards legitimizing world capitalism. For instance, increasing inequalities, as demonstrated by anti-labor attacks among employers and a decline in labor unrest became facts of life (Silver 2003: 171-2; 177-9). Certain features that characterize the current social-economic context resembled those of the nineteenth century. For instance, there are a laissez-faire state, to the freeing up of capital from state regulation, a major shift of investment out of trade and production into finance and speculation, and consequently growing unemployment, escalating inequality, and major disruptions in established ways of life and livelihood for workers.

Nevertheless, the next step of the nation-states is hard to predict. Ultimately, workers' power from the shop floor drives changes in industrial relations. An exemplary case is the workplace bargaining power of workers, which resulted to the GM-UAW contract at a time of both high unemployment and feeble labor organization (Silver 2003: 47). The workplace bargaining power of workers has again increased in the twenty-first century, linked with new production and organization within global networked production. At the moment, although the labor internationalism is yet blocked by protectionism in developed countries through import and immigration restrictions, labor movements in different countries are facing similar challenges and dealing with the same employers at the top of the value chains. In general, workers in respective nation-states are disempowered by current economic and political trends, thereby highlighting the importance of worker solidarity.

4.1.2 The development path of China

Aside from influences of the general economy, industrial relations in a country are shaped by its specific path of development. Indeed, any late comer to industrialization would be unavoidably subjected to a variety of international regulations and practices pre-established by the industrialized world, and may also be impacted by global trends and labor movements in other economies to a certain degree. More importantly, the relationship between the bargaining structure and its macroeconomic outcomes is contingent on the economic or political environment of a given country (Flanagan 1999). In this sense, the development of a country has critical effects on the system of industrial relations, particularly on collective bargaining.

China has been undergoing economic growth at an unprecedented rate worldwide. As commented by McNally (2008: 228), "China seems to be doing everything simultaneously in a much more condensed time frame, in comparison to earlier instances of capitalist accumulation". The development began since the opening-door policy in 1978, when a tremendous amount of Foreign Direct Investment (FDI) and Multinational Corporations (MNCs) entered China and developed local industries. As a whole, foreign-funded enterprises have the largest export share from 2000 to 2004 over 50%, followed by the 25% of SOEs. For the national economy, foreign investments have spill-over effects on technical progress, improving the supplier sector to world standards, better training and disciplining of the workforce, taxes, etc. Also, although many domestic firms remain as Original Equipment Manufacturers (OEMs), which produce products or components that are purchased by another company and retailed under that purchasing company's brand name. Usually those OEMs remain to be unknown in the final product market, because they sell the parts and components to brand name companies without displaying their names in the final products. Chinese domestic MNCs, such as Huawei and Haier, have emerged, earlier than many early-industrialized countries where MNCs only came into being after the domestic capitalism was well developed (Williamson and Zeng 2008: 83). From the 1990s, China became another 'engine' of the world economy following the U.S. For instance, the annual output in the automobile industry increased from 700,000 cars in 2001 to 4 million in 2007, and 13 million in 2009. Over the past century or more, no country as developed as quickly as China.

China's economic boom took place under favorable global economic environments. The late 1970s and the 1980s was a time when the West, particularly the U.S., was overburdened by over-accumulation or over-industrialization (ten Brink 2010). China, still an agriculture-dominated economy at the time, became one of the major beneficiaries of the outflow of investment and production from the West. In addition, the socio-spatial proximity to East Asian Circle such as Japan and South Korea (ten Brink 2010), including a major connection with Ethnic Chinese capitalism (Yeung 2006), created an advantageous industrial environment. Overseas Chinese, including those in Taiwan and Hong Kong, were the first foreign investors that entered China, perhaps due to the familiarity of customs and languages. From 1982 to 1994, more than 70% of foreign investment was from overseas Chinese resources (Hsing 1998: 147). Furthermore, the multilayered subcontracting production networks, centered on Japan and firstly developed in the 1950s and

1960s, gradually shifted production to countries with different levels of economic development in Asia. In the 1980s, it began to relocate low-end and low-cost production to China. All those factors at the early stage of China's industrialization had been very different from those the U.S., Germany or other East Asian countries had experienced.

Among all those differences, the expansion of global production network is noticeable. Over the last few decades, global production networks provided China with great opportunities, in terms of investment and technologies. At the same time, China has made favorable policies, such as providing free land and low taxes for foreign investment, in order to rapidly integrate into these networks. The proportions of foreign investment in the GDP grew 10 times higher than those in the rapid-developing periods of Japan and South Korea (Ernst and Naughton 2008: 48). In this context, the old Japan-centered "flying geese" order in which each national economy exported specific groups of finished consumer products along a hierarchical chain, was replaced by a network whereby "China exports most final consumer goods to the global North on behalf of its Asian neighbors... This provided China with the necessary parts and machines, increasingly high value-added or capital-intensive, for assembly" (Williamson and Zeng 2003).

At the same time, China experienced a distinctive path of development apart from other countries. Besides exemplifying economic openness, China has a booming market as well as the world's largest pool of low-cost labor. Recently China has also seen the emergence of sophisticated lead users and test-bed markets (Ernst and Naughton 2008: 48). Moreover, there are other social and political conditions that make China unique, including the vast geography, rich culture, and communist legacy. For instance, the thousands year old of culture in China, which cultivated several other Asian cultures, has shaped the history, cultural heritage, religious and philosophical traditions, and people's way of life and relations with one another. This partially resulted to the different polices of the socialist Mao or Deng than other former Socialist countries in East Europe (Kornai 1992: 3). As for collective bargaining, for instance, the traditional obedience of mass people to the central state may suggest a more important role of the state in coordinating labor standards than in the U.S. or Germany. In addition, the Communist Party left its mark on all spheres of society, politics, and the economy, even though the command economy came to an end. The reform of China has been initiated, guided and controlled by an ideologically anti-capitalist party-state. In this process, the Party successfully built up the hegemony of the state and the hegemony of the market at the same time, which often discourages workers to organize themselves and collectively bargain with employers (see section 4.4).

Nevertheless, the economic development of China may not appear as different as that of other East Asian countries. Many policy-makers actually followed the "East Asian miracle" as showcased in the early 1990s (Thun 2004: 457). The model of export-oriented industrialization was accompanied by low domestic consumption, and the trade surpluses and high savings rates were translated into the financial power of the national governments, often in the form of large foreign-exchange reserves. Similarly, the financing of China on the US current-account deficit fueled America's appetite for Chinese imports. The additional increase in the trade surplus led to more purchases of U.S. treasury bonds by the Chinese state. Compared to predecessors, China's market and financial dependence on the US increased, due to the high intensity of its export-led and private-consumption-repressing growth. In this sense, the China model is a replication in extreme form of earlier East Asian pattern of economic growth (Ernst and Naughton 2008: 98).

In a word, the development path of China was never a simple replication of the past. China has historically experienced tremendous economic growth and expansion within the specific context in the late 1970s and 1980s. Reflecting many features of primitive capitalism, such as the process of urbanization and infrastructure building, the unique variety of capitalism in China fundamentally includes a rapid integration to global markets and the distinctive role of state institutions in initiating, enabling, and sustaining capitalist development (McNally 2008).

At the same time, the economic and social contradictions inherent within China's development path should not be neglected. Aside from the introduction of mass production and work organizations, the other aspect of Fordism - contractual wage relations and expansion of mass consumption - is at least equally important, even only for the sake of economic growth of the country. Contractual wage relations and expansion of mass consumption were the keys to the economic success in the U.S. and then Germany during the post-war era (Lipietz 1987: 65). Unfortunately, this fact had been largely ignored in China, as in the cases of Latin America and South Korea during the 1970s. So far, China has not seen any significant expansion of purchasing power of workers and peasants, thus restraining the growth of domestic markets within the ruling and middle classes generated by the export economy.

For a long time, the overproduction of industrial goods in China has been digested by consumption in the West. In fact, the problem of overcapacity, a major concern of many industrialized countries in the 1970s and 1980s, has also become a bottleneck of China. For instance, in the automobile industry, profit expectations and incentives for high-volume production have resulted in overcapacity. While the actual sales were 3.3 million passenger vehicles in 2005, the capacity was more than 6 million.[104] In the electronics industry, export orientation alleviates such tension in the domestic market, but when the external demands shrink, as in the case of the 2008/2009 crisis, there is also tremendous pressure on both the production and employment. In the long run, a control on the industries as well as a raising domestic purchasing power will be the only sustainable solutions for the national economy.

The economic and social consequences of the China's current developmental path are apparent. Low wages have constrained domestic consumption and deepened China's dependence on the global North's demand. Accordingly, the basic elements for sustainable development, such as a well-functioning market and a high-skilled mass workforce, are not possible in the wide-spread low-wage regime. For instance, the consumption in the domestic market has been limited by wage stagnation for a long time. Most of the surplus in the export sector has been converted into enterprise savings or further investment, rather than shared by employees. According to the statistic yearbook from the National Bureau of Statistics, from the late 1990s onwards, the total wages declined as a share of GDP from 51% to 20% along with a fall in private consumption, from 45% to 18%, and contrast starkly from the mounting scale of corporate profits from 44% to 31%. At the same time, some problems make the social unbalance in China even worse. One example is urban bias by the Chinese state, which has eventually created the primary accumulation and the perception of "unlimited" cheap labor supply among rural Chinese migrants. Since the 1980s, the state has concentrated investment in the urban industrial sector, especially in coastal areas, while neglecting the financing need and development of the rural area. A study cites an increasing net transfer of resources from the rural agriculture to the urban industrial sector between 1978 and 2000, through taxation, government spending, savings deposits and loans (Huang et al. 2006). As the gap between rural and urban has grown, especially since the township and village enterprises (TVEs) lost favor in policies in the 1990s. Consequently, many young peasants have to seek for jobs in cities. From 1990 to 2003, there were about 220 million migrant workers, according to the 2004 Yearbook of National Bureau of Statistics. In 2011, the Statistic Report of the Ministry of Human Resource and Social Security showed that this number reached to 252.78 million. Although in recent years the central government has attempted to boost domestic consumption by cutting agricultural taxes and raising minimum wages. These policies made little strides for the benefit of rural migrant workers.

As a matter of fact, Chinese industries have the potential or at least the possibilities to develop higher wages and higher skills for workers. For instance,

---

104 Global Insight, 2007, Asian Automobile Industry Forecast Report, April 2007, pp.4

the automobile industry has been highly profitable, due to protection of domestic industries by the government, low percentage of R&D expenses, and the low cost of a single unit in the large-volume production. From 2002 to 2006, although the price of cars decreased 10% annually, the gross profit rates of the industry were maintained to more than 20%.[105] Many predict that the golden period of China's automobile industry is likely to last for another 20 years, through a focus on the market for small- and medium-sized cities and hybrid and new power vehicles.[106] There is room for improvement for wages and other labor standards without substantially risking China's international competitiveness. The actual problem is that the high profitability of capital has never been automatically translated into high wages for employees, without struggles or pressures of collective labor.

Historically, collective labor exerted pressures on the capital through strikes and other industrial actions in the U.S. and Germany, in order to achieve a fair share of the profits. Unfortunately, the labor movement in China is still in the initial stages of formation. Industrial relations in China feature widespread individual bargaining, immature management and labor abuse. While discussions on the improvement of social partnership among trade unions, workers, and state actors can be found in Germany (e.g. Lüthje 2004), Chinese trade unions have begun to explore how to work independently from management. At the same time, trade unions attempt to maintain their traditional cooperation with enterprises and governments (e.g. Taylor et al. 2003; Chan 1994).

Along with the transnational growth of Chinese economy, labor-capital relations had been restructured, exacerbating antagonisms between them. As Taylorist or neo-Taylorist forms of production and management popularized in China, these polices continued to challenge workers' attempts for solidarity. The lean method became popular in China, which did not make work more "humane" but in fact further intensified work and lengthened working hours. Moreover, industries in China became completely dominated by the so-called modern management methods - HRM, unlike a controlled co-regulation in Germany. In the 1980s, just overnight, HRM became the "magic weapon" of reforming the "outworn" wage system in the planned economy. This could be seen in numerous Chinese publications, which included academic research and practical handbooks that touted HRM as the "edging theory" or "research

105 Annual Report on the Automobile industry in China, 2007, http://ar.cei.gov.cn/web/Column.asp?CId3=292

106 e.g. a report co-issued by the State Council, the Society of Automobile Engineers and VW China on July 5, see: People's Daily Online, Golden age of China's automobile industry likely to last 20 more years, 14:28, July 14, 2010

benchmark" in scientifically determining remuneration system. Not a single word in the books mentioned collective bargaining, which indeed remains as the most effective mechanism of setting labor standards in Western countries. As wage determination in China is theoretically and practically up to employers through HRM, there is no much space left for workers or trade unions.

Undeniably, some positive changes have taken place in national policies. Primarily, the 1994 Labor Law has laid the legal groundwork for labor relations. It lays out the institutions for collective negotiation, collective contract, and labor dispute settlement. Significantly, the government claims to be committed to the tasks of workplace inspection and of tripartite negotiations at all levels. To a certain degree, while enterprises in China are managed in a liberal way that resembles the U.S-model, the existing labor legislation on labor relations, social security, and trade unions incorporates certain elements from European countries, in particular Germany (Lüthje 2004). For instance, since 1996 the ACFTU started to promote sectoral collective contracts in an entire region for certain industries, which is similar to German model of industry-wide bargaining. Sectoral collective contracts were also written into the 2008 Labor Contract Law.

Nevertheless, the future fate of the changing industrial relations in China remains yet unclear. One problem is the representation of trade unions and employers' associations. The trade union operates in favor of the party-state interests. At the same time, employers' associations, both public and foreign-invested enterprises, and their branches are established, sanctioned, and licensed by the government (Pearson 1994). The heavy hand of the state in both labor and capital sides is one major characteristic of Chinese industrial relations, although in practice it does not completely control them. This was demonstrated by capitalists' opposition to national law and policies from time to time. For instance, they lobby local governments against the 2008 Labor Contract Law.

Undoubtedly, Silver's prediction (2003) that the shift of automobile manufacturing centers will bring about a radical labor movement has not come true in China, at least up to now, since economic growth does not automatically lead to improvement of labor standards. The fundamental drive of profit sharing through collective bargaining is from workers themselves. According to an influential survey on the beneficiaries and victims of the reform in the 1990s (Ru and Lu 2001), both government officials and urban citizens opined that private business owners benefited the most from the economic reforms, while former SOE workers, peasants and migrant workers received the least. In fact, workers' conditions have reached at the lowest point in years. They are no longer the "masters" of the country. In the market economy, terms like class struggle have been carefully abandoned in political arena since the early 1990s.

Economic modernization and, more recently, harmonious labor relations, a term promoted by the ACFTU echoing the target of building "harmonious society" by the central government, become the mainstream discourse. Unfortunately, these new political slogans rarely have any tangible effects on the daily life and work of Chinese workers.

In sum, the economy of China has benefited from the global shift of investment and production from the West since the late 1970s, although this pattern has led to a path of development that is highly dependent on low-cost exports to external markets. Domestically, Fordism, as practiced through collective contractual relations that guarantee mass consumption, is largely absent in China. Instead, labor policies and practices have been transformed by the global restructuring of industries and a strong emphasis on HRM based job evaluations and performance appraisals. Generally speaking, the current global and national environments are unsustainable and potentially hazardous for the national economy and a fairer society. Without changes towards more balanced industrial relations, e.g. increasing wages through collective bargaining, the social consequences will become even more unbearable for workers.

4.2 Changes of industries and production organization

The methods of organizing production and labor play a significant role in industrial relations. A typical argument among scholars is that "it is the organizational dynamic, rather than the culture itself, that produces and sustains market structures" (Safarian and Dobson 1996). Silver (2003: 41) also states that Ford mass production tends to recreate similar social contradictions wherever it emerges. This research, again, confirms that production regimes strongly influence on industrial relations, particularly the transformation of industrial and production organizations.

Since the 1970s, global networked production, new sectors, smaller and specialized firms, outsourcing and subcontracting have intensified. Industries, including the automobile and electronics sectors, have been dramatically restructured. The electronics sector, particularly microelectronics, has outpaced the dominance of the automobile industry in the twentieth century. Through the "computerization of everything", the semiconductor sector has profoundly impacted almost all industries upon the experience of everyday life and work among ordinary citizens (Silver 2003: 104).

The most significant industrial change has been the disappearance of homogeneous production regimes. For instance,world-wide automobile and electronics industries have witnessed vertical dis-integration along the production chains. In the supply side of the automobile industry and the electronics industry, different types and sizes of enterprises have emerged, a large part of which are union-free. Nevertheless, the degrees of diversification within the two industries are rather different. Recent changes in organization and management have greatly influenced the electronics industry, since they have mirrored the growth of this industry since the 1970s. The automobile industry remains relatively stable on the side of the assembly plants.

In addition, one of the major changes which took place after the collapse of the social contract during the post-war Fordism era is the introduction of new production and management methods that work against collective labor. Among many industrialists, lean production is probably the most profitable method. Since the late 1970s, lean production has become popular, in various forms, in nearly all countries and industries. Fundamentally, the very successes of this model lies in the cooperative relationship between management and labor (Shimokawa 1986: 233), which is often realized through a dual labor market consisting of permanent and temporary workers. In the beginning, this dual structure was stable because temporary workers in Toyota were family members of the former or in some cases rural workers, who unlikely had any motivation to change. However, because this connection between the core and the periphery has long vanished in today's Japan (or it may have never existed in other countries), the lean practices may result in lower pay and worsening working conditions. Moreover, employers claim that work organizations that follow Toyota-style management policies engage workers intellectually through teams in order to solicit ideas for improving the system through employee participation programs and expanding of their work responsibilities. In this way, labor control occurs through a set of far more subtle and carefully contrived strategies than in Fordist factories. However, this concept of "team work" does not genuinely enhance workers' control over work and their participation rights. Primarily, the philosophy of "jointness" in lean production is based on work competition, but true equality between managers and workers do not exist in order to "jointly" determine work and production issues. Along with the eclipse of the union system of shop representation, this new method deprived workers of the ability to resist a new and subtle form of speedup. "Team production" schemes returned to the preunion days in which straw bosses mercilessly drove their workmates to ever-higher levels of production (Lichtenstein 1995: 443). Furthermore, out of the entire pool of workers, only a small number of mostly skilled workers are employed in group work. As in the case of the German automobile industry, works councils found that in 1988, only 7,000 workers out of about 450,000 employees were involved in some form of group work. They were employed only in mechanized and automated processes such as pressrooms, foundries, metalwork shops, body assembly and paint shops (Altmann 1992).

This is the reality of lean production today. Cost reduction and high efficiency are the only goals. For these purposes, lean production does not only uphold flexibility with the use of new technology, but also functionally serve the flexibility of the workforce through staffing and scheduling practices (Moody 1997: 95-101). The biggest divergence of lean production from Taylorism is functional flexibility, which involves job rotation among workers and their ability to work in a number of different jobs, often referred to as "multi-skilling". This is achieved by the reduction or elimination of job descriptions or categories. However, in reality "multi-skilling" should be called "multi-tasking", since the actual work of simple standardized tasks are part of the deskilling of workers in the classical Taylorist sense. Additionally, time flexibility is meant to allow round-the-clock operation in order to fully utilize the firms' capital assets with as few workers as possible. The result is regular overtime and downsizing, a pattern seen from the early days in Japan to many other US imitators in the 1990s or from a new system of time corridor or annualized hours as in Europe. Last, staffing flexibility is achieved through the contracting out and the extensive use of casual labor. In contrast to the temporary workers in the textile industry in early industrialized economies in the nineteenth century, most part-time workers today may have to work on those positions permanently. Although some workers may prefer part-time employment, involuntary part-time work has grown since 1979. Thus, as Moody (1997) commented long ago, lean production touted as a "new way of working" that promised a more humane workplace, has been served as methods of work intensification and of undermining worker unionization. The standardization and intensification of work through "scientific management" are only modifications to Fordism.

Therefore, the outcomes of lean production are characterized by precarious employment and stressful working assignments. These conditions have created clear divisions between a continuously shrinking "core", traditionally featured by permanent or long-term employment and good pay, and a rapidly expanding "peripheral", at the national and international levels of analysis. Increasingly, outsourcing involves low-tech and low-end production as at an early stage and shifts the entire manufacturing processes among traditionally-integrated industries and corporations into specialized companies or factories in low-cost countries or regions, such as China.

In the field of industrial relations, the different features of production organization and new industrial methods brought about various forms of labor-capital relations at the workplace level, thereby changing industrial relations as a whole. For instance, the labor movement of the automobile industry in the twentieth century tended to be large-scaled and well-organized, but today the struggles in the electronics industry appeared more segmented and spontaneous. In many industrialized countries, this transformation accompanied, or even led to, the decline of traditional unionism. Since companies and workplaces were increasingly fractured along vertically dis-integrated production networks, workers' structural bargaining power tended to be weakened. Until the early 1990s, the hard-won social contracts by labor movements in the post-war era had been largely overturned. In this context, trade unionism and high wages were often used by capitalists as the scapegoats of declining profitability or reasons for failure of business. For instance, since GM, the world's number one auto producer for the past 76 years, was replaced by Toyota in 2007, the international media became critical about the high labor costs among the big three American auto makers.[107] At the same time, world-wide capitalists sought for new locations with lower costs and less worker resistance. In light of the combined oppression from capitalists and local governments, new factory locations often had bad labor conditions and inactive trade unions. Nevertheless, as the labor-capital conflict continued to be embedded in everyday work, labor struggles continued. Indeed, the current production regimes, in many cases, endowed new sources of empowerment for workers, in spite of its rather contradictory intentions.

In China, changes in production organizations could be seen as the country continues to integrate itself to the global economy. More importantly, China's growth model predominantly relies on foreign investment. This growth model in particular focuses on vertical dis-integration, as demonstrated by the development of the electronics industry since the 1970s, and on the dissolution of "large corporate complexes" into smaller-sized and more specialized firms. At the same time, some specific configurations of Chinese economy also play a role. For instance, different forms of ownership in China determine certain aspects of industrial relations. Since the reform in 1978, forms of ownership have diversified, which depart from the earlier domination of SOEs. For instance, large-scale foreign joint ventures in the auto industry have become major players, whereas electronics firms are mostly privately-owned, in terms of both value added and exports. This partly explains the different labor practices in the exemplary cases of the automobile and electronics industries.

The two industries are marked by different production organizations, labor standards, and industrial relations. However, they both feature outsourcing and subcontracting at different levels of the production networks. In fact, both

107 E.g. The Financial Times, by: Ma, Jiying, The collapse of 100-year industry, Jan 03,?2008, http://auto.jrj.com.cn/2008/01/032038539534.shtml

extensive and intensive forms of accumulation exist in today China.[108] Some features of intensive accumulation, a model based on accelerated technological development and increased production of relative surplus value exist (e.g. in the production of major auto makers). However, extensive accumulation is seen in auto parts production and at lower levels of the electronics industry, based on the reduction in wages, lengthening of the working day, etc. (Aglietta 1979). This closely resembles the US and German models at the early stages of Fordist development. Although lean production and the following HRM concepts have been selectively introduced in modern firms, mass production, assembly lines and Taylorist division of labor are common.

In the automobile industry, the structure of production organizations and industrial relations is relatively simple. Whole-car makers, which are predominantly foreign-sino joint ventures, remain at the top of the value chain with relatively stable wages and SOE-style labor relations. The tendencies of investing in long-term projects and advanced technologies and production flows give them a strategic role in the economy. When the share of Chinese investment stems from provincial or municipal levels, the joint ventures often have a strong influence from SOE operations, especially in personnel and training policies. As for wages and other labor standards, the "hegemonic" regime featured by relatively skilled workforce and higher standards emerge in spite of slight divergence due to the impact from different foreign countries of origin. Relatively well-paid workforces stand in stark contrast to the massive number of "flexible" workers who face declining labor standards along the suppliers or subcontractors at lower tiers. However, those "core" workforces are shrinking and their labor standards are going declining too. Continuous pressures come from an expanding periphery composed of dispatched labor inside core companies, as well as from workers along the supply chains.

In contrast to the automobile industry, the electronics industry no longer features characteristics of traditional production regimes, namely strong unionism and collective bargaining. Rather, the industry is diverse, with a brand new type of enterprise - contract manufacturers. At the top, the specialized brand name MNCs increasingly emphasize performance in their labor practice. Major contract manufacturers are establishing large-scale high-tech factories with minimum labor standards, while the majority of part and component suppliers and subcontractors follow the classical low-wage model (Hürtgen et al. 2009). Moreover, as the speculative global financial markets and the wildly fluctuating consumer demands exert strong influence on increasingly specialized enterprises,

108 This view is first proposed by Lüthje, Ten Brink and McNally in a research project on China capitalism, 2011

the entire industry has become extremely unstable. Accordingly, employment for the entire manufacturing workforce is highly insecure and wages remain very unstable. These features follow the "lean and mean" model. There is no intention to offer employment security or stable wages to the workforce, especially low-skilled operators. In China, the mixed ownership is credited for the success of many domestic MNCs that emerged from their former SOE or COE background. However, without actual SOE infrastructure, the electronics industry is largely union free. In its place, HRM policies are carefully designed among brand names or first-tier suppliers in order to cultivate workers' cooperation and loyalty. Nevertheless, the remaining suppliers and contract manufacturers view flexible employment and high turnover rates as easy and cheap ways of getting rid of extra workers in case of low customer demands.

It is noted that in both industries, FDI and foreign brand names play an important role. As global MNCs begin production in China, they may bring along their production organization and management traditions from the country of origin. For instance, European firms select suppliers who already enjoy established relationships with their clients in their home country, while Japanese usually invest their key parts suppliers within the same corporate group. These practices are in turn adopted by their Chinese subsidiaries. Since the 1990s, many Western companies began to implement cost-cutting measures that follow lean methods, particularly the extensive use of subcontracting, while abandoning the principle of employment security for the core workforce. This practice is followed in China too.

Many American MNCs, with strong anti-unionism tradition, tend to be innovators of HRM practices, such as emphasizing workforce commitment, high performance work systems, and a strong corporate culture (e.g. Kochan et al. 1997). In practice, precarious practices of hiring and firing, extensive OT and high performance incentives become routine procedures among Chinese branches and subsidiaries. As for German companies, although the characteristics of the high-skill/ high-quality/ high-wage model is notable through the training and wage structure among a few leading companies, the degree of influence from the country of origin depends on the structure of the companies. Since there have been ongoing changes to Germany's traditional unionism and collective bargaining system, some firms insist on the traditional model while others favor the "American" style of flexibility and deregulation. In China, while the former group of industrialists emphasizes multi-skill training, stability, and the development of the workforce, the latter group enhances efficiency through intensified and lengthy working hours, especially in the electronics industry.

In particular, Japanese companies perhaps have been most influenced by the production and management traditions from the country of origin. The classic "lean and dual" model triumphed in Japan within the context of global competition during the 1980s, but such effectiveness will not endure in China. The necessary condition of this model, including the kinship between periphery and core workers (e.g. many periphery workers were the wives or sisters of core workers) and the nature of only working temporary in Japan at the time (e.g. rural migrants only went to factories for seasonal work), does not exist in China. The majority of migrant workers serve as the backbone of China's manufacturing workforce. They are not usually related to urban workers, and they expect to work in the cities at least for several years. In reality, a "lean and mean" model predominates. Nevertheless, both Japanese and Chinese philosophies traditionally emphasize "harmony". In order to keep harmony, extensive communication channels are designed for the purpose of cooperative relations between labor and capital. These channels also facilitate collective negotiation. Furthermore, paternalism in Japanese brand name companies encourages tolerance of enterprise unions. As a result, a few suppliers within traditional Japanese brand names have become well known for their wage negotiation practices in spite of their unfavorable positions in the production network. The cases are very interesting, although it would be hard for such negotiation to continue among other enterprises.

Companies owned by overseas Chinese, especially the Taiwanese, are currently in disrepute in regards to labor standards and management styles. Although many Taiwanese companies, represented by contract manufacturers, are large-scale and produce rather high-tech products, they feature very low base wages, extensive OT, strict work rule, and an authoritative style of management. These companies typically hire migrant workers who have no family life and little other attachment in the cities. The overseas Chinese employees accommodate them in massive dormitories throughout South China. Such free or low-cost accommodation is an important part of compensation, since the majority of migrant workers cannot afford normal rent in the cities. At the same time, this accommodation facilitates extensive OT schedules. Low wages and dormitory living have limited the private lives of workers by stifling other possible attractions outside of work, which in turn coerces workers' desires to work more hours with fewer holidays and fewer opportunities to spend money.

As for Chinese domestic companies, the automobile and electronics industries differ in terms of their positions along the production chains, as well as the products they offer in the global market. Domestic auto makers, in spite of government support and favorable policies, remain in the early stages of development. They still depend on foreign partners for advanced technologies and there is not much incentive for indigenous innovation. Nevertheless, the future is uncertain since several domestic brands currently promote independent technologies, while at the same time large industrial groups with local government connections and large-scale production volumes seek to build their own independent brands now. The electronics industry is quite different. Chinese companies' capacity for rapid learning has made it possible for a number of domestic electronics enterprises to catch up with global brand names. Today there are national champions among dedicated exporters in battery and home appliances, as well as high-tech start-ups which are founded by Chinese overseas returnees.

One special group is foreign-China joint ventures. Apart from the major auto makers, where SOE tradition and foreign brand names have positive effects on labor conditions, some smaller parts suppliers and subcontractors may have shares from the township or village governments. In such cases, it is quite common for the local governments to acquiesce to illegal behaviors of enterprises. At the same time, most of them are non-brand-name companies, and foreign investment comes from individuals. These joint ventures only have loose supplying or subcontracting relationship with brand name MNCs or first-tier suppliers. Accordingly, the influence from the foreign country of origin is weak. Usually, such joint ventures are at the bottom of the value chain with low wage and low-end production.

Besides ownership difference, regional differences are also evident within the geographically vast China. The relationship between the central state and local governments and between states and capital varies distinctively. Generally speaking, local governments, including at regional, city, district, and village levels, play an important role in industrial relations. If ranked by wage levels, YRD would be at the top, Beijing area the second, and then PRD. The YRD's higher wages and better working conditions result from specific local governance practices. As Shanghai exemplifies, the local government keeps a steady intervention in the economy and set up strict rules on the market, which is more developmentalist than others. Additionally, even within the same region, different industrial parks may compete with each other for favorable policies, sometimes beyond the nation's legal limits such as extensive use of interns and lengthy working time. In addition, without coordination of labor standards at higher levels, enterprises within the same industry that produce similar products may have completely different wage structures, working conditions, technological capacities and so forth. At lower levels of the value chains, if a company is regarded as an important engine of growth for the local economy, or if the township or village governments have a share in the company (e.g. a large Chinese color TV maker in Huizhou, Guangdong, or small auto part supplier in the suburb of Shanghai - see chapter 3), this type of labor regime may be the worst kind - repressive and abusive. In recent years, a new problem has emerged while many companies that have begun to "go inland". Cities in the middle and West China - "inland" - are much less developed than coastal regions in the East and South China, but local governments in middle and West China now try to attract investment through favorable policies and their huge low-cost labor pool. Many companies which originally produce in East and South China begin to relocate or expand their production to these cities. For instance, Foxconn has opened several big factories in Chengdu, Zhengzhou, etc.; Geely built up a plant in Lanzhou, Gansu province. The output of the electronics industry in Sichuan and Chongqing has increased to 49.6% and 74.4% respectively in 2010[109]. The expansion into less-developed areas may exert a downward pressures on labor standards within the country as a whole.

To sum up, production regimes in China are influenced by both global trends and domestic conditions. Since from the introduction of China's economic reforms in 1978, a period marked by the late development of the automobile industry and by the restructuring of the electronics industry, manufacturing in China exemplify features common to many global industries. The automobile industry is centered on whole-car joint ventures, but the electronic industry has a largely segmented structure with a distinct group of contract manufacturers. Industrial relations within the electronic industry features flexibilization and deregulation common in all types of enterprises. Many factors, such as the position in the production network, the ownership structure, the country of origin, and local government policies, have collectively shaped the production regimes of individual enterprises. In general, flexible production regimes with low base wages, high turnover rates, no collective contract, and no trade unions are common. In the electronics industry, even in most leading brand name MNCs, employment security and wage stability are absent. Additionally, Western companies, even those with strong trade unionism and collective contracts back in their home countries, highly advocate performance-oriented HRM policies. Those policies pit workers against each other not only within the same enterprise but also between companies, industries, or different countries. The features of major whole-car joint ventures are the closest to a hegemonic factory regime. However, the nearly universal emphasis on flexibility, as demonstrated by the use of dispatched labor as well as by external outsourcing, has endangered the viability of such a regime. Divisions exist between long-term and temporary workers in everyday work and basic

---

109 The Ministry of Industry and Information Technology of the People's Republic of China, 2010 Report on the Economy of the Electronics and IT industry, February 11, 2011

labor standards both inside and among factories. In a nutshell, with the exception of a small percentage of relatively "core" workforce in major auto assemblers, which usually take the form of foreign-sino joint ventures and perhaps a few first-tier auto and specialized electronic part suppliers, the majority of the manufacturing workforce in China experience precarious and repressive labor regimes at the lower end of the global outsourcing and subcontracting networks.

The recent changes n industrial and production organizations have presented both negative and positive results for collective bargaining in China. The new trends of flexibilization, decentralization and deregulation have undermined the power of collective labor in traditional unionism. The diversification of production regimes in both automobile and electronics industries have weakened the voice of collective labor and made coordination at higher levels more difficult. At present, wages and other labor standards have been largely determined by unilateral management decisions. The constant renewal of organizational and management methods by capitalists foretells that the process of establishing an effective collective bargaining system in China, if successful at all, will be lasting and dynamic.

At the same time, possibilities for enhanced bargaining power among workers are also present in the new industrial and production organizations. Within these new production organizations and management methods, the just-in-time delivery system gives workers new leverage. As efficiency of the system depends on the close coordination of production among different enterprises, any disruption on one part of the flow could potentially break down the system. Strikes in one or two major suppliers may completely shut down the entire supply chain. In this way, the workplace bargaining power of workers multiplies. Besides, the dominant low-wage or flexible wage regimes, in contrast to the "five dollars a day" scheme of Henry Ford, tend to create more frequent conflicts along the shop floors. The mass de-skilling of the blue-collared Chinese workforce largely resembles that in the Ford factories in the U.S. and in Germany. Nevertheless, when Ford introduced mass production, affordable and mass-produced housing was designed for workers to recuperate from the rigors of their working lives. Such a careful segregation of factories from workers' homes maintains the illusion of an autonomous, independent self among the workers. In contrast, dormitories in China today are built inside the factory sites to facilitate the intensive production schedule. Family life simply does not exist for the majority of migrant workers. The suicidal wave of Foxconn in the early 2010 resulted from such extremes.

As evidenced by the American and German experiences, such repressive labor regimes tend to be highly unstable. Workers must have a say in the processes closely linked to their everyday work and life. The fact that a huge number of grudging workers with enhanced right consciousness work together in the mass production line and live in concentrated dormitories is potentially unstable. A well-governed and -coordinated system of collective bargaining would be the best solution to guarantee the security of workers and provide incentives to ensure their loyalty and initiative. This is mutually beneficial for workers and capital (e.g. to reduce short-term personnel flexibility and to improve continuity, quality and performance of production). However, the current production regimes are unlikely to change under the enterprise-based labor polity. Thus, an effective model of collective bargaining should at least include jointly-determined contractual wage relationship with higher-level coordination. Given the conditions of China, it would be realistic to first experiment in the automobile industry led by the whole-car makers, with coordination of labor standards along the value chain.

4.3 Chinese State and Labor Policies

At the national level, policies governing collective bargaining are often produced through interactions among major actors of industrial relations. The state, through its role in national socioeconomic regulation, is the most relevant institution governing wage relations (Koch 2006). In industrial relations, the state serves as a tripartite party between labor and capital. During the post-war Fordist era, state intervention, at least in the form of effective and extensive regulations, was indispensable in both the U.S. and Germany. These regulations, including the guarantee of labor rights to collective bargaining, strikes and association, have facilitated the institutionalization of collective bargaining in the long run. The pressure from the labor movements is the essential force in this process.

In China, the role of the state seems to be ambiguous in the process of developing a so-called "socialist market economy" due to its communist tradition and single-party dominance. In this section, I will examine the Chinese state and its stance toward labor law and policy-making, as well as the internal conflicts between central and local states, which has served as a barrier of policy implementation. I aim to identify what favorable factors for collective bargaining exist at the policy level while narrowing those that are currently absent. I will also consider how to institutionalize collective bargaining under the existing conditions.

4.3.1 Labor law and polices

Modern state theories regard the state as a major actor in social relations. Therefore, the relationship between the economic base and its politico-ideological superstructure is inseparable (Jessop 1997). As the foundation of political power, the state order society by enacting regulations and laws, fulfilling economic tasks such as issuing money, building infrastructure, and guaranteeing certain benefits to its citizens. At the same time, the state collects tax revenues in order to accomplish these goals. In time of economic crisis (e.g. the 1930s, the 1970s and 2008/9) the state also attempts to revitalize the capital.

The incorporation between state and capital is obvious. In theory, capital may vie for influence over state power (McNally 2008: 32). In the past, states tended to hold a monopoly over the interests of capital. Nevertheless, capitalism's earliest origins lay in an alliance between state and capital. This alliance emerged again in the first half of the twentieth century when the basic institutions of capitalism were reconstituted.

In China, the priority given to economic growth has been a national policy since the Reform in 1978. The state depends on capital for economic growth in order to secure its internal legitimacy and international power. At the same time, the state does not represent the interest of a single capitalist, but brokers the interests of capitalism as a whole. Thus, the state attempts to maintain the social-political stability for a good environment of capital accumulation.

The relationship between the Chinese state and capital is cooperative, although the anti-capitalist rhetoric from the Socialist tradition has officially continued for the sake of organizational cohesion and ideological legitimacy (Chen 2008). In the early stage of capitalism, capital remains at the mercy of state elites who seek financial guarantees from the state. In this sense, the state depends on economic accumulation and tax revenue to legitimate its ruling, and in turn guarantees a range of social, legal, and infrastructural integration as well as customization services for the maintenance of capitalist socialization (McNally 2008: 234). In the last three decades, this state-capital alliance has led to industrial policies that ensures the priorities of economic growth, while pursuing the re-balancing of efficiency and justice for the society.

Since the Chinese Communist Party (CCP)'s legitimacy rests in great measure on its ability to foster economic wealth, the leverage of capital holders has increased. While the state logic seeks to assure the CCP's monopoly over political organization, the capital logic attempts to create transformative push that expands capital's economic and political space. In fact, capital has been able to assert indirect control over public affairs. The political recognition of private capital in China has advanced since the 1990s. In 1997, private business became officially regarded as one important part of the national economy. Since 2001, private business owners could even join the Party, which claimed to be the Party of workers and peasants. Clearly, through those policies, the CCP attempted to control and co-opt all social interests that could potentially challenge its monopoly (McNally 2008).

To a certain degree, capitalists in China are diverse in their compositions and political backgrounds, which challenges any anti-state movements. Private entrepreneurs differ widely in terms of their employment background, policy concerns, political attitudes, resources, values, and coping strategies (Tsai 2007: 11, 196). Capitalists and domestic MNCs have emerged before capitalism becomes well-developed. According to the survey of official employers' associations in 1995 and 2000, the political composition of private sector was remarkably fluid in the past two decades. Among the new bourgeoisie - the wealthiest group (e.g. 3 million of millionaire in 1998), most were family members of central or local officials and former bureaucrats who relied on their political lineage to derive commercial prerogatives. Even for the rest, such as former SOE employees or those who emerged from the "network capitalism" (McNally 2008: 112) in South China, they were highly enmeshed in the political establishment, either to get political protection or to access public resources. When the government abandoned direct economic command during the reform, some functions expanded abnormally and led to the commercialism of government behaviors. The result was the cooperation of state power with enterprises (Sun 2003:152-155). At the same time, the middle class[110], lack of economic strength and confidence in their class power, was politically risk-averse (Pearson 1997). Thus, there is an absence of a unified capitalist class which may favor democracy in China. Informal networks of entrepreneurs organized by trade, kinship, native place, or former state work unit may support their collective actions. However, it is unlikely that they would take political actions together with the bottom classes of the society (Chen 2008). The reason is Chinese political, economic and intellectual elites are firmly allied, but disadvantaged groups are fragmented and cannot organize (Sun 2003: 15-20).

The power of capital and labor is very unbalanced in Chinese economy and society. Theoretically, capitalists have three different forms of collective action

110 The existence of a middle class in China is a debatable topic. The definition of middle class here is mostly in economical sense. The criteria for the middle class include higher than 5000 RMB monthly wages, minimum of bachelor degree, manager or specialists. They accounted for 11.9% of the total population in 2005. See: Li 2005. In the study of Wei (2004:11), the middle class in China were mainly private entrepreneurs, involving 26.57 million private businesses in 2003, employing more than 200 million people and accounting for 1/3 of the GDP

at its disposal in order to define and to defend their interests, through firm organization, informal cooperation, and the employers or business associations. However, labor only have trade unions.[111] In the past, the establishment of formal employers' organizations emerged only as a defensive response to the formation of unions and to incipient state-interventionism, so they are underdeveloped in China. Their underdevelopment may in turn affect regional and industrial collective bargaining, as there is lack of effective coordination on the side of capital.[112] Nevertheless, since effective trade unions do not exist in China today, from the perspective of the capital, it may not be so urgent to build up their associations. In practice, changes in national laws have pushed some employers to organize themselves firstly to express opposition, such as their opposition to the 2008 Labor Contract Law. During this debate, the voices of workers were mostly individualized and widely scattered. Employers in the export sector in coastal areas made their voices heard by public. For example, the Hong Kong SME association and the European employers' association in Shanghai publicized their opposition against the law.

The central government, in face of such unbalance labor-capital relations, has attempted to make new legislation and policies in recent years. Essentially, economic growth is the primary target of the state for its legitimacy. So far, the large proportion of labor-intensive industries in the economy has grown thanks to 'favorable investment environments' that promote flexibilization, de-regulation, and low labor costs. The current development path of China is centered on low-wage production that represses workers' rights. In fact, wage restraint is typically used by many earlier industrialized countries as a mechanism for improving international competitiveness. Also in the U.S. and Germany, only after the "social contracts" were successfully set up through collective bargaining and guaranteed by the state through laws and rules, wages

111 Compared to the communications between unions and the state, the communication of business associations with the state differ in that they are less visible publicly (because there is a lesser need to mobilize the support of external allies), more technical (because the insight into the political "desirability", that is, factual indispensability, can be presupposed as already agreed upon), more universal (because business associations can speak in the name of all those interests that require for their fulfillment a healthy and continuous rate of accumulation, which, from the point of view of capital and the state, is true of virtually everybody), and negative (because, given the fact that the government has to consider as desirable what is in fact desirable for capital, the only thing that remains to be done is to warn governments against imprudent, "unrealistic", and otherwise inopportune decisions and measures). See: Offe and Wiesenthal 1980

112 e.g. Briefing on annual meeting of the China Law Society, Speech of Mr. Wang, Guoshe, the Director of Shenzhen City Bureau of human resource and social security, August 21, 2010, Vol. 2

began to rise in accordance with productivity. Respective studies of Asia and Brazil also reached the same conclusion (Kittel 2001). In China, as the overcapacity of industrial production requires rising consumption in the domestic market, higher incomes of mass workers are the most common and perhaps the only way to realize it. Further, the shortage of migrant labor has become prominent, especially after Chinese spring festival holidays in coastal regions. Although such shortage tends to be temporary and does not reflect the national oversupply of rural labor, low wages have lost their ability to attract migrant workers. Many factories in coastal regions that offer low wages have to close down temporarily because of insufficient workers. Along this vein, collective bargaining, through fairer income distribution and accordingly higher wages for workers, serves as an essential mechanism in stabilizing the national economy, politics, and society.

At the same time, social and political stability is the other target of the state, apart from economic growth. In the last several decades, as the low-wage, high-welfare system of the planned economy has come to an end, the importance of economic growth in the new market economy has resulted in widespread violations of labor rights. These socioeconomic inequalities undermined the regime's legitimacy among the poor majority, mainly the disabled and elderly without family support, unemployed, and migrant workers. Social stratification gave rise to class conflicts. Disappointed in the failed "social contract" or legal terms (Lee 2007), workers in both old industrial areas in North China and newly developed regions in the South went onto the streets. In 2004, there were 74,000 protests involving 3.76 million people, an increase from 58,000 in 2003 and only 10,000 a decade ago[113]. Thus, the state policy-making apparatus felt the need of turning towards a more pro-labor direction.

Accordingly, the central state has considered of establishing a relatively stable macro-economy with its associated regulations, in order to appear to be labor-friendly. The state is also making a concerted effort to increase domestic consumption in an attempt to lower its reliance on exports and to close the gap between the rich and the poor. Three national statutes, the Labor Contract Law, the Employment Promotion Law, and the Law on Labor Dispute Mediation and Arbitration, were successively promulgated in 2007. These statues have enhanced workers' rights in regards to employment and dismissal, such as encouraging open-term labor contracts and facilitating workers' access to arbitration. Besides, China plans to double employees' wages by 2015,

113 According to the speech of Zhou, Yongkang, former Minister of the Ministry of Public Security, quoted from Yu, Jianrong, Collective incidents and Building Harmonious Society, Sep 08, 2008 http://wenku.baidu.com/view/debd1d563c1ec5da50e270b2.html

according to Huang Mengfu, vice-chairman of the National Council of Chinese People's Political Consultative Conference and chairman of the All-China Federation of Industry and Commerce.[114] Minimum wage standards rose again in early 2010. Moreover, state officials are reconsidering collective bargaining and wage negotiations.

Many observers are optimistic about these changes. Some researchers argue that as the central state looses its control over the economy and administration, social space will allow for the segmentation - and legitimation - of societal interests. Accordingly, the society is becoming less firmly state-dominated than the 'organized dependency' model of the Maoist era (Walder 1984), but more regulated and regimented than the civil society model (Baum and Shevchenko 1999). Additionally, as the economy and social structure develops, some groups of people, such as scholars and journalists in more developed regions, have become more politically sophisticated and assertive in the articulation of their interests. Further, as political successors are selected through the regularized personnel system rather than through personal authority or charisma (e.g. Naughton and Yang 2004: 25), officials are more likely to rely on formal authority and institution building to gain political favors within the Party.

The pressure from mass workers may drive the changes in ruling strategies and accordingly policies. However, such pressure is far from enough. Strikes, labor unrest, and other forms of resistance remind the leadership the potential sources of social instability. Nevertheless, the powers that transformed the post-war orders in the U.S. and Germany were well-organized strong collective labor. In contrast to the absence of such powers in today's China, the power of capitalists and their opposition to pro-labor policies dominate. As for collective bargaining, a majority of managers commonly resist to any coordination of wages and labor standards beyond enterprises. They have a deep-rooted commitment to setting specific wages for individual companies, positions and workers. The change in current ways of determining wages and other labor standards should begin with necessary resistance from workers.

Moreover, rapid changes within certain institutions tend to be incomplete (North 1990). At the moment, national labor laws and policies alone prove to be insufficient. The implementation of labor laws and policies primarily requires support from the state. The current failure of labor law enforcement may be related to de-prioritization given to labor laws by the central government. For instance, policies and regulations on collective bargaining have been issued since 1993, but this mechanism has never been given top priority by the party-

114 South Morning Post, Denise Tsang in Beijing, Firms see pay floor rising 20pc a year up to 2015 Wage increases part of plan to drive up domestic consumption, Sep 21, 2010

state, compared to economic plans. The state often implements its priority policies and controls key local leaders, leaving discretionary power to local agents over the implementation of non-priority policies (Edin 2003). The selective implementation of the central state gives local governments substantial leeway in determining trade-offs. Moreover, the Party allows its cadres to retain considerable power to control the market, which in turn introduces commercialized patron-client ties between state agents and private entrepreneurs (Wank 1999). In this context, enterprises often easily evade labor law and policies in practice. Therefore, apart from the necessity of empowering the voice of collective labor, the enforcement of labor law and policies depends on the governing structures of the state, particularly the relationship between the central and local governments.

4.3.2 Central and local states

The role of the Chinese state has always been significant when discussing the economy, politics, and industrial relations. In practice, besides its sensitive linkages with business and collective labor, the state faces challenges within its own system. Tensions are found even within the huge government apparatus, not only among different branches but more between the central and local states.

The CCP continues to dominate over the market economy, although its direct economic role has retreated relatively. The essential object of reform is certainly not to change the basic structure of the CCP's ruling, but to improve its operation. Despite several decades of capitalist development, no form of organized political opposition has emerged. In other words, there is no Western type of multi-party system in China challenging the dominant position of the CCP as the governing party. Only the specific methods of governance can be altered (Kornai 1992: 83).

In the last decades, the political process was characterized by continued favoritism and factionalism at national and regional levels (Naughton and Yang 2004). Different factions, between former presidents Jiang, Zemin and Hu, Jintao, have shared monopoly power within the Party. In spite of divergent political backgrounds (e.g. former provincial officials from coastal regions vs. from west China) and policy preferences (e.g. urban- or rural-focused), the basic interests of different factions are largely the same; that is, to maintain the ruling of the Party (Li 2003). In general, through the Nomenklatura system of personnel, critical Party positions at different administrative levels are firmly kept within the hegemony of the CCP. At the same time, it has been a common rule that party members are privileged with the titles of civil servants, or joining

SOEs or other public or semi-public institutions. In the industrial sectors, party committees or branches cooperate with joint ventures or with companies that were formerly SOEs. In other words, the government continues to closely follow instructions from the CCP and the CCP rules through the existing Party-state.

Nevertheless, the state and the party could still be regarded as two different political entities. In theory, the separation of powers between the Party and governmental structures used to be debated in national political meetings in the 1980s, but since the 1989 Tiananmen incident, these challenges largely disappeared. Since then, successive leaderships backed away from making progressive changes (Gittings 2005: 13). In practice, the reform after the 1990s was in fact the reform of governance, rather than of the CCP itself. Without any significant changes, the CCP became tightly integrated into other chains of command as the ultimate source of government authority that guarantees political stability and coordinate the processes of global integration (Zheng 2009: 20). In this way, the hierarchical relationship between the government and the Party is tied more closely to material rewards (Naughton and Yang 2004).

The central state has largely initiated and guided the development path of China. Historical experiences have illustrated different roles of state in the development of nations, such as neo-classical laissez-faire state, or centrally planned Leninist state, or East Asian capitalist developmental state. Since the reform, particularly after Deng's South tour in the 1992, the combination of top-down political control and state-guided industrial growth has transformed China into a major economic player. It is now "moving from low-end assembly lines and garment sweatshops to high-end products and innovative approaches to cutting-edge technology, such as solar panels and electric cars" (Dreyfuss 2010). This approach is modeled on the miracle of nearby East Asian countries through exports and controls by developmental states.

Nevertheless, the contemporary Chinese state is far from being a monolithic entity. The relationship between the central and local states is rather complicated. China is characterized as "a diffuse developmental state" or "fragmented authoritarianism" (Lieberthal and Lampton 1992). As compared to the East Asian model of the "developmental states", China is phrased as "competitive liberalism", or "local state corporatism" to illustrate the developmental, market-promoting, and entrepreneurial role of local officials.[115] Consequently, the reform has been entangled by persistent contradictory imperatives and interest conflicts between the central and local governments (Lee 2007: 15).

For a long time, intense rivalries among the Chinese state's various agencies and jurisdictional levels have put considerable constraints on implementing

---

115 A summery in the work of Lee, 2007: 15

national policies. In geographically vast and culturally complicated China, there has been a traditional saying that "the heaven is high and the emperor is far away". Today this is still partly true. In other words, the authority of the central state could not extend many local places, and thus the local states enjoyed quite a freedom in decision-making. Since 1978, the central state has gradually decentralized its control over the economy. In the 1980s, particularly 1984, the redistribution functions of the state were decentralized to the sub-national levels. The ratio of financial revenues between central and local states reached historically low during this period, 22% vs. 78% in 1993. Among the five levels of government - national, provincial, prefectural, counties and townships, the third and fourth levels are in charge of almost all expenditures for social security and other income support and welfare schemes (Naughton and Yang 2004: 25). Accordingly, privately-run enterprises proliferated, including mixed firms and cooperatives owned by cities, districts and communities. Only in the mid 1990s, the central state began to re-centralize power through budget reform, re-distribution of tax revenues, and other financial changes. Afterwards, the administrative and political control of the central state over local leaders gradually increased again.

A large variety of regulations and practices exist at different levels among local states. In particular, the counties and towns with rather strong financial autonomy compete fiercely and have the most leverage in enacting policies, whether they are explicit or implicit, for investors. Such competition is often at odds with the long term plans of the upper levels of government. For instance, in the PRD, while the provincial and many city governments aggressively promote industrial upgrading, towns and villages continue to offer favorable deals for low-end enterprises that are labor intensive and offer workers low wages.

Such investment competition among the different levels of government, by offering free land, cheap credit, and low taxes, has resulted in over-investment and over-expansion of a region's production capacity. In the case of the automobile industry, 30 largest automakers had a combined capacity of producing 14 million units in 2009, according to the official of the National Development and Reform Commission. If their expansion plans among the same automakers continue, their combined capacity would soar to 31 million units by 2015 (Yang 2010). Even if car sales grow 13% annually as the central government predicted, industry sales can only reach a total of 27 million units in 2015 (Yang 2010). Since ambitious officials at city and provincial levels are judged by their performance of local economic development, they encourage state-owned automakers to build more plants and to offer more jobs .

At the same time, the central government critically depends on the performance of these industries as a source of revenue. As tax revenues of the central government decreases, it is not able to provide "public goods". In fact, even if the government can provide public goods without the increase of tax revenues, some measures prove to be ineffective due to its limited allocative power (Wong 2005). For example, in the 1990s the central government distributed transfer payments to the under-developed West China, but these capital flows ended in the East China (Wang and Fan 2004). At the lower levels of government, expansion of local administration power has created local identity, which strengthened the local resistance of implementing central policies. Municipal governments invested in the construction of industrial parks[116], and offered bureaucratic services, fast approvals, and a well-established infrastructure. In particular, policies of decentralization gave priority to the development of the coastal areas, exacerbating the gap between coastal and inland areas (Zheng 2009: 134). In fact, in 2006 the new system of cadre evaluation was promoted by Hu-Wen who cite that "scientific development" and "harmonious society" are the new goals rather than merely economic performance. Nevertheless, problems exist in the evaluation system itself, such as the gaps between central authorities and local power (Guo 2007).

Moreover, locality has strongly impacted bureaucratic and inter-firm relations. Different answers to the question whether there should be "more state or more market" lead to distinctive development patterns at local levels. In general, the YRD, which began to develop at the end of the 1980s, has more active state regulations, whereas the PRD, which developed since the early 1980s without any experience of careful planning by the higher levels of government, is more liberal. Shanghai, in the YRD, is a representative of "local developmental states" with investment-intensive and FDI-privileged growth strategy due to its urban-biased and heavy-handed state interventionism in the 1990s. Guangzhou and Beijing are relatively "laissez-faire local states" featured by fragmented bureaucracy and competitive relations between firms, whereas Changchun and Wuhan are typical "firm-dominated locality" with a fragmented bureaucracy and hierarchical relations between firms (Thun 2006). In practice, different patterns of local institutions tend to have comparative advantages in facilitating different sectors. Shanghai was most successful in the 1980s and 1990s in the auto sector because of its strong state-planning capacity in channeling critical resources to the suppliers and in guiding firms through incremental upgrading. For example, Shanghai VW, which started by producing CKD kits, became dominant in the domestic market with 70% share in the early

116 In China, industrial parks and new development zones are the most vigorously growing points of nation economy with the highest concentration of FDI, high-tech industries and other new economies

1990s. Up to now, Shanghai is the only municipality that has been able to rely heavily on the local supplier sector. At the same time, Beijing was effective in fostering the IT sector. Cities in the PRD became "entrepreneurial cities" with increased autonomy and self-organization. In the less developed regions of China, namely the interior provinces such as Sichuan and Henan, their low cost workforce, natural resources, and favorable investment policies are attracting some large enterprises to expand or relocate production there. In a word, the positions of industries and productions within the global value chains, as well as certain features of the labor force in different regions vary distinctively.

In regards to industrial relations, national laws and policies are often loosened through local implementation provisions. Furthermore, many illegal practices concerning wages, working time, etc., are accommodated or tolerated by the local states. In China, national laws are interpreted at the local level before they are put into practice. Thus local governments at the regional and city levels, and sometimes even at district or village levels, play an important role in local implementation. Most significantly, symbiotic relationships between local governments and capital have been cultivated, based on certain fiscal and political autonomy of local governments (Hsing 1998: 110). Instead of the national law and policies, local rule enacted through local governments, local reform departments, local business administration, and company policies prevail.

In practice, local states centered on different patterns of development tend to have divergent regulations. For instance, the Suzhou Industrial park, with a semiconductor sector that accounts for 16% of the total national output, is a good example of the YRD model. In this industrial park, national labor laws are strictly obeyed, and a special public provident fund is set up[117]. As to the PRD, the law and policies are loosely implemented. Overtime work among workers commonly exceeded the legal limit of 36 hours, and wages lower than that set by the legal minimum wage standards were common among a majority of suppliers before 2008. Because of the low base wages, migrant workers were willing to work OT to earn more money. However, local governments use this as an excuse to give "green lights" to the long working hours in enterprises. Sometimes managers even regard CSR or other voluntary movements of enterprises stricter rules than the laws enforced by local governments. In the PRD, recent changes in national law are largely perceived negatively by

117 The Public Providence Fund is a special scheme of compulsory social insurance in operation in this particular industrial park. As an experimental project modeled after the national social insurance system in Singapore, it substitutes for the national social insurance system under a special authorization from the central government. The fund offers the opportunity for many young employees to get loans for buying an apartment, which is the biggest burden for most people in China today.

enterprises. Many employers threat to relocate toward "inland of China" or other lower-cost countries.[118] Moreover, there are other local rules that lead to different labor practices. For instance, in the PRD, employers often rent a piece of land, so in case of business hardship they may easily disappear, leaving unpaid wages and loans to the local governments. On the contrary, in the YRD, employers usually have to buy the land or the building, which leads to a longer-term business strategy and responsibility.

Although East China tends to have stricter rules than the South, the differentiation between YRD and PRD is far from absolute. Even among villages or township governments in a same city, there may be very different labor policies, as in the case of interns in Wuzhong Industrial Park in contrast to the Suzhou Industrial Park. Although both industrial park belong to Suzhou city, the former employs a large proportion of interns with very low wages, but the government of the SIP officially limits the use of interns. In fact, regardless of regional specificity, personal exchange (e.g. *Guanxi*) continue to play a vital role in the economy (Wang 2001: 177), which protects the close relationships of local governments with local businessmen and foreign investors. As private entrepreneurs continue to manipulate this decentralizing state authority in order to cultivate support, cozy relationships between local government agents and enterprises or their associations has emerged independent of central state authority (Wank 1999: 180; 223).

In consequence, labor bureaus, which are theoretically responsible for enforcing labor laws, are marginalized by local economic and commerce bureaus. Labor officials have reported extreme difficulties in imposing fines and penalties on employers for violation of the law, owing to the general priority by the local governments given to creating a favorable investment climate (Lee 2007: 20). Moreover, the organization and activities of local trade unions are often repressed by governments of the same levels, because many investors do not want trade unions. Accordingly, it is expected that the mechanism of collective bargaining will continue to be underplayed by local governments (e.g. Feng 2006).

To sum up, the role of the state is important, but in practice the central and local states often go in different directions. The recent changes in national labor law, has been primarily for the purpose of ensuring a stable economic growth and creating a peaceful industrial environment that promote a "harmonious society" under the ruling party. In spite of oppositions, new laws were eventually promulgated by presidential orders. Nevertheless, the efforts of the

118 Computer business daily, Foxconn arouses the restructuring of IT manufacturing in the PRD, and a new wave of relocation may come, July 13, 2010

central state to institutionalize conflict resolution through legislations were not very successful since priorities were still given to economic policies by the central state.

Apparently, legislations and policies in paper are far from enough. An ideal model of collective bargaining would require bottom-up forces that push for appropriate institutions. Changes to the current internal structure of the state (e.g. stricter inspection of the central state on the policy implementation of the local states) will facilitate the implementation of labor laws and policies. At the same time, the role of the state should not be over-emphasized. Collective bargaining, at least in its early stages of formation, do not depend on formal regulations. In particular, it is unrealistic to depend on national statues to regulate many details of collective bargaining. This expectation not only goes against the principle of law-making, but it is also never a common practice. For instance, in Germany, where industrial-wide collective bargaining is well known, there are no legal rights or procedures under which workers could claim a collective contract (Lüthje 2004). The essential drive for institution-building for collective bargaining is the power from workers. At present, although strikes and other labor actions have pushed the state to pass new statues and policies, the absent of organized collective labor is distinct. Just as in the U.S. during the early twentieth century, Chinese workers may begin to resist in their workplaces by defending their rights and benefits.

4.4 Trade unions and workers

All of the perspectives mentioned above, such as the anti-labor political and industrial environments, increasing flexibilization and vertical dis-integration of production, and ineffective implementation of national labor law and polices eventually points to the same issue at hand, which is the indispensable role of strong collective labor. On the one hand, these factors have largely limited the space for labor protection in today China. For instance, diversified types of smaller-sized enterprises and the popular HRM methods dis-incentivize workers to organize. On the other hand, new sources of power for workers have also endowed in the new production regimes. At the same time, the Chinese ruling class, under the pressure from below, has gradually realized the necessity of finding a balance between economic growth and social stability.

In this section, I analyze workers and their collective organizations. The status and potential of labor ultimately determine industrial relations, especially collective bargaining within the current socioeconomic and political context of China. As for collective labor, trade unions - the only legal labor organization available to workers - are not genuine representative of labor. Unfortunately, workers' solidarity and class consciousness have been abandoned long ago in the political and economic debates during the reform. In order to institutionalize collective bargaining, there is much work left to be done in China today. Among many factors, the trade unions must reform themselves into inclusive labor organization that function at both factory and industrial levels. In this scenario, workplace control over which American workers struggled for in the early twentieth century is essential, especially since homogeneous production regimes that existed in Germany before the 1990s no longer exist today.

4.4.1 Trade Unions in China

The recent changes in labor law and policies neglect the role of Chinese trade unions. Trade unions have been accepted, in all advanced capitalist states, as an indispensable element in representing workers' interests as well as in promoting social order, the absence of which labor conflict and the disruption of social peace would be much harder to control. As Hyman (2001) identifies, trade unions have three roughly co-equal roles, although each role is more or less evident at different times and in different contexts. First, trade unions are economic actors, who try to improve the welfare of their members through industrial strength and collective bargaining. Second, they are "social partners," who serve as an essential aspect of stable, democratic societies. Third, they are vehicles for class struggle, which fight against the commodification of labor under capitalism. However, ACFTU, as the only official trade union in China, do not fit into these categories.

As a "trade union with Chinese characteristics," the ACFTU merely echoed the decisions of central state, rather than leading labor struggles against the capitalists. Nearly as old as the CCP, the Chinese trade union movement had a splendid history full of struggles and strikes. However, during the Cultural Revolution, it was regarded as unnecessary and thus consigned to complete oblivion (Chan 2008: 73). After it was brought back in 1984, a mediating role was overly emphasized. Although the 11th Trade Union Congress in the 1988 emphasized independence from the Party, this break never came to fruition after 1989. In practice, the major tasks of trade unions in the planned economy, including promoting higher productivity and helping workers through hardship, had not changed. It merely acted as the "bridge", "support", "foundation", and "bond" between the party and workers. This formal status guaranteed the ACFTU a high political rank and resources, but fundamentally restricted its activities (Chan 1993). Consequently, the ACFTU was identified by three approaches - as "corporatist, party organ, and intermediary" (Taylor et al. 2003).

The overall principle is that the trade union is under the control of, if not directly subordinate to, the Party-state. According to the national law, the ACFTU exclusively represents workers in China. Any attempt to build collective labor organizations outside of its framework is restricted, often by the ACFTU. Union cadres are in the personnel system of the government - nomenklatura. The union chairpersons are usually paid and treated the same way as that of deputy officials at the same administrative level. In enterprises with public background, the chairpersons of the enterprise unions are of the similar rank as vice presidents. In many cases, union cadres are even the managers or relatives of the top management members. Employers must pay 2% of payroll to the trade unions, and workers pay 0.5%.

As a consequence, the top concern of Chinese trade unions is to fulfill the missions assigned by the state rather than safeguarding workers' rights and benefits. The major missions include maintaining industrial peace through national labor polices and safeguarding its position as the only legal trade union organization in China. As social stability increasingly becomes the priority of the Party-state, the trade union has closely followed the policy trend of the central government. It responded to the government slogan of "harmonious society", which the central government announced in October 2008, with a new goal of its own - building "harmonious labor relations". This in practice has further emphasized the mediating and coordinating role of trade unions in industrial relations. At the same time, the official trade union keeps any other forms of collective labor organization or movement out. Although the state has abandoned its efforts to monitor and control all of society, it still protects its monopoly on political organizations (Dickson 2010). In the field of labor, the state is alerted of any organized movements either against management or the state. The ACFTU has been put into the position, as an extended state power to control industrial workers, and is expected by the state to forestall any forms of collective action. In fact, the trade union also has all the interests to do this in order to maintain its monopoly and resources. If workers choose to form their own independent organizations, the trade union must firmly adhere to the state's position and spare no effort to forestall, co-opt or prevent them (Chen 2003b).

The most fundamental purpose of trade unions, which is to safeguard the interests of workers, only comes as secondary to protecting the interests of the state. In the past, official documents often listed trade unions' function as labor representatives together with others, such as "to mobilize and organize employees to actively participate in construction and reform", "to represent and organize employees to participate in administrating national and societal affairs and enterprise democratic management", and "to educate employees to continuously improve their ideological, ethical, cultural, and scientific quality". Along with the development of the market economy in China, the trade union has been trying to clarify its role. Noticeably, recent labor policies and law have clarified this function. For instance, in the 2002 amended Trade Union Law and the 2008 amended Trade Union Constitution, the basic role of the trade union was defined as "To safeguard legal rights and benefits of employees". In reality, trade unions found difficulties in meeting all of the contradictory requirements for a long time, such as between focusing on the economic growth of the enterprises versus improving wages and working conditions, or persuading workers to give up strikes versus safeguarding labor rights.

In reality, the administrative orientation of the ACFTU has not really changed. As expressed by the vice president of the ACFTU in 2009, "wage negotiations should be dominated by local government"[119]. However, employees have increasingly demanded a genuine labor representative. The lack of internal democracy as well as disconnection with union members can not be justified for a trade union. In particular, triggered by the recent changes to the labor law, employees have become more aware of their legal rights. Mass workers need to effectively organize to safeguard their interests, and if the trade unions are unable to do so, worker must find other alternatives. For instance, some associations have organized taxi drivers and migrant workers in private- or foreign-invested enterprises. In particular, during the strike wave of 2010, workers abandoned the roles of enterprise unions. Most interestingly, besides wage demands, these strike workers requested their enterprise unions to be elected by and to be accountable to workers[120]. Accordingly, trade unions have been engaged in large-scale propaganda and formal work, while keeping the exclusive legal status and abundant resources. They are engaged in mediating labor disputes, offering legal aid, and helping workers in need. However, usually workers are taken care of, rather than actively participating these union activities. In addition, most activities are only remedies afterwards, rather than prevention or intervention in daily labor-capital interaction (Chen 2003).

Therefore, the state regards the official trade union as indispensable and incompetent at the same time. The necessity for an official union is due to the party's deep fear of uncontrolled collective labor, as the labor movement in Poland in the 1980s. Thus, the party strictly keeps control on the organization of

119 The China Central Government Web, Mr. Zhang, Mingqi, the ACFTU vice president, answer questions regarding industrial-wide wage collective negotiations, interviewed by Workers' Daily, Jul 21, 2009, http://www.gov.cn/jrzg/2009-07/21/content_1370251.htm

120 China Labor News Translations, The Nanhai Honda strike and the?union, Jul 18, 2010, http://www.clntranslations.org/article/56/honda

trade unions. At the same time, the state does not completely trust the ACFTU and thus finds it practically impossible to devolve it real power on labor issues. One example is the legal restrictions on collective contracts. For example, the 1994 Labor Law requires that collective contracts can take effect only after inspection by the labor administration. Unfortunately, the concerns of the state prove to be necessary since the ACFTU has not been able to conduct effective collective bargaining. Moreover, comprehensive law and rules that have been established focus on individual labor relations, which lead to workers' dependency on the law for protection, rather than on trade unions. To a certain degree, the individualized labor relations laws also make workers distrust or feel indifferent toward trade unions. Thus, the limited political and institutional space provided by the state partly causes the incompetence of trade unions in representing workers, while the state becomes distrustful of trade unions because they are unable to fulfill the political task of pacifying workers. Since 2000, some tensions caused by the state's distrust toward trade unions seem to have been alleviated, as evident in the discourse of the 2008 Labor Contract Law. For instance, the trade union, rather than any labor representative, should be the organization that represents workers in collective bargaining processes and arbitrates in disputes. Ultimately, the ACFTU acts as a state apparatus, and the state has no alternative that it trusts.

The extent to which the trade union could represent workers was largely up to the state. Some space had been given, on the precondition that the ACFTU would not mobilize workers against the state or the management (Chen 2003). Within such space, the ACFTU had made some efforts to prove its political significance. In particular, the system of collective bargaining and collective contract was the most prominent mechanism that the ACFTU has ever promoted. The initiation of this mechanism was the result of the ACFTU's persistent lobbying of the government and even enterprises. Experiments started in some enterprises even before collective contracts were firstly written into law in 1994. Moreover, it had also done much work in union organization. The ACFTU no doubt became the largest union in the world in terms of membership, which also began to include migrant workers[121]. Even some anti-union MNCs like Wal Mart and Intel, established trade unions within their Chinese subsidiaries. The main results of those efforts are the impressive numbers of collective contracts and a series of political plans. One of these political plans is called the "Rainbow Plan", which aims to establish enterprise unions and implement collective contract system in all types of enterprises by the end of 2012, with a

121 e.g. four million migrant workers joined trade unions in Jiangsu Province, 36% of all members in the province. http://provincedata.mofcom.gov.cn/label/disp.asp?pid=14426

primary target of 60% for 2010 and 80% for 2011.[122] Furthermore, as a complement to collective bargaining, trade unions also organize and join the tripartite coordination and joint meetings with governments usually at the county level and above.

In practice, however, the dependent and undemocratic nature of trade unions has limited their options, and their political identity is not sufficient to support grass-root unions in representing workers. While the central state has been threatened by labor unrest which highlights the necessity of collective bargaining. China's trade unions are hardly doing anything substantial, except for promoting policies on paper and creating impressive but meaningless numbers of collective contracts. At higher levels, the role of union federations appears to be political. With substantial resources, they are able to issue documents and organize activities according to the policies of the central state. Their influence stems not from organized labor but from their institutional status in the state structure.

At lower levels, the subordination of enterprise unions to employers jeopardizes collective bargaining in the factories, which is the dominant level of collective bargaining and collective contracts in China. Primarily, union cadres are in the administrative ranks (e.g. union chairperson as vice president of the companies) and on payroll of the enterprises. For instance, in many foreign enterprises, the precondition of building trade unions in enterprises depends on the agreement of the employers. Usually HRM departments prepare to set up a trade union, and workers automatically become members without even being informed about it. Enterprise unions are often helpless, in the sense that they are distant from the central authority and have no capability of mobilizing workers. Thus, enterprise unions, voluntarily or not, tend to be close to the management, whose decision-making authorities practically determine the future existence of the unions as well as the positions and wages of union cadres.

Another problem that makes collective bargaining difficult is the representation of trade unions. There is no clear division between "workers" and "employers" in legal and political arena, although the contradiction between the two groups is obvious in reality. The old ideology from the Planned Economy was that everyone could become the "laborer" of building up Socialism. This ideology still influences current laws. According to the 2001 Trade Union Law, any "laborer" can join trade union. As a result, enterprise unions, especially in SOEs, have an overall membership from front-line workers to top management.

---

122 Xinhua Net, data released by Mr. Zhang, Jianguo, the director of collective contract department at the ACFTU, The ACFTU interview on how to implement "rainbow" plan, June 04, 2010, http://news.xinhuanet.com/politics/2010-06/04/c_12181248.htm

However, foreign investors in some areas like Liaoning province, are forbidden to join unions by local regulations.

Fundamentally, there is hardly any support from below, as workers distrust or are indifferent to trade unions. Whereas the trade union is highly centralized, the dominant level of collective bargaining remans within the enterprises. There is not much that enterprise unions can do if individual firms resist collective bargaining. Even if employers agree to bargain and enterprise unions are eager to take action, it is unlikely that the unions would be able to collect adequate information with which to argue. One problem is that enterprises, especially non-listed ones, are experts in hiding profits. According to the field study of this research, wage determination has been the unilateral prerogative of management. Trade unions, if they exist at all, are highly cooperative with management. Workers, who are supposed to be the major actor, are in fact excluded from the bargaining process. The results are low base wages for front-line operators often barely above local minimum wages and a high proportion of performance-based incentives. In other cases, operators only get very low base wages and simply OT pay, which usually means they can earn subsistence wages only through lengthy OT hours. Collective bargaining or wage negotiation, where it does exist, simply echoes general legal clauses. At higher levels, no effective coordination on wages or other labor standards exist. In particular, industrial unions remain inactive and insignificant.

The case of collective bargaining illustrates the fact that Chinese trade unions fulfill political tasks rather than safeguard workers' rights and benefits. At the same time, it shows that there is a significant gulf between rule-making and institution-building. The recent changes in labor law and policies are at the level of rule-making. Without a set of institutions that can respond flexibly to the dynamic economy, the rules can hardly be enforced in practice. When conflicts between labor and capital took place, in the forms of individual complaints, group petitions, slowdowns, and strikes, the state responded with the enactment of the 1994 Labor Law, the establishment of labor dispute mediation committee, and the practice of collective bargaining. Several laws, including the 1994 Labor Law and 2002 amended Trade Union Law, have granted trade unions the right to represent workers within the officially recognized processes of making claims and legally prescribed grievance procedures (Chen 2003). No doubt, this has been one positive change that highlights the focus of policy-making toward laboring people’s livelihood. Nevertheless, without proper institutions, those rules could actually be used as constrains on labor.

Apparently, the power of the state alone cannot create the necessary institutions. However, the state distrusts any civil society institutions and other bottom-up initiatives (Clarke 2007). This distrust is the real obstacle. The laws and policies of the state, no matter in dispute resolution or in wage increases, further put workers in disadvantaged positions. Although workers may be protected in the short term, they remain to depend on external help from the state. In the long run, command or order from the top is not sustainable. The Chinese state has been doing just as Poulantzas (1968: 214) pointed out long ago, in which the juridico-political apparatus of the state purposefully masks the class relations from workers by turning them into the political "individuals-persons" and "subjects of law". In China, labor-capital conflict resolution has been highly regulated and channeled individually through law. The activities of trade union are thus confined by the sanctions of the state.

As a matter of fact, trade unions among different industries and regions are relatively distinct, although they all fall under the umbrella of the ACFTU. For instance, in the automobile industry where major auto makers take the form of foreign-sino joint ventures, union membership is very high. These trade unions organize various activities, such as collective bargaining, workers' congress, and open-factory affairs. As the Chinese side of the joint ventures are usually SOEs, trade unions in those enterprises also follow their SOE tradition. Thus, trade unions play the role of "mediator" or "coordinators", with strong links to the management and a clear target of promoting the economic performance of the enterprises. This coordination rests upon the assumption that workers' interests cannot be separated from the long term development of the companies (Walker 2008). According to an informal survey (Nichols and Zhao 2010), half of employees regard trade unions poor or very poor, although 70% believe it is necessary to have a union. With the exception of training, all workers prefer to rely on their own resources rather than to resort to the union. Given the fact that auto makers have regulated labor practices and stable wages, this SOE-style structure is indeed the most stable among all industries. In the contrary, the rest of the automobile workforce, who work in the lower end or none-core parts of the supply chains, are largely under-privileged. As for the entire electronics industry, no SOE-style trade union system exists. Non-union enterprises are common within highly diversified production regimes.

In the near future, it is impossible for China to have multiple trade unions within the political context. Thus, a more practical option is reforming the existing trade union. Since the political and social status of any trade union should be rooted from their roles on the shop-floors, the change of Chinese unions must start internally, particularly from enterprise unions where the political resistance is diminished. Collective bargaining is only possible if it has the basis of strong shop-floor labor collectivity. Fortunately, some measures, such as the direct election of grassroots union cadres and changes in union finance[123], have taken place. A good example is the industrial level construction union in Guangzhou, independent from enterprise funding and organizing construction workers across the city. Similarly, the Beijing municipal trade union is also experimenting with independent wage negotiations by liberating grassroots union chairs from their economic dependence on employers. In this case, grassroots union leaders are either directly elected by workers or sent from outside of the enterprises by the higher-level unions.[124] Moreover, following the Honda strikes, the Guangdong Federation of Trade Unions has re-adjusted the status of the trade unions as workers' representatives rather than mediators in order to dealing with workers' strikes.[125] It declared that the Honda Nanhai factory will be a pilot site for new democratic accountability mechanisms, including an annual democratic secret vote for union cadres. [126] Wage coordination between brand name corporations and their suppliers in the same industry, at least in the nearby region, is also envisioned by the union federation. Besides, in early 2010, the Guangdong provincial government has drafted democratic management provisions although the draft of the provisions has been shelved partly due to strong oppositions from employers.

4.4.2 Industrial actions and the "recomposition" of the working class?

The associational bargaining power of industrial workers through trade unions, is currently not sufficient. However, repressive regimes did not usually last in history. Ultimately, workers have to express their voice and rely on their collective power to improve their everyday work and life. Industrial actions have been aroused especially since the 1990s in the old industrial base of North China and in the sunbelt region along the coastal line. However, none of those industrial actions fostered a more organized labor movement or preserved lasting institutions like collective bargaining. It is clear that a strong and radical labor movement as in the U.S. in 1930s or in Germany from the 1960s to 1980s does not exist in China.

---

123 There are cases of direct election of union chairmen in some regions with relatively developed private sectors. See: Chen, et al, 2004; Wang, 2006

124 China Daily, Xinhuanet, Unions' role, English.news.cn 2010-09-01 09:32:56, BEIJING

125 According to an interview with Cheng, Weiguang, the chairman of the Guangzhou Federation of Trade Unions, Nov. 2010

126 China Labor News Translations, Plans for election of union chair at Nanhai Honda The Nanhai Honda strike and the union, Jul 18, 2010

It has been recognized that Chinese workers are largely excluded from the tripartite framework of the industrial relations system. In this sense, there is "tripartism with four parties" (Chang et al., 2008), where workers are separated from the state, employers and trade unions. By means of self-organized actions including strikes, the workforce of some plants has managed to become the "fourth" party in industrial relations (Chang et al. 2008). Increasingly, this fourth party is drawing attention through their actions.

This fourth party has significantly expanded since 1978 due to a combination of liberalized policies, foreign investment, and spectacular economic growth (Whyte 1999). Nevertheless, it is composed of highly segmented groups, such as urban workers and migrant workers, former SOE workers and those in private and foreign companies. Different classes emerge based on their common origins, education levels, and skills, but also on the production and ownership structure of the enterprises and industries in which they work. Accordingly, their conditions vary and thus industrial actions also have different causes and display distinctive features.

In the process of developing a market economy, the interests of the mass workers have been widely neglected or largely subordinated by the state to the prioritization of economic growth and industrial development. On average, workers have become substantially less privileged and more insecure than those in the Mao era. Many surveys discovered that workers were among the major "losers" of the reform (e.g. Lu 2002). The pretense that workers were the leading class of the country had largely disappeared from public discourse (Whyte 1999). As for the former SOE workers, they have experienced dramatic changes since the 1990s through restructuring of the SOEs and the associated erosion of their privileged status. For a long time, low wages in the former SOEs had been compensated with comprehensive welfare provided by the state. After the large-scale dismantling of the SOEs, the workers lost the welfare benefits once guaranteed by the state, and many, particularly those in their 40s or 50s, left their jobs without marketable skills. These newly unemployed had little chance of finding a job in the market economy. Besides, migrant workers who were young peasants or who now work in booming industries along the coastal regions usually receive only low wages without the protection offered by social security programs. In many cases, the arbitrariness and exploitation of workers resemble the "low-wage classic" production regime (see Appendix B), the worst type at the early stage of the industrial revolution in the West.

In both situations, the trade union has been of no practical help to workers. According to a survey in the automobile industry (Nichols and Zhao 2010), workers who had direct or indirect (e.g. through parents) experience with the pre-reform planned economy and who had the greatest need for union protection, felt dissatisfied with the existing trade unions. In other words, older urban workers with long-term contracts, the so called "regular workers", along with lower-skilled workers saw trade unions as failures in safeguarding their interests. Therefore in reality, trade unions had been largely abandoned in industrial actions, either in "protests of desperation" in the old industrial bases in the North due to the restructuring of former SOEs, or in "protest against discrimination" in the South, where most migrant workers worked in informal sectors and in privately-owned enterprises (Lee 2007).

The numbers of industrial actions have increased dramatically. Since workers have no capability to negotiate with capitalists individually and trade unions mainly follow political orders, workers possess no formal channels for voicing their concerns. Therefore, they had to resort to unauthorized collective actions. In 2004 alone, 3.76 million Chinese took part in 74,000 protests and riots, an increase from 58,000 cases in 2003 and only 10,000 a decade ago.[127] More than 30% of those were related to labor issues. In the province of Guangdong, almost half of the collective incidences occurred from January to September of 2008 resulted from unpaid wages. In Dongguan, a city in Guangdong province, 40.5% involved blocking public roads and streets by individuals, 22% were collective appeals to higher authorities, and 8.1% were strikes (Ru et al. 2009). Statistics detailing labor-capital disputes also show increasing numbers of social conflicts. Xinhua News, the official media of the Chinese government, reported that 280,000 labor dispute cases were accepted by the civil court in 2008, a 93.93% increase from 2007. Also, in the first half of 2009, 170,000 cases were accepted, another 30% growth compared to the same time in 2008. Collective labor disputes from 2001 to 2008 rose 11% annually. In the first half of 2010, 286 cases were accepted by labor arbitration at different levels, among which 44% were major collective labor disputes.[128] There are no disputes related to collective contracts. The major reason is the existing collective contracts do not contain substantial content in regards to labor standards. Thus, both labor and capital sides are indifferent towards these contracts.

The CCP defined labor-capital disputes as "conflicts among the people" in the national congresses of 2006. It also responded with labor and social policy

127 Chinese Academy of Social Sciences, 2005 Blue book of the Chinese Society, Social Science Academic Press

128 The "collective labor disputes" refer to disputes over rights by more than three to ten individual employees (depending on the cases) with common causes and claims, and "major collective disputes" involve more than 50 employees. quoted from: Legal Daily, collective labor disputes increased rapidly in the last 8 years consecutively, Sep 21, 2010, http://epaper.legaldaily.com.cn/fzrb/content/20100921/Articel06005GN.htm

changes. Nevertheless, in many cases, heavy-handed tactics were still used. The 2007 Emergency Response Law of the People's Republic of China still regarded collective incidents as "social security incidents". Chapter 4 of this law stipulated that above-county level governments could adopt emergency measures, and in case of "seriously-threatening social and security orders", the public security departments could legally send police and take mandatory measures. In practice, when collective disputes occurred, some local government officials intervened to mediate the disputes or to pay the wages that employers owned to workers. If workers strike and/or block roads, governments may also send police force. In some cases, violence against protesting worker was used and local governments often punished the organizers and some participants.[129]

The ACFTU, in light of highly publicized or large-scale violation by employers, often responds rapidly. However, instead of acting as a labor representative, it often acts as a mediator or a consultant in government-led investigations. Some new measures, such as wage negotiations and direct election of grassroots union cadres, have been initiated and supported by the ACFTU. However, the top-down manner in those measures limited the functions of these measures. The governments' distrust towards workers' activism continues. As a result, the trade union further alienated itself from mass workers.

It is noticeable that none of those industrial actions is related to collective bargaining as laid out in the legal framework led by the ACFTU. In some cases, strikes become a channel through which workers put forward their requests for collective bargaining. Workers seek to express their voice, in order to gain attention from government bodies, and to establish an effective means of negotiation. In the existing system of collective bargaining, the ACFTU simply tries to fill the quota as established by the government and is in fact incapable of conducting collective bargaining without the foundation of strong grassroots unions that are trusted and supported by workers. The increase in protests is example and consequence of this failure.

In those industrial actions, the requests of workers vary largely from one group to another, depending on their background, actual status of work and life, knowledge and former experience of collective actions. In many old industrial bases, the pride of being a worker in contrast to the rapid declines in economic and social statuses after Reform has led to major unrest among former SOE workers. Interestingly, workers have a traditional bifurcated perception of the legitimacy of the central and local states (Lee 2007: 122), and rarely blame the central government or even current market conditions for their problems.

129 China Labor Bulletin, Report on Chinese labor movement 2007-2008, http://www.clb.org.hk/schi/files/No%2015%20labormovementreport(S).doc

Typically, laid-off workers from SOEs complain about their former management and local officials. Although migrant workers experience systematic discrimination, through the official registration policy (*Hukou*), they only fight against unfair daily labor practices. There is no sign of a visible connection between the actions of former SOE workers and migrant workers.

By far, most industrial actions remain spontaneous, non-confrontational[130], uncoordinated, and often confined by legalism (Lee 2007). Even in the new wave of Honda workers' strikes, there has been no political claim that may challenge the current ruling. As Scott (1985: 301) comments, everyday resistance is a strategy that the social disadvantaged take according to the local conditions. Instead of overturning the repressive regime, the major purpose among workers' actions is to limit their loss to a minimum in order to survive. Nevertheless, such daily resistance has proved to be the inception of some civil labor movements cultivating the network of collective actions (Silver 2003). It may help workers to increase collective consciousness and lead them to realize that they should not sit and wait for others but take action to protect themselves.

At the very least, workers were more inclined to defend their rights as a "collective". In the 2010 strike wave, from Guangzhou to Tianjin and further to Dalian, the conflicts escalated throughout the country. Beside economic claims, workers asserted the re-election of their own grassroots union leaders. In the strike of Nanhai Honda, the enterprise union, composed of mid- to top managers, was not on the side of workers. Instead, the union merely reported workers' suggestions to the management. Disappointed at the enterprise union, workers realized the importance of a "real" trade union that represents their interests. This trade union could only be democratically elected by workers themselves.

Scholars have begun to pay attention to the possibility of "re-composing" the working class in China. One fundamental problem of the Chinese working class is that the class-based ideology has been wiped out since the 1960s. As the CCP emphasizes more and more the unification of interests for the entire country, the working class has become "de-politicized" (Wang 2008). Terms like working class have long disappeared from the political arena. At the same time, it is unlikely that Chinese workers are willing to challenge the current ruling. Many workers still value a Chinese tradition, according to which they expect themselves or their children to enter the official career thereby becoming elites of the society one day. In fact, workers are also unable to challenge the current ruling, given the divergent structure of contemporary proletariat and the indifference of grassroots towards politics.

---

130 Chinese Academy of Social Science Zhejiang, Survey shows: Zhejiang labor-capital conflicts are mostly non-confrontation ones, Observation and Ideas, June 30, 2010

In general, the ideology of class struggle has been successfully removed in China. Former SOE workers, in spite of their "organized dependency" on state and management (Walder 1984: 13), were once influenced by Maoist class theory, in which the socialist state claimed workers as the "master of the country". Accordingly, in their industrial actions, although associational power based on membership in a class or citizenry are conspicuously absent, those actions may evolve into protests involving multiple enterprises against the same local officials. Class interests and citizens' legal rights are facets of identification among those workers (Lee 2007: 35). Nevertheless, this group of workers has decreased, as most of them have reached retirement age or many joined the managerial ranks.

After more than 30 years of reform, the dominant make-up of the Chinese working class consist of younger urban workers and migrant workers without any real experience of the socialist indoctrination. They simply do not have the political leverage former SOE workers had during the Maoist era. Besides, there are distinctive characteristics among the younger generations of workers. Compared to migrant workers, urban workers may have witnessed or have heard about changes in the ideological, social and economic conditions of the working class from their parents. As indicated in some studies[131], itinerant rural workers have developed a distinctive perspective on work and entitlement that is different from urban workers. Migrant workers, due to their past exclusions from the urban economy as rural residents, tend to feel more sympathy for market economy, although they are still at a relatively disadvantageous status in the market economy (e.g. without urban *Hukou*). Moreover, the new generations are experiencing changing production, work organization, and management control. The reality is that a shrinking number of urban workers operate under a hegemonic production regime mainly created by the favorable policies of the government. At the same time, a majority of migrant workers earn a living through low-wage, unskilled work with long-hours. Urban and migrant workers have been largely divided from each other in terms of education, skill levels, and wage categories.

The diversified and segmented composition of the working class in China is a big problem. Since 1984, the new groups of migrant workers have flow into Chinese cities looking for jobs, primarily to compensate for their family expenses in the countryside. There were 252.78 million migrant workers in 2011,

---

131 e.g. regarding laying-off, migrants said:" I do not think it is unfair. (SOE workers) may blame their situation on changes in the enterprise system or government policy, but from an individual standpoint, unemployment is also a process of winnowing out the incompetent... They still live a better life than villagers. After all, they are from Beijing, have local connections, and are better educated that we migrants." See: Lei 2007

according to official estimation.[132] The same report shows that 36.0% of them work in manufacturing, 17.7% in construction and 12.2% in service sector. Migrant workers account for 80% of the manpower used in the construction industry and 68% in the manufacturing sector. However, only in 2003, the ACFTU started to organize migrant workers.

Boundaries have been drawn between migrant workers and urban residents through government policies for the sake of creating an "unlimited" supply of low-cost labor, and among workers themselves. After a long time of receiving low wages and good welfare in the planned economy, former SOE employees are now thrown out of the system. Younger urban workers, mostly children of former SOE employees, have experienced or at least have witnessed declining political and economic statuses. At present, most companies with state connections, such as central SOEs or large-scaled joint ventures, employ urban workers as a regular workforce. Those companies (e.g. brand name JVs in the auto industry) are shrinking in numbers, but still maintain their leading roles in the industries. They can afford a relatively better pay and welfare to retain core workers. At the same time, migrant workers reman in socially vulnerable positions as dispatched laborers in the informal sector. Urban workers oppose any competition from migrant workers. This divide among urban and migrant workers also mirrors the conflicts among workers in developed and in developing countries.

Consequently, the divided groups have not joint force in safeguarding their common interests, although the waves of labor protests have not stopped. Within the individual-based legal framework, the resistance of workers remains highly individualized primarily among migrant workers. When workers are treated unfairly, such as unpaid OT pay, they usually complain to their supervisors or HR managers. Such complaints do not always get response. In many cases, workers would either drop the case or get jobs in different companies. If they choose to resist, they may appeal to the court. In this process, the idea of collective actions would not occur to workers unless they run out of options. In this sense, the law has become a most contested terrain for class and citizenship formation (Lee 2007). The "cellular activism" of workers closely relates to workers' varied interests that depend on market competition and different local policies since the reform. These distinctions further drive a deep wedge among workers and channels them into dispersed units of activism (Lee 2007: 121).

Importantly, class consciousness is not something superimposed by intellectuals, but rather it grows out of the over determination of economic class

132 The National Bureau of Statistics, 2011 Survey Report on Migrant Workers in China, Apr 27, 2012, http://www.stats.gov.cn/tjfx/fxbg/t20120427_402801903.htm

struggles created by other contradictions and other forms of oppression in society. For instance, the Debsian socialism in the U.S. grew out of an immigrant proletariat that endured economic exploitation along with cultural discrimination in factory towns. The social and cultural base of the American socialism and communism at that time was destroyed in the 1940s and 1950s when the Fordist absorbed immigrant workers and finally "Americanized" them (Davis 1986: 309). However, such absorption has not happened in China in a way that could alleviate the grievances of the various groups of workers.

In this sense, the working classes in China, especially migrant workers, have been forced to re-compose themselves. The counterparts of Chinese migrant workers in the American context is perhaps African-Americans. It was the vigorous second generation of those immigrants that had pushed up labor movements and finally institutionalized collective bargaining (Silver 2003; Piore 1979). In today's China, the majority of migrant workers could be categorized as the second generation of the "floating population" if we consider that the large flow of migrant workers first took place in 1984. In contrast to the elder generation, younger workers regard themselves as "workers", rather than "peasants" or "rural" residents. Sometimes without any experience of working on the land or even owning any land, they have no plan to return to countryside which differs from many migrants of the first generation. More importantly, these younger workers do not seek for mere material interests in the cities, but also dignity, justice, and their need for recognition. According to an investigation-based report from the research office of the State Council in April 2006,[133] migrant workers experience three major transformations, from the identity of "both worker and peasant" to "non-peasant", from "flowing between rural and urban" to "integrating into urban life", and from "striving for living" to "pursuing equality" . In general, they have developed far higher expectations of urban life and work, and are more and more incline to stay in cities. According to official statistics, the population living in rural areas has dropped from more than 70% twenty years ago to only 53% in 2010 (Yang 2010). At the same time, their incomes have barely increased compared to the levels of their parents, but the living costs have skyrocketed. Facing such dilemma, the majority of migrant workers have to seek for new ways for survival.

Apparently, grievances and conflicts are common in today China. The divisions between older and younger generations, urban and rural workers, and regular and dispatched labor have not readily translated into workers' shared anger against the state or the market. It is fair to say that the major groups of

133 Banyuetan, The living status of Chinese migrant workers, May 18, 2006, http://politics.people.com.cn/GB/30178/4384717.html

workers, namely, urban workers including a shrinking number of former SOE employees and their children and migrant workers have not been prepared to unite together as a class, both materially and ideologically. Nevertheless, the increasing industrial actions, as early signs of class struggle and social mobilization, may pave the way for a different future.

4.4.3 The power and potential of Chinese workers

Again, collective bargaining is a more peaceful way to channel the grievances of workers and to avoid the frequent outbreak of labor unrest. Broadly speaking, collective bargaining is also the solution in changing China's developmental path and socioeconomic stability. Since the arrival of mass production in China has engendered certain social contradictions that remain embedded within the specific modes of production, the Fordist wage formula that historically solved many of these contradictions have not yet been established. The absence of such wage regulation under the existing highly diversified production regimes has caused strong grievances and conflicts in factories. As the labor histories of the U.S. and Germany demonstrate, such a wage formula through collective bargaining must be driven by the struggles of workers before the accommodation from the state and the capital can occur. Ultimately, the aggregate power of labor is decisive in collective bargaining. At the same time, labor power is influenced by modern production and management methods, and national policies under global trends.

Generally speaking, there are two major types of bargaining power for workers', structural bargaining power at workplace and the marketplace, and associational bargaining power (Wright 2000). While workplace power is determined by the stability of production, work organization and daily interactions between workers and management, marketplace power is up to both the nature of work and the market conditions of supply and demand. In terms of associational power, all levels, from factory, industrial, national, even to global, are concerned. In particular, the dynamics at the shop-floor level is decisive, whereas trade union organization and national labor politics also affect workers' associational power.

In China, marketplace bargaining power among workers is rather weak. Marketplace bargaining power is based on tight labor markets, characterized by highly-demanded skills, low unemployment rates, and the ability of workers to leave the labor market and live on non-wage incomes. Today the industries tend to homogenize and de-skill the workforce and thus allowing for the possibility to draw on untapped labor pools with little or no industrial experience.

In reality, the majority of Chinese workers are unskilled or semi-skilled. Migrant workers, who serve as the backbone of the manufacturing sector, are easily replaced since most of them only have junior high-school education and low skills. Besides, their jobs are de-skilled with little requirement on training. Accordingly, the general oversupply of labor markets does not provide workers much leverage. Using "dispatched labor" has become a widespread practice in nearly all types of enterprises as a means of reducing costs by paying minimum wages with no redundancy fees, and by minimizing the risks of production fluctuation. One exemplary case involved the 2008-2009 recession in South China when over 20 million migrant workers became jobless overnight.

Noticeably, since 2004, there has been a shortage of migrant labor beginning in the PRD and later along other coastal regions. Again, after the large-scaled closing of factories and labor redundancy in 2008, the early 2009 and 2010 witnessed a dramatic change in the labor market. Enterprises had difficulties in recruiting enough ordinary workers, particularly labor-intensive enterprises in manufacturing sectors (e.g. electronics).[134] Nevertheless, such a labor shortage tended to be only temporary. Some workers did not know the new recruiting advertisement after the crisis, but others were disappointed at the lasting low wages. By far, those periods of "shortage" occurred when migrant workers went back home for the Chinese new year. However, "shortage" disappeared after a couple of months when migrant workers returned to the cities. In other cases, enterprises attracted workers back by making small compromises (e.g. a rising a little bit of wages or benefits). Therefore, at least in the interim, the oversupply of unskilled labor will continue because of the huge surplus labor pool in rural China. This labor pool used to be confined by the state before the 1980s, and later released by policies targeting at creating new workforce for cities.

Only for a small proportion of skilled or high-skilled technicians, particularly those with urban background, higher education, and more advanced skills, may find themselves in relatively better positions in the labor market. According to a survey by the Ministry of Labor and Social Security in April 2004, technicians in 40 cities accounted for less than 4% of the total workforce, whereas the demand of enterprises was at least 14%. At the same time, the combined demand of enterprises on skilled workers and technicians was 31.9%. In regions such as Jiangsu and Guangdong provinces, the shortage of skilled

134 Guangdong textiles and electronics industries in short of workers, http://www.efu.com.cn/data/2008/2008-03-04/230080.shtml; Shenzhen still has "labor shortage" after the new year despite general wage increases, http://finance.qq.com/a/20080220/001355.htm

technicians was even worse.[135] In fact, the shortage of ordinary workers and skilled technicians, on the one hand, reminds us of the importance of education and training for full-scaled industrialization in the long run. On the other hand, it reflects the serious problems of China's low-wage development path.

As a whole, Chinese workers only have weak marketplace bargaining power. For the majority of migrant workers, although rural land rights and recent favorable policies enable them to retreat from labor markets, this avenue is no longer becoming a viable option. Today many young migrant workers identify themselves as workers rather than peasants, and they desire urban work and life.[136] At the same time, urban workers reman vulnerable, since employers can also easily replace them by other workers with higher skills. When employers need to reduce labor costs, increased automation has always been an option. Additionally, the de-skilling of jobs is nothing new since the early introduction of Taylorist division of labor. As work becomes standardized and simplified, outsourcing and using of "dispatched labor" have become widespread. Workers have diminished leverage upon fluctuations based on the supply and demand of the labor market, pitting workers against the employers at the bargaining table.

Workplace bargaining power becomes more important in this sense. Mass production has increased the vulnerability of capital to direct workers' action at the point of production, but the "post-Fordist" organization of production and work, particularly vertical disintegration, are often seen as undermining workers' workplace bargaining power. Empirical studies reveal that in spite of their discourse concerning 'empowerment' or 'cooperation' through methods such as total quality management, employee involvement, quality circles, and team work, employers still rule the workplace and push for intensified work in the name of profit. Behind the "win-win" discourse propagandized by the capital, lean production methods is actually "management by stress", marked by intensification of work, lengthy work hours, just-in-time delivery, outsourcing, subcontracting along a decentralized and deregulated production chain. Nevertheless, workers are increasingly enmeshed in tightly integrated production processes in the form of global production networks rather than in a single company. Therefore, work stoppage at key positions may cause far larger loss for employers. For instance, in enterprises applying just-in-time delivery system, a strike in a key part supplier or the transportation company may completely shut down the production network leading up to assembly plants.

135 According to surveys in Wuxi of Jiangsu province and Shenzhen, Dongguan, Foshan in Guangdong province, enterprises had difficulties in finding skilled workers. http://www.china.com.cn/chinese/zhuanti/jybg/1006318.htm

136 e.g. Foxconn Investigation Report, September 2010, investigation conducted by university scholars and students from both Mainland, Taiwan, and Hong Kong of China.

The effect is similar in the US labor movement during the 1930s when the assembly lines allowed a small number of strategically placed activists to disrupt the output of an entire plant. In the 2010 strikes in Honda and Toyota suppliers in South China, instead of one single plant, nearly a whole production chain was shut down. All four assembly plants of Honda in China which made 3,000 vehicles a day[137] were closed soon after the strike occurred in the factory of a key parts supplier. This shows workers' growing workplace power in a seamlessly-integrated lean production system.

At the same time, the workplace power of workers may be strengthened by the fact that there are usually a large concentration of workers either in the same factories or along industrial clusters of nearby regions. For instance, a few electronics contract manufacturers alone are quite large (e.g. one factory of Foxconn in South China employs more than 400,000 workers). In many enterprises, lack of employment security or high wages has created strong grievances among workers. At the global scale, MNCs pulls workers apart through competition. The same force also pushes them together in common production and employment, which feature a decline of job security and the loss of welfare benefits, as well as the urgent need for interest representation. This also applies to China. The harsh labor practices and growing labor-capital disputes allow workers across enterprises and sectors to begin to identify issues of common concerns. Although recent strikes have not united workers at such a level, on some occasions workers with different origins and in different types of enterprises (e.g. urban workers in auto assembly plants in response to strikers who are mainly migrant workers in part suppliers in nearby areas, according to field study) have begun to raise similar claims to employers. This may be far from class consciousness, but it is at least a sign of common concern regarding the increasingly similar economic conditions of all workers.

Last but not the least, associational bargaining power has become essential today. Since the contemporary global industries featured increasingly heterogeneous production regimes, through vertical disintegration and re-integration "from below" (Lüthje 2002), the structural power of workers largely declined. This is particular severe as the large union-free electronics industry is taking the lead in place of the automobile industry marked by strong traditional unionism. Given the generally diversified and dispersed conditions of the industrial world, the weight of associational power in the overall power strategies of the labor movements has enhanced. Usually, workers' associational

137 China Entrepreneur Magazine, Strikers refused the offer of wage increases and Honda China factories are still closed, June 01, 2010, http://www.iceo.com.cn/shangye/25/2010/0601/194627.shtml

power can be realized through trade unions, political parties, and cross-class alliances with nationalist movements (Silver 2003: 137). Thus, it involves many factors at different levels, such as global industrial trends, national politics and labor policies, and the features of the workforce.

At the global level, a big challenge for workers' associational power is the hypermobility of capital. As capital can flow to any profitable manufacturing locations in the world, it is harder and harder for labor organizations within a nation to defend their workers. This challenge, in turn, de-legitimizes their function in the eyes of workers. This is one of the reasons that labor movements in many industrialized economies have declined in the 1980s. Faced with this challenge, we much remember that retreating from labor collectivity in the name of "competitiveness" or "saving jobs" is only a dead end for workers and trade unions. The attempts of union leaders and local politicians to "save jobs" by conforming to corporate priorities often fail in the end (Moody 1997). This is illustrated in a local strike against GM in Flint in October 1994. This strike was defeated by GM with the assistance of the national union and the mayor of Flint. In the case of NUMMI, a well-known Toyota plant in the U.S. declared its successful lean production standards but ended up relocating its production (Shaiken 2010). In other words, workers' concession can only result in further exploitation, and the production sites which may temporarily keep investment and jobs, would never be able to last through mere cooperation and wage cuts (e.g. the NUMMI case). As Moody (1997) states: "An injury to one is an injury to all". There is no alternative to militancy in collective bargaining and mobilizing workers at shop-floor level. At the same time, a stronger power may be achieved through a broader connection with other social movements at both national and international levels. As for China, due to its role in today's global industrial world, effective collective bargaining may also have positive impacts on other low-cost locations when faced with the problems of capital accumulation for the sake of investment.

Within a specific country, the economic, social and political conditions have impacts on workers' associational power. One of the most distinctive Chinese characteristics is the repressive state-business alliance, in stark contrast to the individualized labor. The state depends on economic accumulation and tax revenue to legitimize its ruling, and it also guarantees a range of social, legal and infrastructural integration and customization services to facilitate the interests of the capital. At the local levels, there is a symbiotic relationship between local governments and capitalists. As a result, workers lose confidence in local states when confronted with the interests of capital. In some cases, workers even went to Beijing and attempted to resort to the central state. Nevertheless, since the central state has been challenged by the pressure from growing labor unrest and imbalance of the economy, its labor legislation and policies have become more strategic particularly since 2000.

In the first place, central policies tend to be relatively labor-friendly or at least have begun to provide a buffer in the process of dramatic privatization and marketization. For instance, during the process of dismantling the socialist work unit system, the pain of many former SOE workers was alleviated to a certain degree, by the fact that they could purchase houses with subsidized prices and peasants were entitled with the right for a piece of land (Lee 2007). Additionally, the re-employment center gave laid-off workers state support in basic living, before they became unemployed. In addition, the last decade has witnessed continuous changes in tax and other policies in rural areas and a gradual relaxation on the entry policies of migrant workers into cities. These polices have released the financial burden of migrant workers from their home, and reduced the procedures they have to go through in order to get jobs in cities. Moreover, following the labor shortage after the 2008/9 crisis, more than twenty provinces increased the minimum wages by about 20% in the early part of 2010. Since many industrial workers, especially front-line operators and newly-recruited workers, only receive minimum wages as their base wages, their incomes may increase because of the increases of minimum wages.

Moreover, the state has worked to reinforce the ideological and structural bases for its hegemony. Scott (1977) argues that workers are more subject to the ideological hegemony of the state than peasants because they are more easily saturated with the state's discursive and symbolic messages. This is proved in China. The Chinese state tries to persuade workers that their problems come not from the state but from the market and their own failure to adapt to it (Blecher 2002). Workers commonly agree that the market policies of the state have brought about economic prosperity in China. With the exception of older SOE workers who came of age during the Maoist era of the planned economy, the majority of Chinese workers believe the state's policies are good, and only the implementation by local governments or employers that is no good. At the same time, the hegemony of the market intensified at a dramatic speed. Citing a general admission of the failure of the past, the market and the Dengist state claim that there is no alternative to the "reforms". According to a survey in Tianjin (Blecher 2002), most workers, even a retired worker and former factory cadre who continues to hold pronounced Maoist sensibilities, have come to accept the core values of the market and of the state as legitimate. In addition, individualized solutions in the market economy, such as the opportunities of finding other jobs in the market and workers' hope of their own children becoming government officials or employers in the future, also make class solidarity less likely.

Further, labor laws and regulations have been promulgated in order to fragment workers' discontent as localized disputes and thus preempt labor agitation (Chen 2003b). Under the precondition of the CCP's monopoly, the legal construction is indeed "a rule by law, not a rule of law that can restrain the government itself" (Lee 2007: 20). In particular, the individual labor law is designed to serve for the CCP's purpose of repressing collective actions of workers. Consequently, labor disputes often appear in the form of "disputes on rights" and are solved individually through mediation, arbitration and court trials. Even collective actions are characterized by legalism (Lee 2007: 20). In other words, the state masks class relations from workers by turning them into the political "individuals-persons" and "subjects of law" who are depicted as "free" and "equal" with each other. The role of trade unions in this process is to accommodate workers into the state's development strategy, through limited channels sanctioned by the state.

Such rule-making without bottom-up institutions may become a constraint rather than actual empowerment to workers. Nevertheless, as workers gradually learn about their legal rights, they are developing some consciousness of labor rights and increasingly use it to defend themselves. The rising number of lawsuits in industrial injuries provides evidence of this. In addition, there have been waves of strikes, protests, and other forms of industrial actions in China in the last three decades.

However, those collective actions by no means reflect organized labor power. Rather than an effective indicator of collective labor strength, strikes often signify cumbersome grievance procedures and inadequate management structures (Tolliday and Zeitlin 1986: 106). If one considers all significant labor movements in history (Silver 2003), such as in 1930s in the U.S and 1960s in Germany, no major victories or strong community support have been seen in China. There is not yet a "turning point" in labor-capital relations that could bring broad political significance there. Most strikes and protests remain spontaneous, single establishment-based, and often directly against unpaid wages and pensions or job loss.

In those actions, the lack of the working class thinking is obvious. The reality is often more complex than Marxist theory of class consciousness, saying there is a spontaneous and almost automatic development, propelled by what is sometimes called a "class instinct" toward the "true" interests of the working class as a whole. Ambiguities of consciousness and interests originated from many factors, such as the ambiguity between individualistic vs. collective improvement of one's condition, and between economic vs. political concepts of one's interest (Offe and Wiesenthal 1980). In particular, Chines workers often face the ambiguity between individual competitiveness and class solidarity.

Without clarifying such ambiguities, existing strikes and protests in China are unlikely to achieve real power for collective labor in the long run.

One important factor that leads to workers' weak associational bargaining power is the wide use of newly-proletarianized unorganized labor. The use of these workers is possible since the capitalists have purposefully achieved high degree of standardization and the de-skilling of industrial work. The majority of migrant workers in China belong to this group, who only began to be organized by the ACFTU in 2013. They resemble to the new rural immigrants in the U.S. back in the early 1950s, many of whom were unaware of trade unions' early struggles and thought that their high wages and fringe benefits as "the philanthropic contributions of enlightened management and not hard-won gains wrested from stubborn bosses" (Lichtenstein 1995: 300). Workers often show gratitudes to employers who provide good wages and legal social welfare. Similar ideas have been commonly heard in Chinese factories. Besides, urban Chinese workers, who may have personal experience of early industrialization in SOEs or witnessed the life of their parents, also rarely have class consciousness or know the importance of unionization and collective bargaining. It is common that none of the two or three generations of Chinese workers has former experience or even knowledge of collective bargaining. In communist regimes, industrialization had proceeded from centralized state investment and organization. In the process, a new, politically-dependent working class had been created, and staff management had enjoyed uncontested control of production and personnel policies. As Walder (1984: 21) commented, shop organization in China did not evolve out of a history of collective conflict and bargaining, nor is it the outcome of management's efforts to wrest control over the production process from foremen and contractors. Although some collective contracts were signed in the early of the twentieth century, it has only been brought back into legislation during the mid-1990s.

Labor history also shows that the driving force of any industrial relations system, including collective bargaining, originates from some combination of actions by both the activist layer and the rank and file. The rank and file in China has not developed their strength, yet neither is there such an activist layer. As for the official trade unions, in the automobile and electronics industries for instance, neither the well-established SOE-type trade unions nor weak and capital-dependent ones could possibly launch or even support radical movements as the unions did in the 1930s/40s in the US or the 1960s/70s in Germany. Furthermore, any labor organization outside of the legal framework is highly restricted or even forbidden. With only one or two exceptions, the continuous waves of strikes have not resulted in genuine grassroots unions elected by the workers themselves; not even in the recent high-profiled strikes in the Honda supplier[138]. It has been gradually recognized that one problem of the Chinese labor movement is that there is little transnational or domestic social movement support. There are a few labor NGOs, which are mainly Hong Kong-based. However, their activities are rather confined to the most needed in a relatively small region (e.g. migrant workers in the PRD).

Under such an economic, social and political context, it is hard to envision a militant revolution by Chinese workers. Even though some industrial actions in recent years appeared to be explosive, most of them originate from direct material needs and have remained unorganized in the longer term. The challenge for the state is primarily economic, and the majority of workers, including the unemployed, remained politically passive (Belcher 2002). As shown in history, the struggle of the working class is the fundamental way in changing the labor regime. The general picture of workers' "sitting and waiting for the state" in China has not precipitated any dramatic reform of industrial relations. State hegemony and the subjection of the mass to the central state is not something new during the post-Mao era. Rather, it had already existed for more than two thousand years of feudalism. Considering the feudalist society of China was eventually turned over only by external forces (e.g. British Army in the Opium War), the current ruling class, with constantly comforting and adaptation strategies are likely to maintain control in the long term. At best, the future could be a more open and diverse society, capable of interacting with others on a broader front, but with its authoritarian features still in evidence (Lee 2007: 39).

In a nutshell, the associational bargaining power of Chinese workers is rather weak. The Chinese working class itself is largely fragmentated. Trade unions that act as labor representatives do not exist. Additionally, workers are commonly obedient to the state and the market, because of the strategic accommodation and individualized solution provided by the state. Unfortunately, this has largely limited the effectiveness of collective bargaining.

The reality in China contradicts the ideal conditions for collective bargaining, as is realized sinc the rise and fall of Fordism in the U.S. and Germany. At present, the diversified production regimes at the factory level are the first big obstacle for a unified voice of workers and unified labor standards. Establishing a higher level of coordination is a difficult task, not only for workers, but also for the majority of union cadres and HR managers. Within a typical modern enterprise (e.g. large auto JVs and brand name electronics

138 Workers' request for a democratically-elected trade union was rejected. Instead, the employers allowed workers to elect their own union sub-groups, which unfortunately was still manipulated by the employers. See: Public information source and, in particular, the field research by several graduate students from Sun Yan-Sen University, in Guangzhou, China, presented on a international conference in October 2010.

companies), HRM policies, especially promotion ladders of internal labor markets, provide incentives for workers' cooperation and loyalty. Detailed work rules and grievance procedures also facilitate the resolution of conflicts. Among the majority of enterprises at lower levels of the value chains, workers have much worse labor standards with limited or even no chance of expressing grievances. Consequently, the small numbers of core workers may be cautious about the competition from large numbers of "peripheral" workers, or in many cases they are indifferent to the conditions of the latter. The huge wage gap or hierarchy between them is also legitimated by the market logic and it might be accepted by the "core" as normal. Such segmentation between different groups of workers makes it difficult to establish a collective basis. In addition, most HR managers have no idea of or no intention of learning what collective bargaining really is. They regard their unilateral power of determining wages and labor standards as givens. Even worse, trade unions, especially among enterprises, are either entirely confined to the management or too weak to make any change. In this context, above-enterprise coordination of wages, at industrial or regional levels, may firstly enhance associational awareness of workers, as interests will become more visibly connected.

Besides above-enterprise coordination, a Chinese model of collective bargaining should include members based on workers' mobilization and democratic shop-floor unions. Only this could realize the direct purpose of collective bargaining; that is, to take wages out of competition. It is important that wages should be viewed as more than a socially determined level of subsistence as in classical political economy, or a price established in external labor markets, as in contemporary neoclassical labor economics (Figart, 2001). Collective bargaining is not only an effective way of pursuing just wages and other labor standards. It also allows for greater democratic participation among workers in the Chinese development path of industrial upgrading from the low-wage regime toward intensive accumulation based on high-tech and higher skills.

This model offers solutions to the ultimate problems to the existing collective bargaining practices and adapts to the characteristics of major actors in industrial relations. Primarily, strong shop-floor power would change the weak position of labor in existing collective bargaining. Although Chinese workers' marketplace power is limited due to the vast oversupply of rural labor and the majority of low-skill and easily substitutable jobs, their workplace power has been enhanced by assembly lines and tightly-integrated production network. Workers have quickly learned to use such power, as indicated in the most recent strike wave of 2010. Furthermore, workers should associate, most effectively among trade unions, to partially compensate for their power disadvantage in relations to the capitalists. The Chinese trade union shares similar problems with other labor movements, like the difficulty of collective identity due to diverse interests of workers, it also has its peculiar problem of dependence upon the state politically and on the capital financially. It has failed to represent workers for a long time. Nearly all recent strikes have excluded the official trade unions. There are two urgent tasks that the trade union has no way to avoid - clarifying its essential role as a labor representative and mobilizing the rank and file. The first step should be establishing democratic trade unions at shop-floor levels. Fortunately, some local unions have already started such experiments. At the same time, it is important to remember the basic flaw of Fordism is that the concession or trade-off in collective bargaining is devastating in the long run. For instance, concessionary bargaining had caused the decline of the U.S. labor movement after the 1940s and also the crisis of German industry-wide bargaining since the 1990s. In China, the wage negotiation of Honda strike workers may be regarded as the first step of effective collective bargaining, but the resistance by workers remained to be strengthened (See Chapter 3). Necessary resistance by workers is essential in collective bargaining. This lesson is particularly important in China today, since Honda workers may lead the practice of collective bargaining into a new stage.

Furthermore, proper institutions can guarantee workers' rights in collective bargaining in the long run through the combined efforts of workers, trade unions, the state and the capital. The strong state in China should provide basic rules. A comprehensive national social security program with wide coverage, especially health insurance, is important in reducing labor-capital conflicts and letting trade unions concentrate on key labor standards like wages, as shown in the German model. China has a social security program, but it only provides low-levels of benefit. It is also exclusionary due to its limited coverage and discriminative against migrant workers. In regards to the mechanisms of collective bargaining, the greatly diversified production regimes in China urgently need above-enterprise-level wage coordination, which could in the long run, serve as a general contract for an entire industry or region. Leading enterprises in the industry, like the major assemblers in the automobile industry, may set a precedent for labor standards along the production network. In industries that are dominated by small and union-free enterprises, like the electronics industry, industrial or regional trade unions should take the lead in above-enterprise bargaining for all workers. In both situations, the local states, specifically the labor bureaus, have a key role in guiding and controlling labor standards.

Nevertheless, in practice, some variables that may impact this model remain uncertain. First is the future role of the state. In the recent strike wave in 2010, local governments handled strikes with noticeably different methods. The attitudes of politicians and the measures of the higher-level trade unions are much more pro-labor in the relatively liberal South (e.g. Guangzhou[139]) than in the more politically conservative North (e.g. Tianjin). Optimists may find it promising that the 2010 strikes were assessed by Guangdong provincial government as reasonable. Such positive attitude of the government toward strikes was perhaps the first time in China. New policies with regard to employees' engagement in wage negotiation and wage coordination within industries are also being drafted. However, it is most likely that any significant change would still take place under the control of the party-state, given the political monopoly and inherent distrust by the state toward collective actions. When this does happen, it is necessary to keep in mind that without bottom-up institutions, these rules may constrain rather than empower workers.

139 South China Morning Post, Strikers feel force of Tianjin's heavier hand, Jun 25, 2010

Concluding remarks

In sum, I argue that Fordism is not likely to return to China. Although the industrialization process in China features mass production and assembly lines, the social relations of Fordism, in the form of a collective wage contractual relationship that guarantees mass consumption, has clearly not been established in China today. Nevertheless, collective bargaining has been increasingly regarded as the reformist and democratic answer to the existing problems of China. It is urgently needed for the national economy. More importantly, collective bargaining is increasingly demanded by workers. Therefore, collective bargaining has drawn much attention from the police-making of the state. The future of collective bargaining is highly contingent on China's specific transformations as a result of local, national, and global forces. The potential for establishing an effective model of collective bargaining that adapts to the socioeconomic conditions of China do exist, not solely through the rule of the state, but through institution-building with the combined efforts from workers and from industrial and national policy-making bodies.

The analytic model of this study is based on the Regulation Approach. The accumulation process impacts regulations. At the same time, regulations in an industrial society "normalize" existing regime of accumulation and "guide" its future. In this way, collective bargaining serves as a form of wage regulation that makes sure the allocation of social production between accumulation and consumption is properly adjusted. The model of collective bargaining is impacted and restrained by the current regimes of accumulation. Moreover, the tensions or defects within such regimes may push forward more effective collective bargaining. In this study, I outline the types of production regime that are illustrated by the organization of work and production, and the determination of wages and other labor standards within factories. Additionally, regulations refer to labor-related policies, as they are impacted by the national development path, political framework, and also current global industrial and political trends. In consequence, three levels of the following most relevant factors are explored: production and accumulation regime in factories, national policies on economy and politics, and global industrial and political tendencies. At all the three levels, major actors of industrial relations are involved: workers and trade unions, employers, and the state. The institutionalization of collective bargaining is a combined result of all these factors.

Primarily, the processes of formation and institutionalization of collective bargaining, in the U.S. and Germany, are excellent references for China. Similar factors may influence industrial relations in countries that differ greatly in other respects. I assess the advantages and disadvantages of the two models of collective bargaining and their systems of respective industrial relations on the basis of whether they facilitate or block the development of intensive accumulation regimes. Moreover, I also summarize the essential forces and factors contributing to the institutionalization of collective bargaining.

Collective bargaining should at least fulfill the fundamental goal of channeling the labor-capital communication and of realizing a fairer allocation between profit and wages. It should also meet major policy targets, such as quelling labor militancy and reaching compromise between labor and capital within the framework of capitalism. In this sense, Germany has a better model than the U.S.. Germany has created a virtuous development cycle between high wages, high skills, and high productivity, which not only had maintained industrial peace but also kept up the quality manufacturing and economic growth at least up to the early 1990s. Wages of the majority of workers had regularly increased and accordingly the social cleavage had been much smaller than in the U.S.

The U.S. and German models of collective bargaining mainly vary in the degrees of centralization, coordination and coverage. In contrast to the uncoordinated bargaining and company-based agreements only covering a limited group of union members in the U.S., the "one general contract" in Germany applies to the entire sector on a regional basis. The German model has wide coverage and generally keeps limited variations on wages across the economy. In addition, industrial bargaining in Germany highly focuses on wages, and only recently on working hours, since other labor standards are either taken care by the state or are decentralized to works councils and individual employers according to work agreements. However, the U.S. trade unions have to bargain for multifarious topics beside wages, particularly health care. These topics not only distracted trade unions from core labor standards like wages, but also led to concessions. For instance, trade unions had to give up wage and benefit gains to keep their jobs in the late 1970s (e.g. the Chrysler bailout of 1979). Since the 1990s, typical concessions were workers gave up more wages in exchange for keeping health benefits. Nevertheless, although the German model seems to have more advantages, the U.S. experience also has its own merits. A major problem of the German system was the overly cooperative works councils with management at shop-floor levels, which partly caused the crisis of the German model after the 1990s. In contrast, the strong shop stewards and workplace control in the U.S. were the basis for the success of the labor movement in the 1930s and 1940s.

Moreover, there are common forces and factors contributing to the institutionalization of collective bargaining in the two countries. In general, the success of collective bargaining in Fordism is the result of long-term struggle among workers in the first place. The institutionalization of collective bargaining is later facilitated by the crisis-solving policies of the state and compromise of employers under certain economic and social circumstances. The conditions that had cultivated the mechanism of collective bargaining firstly include the Fordist mass production with its inherent labor-capital conflicts, strong structural bargaining power of workers, especially workplace power. Ultimately it is the strong labor movement that initiated struggles at shop-floor level and pushed forward national policies. Industrial unionism and class consciousness particularly are important. Besides, the affirmative policies from governments are necessary. Under pressures from rising labor unrest, lack of mass consumption, and political and ideological rivalry, the states introduced legislation on collective bargaining as a less militant way of reform than revolution. At the global level, the establishment of Soviet Union and China in the first half of the last century put pressure on industrialized countries in the West. The nation-states were forced toward pro-labor direction in order to pacify workers. In this context, national policies began to facilitate mass consumption norm and developmentalist social contracts.

As a whole, the historical experiences of the U.S. and Germany since the end of the WWII show that collective bargaining is likely to develop under favorable conditions, particularly homogeneous production regimes, strong collective labor, and affirmative polices of the state. As for the mechanism itself, collective bargaining is most effective when it features wide coverage and coordination above individual enterprises. For instance, the German model of industrial bargaining covers the entire sector of a region and wages in all enterprises are coordinated at the sectoral level. Noticeably, power building among workers had led to the very successes of industrial unionism in achieving social contracts in both the U.S. and Germany. Later, the compromise on workplace control in exchange for employment security or so has become the largest flaw in the post-war Fordism, which precipitated the decline of labor movements. In light of today's popularity of the lean production and management methods under neoliberalism, two factors become particularly significant in guaranteeing the effectiveness of collective bargaining - workplace control and institutional guarantee.

Certainly, there are significant differences between today's China and the two other countries being discussed at respective historical stages. In particular, there is no distinctive turning point in China as the WWII was in the history of the U.S. and Germany. At large, the continuity of regulation modes in China, especially in wage regulation, is rather distinctive. Besides, instead of a transformation from extensive to intensive accumulation regimes, both types of production and accumulation actually co-exist in China today. In this context, the general trends of history may help find the future direction of industrial relations and collective bargaining, but specific economic, social, and political conditions also matter.

As the overall background, the global political and economic environments are unsustainable and potentially hazardous for the Chinese economy and industrial relations. Primarily, some changes have taken place in the past decades, from the relatively labor-friendly environment in the post-war era toward a less favorable one for workers all over the world. Unfortunately, since the 1970s in the U.S. and more recently in Germany, social contracts and Fordist wage regulation collapsed or came into crisis. The labor movements in most nations were weakened by global industrial restructuring, downsizing, and lean production. Additionally, today the capital becomes hyper-mobile. The emergence of new sectors and smaller enterprises and the widespread practices of outsourcing and subcontracting have further weakened labor collectivity. As a result, competition over jobs and wages among workers has risen in different countries and workers are pitted against each other. Furthermore, the absence of ideological rivalries following the collapse of former socialist countries makes capitalism the dominant ideology. Thus, labor movements worldwide, with only a few exceptions, have suffered from declining membership and decentralization of collective bargaining. As to China, while the economy has largely benefited from the global shift of investment and production from the West since the late 1970s, its development path is overly dependent on low-cost exports to external markets. Domestically, the necessary social relations of Fordism are absent. Rather, labor policies and practices have been strongly impacted by the global restructuring of industries, neoliberalism and HRM. Without changes, e.g. increasing wages, the social consequences have become unbearable for workers.

Following these global trends, the industries in China, demonstrate large-scaled "vertical disintegration" as the examples of the automobile and electronics industries clearly show. The exceptions are still relatively integrated major auto makers and for the electronics industry the contract manufacturers which "re-integrate" manufacturing at the bottom. This leads to distinctive structures of industrial relations with a top auto assembler-dominating the automobile value chain and a greater diversity of enterprises in the electronics industry. At the same time, lean production methods have become widespread, thereby intensifying the standardization of work, increasing work load and/or speed and creating a contrasting division between a shrinking "core" and a majority of peripheral workers. In this sense, the production regimes in contemporary China have become more diverse than ever with the majority of workers working in de-skilled and standardized jobs. Moreover, the dominance of HRM in wage relations has led to highly individualized wage determination, which is often based on performance appraisal. It is fair to say that the labor-capital conflicts in the early Ford factories have only intensified in China today. As such repressive labor regimes appear to be highly unstable, a well-governed and -coordinated system of collective bargaining could be the best solution of guaranteeing security of workers and improve continuity, quality and performance of production for employers. Given the current industrial conditions, it may be realistic to first experimented in the automobile industry led by the auto assemblers. Since auto assemblers play a dominant role in the industry and their parts and components suppliers are often built surrounding them in the nearby regions, they are able to coordinate labor standards throughout the value chain.

At the national level, social, political and ideological conditions do not favor collective labor. Rather, liberalism has become the mainstream since the beginning of the reform in 1978. As the economy boomed in the last decades, a bigger economic space has emerged for a more balanced development, where the government and capital are able to provide better pay, at least higher than in the existing regimes. However, economic and industrial policies in the last decades have not given priority to labor. Besides, the decentralized relationship between central and local states and competition among local states lead to divergent labor standards from one place to another. Labor standards are often lowered by a tacit alliance between the capital and local governments, and many even act against the national law.

The recent promulgation of pro-labor legislation and policies by the state, since the early 2000s, are aimed primarily for the purpose of creating more stable economic growth model and more peaceful industrial environments, under the banner of state-led "harmonious society". In fact, the "labor shortage" and increasing strike waves have driven the state to pursue these policies. Nevertheless, such efforts have not successfully institutionalized conflict resolution through legislation, since the central state still give priorities to economic policies and the local states keep the cozy relationships with capital. In fact, whereas those new rules have channeled or alleviated labor-capital conflicts to a certain degree, the orientation of individualization and legalism actually becomes a barrier to developing collective consciousness among workers.

All the above-mentioned perspectives, such as the flexibilization and vertical dis-integration of production and ineffective implementation of national labor polices, have eventually pointed at the same question - the indispensable role of strong collective labor. Unfortunately, the interconnected relations between the state and trade unions lead to the absence of genuine labor representative in China. Chinese trade unions, as the only legal form of collective labor, have obvious limitations. Priorities are given to following the direction of the ruling party and to maintaining its own monopoly as labor organization. This has led to problematic implementation of state labor policies. Even worse, it is difficult for the union itself to survive in the market economy since it fails to pacify workers as the government has expected. In fact, workers increasingly seek for other alternatives. In many cases, they abandoned trade unions in their protests and strikes. In practice, trade unions at upper levels depend on the party-state for both resources and power, and those at the establishment level are financially and organizationally subject to employers and consequently unwilling or unable to mobilize workers. In fact, some small-sized labor NGOs in mainland and in Hong Kong target workers who are most in need, which has proved to be fairly effective. However, any labor organization outside of the legal trade union framework is not allowed. The only option is to reform the existing trade unions. Because the political and social status of any trade union should be rooted from their role at shop-floors, the change must start from enterprise unions, where the political resistance is much weaker. Some pilot projects have started in a few regions like Guangdong, with a focus of making sure the economic independence and democracy of grass-roots trade unions.

Workers who serve as fourth party outside of the tripartite mechanism now possess increasing workplace bargaining power, but they have weak marketplace and associational bargaining power. More importantly, since workers are increasingly enmeshed in tightly integrated production processes, work stoppage at key positions may cause far larger loss, in some cases even close down the entire network. Their workplace power may also be strengthened by the fact that there has been a large concentration of mass workers with common concern and grievances, either in the same factories or along industrial clusters in the nearby regions.

The associational bargaining power of Chinese workers is rather weak. Primarily, the heterogeneous production regimes and hypermobility of capital largely divide the workforce and increase the competition among workers. This division makes solidarity strategically more important. The Chinese workforce is also highly segmented, between rural and urban workers, among workers in different ownership of enterprise, and between regular and dispatched labor. Their consciousness of collective rights and solidarity is still conspicuously absent, particularly class consciousness that extends beyond single enterprises. Thus, it is difficult to establish a collective basis for a strong labor movement. Moreover, the common obedience of Chinese workers to the state and the market, which has resulted from political indoctrination since the economic reform as well as the individualized solutions provided by the market and the legal system, have all limited their associational bargaining power. The struggle of the working class is the fundamental means of changing the labor regime. At present, workers' general subordination to the central state has not prepared any dramatic reform of industrial relations. Even though some industrial actions in recent years appeared to be explosive, most of them originate from economic needs and have remained unorganized in the longer term. Nevertheless, the increasing industrial actions, as an early sign of class struggle and social mobilization, may pave the way for more radical labor movements.

Apparently, the current situations of China at all levels have, on the one hand, largely limited the space for labor. This explains the reason why there is no real collective bargaining in China. However, new sources of power are also endowed in the new organization of production, and the Chinese ruling class, under the pressure from below, has gradually realized the necessity of finding a balance between economic growth and social stability.

At present, collective bargaining does not exist in China, although it has been legislated and promoted by the state and the official trade unions, particularly in recent years. The law and policies are ambiguous; that is they intentionally minimize any confrontation and are silent on the right to strike. Within enterprises - the dominant level of collective bargaining - the determination of labor standards remains predominantly a unilateral prerogative of management, and enterprise unions are unwilling or unable to make any resistance. Even worse, workers are excluded from collective bargaining. In practice, the majority of collective contracts are signed either as a way for enterprise unions to fulfill the official quota of upper-level trade unions, or as a perfunctory effort among employers to fulfill the expectations of the local labor administration. At the same time, coordination at the above-enterprise level does not exist. In fact, such coordination may help avoid direct confrontation within enterprises by reducing the control of management over enterprise unions, and thereby achieve a more balanced and professional bargaining.

In general, the reality in China is rather contrary to the ideal conditions for collective bargaining, as is evidenced by the rise and fall of Fordism in the U.S. and Germany. Many necessary conditions for the formation of collective bargaining are widely absent, especially strong collectivization of the labor force. In today's China, there is lack of the pressure for a strong labor movement from below. The working class is economically-segmented and largely de-politicized. Although the use of state power may help to achieve direct and immediate effects, in the long run, commands or orders from the top are neither applicable nor sustainable. The diversification of production regimes and the widespread HRM practices at the factory level are a big obstacle for a unified voice of workers and for unified labor standards. Establishing a higher level of coordination is a difficult task, not only for workers, but also for the majority of union cadres and HR managers. At the same time, above-enterprise coordination of wages, at industrial or regional levels, may firstly enhance the associational awareness of workers, as their interests become more visibly connected.

Given all the differences, we expect that the processes of establishing effective collective bargaining and the driving forces behind it are very different from those in the past. In fact, collective bargaining is the practical choice for all major actors of industrial relations in China. The current ruling class are likely to maintain control in the long term. Nevertheless, the necessities of industrial upgrading and the growing rates of domestic consumption due to overproduction may become a catalyst for the capital and for the state to change. If we compare the crisis of 2008-2009 to those in the 1930s and the 1970s, it is clear that we need to renew existing regulations. Furthermore, under the existing economic, social and political context in China, it is hard to envision a militant revolution by Chinese workers. Workers try to express their voice or to draw attention from the government through strikes, labor disputes, and passive ways like quitting, when there is no effective channel of communication with management.

What then constitutes a Chinese model of collective bargaining? This question has drawn attention from scholars. The cases of a few Japanese JVs in the empirical study are regarded by Xu (2003) as a possible model, which features "paternalism, hierarchy and the rule of people". Although this may fit into the popular argument of Chinese particularity as well as the common cultural background in East Asia, the cases contain too much specific Japanese management styles. Besides, they only follow existing legal clauses (see Chapter 3). This is not effective collective bargaining. The approach of Peng (2009), recognizing both the effectiveness and limitation of these cases, attempting to integrate such negotiation with other communication channels such as dispute prevention and information sharing, and transitioning to collective bargaining seem to be more pragmatic. This indeed could be a possible way of developing the ideal model for collective bargaining among enterprises.

This study finds that an ideal model of collective bargaining in China should not only integrate the essence of collective bargaining in the practices of industrialized countries, but it should also fit into the specific conditions of the country. Learning from workers' experiences in in the U.S. and Germany, mobilization and participation in democratic unions at the shop-floor level, and centrally-coordinated bargaining are indispensable. The solidarity of the working class should always be valued, since the narrow focus on American trade unions and the abandonment of the unemployed and of the temporary workers by German unions have resulted to cleavages in the workforces and societies. At the same time, the ideal model should adapt to Chinese conditions.

For instance, the highly diversified production regimes in China indeed urgently need above-enterprise-level wage coordination, and in the long run, perhaps a general contract for an entire industry or region. There are also large differences between the automobile and electronics industries. Thus, leading enterprises, like the major assemblers in the automobile industry, may set a bottom line for the labor standards along the production network. In contrary, in industries that are dominated by small and union-free enterprises, like the electronics industry, industrial or regional trade unions should take the lead in above-enterprise bargaining for all workers.

The ideal model, to begin with, should have a stronger voice of workers at the shop-floor level. The enterprise unions should be led by a democratic labor representative, which can be done through actions like the current experiments of direct election of union cadres. A universal coverage of collective contracts is necessary to realize the direct purpose of collective bargaining - taking wages out of competition. Collective bargaining is not only an effective way of pursuing just wages and other labor standards, but also engenders a greater democratic participation of workers in the development path of China from the low-wage regime toward intensive accumulation based on high-tech and higher skills. At above-enterprise levels, the leading companies (e.g. auto assembly plants), or above-enterprise unions (e.g. in the electronics industry), coordinate wages throughout respective supplying network in the region. In both situations, the local states, specifically the local labor bureaus, have a key role in guiding and controlling wages and other labor standards. At the top, the central state accommodates the basic claims of workers by guiding the group of employers and regulating local states more strictly in the labor field. In fact, the theoretical debate on labor law and education of labor polices and practices in China is helping non-experienced Chinese laborers and employers to realize the logic of market economy and its embedded labor-capital conflicts. Some regions have been engaged in this (e.g. through public lectures offered in trade union cadre schools and by labor scholars), but still need to develop it much deeper in understanding and broader in terms of people involved.

At the same time, the ideal model is also realistic since it offers solutions to the ultimate problems of current collective bargaining system in China and fits into the power status of the major actors in industrial relations. In the beginning, the reality that enterprise unions depend financially and organizationally on employers and workers are excluded outside of collective bargaining practices has to be fundamentally changed. In fact, workers have increasing bargaining power and they more and more incline to demonstrate it in case of conflicts with employers. Additionally, a strong state that coordinate labor relations may facilitate a more peaceful processes of collective bargaining in the foreseeable future. It is most likely that any change would take place under the control of the Party-state, given the political monopoly and inherent distrust of the state toward collective actions. Since the reign of the Party relies on its capacity of representing the interests of the majority for political legitimacy, further policy adjustment toward a labor-friendly society may be expected. The active institution-building led by cities in South China, particularly following the 2010 strike wave, may be the first step. The role of the state is necessary for better regulation and effective inspection of collective bargaining, particularly because current labor relations in China are completely unbalanced and labor rights are widely neglected and violated in enterprises.

Most importantly, there is no alternative to the strong power of collective labor at shop-floors as the ultimate drive in collective bargaining and industrial relations. Fortunately, along with the development of a market economy and recent changes of labor law, employees' consciousness of their rights has been considerably enhanced, as indicated by the growing number of court cases and protests. In fact, workers' resistances in the form of industrial actions have never stopped, although such "everyday resistances" remain spontaneous and localized since they only target at direct material needs. At the very least, these experiences might train their organizational capability, cultivate collective action networking, and most importantly, develop collective consciousness of workers in defending their own rights and benefits. Additionally, the bargaining power of Chinese workers, in spite of the inactivity of trade unions, has continued to develop. Although most of the workers particularly those with low education and low skills may be easily substituted in the surplus labor market, their workplace bargaining power is nonetheless enhanced by the concentration of production and by the integration of production networks through new methods like just-in-time delivery.

Following the strike wave in the automobile industry of early 2010, collective bargaining in China has entered a new stage. The successes and mistakes of the U.S. and German experiences become especially relevant. In particular, workers' resistance, rather than mere cooperation, is always necessary in collective bargaining. Concessions or trade-offs by workers is the basic flaw of Fordism, which only proved to be devastating in the long run. In the U.S. and later in Germany, trade-offs were made through concessional bargaining, which eventually led to broken social contracts and the decline of the labor movements. The 2010 Honda Nanhai strike and the following rounds of collective bargaining show the most recent development in China. The shop-floor power of workers is strong. However, the results of bargaining seem rather unsatisfactory for many workers, since the wage increase of 800 RMB is not for base wage as they demanded and does not apply to all workers. An important lesson that Chinese workers like those in Honda Nanhai should keep in mind is that resistance against employers' prerogative is always necessary and too much concession would only lead to further weakening the positions of workers.

Further, workers should associate in the form of trade unions, to partly compensate for the power advantage of capitalists. Chinese trade union has its peculiar problem - dependency on the state politically and on the capital financially, beside similar problems to other labor movements, like the difficulty of collective identity due to diverse interests of workers. It has failed to represent workers for a long time. Therefore, nearly all recent strikes have excluded the official trade unions. There are two urgent tasks that the trade union has no way to avoid - clarifying its essential role as labor representative and mobilizing the rank and file. The first step should be to establish democratic trade unions at shop-floor levels, and indeed, some local unions have already started such experiments.

Moreover, institution-building is essential to guarantee a long-standing system of collective bargaining. In the last decades, the labor law and policies of the state pertain to rule-making. Without the active participation of major actors, a law becomes meaningless on paper and fail to build the relevant institutions necessary to carry out the rules. In fact, without such institutions, rules might become counter-productive rather than serve as a means of worker empowerment. The state along cannot build these institutions. Rather, the solution rests upon the combined efforts among workers through democratic trade unions, the state, and industrialists. Importantly, only the establishment of proper institutions can guarantee workers' rights in collective bargaining in the long run. The Chinese state should provide basic rules for labor issues. For instance, a comprehensive national social security program with wide coverage, especially health insurance, is important in reducing labor-capital conflicts and is critical for trade unions to concentrate on key aspects like wages, as shown in the German model. The social security program should be improved since it only allows for minimal guarantees, low coverage, and discrimination against migrant workers.

Nevertheless, in practice, some variables that may impact this model remain uncertain. First is the future role of the state towards collective actions and industrial unions. In the recent strike wave in 2010, local governments handled strikes with noticeably different methods. The attitudes of politicians and the measures of the higher-level trade unions are much more pro-labor in the relatively liberal South (e.g. Guangzhou[140]) than in the more politically conservative North (e.g. Tianjin). Optimists may find it promising that the 2010

---

140 South China Morning Post, Strikers feel force of Tianjin's heavier hand, Jun 25, 2010

strikes were assessed by Guangdong provincial government as reasonable, perhaps for the first time in China. New policies with regard to employees' engagement in wage negotiation and wage coordination within industries are also being drafted. However, it is most likely that any significant change would take place under the control of the party-state, given the political monopoly and inherent distrust of the state on collective actions. In addition, it is uncertain whether workers would be able to resist or confront with employers within factories through existing trade unions. The question of how local states might retreat from their role as the partners of capital to become genuine enforcers of labor standards remains uncertain. These would be meaningful topics for future research on industrial relations in China.

Given the complex relationships among the major actors in industrial relations as well as the divergent social-economic environments and workers' characteristics, the formation of collective bargaining could be a long and gradual process. A lasting period of struggles and compromises between workers, employers and states, is likely in the future. It is also unlikely that "harmonious labor relations", which resembles the project of "social partnership" in Germany, can take place overnight due to the strong state and the absence of certain balances of power among capitalists and workers. The current wage regulation may continue temporarily. However, the historical experiences of the U.S. and Germany remind us that institutionalized collective bargaining are results of long periods of social mobilization and struggle. Migrant workers in China, the backbone of the industrial workforce, may potentially break new ground in collective bargaining. In particular, the second generation of migrant workers resembles the immigrants in both the U.S. and, to a lesser degree, Germany at different periods of time, who had actively led or engaged in labor movements. It is true that migrant workers in China face tremendous difficulties than those by immigrant workers in the West decades ago. The two or three generations of migrant workers have little experience or even no common knowledge about collective bargaining. In the end, the land right system together with other new rural policies still gives an alternative, however unattractive it might seem. Nevertheless, workers have quickly learned to use their power, as indicated in the most recent strike wave of 2010. The rising bargaining power of workers, both structural and associational, may eventually bring about the institutionalization of collective bargaining in China.

References

Abel, I. W. 1976, Collective bargaining - labor relations in steel: Then and Now. 1975 Benjiamin F. Fairless Memorial Lectures. Pittsburgh: Carnegie-Mellon University Press

Aglietta, Michel, 1979, A theory of capitalist regulation: the US experience, (translated by David Fernbach), London: NLB, 1979

Altmann, Norbert, 1992, Unions' Policies Towards New Technologies in the 1980s - An Example from the Metal Industry, p361-384, (ed.) by Altmann, Christoph K?hler, Pamela Meil, Technology and Work in German Industry, Routledge, London and New York, 1992

Amin, Ash (ed.), Post-Fordism: a reader, Blackwell publishers Ltd., 1994

Artus, Ingrid, 2006, Im Schatten des duale n Systems: Zur Bedeutung tariflicher Normen in Betrieben ohne Betriebsrat, in Artus, et al, Betriebe ohne Betriebsrat, pp 141-170. Frankfurt: Campus Verlag

Arrighi, Giovanni , 2007, Adam Smith in Beijing. Lineages of the Twenty- first Century. London: Verso

----- 1990, Marxist-Century, American-Century: the making and remaking of the world labor movement, New Left Review, 179, Jan-Feb, 29-63

Baum, Richard and Shevchenko, Alexei, 1999, The state of the state, in Merle Goldman and Roderick MacFarquhar (eds.), The Paradox of China's Post-Mao Reforms, Cambridge, MA: Harvard University Press

Baumol, William J., Litan, Robert and, Schramm, Carl J., 2007, Good capitalism, bad capitalism, and the economics of growth and prosperity, Yale University Press

Berg, Peter, 2008, Working time flexibility in the German employment relations system: implications for Germany and lessons for the United States, Industrielle Beziehungen, Vol. 15, Iss. 2

Blecher, J. Marc, 2002, Hegemony and workers' politics in China, The China Quarterly, p283-303

Bonefeld, Werner and Holloway, John (ed.), 1991, Post-Fordism and Social Form: A Marxist Debate on the Post-Fordist State, Macmillan Academic and Professional Ltd

Borrus, Michael and Zysman, John, 1997, Wintelism and the Changing Terms of Global Competition; Prototype of the Future? BRIE Working Paper, 96B, University of California, Berkeley

Boyer, Robert, 2005, How and why capitalisms differ, MPIGF 05/4

Braverman, Harry, 1974, Labor and Monopoly Capital: the degradation of work in the twentieth Century, New York: Monthly Review Press

Brown, C. Ronald, 2006, China's Collective Contract Provisions: Can Collective Negotiations Embody Collective Bargaining? Duke Journal of Comparative & Intl Law, Vol 16:35, pp35-77

Burawoy, Michael, 1979, Manufacturing Consent: Changes in the Labour Process under Monopoly Capitalism, University of Chicago Press

---- 1985, The Politics of Production: Factory Regimes under Capitalism and Socialism, London:Verso

-----1996, The State and Economic Involution: Russia Through a China Lens, World Development, Vol.24, No.6, pp1105-1117

---- 2000, Involution and Destitution in Capitalist Russia, Ethnography, Vol. 1, No. 1,pp 43-65, SAGE publications

---- Jan 2001, Review Symposium: Neoclassical Sociology: From the End of Communism to the End of Classes, University of Chicago, AJS Vol. 106 No. 4, pp 1099-1120

Burawoy, Michael and Lukacs, Janos, Dec 1985, Mythologies of work: a comparison of firsms in State Socialism and advanced capitalism, American Sociological Review, Vol. 50, No. 6, pp. 723-737

Camuffo A., and Volpato G., 1995, The Labor Relations Heritage and Lean Manufacturing at Fiat, International Journal of Human Resource Management, vol.6, n.4.

Caprile M., 2000, Outsourcing and industrial relations in motor manufacturing, http://www.eiro.eurofound.eu.int/2000/08/study/tn0008201s.html

Chamberlin, Waldo (ed.), 1942, Industrial relations in Germany 1914-1939, Stanford University Press, New York

Chan, Anita, Jan. 1993, Revolution or corporatism? workers and trade unions in post-Mao China, the Australian Journal of Chinese Affairs, No.29, p31-61

---- 2008, China's trade unions in corporatist transition, in J. Unger (ed.), Associations and the Chinese state: contested spaces, New York: Sharpe, pp69-85

Chang, Kai, 1995, Labor relations, laborers, labor rights (Laodongguanxi, laodongzhe, laoquan), China Labor and Social Security Publishing House

---- 2003, Legislation on right to strike in China, Studies on law and policy, Vol. 69, No. 3

---- 2004a, Labor Rights - Research on the legal adjustment of labor relations in contemporary China (Laoquanlun - dangdai zhongguo laodongguanxi de falv tiaozheng yanjiu), China Labor and Social Security Publishing House

---- 2004b, The major role and function of the government in labor legal relations (Lun zhengfu zai laodong falvguanxi zhong de zhutidiwei he zuoyong), China Labor, 2004, Vol. 12

---- 2008, The legal foundation and position of Labor Contract Law (Lun laodonghetongfa de lifayiju he falvdingwei), Legal Forum, Vol. 2.
Chang, Kai/ Lüthje, Boy/Luo, Siqi, 2008, Die Transformation der Arbeitsbeziehungen in China und ihre Besonderheiten. Working Paper Institut für Sozialforschung Frankfurt/M.
Chen, An, Why does capitalism fail to push China toward democracy? In: McNally, 2008
Chen, Feng, 2003a, Reform of state-owned enterprises and workers' protests (Guoqi gaizhi yu gongren kangzheng), paper presented on the "Chinese trade union movement, trade unions and state" conference, jointly held by Hong Kong Baptist University and Chinese University of Hong Kong
---- 2003b, Between the state and labour: the conflict of Chinese trade unions' double identity in market reform, The China Quarterly
Chen, Shengyong, Wu, Wei, and Chen, Yan, 2004, Direct election of trade union: New development of local democracy in China - the case of Yuhang, Yuyao and Wenling, Zhejiang Social Science, No.1, pp63-73
Clarke, Donald C., Sep 2007,Legislating for a Market Economy in China, The China Quarterly, Vol. 191, pp. 567-585
Clarke, Simon, Lee, Changhee and Li, Qi, 2004,, Collective Consultation and Industrila Relations in China, British Journal of Industrial Relations, Jun 2004 0007-1080, pp235-254
Davis, Mike, 1986, Prisoners of the American dream?: politics and economy in the history of the US working class, London?: Verso
Dickson, Bruce J., 2010, Dilemmas of Party adaptation: the CCP's strategies for survival, in Chinese politics: state, society and the market, edited by Peter Hays Gries and Stanley Rosen
Dicken, Peter, 1998, Global Shift, 3rd ed. Paul Chapman Publishing
Dilger, Alexander, 2003, Economic Effects of Co-determination, The Changing Contours of German Industrial Relations, Walther Müller-Jentsch and Hansj?rg Weitbrecht, eds., Munich and Mering, pp. 119-135
Dinges, Thomas, Jan. 24, 2011, Electronics Contract Manufacturing Market Growth Slows in 2011, Isuppli
Doellgast, Virginia and Greer, Ian, March 2007, Vertical Disintegration and the Disorganization of German Industrial Relations, British Journal of Industrial Relations, 45:1, 0007-1080 pp. 55-76
Dong, Baohua, 2006, Socialization and internaitonalization of labor relation adjustment (Laodong guanxi tiaozheng de shehuihua yu guojihua), Shanghai Jiaotong University Press
Dreyfuss, Robert, September 2, 2010, China in the Driver's Seat, published on The Nations, http://www.thenation.com/article/154484/china-drivers-seat

Edin, Maria, 2003, State capacity and local agent control in China: CCP cadre management from a township perspective, The China Quarterly

Edwards, P.K, 1986, Conflict at Work: A Materialist Analysis of Workplace Relations, Oxford: Basil Blackwell Ltd

Ernst, Dieter and Naughton, Barry, 2008, China's emerging industrial economy: insights from the IT industry, in: Christopher McNally (ed.), 2008

Feng, Gang, "Institutional disadvantages" of enterprise unions and the background, Society, 2006.3, Vol. 26

Feng, Tongqing, 2002, The fate of Chinese Workers - Workers' actions since the reform (Zhongguogongren de mingyun - gaige yilai gongren de xingdong), Social Sciences Academic Press

-------2005, Chinese experience: enterprise governance and employees' democratic participation in a transitional society (Zhongguo jingyan: zhuanxingshehui de qiyezhili yu zhigong minzhucanyu), Social Sciences Academic Press

Figart, M. Deborah, 2001, Wage-setting under Fordism: the rise of job evaluation and the ideology of equal pay, Review of Political Economy, Volume 13, No. 4

Flanagan, Robert J., Sep., 1999, Macroeconomic Performance and Collective Bargaining: An International Perspective, Journal of Economic Literature, Vol. 37, No. 3, pp. 1150-1175

Gallagher, Kelly Sims, 2006, Limits to leapfrogging in energy technologies? Evidence from the Chinese auto industry, Energy Policy 34, 383- 394

Gartman, David, 1998, Postmodernism; or, the cultural logic of Post-Fordism? The Sociological Quarterly, Vol. 39, Number 1, pp 119-137

Gerber, Larry G. 1995, Corporatism and State Theory: A Review Essay for Historians, Social Science History, Vol. 19, No. 3, pp.316

Gittings, John, 2005, The changing face of China: from Mao to Market, Oxford University Press

Gordon, D.M, Edwards, R. and Reich, M. (1982) Segmented Work, Divided Workers: The Historical Transformation of Labor in the United States. New York: Cambridge University Press

Grove, Andrew S. 1996, Only the Paranoid Survive: How to Exploit the Crisis Points that Challenge Every Company and Career. New York: Doubleday.

Gu, Xin, and Wang, Xu, 2005, From Nationalism to Corporatism - the evolution of the relationship between the state and professional organizations in the transition to the market economy (Cong guojiazhuyi dao fatuanzhuyi - zhongguo shichangzhuanxing guocheng zhong guojia yu zhuanyetuanti guanxi de yanbian), Sociological research, Vol. 2, 2005

Guo, Baogang, 1999, Comparison of the labor policies between mainland China and Taiwan (Zhongguo dalu he taiwan laogongzhengce zhi bijiao), Modern China Studies, Vol. 1999, No. 64

Guo, Liangping, March 2007, China's new cadre evaluation system, EAI Background Brief No. 324, 15

Guo, Yue, 2004, Research on Chinese labor relations in the transition period (Zhuanxing shiqi zhongguo laodong guanxi yanjiu), Jan 9, 2004

Guo Yue, 2005, Balancing labor relations: building up real collective bargaining institutions (Pingheng laodongguanxi), China Labor, Vol. 2 p 22-24

Hall, Peter A. / Soskice, David, 2001, An Introduction to Varieties of Capitalism, pp1-68, in: dies. (Hg.): Varieties of Capitalism: The Institutional Foundations of Comparative Advantage, Oxford

Han, Deqiang, 2006, How neo-liberlists influence reform vs. How mainstream economists misguide reform (Yixie xinziyouzhuyi xuejia ruhe yingxiang gaige, yixie zhuliujingjixuejia ruhe wudao gaige), Probe, Vol. 2, p183-188

Herrigel, Gary, 2008, Roles and rules: ambiguity, experimentation and new forms of stakeholderism in Germany, Industrielle Beziehungen, Jahrgang 15, Heft 2

Hirsch, Joachim, 1991, Fordism and post-Fordism: the present social crisis and its consequences, Werner Bonefeld and John Holloway (ed.), Post-Fordism and Social Form: A Marxist Debate on the Post-Fordist State, Macmillan Academic and Professional Ltd

---- 2000, The Concept of Materialist State Theory and Regulation Theory' , in J.D. Schmidt and J. Hersh (eds) Globalization and Social Change, pp. 101-18. London: Routledge

Höpner, Martin, 2001, Corporate governance in transition: then empirical findings on shareholder value and industrial relations in Germany, MPIfG Discussion Paper 01/5, Köln

Hsing, You-tien, 1998, Making Capitalism in China: The Taiwan Connection. New York: Oxford University Press

Hu, Jun, Tao, Feng, and Chen, Jianlin, Aug., 2005, Development paths of OEM firms in Pearl River Delta, China Industrial Economy, Vol. 8

Huang, Yasheng, 2008, Capitalism with Chinese characteristics: Entrepreneurship and the state, Cambridge University Press

Huang, Jikun, Scott Rozelle and Wang Honglin, 2006, Fostering or Stripping Rural China: Modernizing Agriculture and Rural to Urban Capital Flows, The Developing Economies, vol. 44, no. 1, pp. 1-26

Hürtgen/Lüthje/Schumm/Sproll, 2009, Von Silicon Valley nach Shenzhen: Globale Produktion und Arbeit in der IT-Industrie, Verlag

Hugins, Walter, Jacksonian, 1960, Democracy and the Working Class: a Study of the New York Workingmen's Movement, 1829-1837, Stanford

Hyman, Richard, 2001, Understanding European Trade Unionism: Between Market, Class and Society. London: Sage

Jacobides, M. G., 2005, Industry change through vertical disintegration: how and why markets emerged in mortgage banking. Academy of Management Journal, 48 (3): 465-498

Jiang, Ying, 2004, Reflection on the formality of collective contracts (Dui jitihetong xingshihua de fansi), Theory & Practice of Trade Unions, Vol. 18, No. 6, pp45-49

Jenson, Jane, Dec. 1990, Representations in Crisis: The Roots of Canada's Permeable Fordism, Canadian Journal of Political Science, Vol. 23, No. 4

Jensen, Carsten Storby, Feb. 2006 , Trade unionism: differences and similarities - a comparative view on Europe, USA and Asia, Journal of industrial relations, vol. 48 no.1, p59-81

Jessop, Bob, 1991, Regulation Theory, Post-Fordism and the State: More than a Reply to Werner Bonefeld, in BONEFELD, Werner and HOLLOWAY, Jon (eds.), pp. 69-91

---- 1992, Fordism and post-Fordism: a critical reformulation', in Michael Storper & Allen John Scott (Eds.), Pathways to industrialization and regional development. London, New York: Routledge

----- 1994, Post-Fordism and the state. Post-Fordism: A Reader. A. Amin (ed.) Oxford: Blackwell. 251-279

---- Nov. 1997, L'Economia Integrale, Fordism, and Post-Fordism, Lecture prepared for Italian-Japanese conference on Gramsci, Tokyo, Nov. 15-16

Jessop, Bob and Sum, Ngai-Ling, 2006, Beyond the regulation approach: putting capitalist economies in their place, Cheltenham: Edward Elgar Publishing

Jürgens, U., Naumann, K. & Rupp, J., 2000, Shareholder value in an adverse environment: the german case, Economy and Society, 29(1), pp. 54-79.

Katz, Harry, 1986, Recent developments in US auto labor relation, see: The automobile industry and its workers: between Fordism and Flexibility, ed. by Tolliday, Steven and Zeitlin, Jonathan, Polity Press

Katzenstein, Peter J. (ed.), 1988, Industry and political change in West Germany, Cornell University Press

Kenworthy, Lane, Nov. 2000, Quantitative indicators of corporatism: a survey and assessment, MPIfG discussion paper 00/4

Kittel, Bernhard, 2001, How bargaining mediates wage determination: an exploration of the parameters of wage functions in a pooled time-series cross-section framework, MPIfG discussion paper 01/3, July 2001

Kochan, T., Lansbury, R., MacDuffie, J.P. Eds, 1997, After Lean Production: Evolving Employment Practices in the World Auto Industry, Ithica, New York: ILR Press

Kochan, A. Thomas, 2012, Collective bargaining: crisis and its consequences for American society, Industrial Relations Journal, 43:4, 302-316

Koch, Max, 2006, Roads to Post-Fordism: labour markets and social structures in Europe, ASHGATE

Kong, Xianghong, On the construction of harmonious labor relations: three rounds of collective wage negotiation in Nanhai Honda, Presentation made on the 2012 international conference of the International Center for Joint Labor Research of Sun Yat-sen University, Guangzhou

Kornai, JĐnos, 1992, The socialist system--the political economy of communism, Oxford University Press

Lee, Ching Kwan ,1995, Production Politics and Labor Identities :Migrant Workers in South China. China Review

---- 1998, The labor politics of market socialism: collective inaction and class experience among state workers in Guangzhou, Modern China, vol24, no1

---- 1999, From organized dependence to disorganized despotism: changing labor regimes in Chinese factories, The China Quarterly, No.157, pp44-71

---- 2007a, Against the law: labor protests in China's rustbelt and sunbelt, University of California Press: Berkeley and Los Angeles, California

Lei, Guang, 2007, Rural "guerrilla" workers and home renovation in urban China, p56-73. In Lee (ed), Working in China: Ethnographies of labor and workplace transformation, Routledge: London and New York

Li, Cheng, 2003, The 'New Deal': Political and Policies of the Hu Administration, Journal of Asian and African Studies, 38 (4-5); 329-346

Li Qiang, 2004, Migrant workers and social stratification of China (Nongmingong yu shehuifenceng), Social Sciences Academic Press

Li, Zhongxin, 2001, Economic development and social stability of China in the new century (Shijichu zhongguo jingjifazhan yu shehuiwending), China Politics, Vol. 12

Lichtenstein, Nelson, 1995, The most dangerous man in Detroit: Walter Reuther and the fate of American labor, BasicBooks

Lieberthal, Kenneth G. and Lampton, David M. (eds.), 1992, Bureucracy, politics and decision-making in Post-Mao China, Berkeley: Princeton University Press

Lipietz, Alain, 1987, Mirages and Miracles: the crises of global Fordism, translated by David Macey, London: VERSO

------ 1994, Post-Fordism and democracy. Post-Fordism: A Reader. A. Amin. Oxford: Blackwell. 338-358.

---- 1997, translated by Angus Cameron, The post-Fordist world: labour relations, international hierarchy and global ecology, Review of International Political Economy 4:1, Routledge

Lu, Xueyi, 2002, Research report on social classes in modern China, (Dangdai zhongguo shehuijieceng yanjiubaogao), Beijing: Social Sciences Academic Press

Luo, Siqi, 2011, Collective contract, no collective bargaining, in China's labor question, Christoph Scherrer(ed) Munich: Rainer Hampp Verlag, pp49-69

Lüthje, Boy, 2001, Standort Silicon Valley: ökonomie und Politik der vernetzten Massenproduktion. Frankfurt/New York: Campus

------ Dec. 2002, Electronics contract manufacturing: global production and the international division of labor in the age of the internet, Industry and Innovation, special issue: Global Production Networks, Vol. 9, No. 3

---- 2004, Co-Determination and Collective Bargaining in Germany - A Model Under Stress, Presentation at International Labor Law Forum: Reform and Development, at Peking University, February 26-28

Lüthje, Boy, Luo, Siqi, and Zhang, Hao, 2013, Beyond the Iron Rice Bowl - Regimes of Production and Industrial Relations in China. Frankfurt/New York: Campus. 2013

Ma, Xiaohe, Sep. 15th 2005, Development trends and policy choice of Chinese auto industry, Institute for industrial development at the National Development and Reform Commission

Manow, Philip, January 1999, The uneasy compromise of Liberalism and Corporatism in Postwar Germany, working paper 5.88 Univ. Of California, Berkeley Center for German and European Studies

Marsden, David, 2008, Symposium: overseas perspectives on the future of German employment relations, Industrielle Beziehungen, Jahrgang 15, Heft 2

Marx, Karl, Capital Volume One, 1st english edition, 1887 (4th German edition), translated by Samuel Moore and Edward Aveling, edited by Frederick Engels, Progress Publishers, Moscow, USSR. (transcribed by Hinrich Kuhls), http://www.marxists.org/archive/marx/works/1867-c1/ch06.htm

McCammon, Holly J., May, 1990, Legal Limits on Labor Militancy: U. S. Labor Law and the Right to Strike since the New Deal, Social Problems, Vol. 37, No. 2 , pp. 206-229, URL: http://www.jstor.org/stable/800649

McNally, A. Christopher, 2008, China's Emergent Political Economy: capitalism in the dragon's lair, Routledge

Meyer, Stephen III, 1981, The Five Dollar Day: Labor Management and Social Control in the Ford Motor Company, 1908-1921. Albany: State University of New York Press

Moore, Barrington, 1966, The social origins of dictatorship and democracy: lord and peasant in the making of the modern world, Boston: Beacon Press

Moody, Kim, 1997, Workers in a lean world: unions in the international economy, Verso

---- 2007, U.S. labor in trouble and transition, Verso

---- 2010, A pattern of retreat: the decline of pattern bargaining, Labor Notes February, p7-9

Müller-Jentsch, Walther, 2003, Re-assessing Co-determination p39-56; see, Müller-Jentsch, Walther and Weitbrecht, Hansjörg (ed.), The changing contours of German industrial relations, Rainer Hampp Verlag, München

Naughton, Barry J. and Yang, Dali L., 2004, Holding China together: diversity and national integration in the post-Deng era, Cambridge University Press

Nichols, T., Cam, S., Grace Chou, W., Chun, S., W. and Feng, T, 2004, Factory regimes and the dismantling of established labor in Asia: a review of cases from large manufacturing plants in China, South Korea and Taiwan' Work, Employment & Society, 18: 663-685

Nichols, Theo and Zhao, Wei , 2010, Disaffection with Trade Unions in China: Some Evidence from SOEs in the Auto Industry, Industrial Relations Journal, Vol. 41, Issue 1, pp. 19-33

Nielsen, K., 1991, Towards a flexible future - theories and politics, The Politics of Flexibility. B. Jessop et al (eds). Aldershot: Edward Elgar

North, Douglass C., 1990, Institutions, Institutional Change and Economic Performance, Cambridge: Cambridge University Press.

Offe, Claus, and Wiesenthal, Helmut, 1980, Two logics of collective action: theoretical notes on social class and organizational form, Political power and social theory, Volume 1, pages 67-115 by JAI Press Inc.

Okayama, Reiko, 1986, Industrial relations in the Japanese auto industry 1945-70: the case of Toyota, in Tolliday and Zeitlin (ed.), Polity Press

Pearson, Margaret M., Jan. 1994, The Janus Face of business Associations in China: socialist Corporatism in Foreign Enterprises, The Australian Journal of Chinese Affairs, No. 31, pp25-46

----- 1997, China' s New Business Elite: The Political Consequences of Economic Reform. Berkeley and Los Angeles: Univ.of California Press

Peng, Guanghua, April 2003,Theories and research methods of collective labor law, Trade Union Theory and Practice, No. 2, Vol. 17, pp1-5

---- 2009,Collective negotiation and collective contracts, New manpower,No272

Perry, J. Elizabeth, Mar. 1994, Shanghai's Strike Wave of 1957, The China Quarterly, No. 137

Piore, Michael J., 1979, Birds of Passage: Migrant Labor and Industrial Societies. Cambridge: Cambridge University Press

Piore, Michael J., and Sabel, Charles F., 1984. The Second Industrial Divide: Possibilities for Prosperity. New York: Basic Books

Polanyi, 1944, The Great Transformation. Boston: Beacon

Pontusson, Jonas, 2005, Inequality And Prosperity: Social Europe Vs. Liberal America, Cornell University Press

Poulantzas, Nicos, 1968, Political power and social classes, London: New Left Review

Pringle, Tim, 2005, Barriers and Barricades: Union Rights and Free Trade in the context of China, ACTU/NZCTU/Monash University China Symposium, 14-15 Feb 2005, Melbourne

Rafalski, Traute, 1988, Social planning and corporatism: modrnization tendencies in Italian Fascism, in Tilla Siegel (ed.), Fordism and Fascism, International journal of political economy, Vol. 18, No. 1, Spring 1988

Ren, Xiaoping, 2010, Remuneration in SOEs: unfairness and fairness, Chinese Workers, 2010 (8)

Ren, Yan and Pun Ngai, 2006, Space politics of international labor process: dormitory system in globalization (Kuaguo laodongguocheng de kongjian zhengzhi: quanqiuhua shidai de sushe tizhi), Sociological studies, Vol.04

Reynolds, Lloyd G., 1971, The three worlds of economics, New Haven: Yale University Press

Ru, Xin, Lu, Xueyi, 2001, and Shang, Tianlun, ed., Blue Book: Analysis and Prediction of Chinese Society, China Social Sciences Publishing House

Ru Xin, Lu Xueyi, Li Peilin, (ed.), 2009: analysis and forecast of the social trends in China (2009 nian: zhongguoshehuixingshifenxiyuyuce), China Social Sciences Publishing House

Sachse, Carola, Spring 1988, a flow of people and a flow of goods: factory family policy at Siemens, 1918-1945, p14, in Tilla Siegel (ed.), Fordism and Fascism, International journal of political economy, Vol. 18, No. 1

Safarian, A. E. and Dobson, Wendy (ed.), 1996, East Asian capitalism: Diversity and dynamism, Hongkong Bank of Canada Papers on Asia, Volume 2

Sauer, Dieter, 1999, Corporate reorganization, human resource management and the flexibilization of work and employment: A German view, Paper presented to the International Conference on "Business Transformation and Social Change in East Asia", Taichung, Taiwan, June 10/11, 1999

Schmidt, Ingo, 2008, Comparing Crises: The 1930s, the 1970s, and Today, The Bullet, A Socialist Project e-bulletin, No. 141, September 28, 2008

Schmitter, Philippe C., Jan., 1974, Still the Century of Corporatism? The Review of Politics, Vol. 36, No. 1, The New Corporatism: Social and Political Structures in the Iberian World, pp 81-135
Schumpeter, Joseph A., 1942, Capitalism, Socialism and Democracy
Schr?der, Wolfgang, 2002, The Europeanization of collective bargaining? Lessons of the strike in the German metalworking industry in 2002, in: Transfer 4/2002, pp707-711
Scott, James, 1985, Weapons of the Weak: Everyday Form of Peasant Resistance, New Haven, CT: Yale University Press
---- 1977, Hegemony and the peasantry, Politics and Society, Vol. 7, No. 3, pp267-296
Shaiken, Harley, 2010, Commitment is a Two-Way Street: Toyota, California and NUMMI. UC Berkeley: Institute for Research on Labor and Employment. Retrieved from: http://escholarship.org/uc/item/0rx6q86w
She, Yunxia and Fu, Lin, 2001, International debates on free trade and international labor standards (Guojishehui dui maoyiziyouhua yu laogong biaozhun de bianlun), Theory & Practice of Trade Unions, Vol. 06
Shimokawa, Koichi, 1986, Product and Labor Strategies in Japan, in: Tolliday and Zeitlin (ed.), 1986, Polity Press
Sit, F. S. Victor, and Liu, Weidong, 2000, Restructuring and spatial change of China's auto industry under institutional reform and globalization, Annals of the Association of American Geographers, Vol. 90, No. 4, pp. 653-673
Silver, Beverly J., 2003, Forces of labor: workers' movements and globalization since 1870, Cambridge University Press
---- 1993, Labor Unrest and the Successive Geographical Restructuring of the World Automobile Industry, 1930's to the Present, http://www2.cddc.vt.edu/digitalfordism/fordism_materials/Silver.htm
Soskice, David (1999) Divergent production regimes: coordinated and uncoordinated market economies in the 1980s and 1990s. In: Kitschelt, Herbert et al (eds.) Continuity and change in contemporary capitalism. Cambridge studies in comparative politics, pp. 101-134
Steinmetz, G. 1993, Regulating the social, the welfare state and local politics in imperial Germany, Princeton: Princeton University Press
Strauss, Georgy, 1984, Industrial Relations: times of change, Industrial Relations 23, No.1: 1-15
Streeck, Wolfgang, 1984, Industral relations in West Germany: a case study of the car industry. London: Heinemann
---- April 1987, Industrial relaions in west Germany: agenda for change, IIM (Research Unit Labour Market and Employment)/ LMP 87 - 5

----- Jan 1988, Successful adjustment to turbulent markets: the automobile industry, discussion paper IIMV

----- 1997: German Capitalism: Does It Exist? Can It Survive? In: New Political Economy Vol. 2, No. 2, 237-256.

Streeck, Wolfgang and Thelen, Kathleen (eds.), 2005: Beyond continuity: institutional change in advanced political economies, Oxford Univ. Press

Streeck, Wolfgang and Visser, Jelle, April 1998, An evolutionary dynamic of trade union systems, MPIfG Discussion Paper 98/4

Sun, Liping, 2003, Split: the Chinese society since the 1990s, Social Sciences Academic Press

Taplin, I.M. (1995) Flexible production, rigid jobs: Lessons from the clothing industry. Work & Occupations. 22, pp412-438

Taylor, Bill, Chang, Kai and Li, Qi, 2003, Industrial relations in China, Edward Elgar Publishing

Ten Brink, Tobias, 2010, Strukturmerkmale Des Chinesischen Kapitalismus, MPIfG Discussion Paper 10/1

Thelen, Kathleen, 2004, How institutions evolve: the political economy of skills in Germany, Britain, the U.S. and Japan, Cambridge Univ Press (KU 0703)

Vitols, Sigurt, 2001, The origins of bank-based and market-based financial systems: Japan, Germany, and the US, in The origins of nonliberal Capitalism, W. Streeck and K. Yamamura(ed.), Ithaca:Cornell Univ. Press

Thun, Eric, 2006, Changing Lanes in China: Foreign Direct Investment, Local Governments, and Auto Sector Development. New York: Cambridge University Press

Tolliday, Steven and Zeitlin, Jonathan (ed.), 1986, The auto industry and its workers: between Fordism and Flexibility, Polity Press

Tong, Xin, 2005, Active actor: Trade union practice in B enterprise, See: Feng, Tongqing (ed.), Chinese experience, Social Sciences Publishing House

Tsai, Kellee S., 2005, Capitalists without a class: political diversity among private entrepreneurs in China, Comparative Political Studies, Vol. 38 No. 9 Nov 2005 1130-1158, Sage Publications

---- 2007, Capitalism without democracy: the private sector in contemporary China, Cornell University Press

Turner, Lowell, 1991. Democracy at Work. Ithaca: Cornell University Press

----- 1998, Fighting for partnership: labor and politics in united Germany, Cornell University Press, Ithaca and London

T㉆selmann, Heinz and Heise, Arne, 2000, The German model of industrial relations at the crossroads: past, present and future, industrial relations journal 31:3, Blackwell Publishers Ltd. p162-175

Unger, Jonathan and Chan, Anita, Jan 1995, China, Corporatism, and the East Asian Model, The Australian Journal of Chinese Affairs, No. 33., pp29-53
Unger, Jonatan and Chan,Anita, 2008, Associations in a bind: the emergence of political corporatism, in J. Unger (ed.), Associations and the Chinese State: Contested Spaces, New York: Sharpe, p48-68
Walder, G. Andrew, 1984, Communist Neo-Traditionalism: Work and Authority in Chinese Industry, University of California Press
Walker, Cathy, Jan. 2008, Unions in China: A View from a Canadian Unionist, Relay - A Socialist Project Review, p26-29
Wang, Hongying, 2001, Weak State, Strong Networks: The Institutional Dynamics of Foreign Direct Investment in China, Oxford University Press
Wang, Yijiang, 2004, Market mechanism could effectively protect labor rights and benefits (Shichang jizhi ke youxiao baohu laodongzhe quanyi), Caijing, Vol. 21
Wang, Gaoshe, and Zhao, Zhiping, 2005, Problems and countermeasures of implementing collective bargaining (Jiti tanpan zhidu tuixingzhong de wenti yu duice), Inquiry into Economic Issues, No. 2, 2005
Wang, hui, Sep 2008, Das Vergessen der sechziger Jahre: Entpolitisierte Politik und Hegemonie im neuen China. In: Prokla - Zeitschrift fuer kritische Sozialwissenschaften, H. 152, Jg. 38, pp. 459 - 477
Wang, Jinhong, 2006, Union reform and new development at grassroots democracy, Economic and mangement digest, No. 19, pp17-22
Wang, Xiaolu, and Fan, Gang, 2004, The changes and influential factors on the regional differences in China (Zhongguo diquchaju de biandongqushi yiji yingxiangyinsu), Economic Research, No. 1
Wank, David L., 1999, Commodifying Communism: business, trust, and politics in a Chinese city, Cambridge University Press
Wächter, Hartmut, Peters, Rene, Tempel, Anne, and Müller-Camen, Michael, 2003, The country-of-origin effect in the cross-national management of human resources: results and case study evidence of research on American multinational companies in Germany, Rainer Hampp Verlag
Wei, Jie, Aug. 23, 2004, Specially-made Chinese "manufacturing center" (Liangshendazao zhongguo de "zhizao zhongxin"), Info website of the development research center of the State Council, http://www.drcnet.com.cn/DRCNet.Channel.Web/expert/showdoc.asp?doc_id=198432
Weiss, Manfred, 1989, Labour law and industrial relations in the Federal Republic of Germany, Deventer: Kluwer Law and Taxation Publishers
White, Gordon, 1996, Chinese trade unions in the transition from socialism: towards corporatism or civil society. British Journal of Industrial Relations, 34(3): 433-457

Whyte, Martin King, 1999, “The Changing Role of Workers”, in Merle Goldman and Roderick MacFarquhar (eds.), The Paradox of China’s Post-Mao Reforms, Cambridge, Harvard University Press, pp. 173-196.
Williamson, Peter J. and Zeng, Ming, Oct 2003, The hidden dragons, HRB spotlight, China Tomorrow, Harvard Business Review, p 92-99
---- 2008, The global impact of China’s emerging multinationals, McNally, 2008
Windolf, P., 1989, Productivity Coalitions and the Future of European Corporatism, Industrial Relations vol. 28, pp1-20
Wong, Christine, April 2005, Can China change development paradigm for the 21st century? Fiscal policy options for Hu and Wen after two decades of muddling through, working paper FG 7, 2005/ 03, SWP Berlin
Wood, Stephen, 1991, Japanisation and/or Toyotism? Work, Employment and Society, Vol. 5
Wright, Erik Olin, 2000, Working-class power, capitalist-class interests, and class compromise, American Journal of Sociology, 105(4), pp957-1002
Xu, Xiaohong, 2003, Labor relations in the Chinese Auto industry, unpublished draft
Yang, Jian, September 10, 2010, The government has caused China's excess production capacity, Automotive News
---- June 08, 2010, China's auto industry should prepare for higher wages, Automotive News, Shanghai, http://www.autonewschina.com/en/printarticle.asp?id=5187
Yao, Xianguo and Lai, Puqing, 2004, The rural-urban registration differences in the labour-capital relations in China (Zhongguo laoziguanxide chengxiang huji chayi), Economic Research Journal, Vol. 7
Ye, Xiaoming and Xu, 2005, Huiping, Discussion on collective contract system in China (Shilun woguo de jitihetong zhidu), Enterprise Economy, No. 12
Zhang, Jing, 2001a, Interest organization - case study of workers' congress in enterprises (liyi zuzhi danwei - qiye zhidaihui anli yanjiu), China Social Sciences Publishing House
----2001b, The role of trade union in the model of "Corporatism" ("Fatuanzhuyi" moshi xia de gonghui juese, Trade union theory and practice, Vol. 1
Zhang, Lu, Spring 2008, Lean Production and Labor Controls in the Chinese Automobile Industry in An Age of Globalization, International Labor and Working-Class History, No. 73, pp. 24-44
Zhang Yu & Zhao Feng, 2006, The rate of surplus value, the composition of capital, and the rate of profit in the Chinese manufacturing industry: 1978-2005, the 2nd Conference of International Forum on Comparative Political Economy of Globalization

Zhao, Aixue, Oct. 2004, New collective contract provision is better regulated (Xin jitihetongguiding gengguifan), Trade Union Theory & Practice
Zheng, Yongnian, 2009, Globalization and state transformation in China, (Chinese edition - translated by Yu, Jianxing and He, Ziying), Zhejiang People's Publishing House
Zhu, Xiaoyang, and Chan, Anita, 2003, The institutional channel of collective expression of employees' interest in a time of governance - Workers' Congress (Zhilishidai zhigong liyi jizhongbiaoda de zhiduhua qudao - zhigongdaibiaodahui), Open Times, Vol. 3, pp120-132

Newspapers and Periodicals
Statistics Yearbooks, National Bureau of Statistics
Yearbooks of Chinese electronics industry
Reports of the second national economic survey, December 25, 2009
CATARC - China Automotive Technology and Reseach Center
Global Insight
Automotive news
Computer business daily
Caijing news

Websites:
Ministry of Industry and Information Technology of China
The Customs
Xinhua news
CCID net, e.g. http://www.ccidcom.com/html/yaowen/201001/29-93499.html
Sohu news
www.made-in-china.com
Information Center for Social Sciences, Renmin University of China
People's Net
First Financial Daily
Chosun News
OECD observer

Appendix A

Table 1 - The Percentage of the Three Industries in Gross Domestic Product

Year	Primary Industry	* Secondary Industry	Industry	Tertiary Industry
1978	28.2	47.9	44.1	23.9
1980	30.2	48.2	43.9	21.6
1985	28.4	42.9	38.3	28.7
1990	27.1	41.3	36.7	31.6
1995	19.9	47.2	41.0	32.9
1996	19.7	47.5	41.4	32.8
1997	18.3	47.5	41.7	34.2
1998	17.6	46.2	40.3	36.2
1999	16.5	45.8	40.0	37.7
2000	15.1	45.9	40.4	39.0
2001	14.4	45.1	39.7	40.5
2002	13.7	44.8	39.4	41.5
2003	12.8	46.0	40.5	41.2
2004	13.4	46.2	40.8	40.4
2005	12.2	47.7	42.2	40.1
2006	11.3	48.7	43.1	40.0
2007	11.1	48.5	43.0	40.4
2008	11.3	48.6	42.9	40.1

Employment	1978	1990	2000	2008
Primary Industry	70.5	60.1	50.0	39.6
Secondary Industry	17.3	21.4	22.5	27.2
Tertiary Industry	12.2	18.5	27.5	33.2

Source: Statistic Yearbook 2009, Table 1-3, 4-3, http://www.stats.gov.cn/tjsj/ndsj/2009 /indexch.htm; Note: Secondary Industry includes mining, manufacturing, producers and suppliers of electricity, gas and water, and construction.

Table 2 Distribution of industrial enterprises with legal entities and their employees

	Enterprises (10,000)	**Employees (10,000)**
Transportation vehicle manufacturing	7.6	577.3
Electric machinery and equipment manufacturing	8.9	624.8
Communication equipment, computers and other electronics equipment manufacturing	4.3	698.8

Source: The No. 2 report of the Second National Economic Survey, released on December 25, 2009 by the State Council and the National Bureau of Statistics.

Table 3 Industrial Value-added in the Electronics Industry (Unit: 100million RMB)

	2000	2001	2002	2003	2004	2005	2006
Electronic & telecom equipments	1471	1623	1939	2572	3366	4016	5118
Computers and office equipments	374	432	604	1022	1226	1824	2111

Source: National Bureau of Statistics, China Statistics Yearbook on High Tech Industry 2007

Table 4 Output of Automotives and Auto Parts, 2004

	Total Output Value (100 million RMB)	Share of Auto Parts
National Total	9,463	21.3%
Jilin	1,681	11.9%
Shanghai	1,164	30.6%
Hubei	1,142	8.0%
Chongqing	687	12.1%
Guangdong	604	12.6%
Beijing	547	11.2%
Shandong	527	24.6%
Jiangsu	497	29.0%
Zhejiang	384	60.7%
Liaoning	253	29.5%

Source: Almanac of China's Automotive Industry 2005

Appendix B

Table 1 Typology of regimes of production

Type	**Production Model**	**Work/ Human Resource**	**Labor Relations**
State bureaucratic	Integrated Med to high tech Brand name	Stable after restructuring Urban workers High wages Low base, allowances	Stable TU, party, gov rules Collective contract Weak collective bargaining Few labor conflicts
Corporate bureaucratic	Integrated High tech Strong brand Market control	Stable employment Urban workers, skilled High wages, benefits High base pay Career incentives	TU, cooperative Mostly collective contract Weak collective bargaining Labor conflicts, few collective, often individual
Corporate high performance	Integrated High tech Strong brand High flexibility	Flexible employment Urban workers High wages, benefits Low base, high variable and OT	Weak or no TU Employee involvement Often no collective contract No collective bargaining Occasional labor conflict
Flexible mass production	Integrated Med to high tech No brand name High flexibility	Flexible employment Rural workers Neo Taylorism Low wages, benefit Very long work hours	Mostly non-union No collective contracts Occasional labor conflicts, sometimes militant Violations of legal standards
Low wage classic	Low integration Low tech No or weak brand High flexibility	Flexible employment Rural workers Low wages, benefit Personalized control Very long work hours	Mostly non-union No collective contracts Frequent violations of legal standards

(Source: Luethje, Luo, and Zhang, 2013. The project was supported by Hans Böckler Stiftung)

Table 2 Major Laws & Regulations on Collective Bargaining & Collective Contract

Title	**Year**	**Organization**	**Relevant articles**
Trade Union Law	1992	Standing Committee, the National People's Congress	Article. 18
	2001 (amended)	Standing Committee, the National People's Congress	Article 6, 20
Labor Law	1994 (effective 01.01.1995)	Standing Committee, the National People's Congress	Article 33-35; 84
Labor Contract Law	2008	Standing Committee, the National People's Congress	Article 6; 11; 18; 51-56; 75; 78
Regulations			
Collective Contract Provisions	1994 (effective 1995; abolished 2004)	Former Ministry of Labor	
	2004	Former Ministry of Labor and Social Security	
Proposed Regulations on Wage Collective Negotiation	2000	Former Ministry of Labor and Social Security	
Wage Regulation	Not yet	Ministry of Human Resource and Social Security.	

Source: Luethje, Luo, and Zhang, 2013. The project was supported by Hans Böckler Stiftung

Arbeit, Bildung & Gesellschaft
Labour, Education & Society

Herausgegeben von Prof. Dr. György Széll, Prof. Dr. Heinz Sünker,
Dr. Anne Inga Hilsen und Dr. Francesco Garibaldo

Bd. 1 György Széll (ed.): Corporate Social Responsibility in the EU & Japan. 2006.

Bd. 2 Katja Maar: Zum Nutzen und Nichtnutzen der Sozialen Arbeit am exemplarischen Feld der Wohnungslosenhilfe. Eine empirische Studie. 2006.

Bd. 3 Daniela De Ridder: Vom urbanen Sozialraum zur kommunikativen Stadtgesellschaft. 2007.

Bd. 4 Heinz Sünker / Ingrid Miethe (Hrsg.): Bildungspolitik und Bildungsforschung: Herausforderungen und Perspektiven für Gesellschaft und Gewerkschaften in Deutschland. 2007.

Bd. 5 Anja Bastigkeit: Bildungsbiographie und elementarpädagogische Bildungsarbeit. 2007.

Bd. 6 Antônio Inácio Andrioli: Biosoja versus Gensoja. Eine Studie über Technik und Familienlandwirtschaft im nordwestlichen Grenzgebiet des Bundeslandes Rio Grande do Sul (Brasilien). 2007.

Bd. 7 Russell Farnen / Daniel German / Henk Dekker / Christ'l De Landtsheer / Heinz Suenker (eds.): Political Culture, Socialization, Democracy, and Education. Interdisciplinary and Cross-National Perspectives for a New Century. 2008.

Bd. 8 Francesco Garibaldo / Volker Telljohann (eds.): New Forms of Work Organisation and Industrial Relations in Southern Europe. 2007.

Bd. 9 Anne Marie Berg / Olav Eikeland (eds.): Action Research and Organisation Theory. 2008.

Bd. 10 György Széll / Carl-Heinrich Bösling / Ute Széll (eds.): Education, Labour & Science. Perspectives for the 21st Century. 2008.

Bd. 11 Francesco Garibaldo / Philippe Morvannou / Jochen Tholen (eds.): Is China a Risk or an Opportunity for Europe? An Assessment of the Automobile, Steel and Shipbuilding Sectors. 2008.

Bd. 12 Yunus Dauda: Managing Technology Innovation. The Human Resource Management Perspective. 2009.

Bd. 13 Jarmo Lehtonen / Satu Kalliola (eds.): Dialogue in Working Life Research and Development in Finland. 2009.

Bd. 14 György Széll / Werner Kamppeter / Woosik Moon (eds.): European Social Integration – A Model for East Asia? 2009.

Bd. 15 Benedicte Brøgger / Olav Eikeland (eds.): Turning to Practice with Action Research. 2009.

Bd. 16 Till Johannes Hoffmann: Verschwendung. Philosophie, Soziologie und Ökonomie des Überflusses. 2009.

Bd. 17 Denis Harrisson / György Széll / Reynald Bourque (eds.): Social Innovation, the Social Economy and World Economic Development. 2009.

Bd. 18 Werner Weltgen: Total Quality Management als Strukturierungsaufgabe für nachhaltigen Unternehmenswandel. 2009.

Bd. 19 György Széll / Ute Széll (eds.): Quality of Life and Working Life in Comparison. 2009.

Bd. 20 Francesco Garibaldo / Volker Telljohann (eds.): The Ambivalent Character of Participation. New Tendencies in Worker Participation in Europe. 2010.

Bd. 21 Richard Ennals / Robert H. Salomon (eds.): Older Workers in a Sustainable Societey. 2011.

Bd. 22 Christoph Sänger: Anna Siemsen – Bildung und Literatur. 2011.

Bd. 23 Nam-Kook Kim: Deliberative Multiculturalism in Britain. A Response to Devolution, European Integration, and Multicultural Challenges. 2011.

Bd. 24 Mirella Baglioni / Bernd Brandl (eds.): Changing Labour Relations. Between Path Dependency and Global Trends. 2011.

Bd. 25 Rüdiger Kühr: Japan`s Transnational Environmental Policies. The Case of Environmental Technology Transfer to Newly Industrializing Countries. 2011.

Bd. 26 Francesco Garibaldo / Dinghong Yi (eds.): Labour and Sustainable Development. North-South Perspectives. 2012.

Bd. 27 Francesco Garibaldo / Mirella Baglioni / Catherine Casey / Volker Telljohann (eds.): Workers, Citizens, Governance. Socio-Cultural Innovation at Work. 2012.

Bd. 28 Simone Selva: Supra-National Integration and Domestic Economic Growth. The United States and Italy in the Western Bloc Rearmament Programs 1945-1955. Translation by Filippo del Lucchese, revision by Simone Selva. 2012.

Band 29 György Széll / Roland Czada (Hrsg.): Fukushima. Die Katastrophe und ihre Folgen. 2013.

Band 30 Siqi Luo: Collective Bargaining and Changing Industrial Relations in China. Lessons from the U. S. and Germany. 2013.

www.peterlang.de

www.ingramcontent.com/pod-product-compliance
Ingram Content Group UK Ltd.
Pitfield, Milton Keynes, MK11 3LW, UK
UKHW020121290926
15471UKWH00003B/213

9 783631 626467